Processing

*Creative Coding and Generative
Art in Processing 2*

Ira Greenberg, Dianna Xu, Deepak Kumar

friendsof

DESIGNER TO DESIGNER™

an Apress® company

PROCESSING

ISBN 978-1-4302-4464-6

ISBN 978-1-4302-4465-3 (eBook)

Distributed to the book trade worldwide by Springer Science+Business Media New York, 233 Spring Street, 6th Floor, New York, NY 10013. Phone 1-800-SPRINGER, fax (201) 348-4505, e-mail orders-ny@springer-sbm.com, or visit www.springeronline.com.

For information on translations, please e-mail rights@apress.com or visit www.apress.com.

Apress and friends of ED books may be purchased in bulk for academic, corporate, or promotional use. eBook versions and licenses are also available for most titles. For more information, reference our Special Bulk Sales–eBook Licensing web page at www.apress.com/bulk-sales. APress Media, LLC is a California LLC and the sole member (owner) is Springer Science + Business Media Finance Inc (SSBM Finance Inc). SSBM Finance Inc is a Delaware corporation.

Any source code or other supplementary materials referenced by the author in this text is available to readers at www.apress.com. For detailed information about how to locate your book's source code, go to www.apress.com/source-code/.

The front cover image was generated by the Processing sketch noise.pde found in Chapter 9.

Credits

President and Publisher:
Paul Manning

Lead Editor:
Ben Renow-Clarke

Technical Reviewer:
Ryan Rusnak

Editorial Board:
Steve Anglin, Mark Beckner, Ewan Buckingham, Gary Cornell, Louise Corrigan, Morgan Ertel, Jonathan Gennick, Jonathan Hassell, Robert Hutchinson, Michelle Lowman, James Markham, Matthew Moodie, Jeff Olson, Jeffrey Pepper, Douglas Pundick, Ben Renow-Clarke, Dominic Shakeshaft, Gwenan Spearing, Matt Wade, Tom Welsh

Coordinating Editor:
Anamika Panchoo

Copy Editors:
Michele Bowman, Linda Seifert

Compositor:
SPi Global

Indexer:
SPi Global

Artist:
SPi Global

Cover Image Artist:
Corné van Dooren

Cover Designer:
Anna Ishchenko

To Robin, Ian, and Sophie, and to Hilary, Jerry, and Eric
—Ira Greenberg

To Marcus and Kira
—Dianna Xu

To Debika and Sameer
—Deepak Kumar

Contents at a Glance

Contents

Foreword

One of the very best things about writing a book is the opportunity it presents to meet new people. After the release of *Processing: Creative Coding and Computational Art*, in June 2007, I received many thoughtful notes from creative coders around the world. Most of these readers, similar to me, came from the arts and were just discovering the exciting creative potential of code. I also received some notes from professional programmers and computer scientists, which at the time was very surprising. As a self-taught coder, I wasn't sure what I could offer trained computing professionals, or even if I would be taken seriously.

Two of the computer scientists I met at the time were Deepak Kumar and Dianna Xu, both professors in the Department of Computer Science at Bryn Mawr College. Deepak and I first communicated (virtually) in the Processing online forum, during a somewhat heated discussion thread about the disconnect between the creative coding and computer science communities, especially within academia. You can read the original thread at: http://processing.org/discourse/beta/num_1212418008.html. Near the end of the thread Deepak graciously extended an open invitation to visit Bryn Mawr, to present Processing and explore the connections between our two communities. What especially motivated me to follow-up on Deepak's invitation was the last sentence of his comment:

"Let's work together and see how we can bring about some radical change!"

During my initial visit to Bryn Mawr I met Dianna and Deepak. Though I had been coding for a fairly long time by now and had regular interactions with computer science faculty from the institution where I was teaching, it was still intimidating sitting across the table from them–*with actual PhDs in Computer Science*–but it was also equally exhilarating! Dianna and Deepak were very seriously exploring new ways to teach Computer Science, including how to make programming more engaging and accessible to the widest possible audience. They had been very successful pioneering an earlier approach utilizing robots in the introductory computing classroom. It was such a thrill to learn about their work and to be able to talk so intensively about coding and computer science pedagogy. Though we started from very different places–the arts and computer science–we somehow ended up in a pretty similar place, with a shared passion for presenting computation as a powerfully creative and fascinating medium, and spreading "the word" to future generations.

Over the next few years, Deepak, Dianna, and I worked closely presenting lectures and workshops on Processing and our emerging "creative coding" approach. We were very fortunate to receive funding from the National Science Foundation enabling us to more formally explore our approach in the Computer Science 1 (CS1) classroom, which we did at our respective schools. During this period we also began discussing the idea for a new CS1 book, based on Processing and creative coding. These discussions, along with the result of our research, directly led to the creation of the book you're holding in your hands.

This book is a departure from the existing Processing and CS1 literature in that it attempts to present the spirit and excitement of creative coding, while rigorously covering the fundamentals taught in the CS1 classroom. We structured the book to be useful to the autodidact, but equally useful to the CS1 instructor, at both the secondary and post-secondary levels. We've each had very positive results utilizing the book's approach within our own classrooms and are very excited to now help others do the same.

Finally, I want to very publically thank Deepak and Dianna for "taking me in" to the Computer Science fold (including tolerating my artistic ways) and also for agreeing to co-author this book. I've learned a great deal working with them and know this book is far richer because of their generous and thoughtful collaboration, AND I'm hopeful we will indeed *"...bring about some radical change!"*

Ira Greenberg, 2013

About the Authors

Ira Greenberg directs the Center of Creative Computation and is Associate Professor of Computer Science at Southern Methodist University in Dallas, TX. He is the author of the first major reference on the Processing language, *Processing: Creative Coding and Computational Art* and also wrote *The Essential Guide to Processing for Flash Developers*, both by friends of ED. A formally trained painter (BFA, Cornell University, MFA, University of Pennsylvania) turned computational autodidact; Ira has spent the past 20+ years searching for ways to make code drip. When not programming or hanging out with his family, you can find Ira playing and coaching ice hockey around the Dallas-Fort Worth metroplex.

Dianna Xu is an Associate Professor of Computer Science at Bryn Mawr College, PA. She devotes considerable time and effort rethinking the CS curricula to include contemporary, diverse examples of computing in a modern context, and to attract interdisciplinary and non-conventional students to the field. Her research interests include Computer Graphics, Computational Geometry, Visualization, Creative Computation, and Computer Science Education. She received her B.A. in Computer Science from Smith College and her M.S. and Ph.D. in Computer and Information Science from the University of Pennsylvania.

Deepak Kumar is a Professor of Computer Science at Bryn Mawr College and the associate director for education and diversity of the Center for Science of Information, a National Science Foundation Science & Technology Center (www.soihub.org). His research interests include artificial intelligence, science of information, data visualization, creative computing, and computer science education. He received a MS in Instrumentation from Birla Institute of Technology & Science, and a MS and PhD in computer science from the University at Buffalo.

About the Technical Reviewer

Ryan Rusnak is a software developer with a passion for creative coding. He holds a master's degree from Carnegie Mellon University in Human-Computer Interaction. His projects have been featured in *WIRED*, *Popular Science*, and on the Science Channel and the *Graham Norton Show*. He currently resides in Arlington, VA with his wife Kirby Rusnak.

About the Cover Image Artist

Corné van Dooren designed the front cover image for this book. After taking a break from friends of ED to create a new design for the Foundation series, he worked at combining technological and organic forms, with the results now appearing on the cover of this and other books.

Corné spent his childhood drawing on everything at hand and then began exploring the infinite world of multimedia—and his journey of discovery hasn't stopped since. His mantra has always been "the only limit to multimedia is the imagination," a saying that keeps him moving forward constantly.

Corné works for many international clients, writes features for multimedia magazines, reviews and tests software, authors multimedia studies, and works on many other friends of ED books. If you like Corné's work, be sure to check out his chapter in *New Masters of Photoshop: Volume 2* (friends of ED, 2004). You can see more of his work (and contact him) at his website, www.cornevandooren.com.

Acknowledgments

The authors would like to thank Aaron Cadle, Eric Eaton, Mark Russo, and Paul Ruvolo for their willingness to try this new approach of teaching Introduction to Computer Science with us; and for their support, encouragement, and assistance on this project in general. We would also like to thank our numerous students who took a course from us as we were developing these materials, with special thanks to Amanda Guadalupe, a student, whose project work on visualizing her Twitter tweets is included in Chapter 5.

We would like to express gratitude to Ben Fry and Casey Reas for their responsiveness to questions on the Processing 2.0 transition.

In addition, we would like to thank our families, who supported and encouraged us in spite of the time it took us away from them.

This work was partially supported by funds from Bryn Mawr College, Southern Methodist University, the Mellon Foundation, and the National Science Foundation under Grant No. 0942626, No. 0942628, No. 1140519, and CCF-0939370. We sincerely thank them for their support.

Introduction

Creative Coding grew primarily out of the digital art and design community, as an approach to programming based on intuitive, expressive, and organic algorithmic development, with an iterative leap-before-you-look style. Related, but broader, is the idea of Creative Computation, which explores computation as a universal, generative, and primary creative medium. We find these paradigms well suited for introducing computing to a new generation of students, who respond well to creative tasks and visual feedback. This book attempts to introduce programming and the fundamentals of computing and computer science by engaging you, the reader, in Creative Coding and Creative Computation contexts.

This book is designed for independent learning as well as a primary text for an introductory computing class (also known as CS1, or CS Principles, in the computing education community). A lot of the material grew out of our very successful NSF TUES funded project to develop a complete CS1 curriculum using Processing and Creative Coding principles. The central goal of the project was to strengthen formative/introductory computer science education by catalyzing excitement, creativity, and innovation. The digital representation of data, access to authentic sources of big data, and creative visualization techniques are revolutionizing intellectual inquiry in many disciplines, including the arts, humanities, and social sciences. We strongly believe that the introductory computing curriculum should be updated with contemporary, diverse examples of computing in a modern context.

We developed our introductory computing curriculum based on the philosophy that it should cover the same set of core CS1 topics as any conventional Java-based CS1, but show applications in the visual arts and interactive media, as well as through clean, concise, intuitive examples of advanced areas not typically accessible to CS1 students, including physics-based simulations, fractals and L-systems, image processing, emergent systems, cellular automata, aspects of data science and data visualization.

While it is entirely possible to learn to program on your own with this book, teaching with this book will require additional organization and initiative on the part of the instructor. This is an unconventional CS1 text in that our priority was to demonstrate the Creative Computation way of thinking (or way of teaching) and how it connects to the introductory computing curriculum, rather than to provide systematic/detailed lesson plans. Many standard, but basic programming constructs have not received the typical amount of attention because we trust a certain level of instructor experience and comfort to fill the gaps in the classrooms. It is our hope and belief that once shown the creative possibilities, following the same philosophy and adapting the material to your own classrooms will be an enjoyable and motivating task.

Resources

The home of the Processing project is the website:

`http://processing.org`

First and foremost, install Processing from their Download section. At the time of this writing, Processing 2.0 is still in later stages of Beta (the most current version is 2.0b8). The stable release remains to be 1.5.1. The Processing installation comes with an extensive collection of examples directly accessible from the IDE through the File➤Examples pull-down menu that should not be overlooked. This book includes coverage of most of the key features included in Processing 2.0. Those using Processing 1.5.1 release should bear this in mind.

Besides the Download section, the Processing website maintains a complete API Reference. We refer to it as the Processing Reference in this book and would encourage the reader to become familiar with navigating their browsers to it as well as to learn to read the rich documentation and examples it provides. Much learning can and will take place with increased usage of the Processing Reference. Equally important for the beginner (as well as the instructor) is the Learning section of the `Processing.org` website. The set of tutorials provided there will be valuable for anyone starting to learn Processing from this book. These comprehensive tutorials are good starting points for the basics, as well as additional information. In fact, these should be treated as ancillary materials for the earlier chapters. Both reference and tutorials are also conveniently accessible from the Processing IDE from the Help pull-down menu (just access the Help➤Reference and Help➤Getting Started options).

We have taught using the approach presented here well over a dozen times in the past few years. Consequently, we have accumulated a wealth of curricular material, much more than there is room for in this book. Instructors interested in gaining access to complete syllabi, lecture notes, class examples, assignments, and problem sets, please write to us.

The book is sprinkled with a number of "Try This" suggestion boxes, which we have chosen to place wherever they are relevant. Some merely test a grasp of the current discussion; others require more substantial thought and even full-fledged programming work. The complete code examples in the book can be downloaded from the book publisher's resource website:

`http://apress.com/9781430244646`

While it would be trivial to copy the code and run it, we strongly urge everyone to actually type the programs yourselves. This is a book about learning after all, and there is no substitute for experiencing the coding process first hand. Entering your own code from scratch, even if you are copying from these examples, is essential to learning the concepts that are being communicated. Question every word in every line of the code as you type, and don't be afraid to experiment. You will learn more!

We also recommend visiting the online community OpenProcessing:

`http://www.openprocessing.org`

This website is devoted to sharing open-source Processing sketches. There is much to learn from and get inspired by from the sketches shared there by creative coders, students, and teachers alike from across the globe. We hope that, as you learn and evolve your own creative style, you will contribute your own sketches.

Finally, the Processing.org website itself has its own discussion forum where you can post queries and get involved in discussions involving all things Processing. We urge you to support these efforts in any way you can. Buy a Processing t-shirt!

In the Book

In line with the philosophy of leap-before-you-look we begin by literally diving into the shallow end (Chapter 1) where we provide background and introduction to creative coding, Processing, its origins, and its relationship with Java. We offer a 30,000 feet overview of creative coding, the distinction between programming and the discipline of computer science. We also provide a detailed tour of the Processing IDE, which could be skimmed in the initial encounter but returned to later as the need arises. We follow this, in Chapter 2 (Art by Numbers) with a whirlwind tour of pseudocode, algorithms, and basic programming constructs: variables, simple types, expressions, and comments. Drawing with these coding primitives is presented by introducing Processing's coordinate system and commands for drawing 2D shapes. This sets the stage for a deep immersion in Processing and creative coding. By taking a boot camp approach (Chapter 3), we introduce functions, all the basic control structures (conditionals and loops), and additional drawing concepts like transformations, and drawing contexts. Instructors of introductory computing courses may want to take a more deliberate approach here especially with the key programming constructs. These are further developed in Chapter 4 to enable a deeper understanding of structuring programs. At the same time, we introduce the dynamic mode in Processing, including handling mouse and keyboard events, as well as a deeper treatment of drawing curves. By this time, most of the basics of programming as well as Processing have been introduced. We would encourage the readers to take some time to reflect, take stock, and review before moving on into the book.

Beyond the basics, we next delve into some of the core CS1 topics: arrays, object-oriented programming, and recursion. We use the backdrop of learning about arrays to introduce concepts in data science and visualization. Arrays are introduced as mechanisms for storing, processing, and visualizing datasets (Chapter 5). Also, one of the core computer science ideas: algorithms and space-time complexity are given an informal treatment. Object-oriented programming and its manifestation in Processing is introduced in Chapter 6 as a mechanism for organizing the chaos of large programs and also as a way of modeling "live" or animated entities in a sketch by way of particles and physical motion models. We introduce Processing's PVector class and go beyond basic physics by providing a detailed example of Verlet Integration for natural looking motion and behaviors in sketches, thereby truly enhancing a creative coder's conceptual toolbox. We go deeper into creative data visualization (Chapter 7) by deconstructing (and reconstructing) a popular visualization application: word clouds. In the process, strings, ArrayLists, sorting algorithms, and font metrics are introduced. In the context of a fairly non-trivial example, we have attempted to illustrate program design and redesign principles and how object-oriented programming facilitates well-designed, maintainable, clean code. More creative fun follows with recursion (Chapter 8) as a computational medium for creating and experimenting with models of biological systems, fractal geometry, and advanced data visualization.

Our journey continues deeper both into computing and creative computing where in Chapter 9 we explore painting with bits in the context of image processing and manipulation. Two dimensional arrays and pixel buffers as underlying computing concepts come together in manipulating images to create stunning visual effects. We go beyond, by using bitwise operations and Processing's color component functions to see examples of steganography. Further, iterative solutions are presented as solutions for modeling emergent systems, cellular automata, and glorious tiling patterns. We build further on image manipulation in Chapter 10 where we try to impress upon the idea that image processing is a creative medium with wider range of applications that go beyond traditional "photo manipulation." This is also where the fact that Processing is designed by artists and creative coders really pays off: We introduce several built-in image manipulation functions that are typically not accessible to students in an introductory computing course.

If you consider this book a (big) meal, you can think of the last chapter as dessert–a hard earned and guilt free dessert! It is truly a buffet, with a glimpse into the three-dimensional world, developing sketches for Android devices, and going beyond Processing into Java, OpenGL, C++, and other programming environments. In today's ubiquitous world of computation, the boundaries between languages, environments, and devices are blurring. Processing gives you a handle on the myriad of techniques and tools that serve as building blocks at first and then takes you to the very cusp of exciting new frontiers of creative computing. We hope you will enjoy this gradual, yet deliberate computational, intellectual, and visual feast. If we have not been successful at any aspect of the book, please write to us, we want to know.

Bon appétit and happy creative coding!

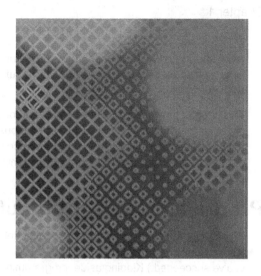

Chapter 1

Diving into the Shallow End

Imagine enrolling in a class to learn a new sport, perhaps Irish Hurling. (This type of hurling involves a ball and bat.) You arrive at class on the first day excited to dive into this exotic new hands-on activity, only to be confronted by a long lecture on the theoretical foundation of hurling. Over the next fourteen weeks, the course proceeds in a similar fashion, with maybe a couple of contrived on-the-field exercises to reinforce the lectures. We don't know about you, but we're not so sure we'd make it through this class long enough to get to the on-the-field part (the part that got us excited about learning hurling to begin with.) This is what many students experience when they take their first computer science class.

Of course, learning the theory behind Irish Hurling might provide you with pretty interesting and ultimately valuable information, especially if your goal is to become a world-class Hurler. However, for most of us, diving directly into the theoretical aspects of an activity such as hurling, or computer science, before getting a handle on why the theory might actually be useful can be intimidating and off-putting (and very few of us are destined for the Hurling Hall of Fame.) Worst of all, this approach can lead to wider societal misconceptions, such as: *computer science is obscure, difficult, and even boring.* These misconceptions can also become self-fulfilling prophecies, ultimately attracting only the *types* of students who buy into the misconception, leading to a population of students and practitioners lacking in diversity and varied perspective.

In the last few years, some computer scientists and other computing professionals, the authors of this book included, have begun challenging the entrenched and narrow approach to teaching computer science. This book champions a new way–*a creative coding approach*, in which you'll learn by doing. Building creative code sketches, you'll learn the principles behind computer science, but in the context of creating and discovery. Returning to the hurling analogy, first you'll learn how to whack the hurling ball (*the silotar*) with the hurling bat (the *hurley*) wicked hard; then you'll learn the physics behind it. Or, to use some computing lingo, first you'll learn to code a cool app, then you'll learn about the fundamental principles behind it. Not only will this make coding easier and more fun to learn, but it will make the theory part much more relevant and hopefully even fascinating.

This chapter provides just a little context and background for the rest of the book. You'll learn about the history of Processing, including its origins at the famous MIT Media Lab. We'll discuss the creative coding approach in a bit more detail, including some relevant research into its effectiveness. Finally, you'll have a detailed tour of the Processing language and development environment.

Programming vs. Computer Science

If you want to tick off a computer scientist, tell him that you *know* computer science because you can write some code. (Of course, many computer scientists don't show a lot of emotion so you may not even be sure you've succeeded.) Kidding aside, programming is not computer science. BUT, from our perspective, it is often the most fun part of it. Yet, there are computer scientists who don't actually program. These are theoreticians who see computation more as applied mathematics than as hands-on implementation. Such a theoretician might be interested in proving something about computing, using mathematical proofs. However, to the average end-user, programming is often equated with computer science.

According to Dictionary.com, computer science is defined as:

> *the science that deals with the theory and methods of processing information in digital computers, the design of computer hardware and software, and the applications of computers.*

The first part of the definition, *the theory and methods of processing information* is concerned with more fundamental mathematical principles behind computing. This is perhaps the most pure scientific part of computer science. Research in this area affects things like the speed, efficiency, and reliability of computers. Arguably, this area of research provides the bedrock for all other aspects and applications of computing. Though programming is a part of this branch of computer science, its role is primarily for testing and verifying theory.

A company like Apple spends a great deal of time and resources researching how its hardware and software should look, feel, and function in the hands of users. This area of computer science research, the second part of the dictionary.com definition, the *design of computer hardware and software,* is where science gives way to engineering and design—where theory is applied, creating tangible systems. Another way of describing this area might be: the interface between the mathematical and theoretical aspects of computing and the incredible things we can do with it. Programming is a huge part of this area and is commonly referred to as software engineering.

The last part of the definition, *applications of computers* (not to be confused with computer apps) is about how computers (really computation) can be applied in the world. This part of the definition may be too general, as computers impact nearly all aspects of life, and it's extremely likely this impact will only increase in the future. It's not such a leap to imagine our cars driving themselves, our walls and countertops acting like smart touch screens, and our communication devices shrinking and getting even further integrated into perhaps even our physical bodies. Programming is very relevant to this part of computer science as well, mostly in the development of specialized software and hardware targeting specific application domains.

Google developed and released the Android Software Development Kit, which includes libraries of code and application software for creating custom Android apps. Apple has its own similar development platform, as do many other companies. These development environments enable people to efficiently program applications, without the need of years of formal computer science training. Clearly, this evolution in software development is challenging long held notions of required technical expertise. There are high school students writing highly successful mobile applications, artists programming interactive artworks, and many other "non-experts" creating small software businesses overnight. So no, programming is not computer science, but apparently computer science is not necessarily required for programming either.

Art + Science = Creative Coding

At Southern Methodist University in Dallas there is a Center of Creative Computation (C³) that explores computation as a fundamental creative medium. C³ considers computer code (as well as other aspects of computation) the same way a painter thinks about paint, or a musician sound or even how a dancer thinks about gesture. C³ is less concerned with why computation solves a specific problem and more interested in how it is solved, and most importantly, how it can be solved in a more interesting and novel way. Yet in spite of this creative approach, C³ requires students to take very challenging courses in computer science, math, and physics. It also requires an equal amount of rigorous creative courses. This integration of quantitative material with creative practice can be a daunting challenge for some students, especially those who were labeled at an early age: "the artist" or "the geek," but probably not both.

C³ has been successful (as has a similar interdisciplinary approach at Bryn Mawr College) integrating difficult quantitative material with creative practice in the classroom, and research lab, utilizing a "Creative Coding" approach. This approach was originally developed at the Massachusetts Institute of Technology (MIT) Media Lab, by past lab director John Maeda, who you'll hear more about shortly. Creative coding combines approaches from the arts classroom, such as critiques, portfolio development and emphasis on aesthetics and personal expression, with fundamental principles from computer science. Creative coding uses computer code as the creative medium by which students develop a body of art, while developing core competency in programming.

In 2010, researchers from Bryn Mawr College and C³ at Southern Methodist University received a National Science Foundation grant to explore the use of creative coding in the introductory computer science classroom. Based on early research results, it is very promising that students learning the creative coding approach develop significantly greater personal interest in programming as compared to students in a more traditional computer science class.

To help facilitate this integration in the classroom, the creative coding approach relies on some innovative programming languages and development environments, especially Processing, which grew directly out of work done at the MIT Media Lab.

MIT Media Lab

The MIT Media Lab was founded by MIT professor Nicholas Negroponte and then-MIT President Jerome Wiesner in 1985. Its mission, as stated on the Media Lab site (http://www.media.mit.edu/about), is to:

> envision the impact of emerging technologies on everyday life—technologies that promise to fundamentally transform our most basic notions of human capabilities.

Though an academic lab at MIT within the School of Architecture and Planning, the Media Lab has always radically crossed disciplines and blurred distinctions between theory and implementation, academia and industry, and science and art. It has been involved in fundamental breakthroughs of the digital age since its founding, including the World Wide Web and wireless networks. The lab has also pioneered innovative research and development in radically new areas, such as smart toys, ubiquitous computing, and aesthetics and computation.

The Aesthetics + Computation Group (ACG) at MIT was created in 1996 by John Maeda, a formally trained computer scientist and graphic designer. Maeda and ACG explored novel approaches to software tools and language development, as well as computational artistic practice. One of the projects developed at the Media Lab was a new programming language and programming environment named "Design By Numbers" (DBN). DBN is a very simplified programming language built on top of the Java programming language (explained a bit later in this chapter). DBN greatly simplified the process of graphics programming using Java by creating a simplified language syntax (the commands and rules used to program) and a development environment that enabled fast prototyping of simple graphics patterns, code art, and designs. DBN was never intended as a full-featured programming language, but rather a proof of concept for a radically new approach to language design; it was tested primarily in the design arts classroom to teach programming to beginners.

DBN as a proof of concept was a big success, though as a usable language, it wasn't much more than an academic exercise. Two of Maeda's students in the Media Lab, Ben Fry and Casey Reas, worked on DBN. After finishing their studies at the Media Lab, Fry and Reas decided to take the lessons learned developing DBN and build a more full-featured language. They named their new project Processing, which they kicked off in 2001.

What Is Processing?

In the very simplest sense, Processing is a software application that allows you to write, edit, compile (which will be explained shortly), and run Java code. However, before discussing Processing further, it will help you to understand a little bit about Java, but even before we talk about Java, we need to talk briefly about computing in general. (Please note, this will be one of the only places in the book where we throw some theory at you without a fun, hands-on activity.)

Bits and Bytes

You probably have some sense that computers and 1's and 0's go together. But it may not be so clear to you how a bunch of 1's and 0's can lead to Shrek running through a field of blowing grass, your computer's operating system, or Facebook. It really is truly remarkable what has been done with a bunch of 1's and 0's. Though really, it's not about 1's or 0's, but instead a state of being true or false, or more accurately, something being open or closed. If you've ever looked inside your computer, at the beautiful and mysterious boards, cards, chips, wires, etc., it should be obvious that everything in there is fundamentally reliant on electricity. However, electricity is a pretty mysterious force unto itself, and it will be simpler for this discussion to think of electricity in a much more general form, as a flowing source, something akin to water. (Though we can't recommend filling the inside of your computer up with a hose.)

Using the water metaphor, you can think of the guts of your computer as a series of incredibly complex canals with controllable dams. If a dam is down or closed, water doesn't flow past it; if it's up or open, water does pass through. As a complex interconnected system, some dams control the availability of water for thousands of other dams. By systematically controlling dams, you can control how, when, and where water flows through the system. Perhaps some of the dams are controlled by water pressure in parts of the system; when water starts flowing they open up and remain open. You can think of this like a water loop that keeps flowing. Other dams might be open by default and water pressure closes them. Some of the dams can even be constructed in a series where one dam's state (open or closed) controls another's state. As the dam master, you can design complex systems to precisely control how water (and ultimately ships) move through the system, based on certain conditions. For example, if dam A and dam B are both open then perhaps a ship can safely pass through canal C, but if either dam is shut it can't. So even though we're just describing dams and canals, you can see how simple logic–if a certain condition is true, something occurs–can be constructed in the system. By simply opening or closing dams, we can control specific outcomes to the larger system.

Of course, computers use flowing electricity instead of water, but the system works in a similar way. Gates, the computer's version of dams, control the passage of electrons. Gates in modern transistors–the fundamental electronic components in devices such as our computers–can be open or closed, just like the dams. We can use a 1 or 0 to represent the two discrete states, which we refer to technically as binary digits, or more commonly as "bits."

A binary number system is based on only 2 unique digits (0 or 1), as opposed to our more familiar decimal system that uses 10 unique digits (0–9). We can design number systems with any number of unique characters. For example, another commonly used number system in computing is hexadecimal, with 16 unique characters (0–9 and A–F). Since computing is fundamentally based on those previously mentioned open or closed gates, it's efficient for computers (not us) to utilize a binary system.

A bit, at any one point in time, can either be 1 or 0, but never both. When we group eight of these bits together, we refer to this as a byte: one thousand bytes is a kilobyte, one thousand kilobytes is a megabyte, and a thousand of these is a gigabyte, and it keeps going. Hopefully, the common "buzz" terms people throw around when comparing their mobiles devices (*"Dude, my phone has 20 gigs of memory…"*) have a little more context now. If you think back to the dams and canals analogy, imagine the complex ship movement you could get with billions of individual dams. You can probably now imagine how, as seen from a plane above, millions of different boats moving through such a complex system of dams could create organized patterns–even approximating a running Shrek perhaps, or forming the basis for complex logic determining the rules about how to friend someone on Facebook.

Mnemonics

Manipulating individual bits to represent everything a computer does, though theoretically possible, is extremely impractical. The computer's language is purely mathematical–it breathes 0's and 1's. We humans, however, are not quite as numerate as our machines, and we rely on more descriptive, symbolic systems to communicate, such as our natural spoken and written languages. While a computer might be happy with the binary code 0110011 to signify an operation such as adding two numbers together, humans prefer something more along the lines of the word "add." Though a series of 0's and 1's is efficient, it's difficult for most of us to efficiently decipher binary patterns and then remember what each unique pattern means. This divide between how computers *process* information as compared to how we *comprehend* it has led to the development of programming languages.

At a fundamental information processing level, our brains work quite similarly to our computers. Instead of a complex array of transistors, we have an interconnected network of neurons. The individual neurons can be thought of as analogous to individual transistors. Though instead of having gates, neurons utilize something called an action potential. The action potential, like a transistor's gate, is controlled by an electrical impulse, determining when the neuron transmits information, or fires. It's an all or nothing response, like an open or closed gate.

Information processing–whether in the brain or computer–is quite distinct from human comprehension. The computer is sort of a silicon brain in a shiny box. As mentioned earlier it groks on 1's and 0's, or what is more technically called machine language. When computers were first developed if you actually wanted to do something with them, you needed to learn to speak their native machine language. This was a very difficult, tedious, and slow process. Computer scientists quickly realized they needed to simplify the programming process and began to develop higher-level languages. By higher-level, we mean languages less directly mapped to how computers process information and more closely aligned with how we understand it. One of the first such languages developed was Assembly language.

Assembly language by today's standards is still a very low-level language–*pretty darn close to the 1's and 0's*–but it was a huge step forward in simplifying programming. Assembly language converts machine language commands from pure numbers to statements, including familiar words such as: `set`, `store`, `load`, and `jump`. In the context of the machine's native language, we can refer to these more natural language terms as mnemonics, or devices to help us understand and remember the underlying machine commands.

Though Assembly was a big step forward in simplifying programming, it's still a dense and complex approach. Because Assembly maps individual machine language commands with mnemonics, it still takes a lot of code to do relatively simple things. For example, the following is Assembly code to output the phrase: "Happy Creative Coding!"

```
; code based on example: http://michaux.ca/articles/assembly-hello-world-for-os-x
; A "Happy Creative Coding!" program using NASM
section .text
global c3Start
c3Start:
    push dword msglen
    push dword mymsg
    push dword 1
    mov eax, 0x4
    sub esp, 4
    int 0x80
    add esp, 20
    push dword 0
```

```
    mov eax, 0x1
    sub esp, 4
    int 0x80
section .data
  mymsg db "Happy Creative Coding!", 0xa
  msglen equ $-mymsg
```

By comparison, here is code to do the same thing in Java:

```
// A "Happy Creative Coding!" program using Java
public class Happy {
    public static void main(String[] args){
        System.out.println("Happy Creative Coding!");
    }
}
```

And finally, here's the same program in Processing

```
// A "Happy Creative Coding!" program using Processing
println("Happy Creative Coding!");
```

If it wasn't obvious, Java, and especially Processing, greatly reduced the number of lines in code. Also, if you read through the example code, we suspect you were able to understand much more of the Java and Processing code than the Assembly.

The first language assemblers, the software that converts Assembly code to machine language, emerged in around 1950. Java was released in the mid-1990s. In the forty or so years between Assembly and Java, many other programming languages were developed. One of the most important languages that emerged, which strongly influenced Java and ultimately Processing, was the C programming language. For our discussion, it's not necessary to say too much about C, other than that it was considerably more high-level than Assembly, and it became very widely adopted. Compared to Assembly, C greatly reduced the lines of code necessary to program the computer, allowing single programming calls to internally map to many lines of Assembly code; it was no longer a 1 to 1 translation with just added mnemonics. The grammar of the Java programming language, more commonly referred to as the syntax of the language, is heavily based on C, but as you'll learn, Java is an even more high-level language approach than C.

Java

The development of Java was, by some standards, a failure. Java was initially developed for interactive television and ultimately to connect "smart" devices, which didn't really catch on until about fifteen years after Java's release. We take it for granted now that our newer flat screen TVs are Internet ready, allowing us to surf the Net while we watch shows on demand and check our email. Back in 1995, this was a pipedream held by a few technology zealots, certainly not by the mainstream public. What arguably saved Java was the proliferation of the Internet, which we'll say more about in a moment. From near failure to ultimate success, Java is today one of the most popular programming language in the world, according to the TIOBE Programming Community Index (http://www.tiobe.com/index.php/content/paperinfo/tpci/index.html).

Java was designed as a full-featured programming language, like C, but with one very big difference–universal portability. Java's original slogan was "Write once, run everywhere." The idea was that a programmer could write a Java program on any machine, and the program would run consistently on any other machine. This may not seem like such a big deal at first glance, but computers are not simply just the buzz words we've reduced them to: Mac, Windows, Linux. Computers are composed of lots of complex parts, such as central processing units (CPUs), graphical processing units (GPUs), and random access memory (RAM), just to name a few. These parts, especially the CPU, the main brain of the computer, rely on specific instructions, the machine language, to do their magic. Unfortunately, these machine instructions vary widely across not only computer brands, but also specific hardware components like CPUs.

Thinking back on our discussion about the Assembly programming language, you learned that Assembly wraps machine language with mnemonics–adding somewhat more normal-sounding language commands to the underlying binary math. The C language takes the process a step further, in a sense wrapping the Assembly language with a much higher-level language construct, greatly simplifying programming. For example, one line of C code might replace ten lines of Assembly. The problem with the way this approach works is that the code (regardless if it's Assembly or C) all still reduces down to machine language, and as previously mentioned, machine language code is specific to the machine hardware you're working on. To run a C program, you need to explicitly convert your C code to machine language for your specific CPU. We refer to this process as compilation or compiling. A C language compiler is software that makes the conversion from the C source code you write to the machine's native language, the binary code (1's and 0's).

So how did Java improve this situation? Java incorporates an additional layer of software, called a language interpreter, or to use Java speak, a Java Virtual Machine (commonly shortened to JVM). Java code, like C code, is compiled. However, the Java code is not compiled down to the native machine level, which again would be hardware specific. Rather, Java code is compiled to a higher universal form, called bytecode. The Java bytecode is universal, in that it should be able to run on any machine, regardless of the underlying hardware architecture, as long as the machine includes a Java Virtual Machine. If you think back to our earlier discussion, we wrote that Java was an initial failure saved by the proliferation of the Internet. The Internet is a vast network of computers, with widely varied hardware configurations, running various operating systems. The Java environment, including its compiler (to bytecode) and its interpreter (JVM), became the perfect solution to connect all these disparate devices. In addition, some Web browsers include their own Java Virtual Machine, allowing Java programs (referred to as applets in this context) to also run on the Web. To learn more about Java's interesting history, see: http://www.oracle.com/technetwork/java/javase/overview/javahistory-index-198355.html.

In addition to the Internet, Java is also having a dramatic impact on mobile, and more generally, ubiquitous computing, with Java Virtual Machines widely available for many of our portable and handheld devices. For example, Google's Android operating system is based on Java.

So in the end, it seems Java, like other revolutionary ideas, was not so much a failure as ahead of its time. That's not to say that Java is without its critics. Java is still a fairly complex language and environment to work with and also challenging to teach with in the introductory computing classroom. Some critics also fault Java for being slower than a purely compiled language like C, which doesn't need to be run through a language interpreter. (It's quite a hot topic as to how much slower Java actually is compared to a purely compiled language like C.) Since Java's release, many other new languages have been developed that aim to further reduce the complexity of programming. One of these is Processing, which has been steadily growing in popularity since its release in 2001. Though Processing is indeed an independent programming environment, with its own language, you'll learn next that it is also inextricably linked to Java.

Processing

As we mentioned earlier, Processing emerged out of the MIT Media Lab, inspired by the simple DBN language. While DBN was developed as a proof of concept, a showcase to demonstrate an approach to programming, Processing was created as a full-featured programming environment for "real" creative development (*creative coding!*) However, DBN provided important lessons for Processing's initial developers, Reas and Fry:

- **Keep it simple!**
  - The Processing interface, which you can see in Figure 1-1, is incredibly minimal, *by design*. Reas and Fry conceived of Processing as a sketchbook of a sort, with essentially a blank page to begin creating on. Though Processing greatly simplifies the programming process, it was never intended to reduce the complexity of the creative process. The language is devoid of most slick filters and effects you might find in a software application like Adobe PhotoShop, again by design.

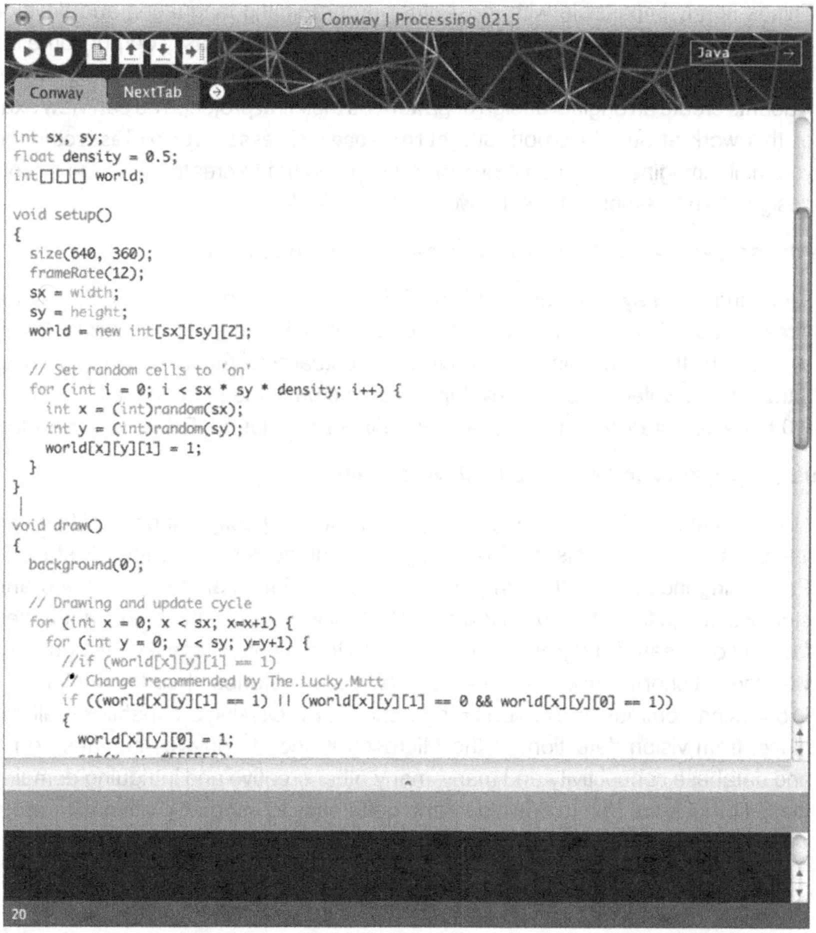
Conway | Processing 0215
Java
Conway
NextTab
int sx, sy;
float density = 0.5;
int[][][] world;
void setup()
{
size(640, 360);
frameRate(12);
sx = width;
sy = height;
world = new int[sx][sy][2];
// Set random cells to 'on'
for (int i = 0; i < sx * sy * density; i++) {
int x = (int)random(sx);
int y = (int)random(sy);
world[x][y][1] = 1;
}
}
void draw()
{
background(0);
// Drawing and update cycle
for (int x = 0; x < sx; x=x+1) {
for (int y = 0; y < sy; y=y+1) {
//if (world[x][y][1] == 1)
// Change recommended by The.Lucky.Mutt
if ((world[x][y][1] == 1) || (world[x][y][1] == 0 && world[x][y][0] == 1))
{
world[x][y][0] = 1;
20

Figure 1-1. Main Processing interface

- **Create an easy-to-use environment to write, test, and run your code, also referred to as an integrated development environment, or IDE**

  - Processing is a completely self-contained executable application. You simply launch it by double-clicking and begin coding. Most other programming environments require a fair amount of fussing with system settings and preferences to get working. In addition, many of these other environments are temperamental and can easily *break*, as files get accidentally moved or saved. Also, the programming environments themselves (not even the programming languages you use within them) can be extremely complex to master. The Processing environment by contrast is simple and intuitive to use and doesn't add to the complexity of coding.

- **Create a zero-entry approach to coding**

  - On the first day of the introductory Computer Science class we have students who have never programmed before coding interesting creative work with Processing. This is nearly impossible with most other programming languages and development environments. Some languages will allow you to relatively easily output some text–the old school tradition is for CS 1 students to output "Hello World." Using processing, students create an original design or pattern as their first project. You can view examples of this work at our classroom site http://openprocessing.org/classroom/1262. As you might imagine, it's much more interesting and fun to create an image of your own design, than to simply output the words "Hello World."

- **Give the software away for free and release the source code**

  - Reas and Fry may have lost millions of dollars based on their "give it away for free" strategy, but this model also allowed Processing to be adopted worldwide. In addition, by releasing the Processing source-code, the actual code that created Processing, they attracted a devoted group of developers to help push the language along. Processing 2.0 benefited greatly from the extended team of passionate Processing developers.

- **Focus on graphics and multimedia development**

  - Like John Maeda, Reas and Fry have graphic design backgrounds, and that spirit has influenced many aspects of Processing. We sometimes joke with our students that Processing includes all the fun parts of Java and hides all the boring and annoying stuff; it's not quite that simple. However, Processing is a programming language that is focused on creative programming. In addition to the core Processing language, which we'll look at shortly, Processing includes extensive libraries of code contributed by the Processing community. These libraries extend Processing's capabilities all over the place, from vision detection, to the Microsoft Kinect, to physics engines, to network and database connectivity and many, many other creative and intriguing domains. And these libraries are free to download and quite easy to integrate within your projects.

■ **Build it on Java**

■ DBN was initially developed in Java because it could be built as a stand-alone application, a program you double-click on your hard drive, and also as a Web-based applet. You'll remember that Java's language interpreter, JVM, lives in some browsers, as well as on nearly all desktop computing environments, and now of course on mobile and other handheld devices. Processing followed this approach, allowing Processing programs to be run from the desktop, but also on the Web showcased in online galleries, like at openProcessing.org. In addition, by developing in Java and relying on the JVM, Reas and Fry minimized the need to develop and maintain many different versions of the software, to accommodate all the different potential machine hardware and operating system configurations out there. Processing's relationship to Java also allows Processing sketches to be fully integrated in stand-alone Java applications. This advanced functionality allows a truly seamless transition from Processing to Java, which is very useful in the computing classroom and also for you as you advance in your coding skills.

In addition to the lessons learned from their work on DBN, Reas and Fry took Processing much further, adding new features, capabilities and resources, including:

■ **A worldwide support network**

■ Processing has always been an active online community–a social network of a sort. Processing was born of the Web, and for years the only information about Processing was what was posted on the processing.org site and perhaps an annual email or two. As Reas and Fry developed Processing, going back to 2001, they released new versions, sometimes as many as a few a week. This *early and frequent* release model is very different from commercial software projects, which have infrequent, controlled software releases. Reas and Fry also listened to users' suggestions and encouraged active bug reporting, as users found broken or "buggy" parts of Processing. This transparent and interactive approach to development created a very loyal and passionate following, which continues today.

The Processing discussion forum (http://forum.processing.org/recent) has always been an active place to discuss all things Processing. If you have an obscure Processing question, chances are a search of the forum will turn up an answer and lively discussion.

■ **An open-architecture for expanding Processing's capabilities and even its look and feel**

■ The Processing core language, published at http://processing.org/reference/, has been very stable since around 2006. There have been steady minor tweaks to the language and environment, as well as substantial ones with the new 2.0 release. The major growth and development in Processing has been primarily through user-submitted libraries (over 130 as of this writing) and tools. Processing includes a system for expanding and even altering itself, sometimes referred to as an open-architecture. There is a relatively simple process for creating both new features in the language, through external libraries, and changes and additions to the development environment, through tools.

- **3D support**

  - One of the most interesting and fun parts of Processing is its 3D support. Processing utilizes OpenGL, an industry standard 3D software specification that utilizes your computer's hardware for acceleration, providing very robust performance. Though 3D typically requires advanced programming and mathematics, Processing simplifies the process significantly.

- **Extensive support materials**

  - Processing was originally built on the autodidactic principle, with the assumption that motivated individuals would teach themselves the language. Though some "creative coding evangelist" types did do this, Processing now has extensive support resources–from numerous books, to online tutorials, to classes and workshops offered around the world. On the processing.org website, you'll find lots of code examples, as well as longer tutorials. One of the best ways to learn to program is to start with existing code and tweak it–to see what happens. Throughout the book, you'll see *Try This. . .* sections after code examples, where you'll be encouraged to tweak the book examples.

Quick Tour

Now that you have some sense of what Processing is, at least in theory, let's next take a quick tour of the software. The first thing you'll want to do (if you haven't done so already) is download Processing from: `http://processing.org/download`. You should download the current release of the software (**not** a pre-release) for your specific operating system. Windows users should download the software using the Windows link, not Windows (Without Java), To install the software, simply double-click to extract the downloaded .zip file, for OSX and Windows, or .tgz for Linux.

Figure 1-2 shows the main Processing interface.

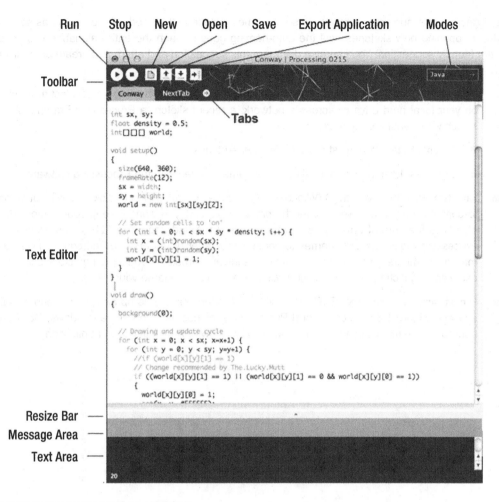

Figure 1-2. Main Processing interface with labels

As we mentioned earlier, the Processing interface is minimal by design. Since Processing is a text-based programming language, the Processing environment is essentially a simple text editor, with basic programming capabilities. Next are brief descriptions of the toolbar interface elements, labeled in Figure 1-2:

- Run Cmd+R (OS X) or Ctrl+R (Windows): Compiles your code, launches a display window and executes your sketch within this window.

- Stop: Terminates your running program.

- New Cmd+N (OS X) or Ctrl+N (Windows): Creates a new sketch within a new directory. Both the directory and the PDE file (Processing's own file format) will share this name. By default, new sketches are saved with the root "sketch_□," the date (in the form year/month/day), and a secondary character beginning with the next alphabetically available character. For example, today's date is November 16, 2012, so a new sketch by default will have the name "sketch_121116a", the next one: "sketch_121116b", etc.

Easter Eggs are little surprises programmers sometimes include in their code. Processing has some as well. For fun, try opening new sketches until the auto-naming goes through the entire alphabet; you should then receive a friendly suggestion. You can also disregard this suggestion and attempt to create an additional new sketch, which will prompt yet another response.

- Open Cmd+O (OS X) or Ctrl+O (Windows): Opens a submenu where you can select a sketch residing on your local hard drive or across a network, a recent sketch, a Processing Example sketch, or a sketch within your Sketchbook.

    - Recent: Select from a list of recently used sketches.

    - Examples: Load an example sketch that came bundled with the Processing software.

- Save Cmd+S (OS X) or Ctrl+S (Windows): Writes the current sketch to disk. You will not be prompted to confirm that you are writing over the previous state. If you want to keep your original sketch and also save the current one, you should use Save As, found under the File menu. Please note that Processing requires sketch names to begin with a letter or underscore and contain no spaces. You may use numbers in the sketch name after the initial character. If you try to name a Processing sketch using an illegal character, Processing will bark at you and rename your file.

- Export Application Cmd+E (OS X) or Ctrl+E (Windows): Opens up an Export Options dialog box, shown in Figure 1-3. You can export Processing sketches as stand-alone Windows, OS X and Linux applications, either running within a contained window or as a full-screen application.

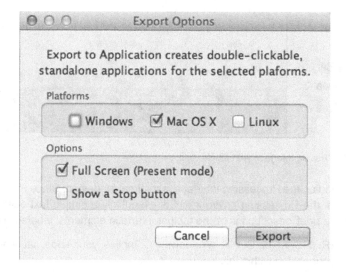

Figure 1-3. Export Options window

- Modes is a very exciting new feature in Processing 2.0. Figure 1-4 shows the modes pop-up menu.

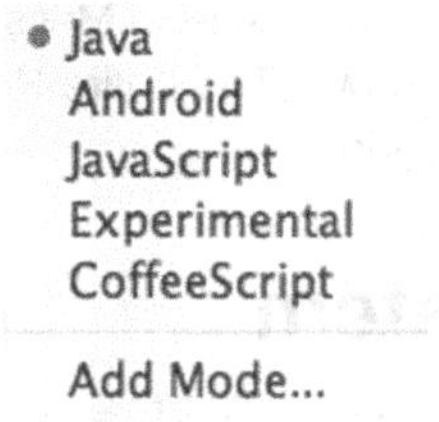

● Java
Android
JavaScript
Experimental
CoffeeScript

Add Mode...

Figure 1-4. Modes pop-up menu

- Java mode is the default Processing mode, which utilizes Java under the hood to create stand-alone applications. Java (formally called Standard) mode is all there was prior to Processing 2.0. It's essentially Processing 1.0.

- Android mode was added in Processing 2.0. It allows you to develop Android apps using Processing. The apps can even automatically be saved to your Android device. This mode does require the Android Software Development Kit (SDK), which can be downloaded at http://developer.android.com/sdk/index.html. Once the Android SDK is installed, you're able to select Android mode in Processing, which opens up a contextually altered version of the development environment. If you mouse over some of the familiar toolbar elements, you'll notice some things have changed: instead of Run, it now shows Run on Device and instead of Export Application, it now shows Export Signed Package and Export Android Project. There are also some changes to the menus.

- JavaScript mode was added in Processing 2.0, essentially as replacement for the Java Applet export feature in Processing 1.0. Applets ran in a Web browser using the Java plug-in (a Java virtual machine embedded within the browser). Java applets were historically buggy within the browser, often with long load times. In addition, some browsers no longer enable applets by default. HTML 5.0 and JavaScript can now provide most of the functionality of Java applets, with considerably faster load times and new capabilities and functionalities actively being developed. JavaScript mode relies on the JavaScript library Processing. js, originally developed by John Resig. Processing.js allows Processing sketches to run within a browser, without the need for the Java plug-in. it works by converting the Processing code into JavaScript code and utilizing the canvas element introduced in HTML5. To learn more about the canvas element and HTML5 see https://developer.mozilla.org/en/Canvas_tutorial (4/11/2012). Processing.js is a stand-alone JavaScript library that may be used independently of the Processing environment, such as in an HTML editor. However, Processing's new JavaScript mode greatly simplifies the process of creating real-time Web graphics, animation, and even 3D content. Similarly to Android mode discussed earlier, switching to JavaScript mode alters the naming of some of the toolbar elements in the Processing environment: Run becomes Start Server, and Export Application becomes Export for Web.

- Experimental mode introduces a debugger into Processing. Debuggers allows you to incrementally move through your code as it is being Processed, helping you identify bugs and logical errors.

- Additional modes will be listed here. As of this writing CoffeeScript mode was included, allowing you to use CoffeeScript language syntax to create Processing sketches. You can read more about CoffeeScript here: https://github.com/fjenett/coffeescript-mode-processing.

- Add Mode... opens up a Mode Manager allowing you to add other custom modes to Processing, as they become available. This will allow coders who work in other languages, such as Python or Ruby, just to name two popular ones, to be able to integrate Processing code in their projects.

Finally, you can change the ratio of Text Editor size to Message Area size by dragging the resize bar with the embossed dot (see Figure 1-2) up and down. The entire Processing application window is also resizable by dragging the lower right corner of the window.

Processing Menu System

The overall menu system is pretty straightforward, and most of it should be self-explanatory. However, Processing 2.0's new modes feature does recontextualize the menus somewhat when different modes are selected. First we'll look at the menus in Java mode and then discuss the changes in Android and JavaScript modes respectively. Please note that in Windows, the Processing menu is contained within the Processing application window, while in OS X, the menu system is separate from the Processing application. Aside from appearances, the two menus on the different platforms have identical functionality and command sets.

The Java mode File menu, shown in Figure 1-5, contains the following commands:

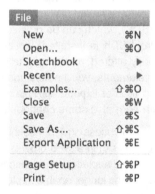

Figure 1-5. Processing's File menu

- New Cmd+N (OS X) or Ctrl+N (Windows): This has the same functionality as the New button on the toolbar.

- Open... Cmd+O (OS X) or Ctrl+O (Windows): This has the same functionality as the Open button on the toolbar.

- Sketchbook: The Sketchbook submenu includes sketches you've created, residing at your sketchbook location, specified in the Processing preferences. The Sketchbook submenu checks for PDE files, each enclosed within their own directory, within the specified Sketchbook directory. The PDE file and its directory must have the same name. You can also create additional outer directories (for organizational purposes) around your related sketches. Processing's Examples directory, which we'll discuss in a moment, is organized this way. PDE files not enclosed within a same-named directory will not be visible from the sketch submenu. You can still explicitly open them with the Open command, but Processing will alert you that a directory is required and will actually create one and move your file into it when you press OK.

- Recent: This includes a list of recently saved sketches, with the most recent at the bottom of the list.

- Examples...: The Examples command opens up a file dialog allowing you to select one of Processing's standard examples, installed with Processing. Experimenting with Processing's examples is a great way to learn Processing.

- **Close** Cmd+W (OS X) or Ctrl+W (Windows): This has the same functionality as the Open button on the toolbar.

- **Save** Cmd+S (OS X) or Ctrl+S (Windows): This has the same functionality as the Save button on the toolbar.

- **Save As** Cmd+Shift+S (OS X) or Ctrl+Shift+S (Windows): This is similar to the Save function, except that it prompts you for a new sketch name, allowing you to save the current changed version of your sketch without overwriting the original.

- **Export Application** Cmd+E (OS X) or Ctrl+E (Windows): This has the same functionality as the Export Application button on the toolbar.

- **Page Setup** Cmd+Shift+P (OS X) or Ctrl+Shift+P (Windows): Opens standard Page Setup dialog box to specify printing options.

- **Print** Cmd+P (OS X) or Ctrl+P (Windows): Prints all the code within the main tab or the currently selected tab.

In Android mode, Export Application becomes Export Signed Package and Export Android Package respectively. Both of these export functions create an Android application package file (APK), which is a single file bundle of all the elements necessary to distribute or install an Android app.

In JavaScript mode, Export Application simply become Export, which creates a Web-export directory that includes: index.html, processing.js and "sketchName".pde file.

Edit Menu

Figure 1-6 shows a screenshot of Processing's Edit menu.

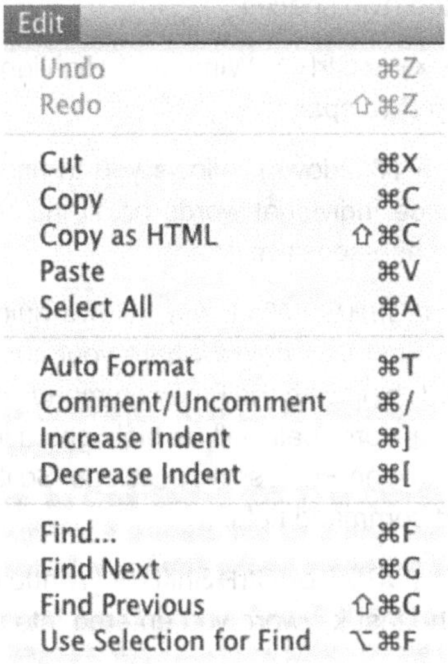

Edit	
Undo	⌘Z
Redo	⇧⌘Z
Cut	⌘X
Copy	⌘C
Copy as HTML	⇧⌘C
Paste	⌘V
Select All	⌘A
Auto Format	⌘T
Comment/Uncomment	⌘/
Increase Indent	⌘]
Decrease Indent	⌘[
Find...	⌘F
Find Next	⌘G
Find Previous	⇧⌘G
Use Selection for Find	⌥⌘F

Figure 1-6. Processing's Edit menu

The Edit menu contains the following commands:

- Undo Cmd+Z (OS X) or Ctrl+Z (Windows): Cancels the previous action, including any addition or deletion of code within the text editor. To reverse Undo, select Redo.

- Redo Cmd+Shift+Z (OS X) or Ctrl+Shift+Z (Windows): Reverses the last Undo command, restoring your sketch to the state immediately prior to selecting Undo.

- Cut Cmd+X (OS X) or Ctrl+X (Windows): Copies the selected text into clipboard memory and removes the selected text from the text editor.

- Copy Cmd+C (OS X) or Ctrl+C (Windows): Copies the selected text into clipboard memory and leave the copied text as is within the text editor.

- Copy as HTML Cmd+Shift+C (OS X) or Ctrl+Shift+C (Windows): Copies the selected text into clipboard memory and formats it for correct display in a Web browser. The command leaves the copied text as is within the text editor.

- Paste Cmd+V (OS X) or Ctrl+V (Windows): Adds the contents of the clipboard memory to the text editor window at the cursor's position, replacing any selected text.

- Select All Cmd+A (OS X) or Ctrl+A (Windows): Highlights all the text within the text editor window.

- Auto Format Cmd+T (OS X) or Ctrl+T (Windows): Attempts to visually organize the code, removing some unnecessary white space and correcting the indenting.

- Comment/Uncomment Cmd+/ (OS X) or Ctrl+/ (Windows): Adds two forward slashes (//) in front of any highlighted text in the text editor. The double forward slashes prevent Processing from running the commented lines of code.

- Increase Indent Cmd+] (OS X) or Ctrl+A (Windows): Highlighted text within the text editor window is shifted to the right one tab stop (two spaces.)

- Decrease Indent Cmd+[(OS X) or Ctrl+A (Windows): Highlighted text within the text editor window is shifted to the left one tab stop (two spaces.)

- Find Cmd+F (OS X) or Ctrl+F (Windows): Allows you to find and replace keywords within the text editor window. You can replace individual words or all instances of words, and optionally specify whether searches should be case-sensitive or not.

- Find Next Cmd+G (OS X) or Ctrl+G (Windows): Allows quick and persistent searches of the last keyword you entered into the Find field below where your cursor is in the text editor. For example, if we attempt to find the keyword "ball" with the Find command, later on we can simply select Find Next, and the next occurrence of the word "ball" will be highlighted in the text editor. The keyword, used by Find Next, does not persist between Processing sessions. So if you quit and restart Processing, you'll lose your keyword in the Find command field.

- Find Previous Cmd+Shift+G (OS X) or Ctrl+Shift+G (Windows): Similar to Find Next, allows quick and persistent searches of the last keyword you entered into the Find field above where your cursor is in the text editor.

- Use Selection for Find Cmd+Option+F (OS X) or Ctrl+alt+F (Windows): The command is useful for quickly setting a keyword to be used in persistent searches, with Find Next or Find Previous, without needing to open the find dialog box. Set the search keyword by highlighting a word in the text editor and selecting the command.

Sketch Menu

Figure 1-7 shows a screenshot of Processing's Sketch menu.

Figure 1-7. Screen capture of Processing's Sketch menu

The Sketch menu contains the following commands:

- Run Cmd+R (OS X) or Ctrl+R (Windows): Has the same functionality as the Run button on the toolbar.

- Present Cmd+Shift+R (OS X) or Ctrl+Shift+R (Windows): Creates a full-screen display of your executing sketch. You can stop the display by selecting the Stop command in the lower-left corner of the screen, or by pressing the Esc key.

- Stop: Stops a running sketch.

- Import Library: Figure 1-8 shows a screenshot of the Import Library submenu.

Figure 1-8. Import Library submenu

- The Add Library... command opens up a Library Manager window, as shown in Figure 1-9. The Library Manager includes a scrollable list of external Processing libraries that you can automatically install in Processing. By default, installed external libraries are contained within the Libraries directory, within Processing's default Sketchbook directory. Processing's Sketchbook location is specified under preferences.

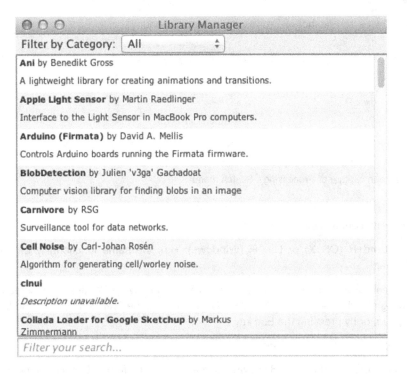

Figure 1-9. Library Manager

- Directly under the Add Library... command are Processing's core libraries that come preinstalled and are not referenced though the Library Manager.

- Below the core libraries are any additional user contributed libraries that you have installed, by using the Add Library... command. Figure 1-10 shows some installed contributed libraries.

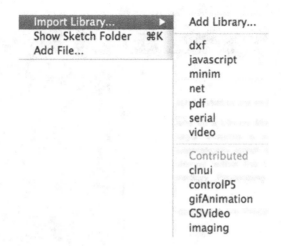

Figure 1-10. Installed contributed libraries below Processing's core libraries

To use a library, you need to first select it in the list of installed libraries under Sketch ➤ Import Library. For example, if you select dxf, the following line of code is added to the top of your sketch: import processing. dxf..*;. Using import statements is standard practice in Java, for which related classes of code are grouped in directories called packages. Packages allow you to organize code libraries for reuse and distribution. They also provide a way of helping to ensure that certain names don't collide or interfere with one another, if libraries include the same named structures.

- `Show Sketch Folder` Cmd+K (OS X) or Ctrl+K (Windows): Opens up the directory of your current sketch. Normally, your current sketch directory will reside within your main sketchbook directory. If you remember, your main sketchbook location is specified in the preferences.

- `Add File`: Opens a file navigator, allowing you to load an image, font, or other media into a data sub-directory within your sketch directory. If no data directory exists, Processing will automatically create one for you.

In `Android` mode, Run becomes `Run on Device`, and `Present` becomes `Run in Emulator`. `Run in Emulator` opens up a virtual Android device (the Android emulator), shown in Figure 1-11. Please note that the emulator is part of the Android SDK and is not installed with Processing. `Run on Device` will actually install your Processing sketch, cleverly converted into an Android app, onto a connected Android device. Please note, as of this writing external libraries will not work in Android mode.

Figure 1-11. Android emulator

In JavaScript mode, the Sketch menu changes more dramatically, as shown in Figure 1-12.

Figure 1-12. Sketch window in JavaScript mode

The Run command is replaced by `Run in Browser`, which creates a local Web server on your machine and loads the sketch in a browser window at IP address `http://127.0.0.1`, followed by a port address, such as `http://127.0.0.1:53312`. The numbers 127.0.0.1 specify the address of the local host, or the address you'll use when you access a sketch in `JavaScript` mode from the same machine as the one running the Web server. The numbers after the colon (53312) are a dynamically assigned port. (This port number may be between 0 and 65535.)

Because Processing runs your JavaScript sketch in a Web server, it is viewable across your local area network. However, to access the running sketch from another device, you need to replace the 127.0.01 (local host) address with the actual IP address of the machine running the Web server. For example, if the running sketch is on your machine, which has IP address 192.168.5.3 and port 62004, the sketch is viewable across the local area network at address `http://192.168.5.3`: 62004; (it will still be viewable from your machine at `http://127.0.0.1`: 62004.)

The `Reopen in Browser` command opens an instance of the running sketch in another browser window/tab. The `Stop` command stops the Web server.

Please note, as of this writing no external libraries work in JavaScript mode.

Tools Menu

Figure 1-13 shows a screenshot of Processing's `Tools` menu.

Figure 1-13. Processing's Tools menu

The `Tools` menu contains the following commands:

- `Create Font`: One of the challenges of designing for the Web is the incompatibility of system resources such as installed fonts, which will often be different from machine to machine and across platforms. One solution is to use only a very limited set of fonts that can be assumed to be installed on most systems—such as Arial, Times, and Sans. However, from a design perspective, this is pretty limiting. Another solution is to bundle bitmap glyphs—or actual raster graphics of each character in a font family—with a project to allow the use of fonts that aren't likely to be installed on a user's machine. The `Create Font` command does just this. The command opens the `Create Font` dialog box, shown in Figure 1-14, which allows you to select any font installed within your system.

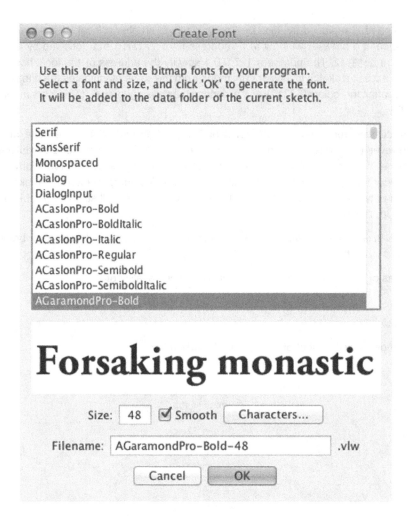

Figure 1-14. Processing's Create Font dialog box

- This dialog box includes the options Size, Filename, and Characters. The font generated is a copy of an existing font in your system, created in Processing's VLW font format and installed within a data subdirectory in the current sketch directory. Similar to loading other media into Processing, a data directory is automatically created, if one doesn't already exist. There are some memory concerns involved in creating fonts this way. The larger the font size you specify, the more memory the font will use, as each font includes the actual raster information needed to draw the individual characters; normally, fonts are created using vector data. In addition, the Smooth option also requires a little more memory. The Character button opens the Character Selector dialog box, shown in Figure 1-15, allowing you to include non-English characters, such as ü and Å. This option increases the memory size of the created fonts, so unless you need these languages features, it's best to leave the Default Characters option selected.

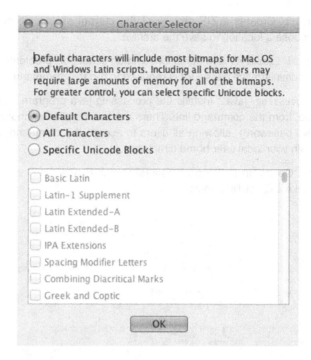

Figure 1-15. Character Selector dialog box

■ `Color Selector`: This is a simple color picker, showing you the Hue Saturation and Brightness (HSB), Red, Green and Blue (RGB), and hexadecimal color values of the color selected (see Figure 1-16).

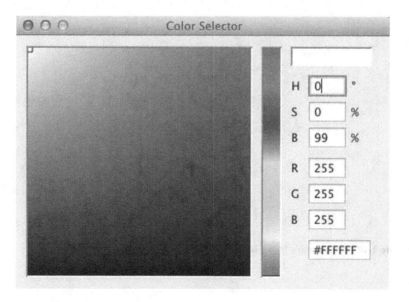

Figure 1-16. Screen capture of Processing's Color Selector tool

■ `Archive Sketch`: Creates a ZIP archive of the current sketch, prompting you with a Save dialog window to choose a location to save the archive.

■ `Fix the Serial Library`: Attempts to fix common serial port problems, enabling Processing s Serial library. Your administrative password is required to run this command.

■ `Install "processing-java"`: Installs the processing-java program enabling you to run Processing, in Java mode, from the command line. There are two installation choices: system-wide (requiring an administrative password) allowing all users to access the command, or user-defined: installing the program within your local user home directory.

■ `Movie Maker`: Opens up a dialog window (shown in Figure 1-17) allowing you to select a folder of images to make a QuickTime movie.

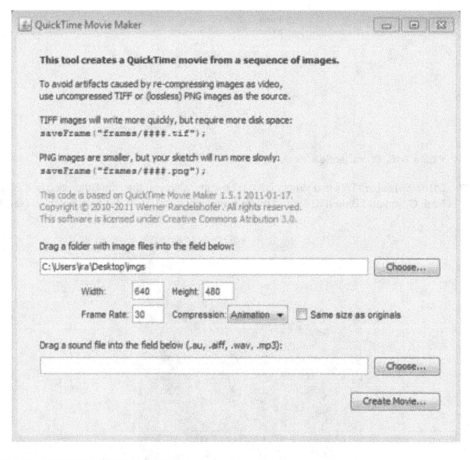

Figure 1-17. Processing's Movie Maker tool

■ Add Tool...: Like the Add Library... command, Add Tool... opens up a Tool Manager allowing you to install user-contributed Processing tools. Any installed user contributed tools will be listed between the Movie Maker and Add Tool... commands. For example, Figure 1-18 shows a screenshot of our Tools menu with some user-contributed tools installed.

Figure 1-18. Tools menu with user-contributed tools added

The Tools menu in Android and JavaScript modes stays the same as in Standard mode.

Help Menu

Figure 1-19 shows a screenshot of Processing's Help menu.

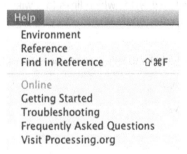

Figure 1-19. Processing's Help menu

The Help menu contains the following:

- **Environment**: This launches your default Web browser, loading information on the Processing environment.This functionality does not require an Internet connection, as the information is stored locally within the Processing application directory. The environment page gives an overview on Processing, similar to this chapter.

- **Reference**: This provides you with reference to the Processing language API, which is stored locally on your hard drive. This is the place to go to learn about specific commands in the Processing language. For the very latest information, refer to http://processing.org/reference/index.html.

- **Find in Reference** Cmd+Shift+F (OS X) or Ctrl+Shift+F (Windows): Select a word in your sketch and then select Find in Reference. If the word exists in the Processing API, the relevant reference information will be opened in your default Web browser.

- **Online** (Not currently implemented as of this writing)

- **Getting Started**: This launches your default Web browser, loading information on the Processing environment. This functionality does not require an Internet connection. Getting Started includes a tutorial on how to build your first sketch.

- **Troubleshooting**: This page covers many of the common "Help me, something's not right with the processing universe!" concerns voiced on the discourse board; you can think of this page as the triage FAQ.

- **Frequently Asked Questions**: This command opens a list of questions and answers to some common Processing issues. The online version is at http://processing.org/faq.html.

- **Visit Processing.org** Cmd+5 (OS X) or Ctrl+5 (Windows): This command launches your default Web browser and loads http://processing.org/.

In Android mode, the Help menu remains much the same as in Standard mode. However, two additional menu items are added: Processing for Android Wiki, which links to a wiki that provides the most up-to-date information about Processing's Android mode; and Android Developers Site, which links to Google's Android reference site.

JavaScript mode's Help menu includes links to reference information at http://processingjs.org, including:

- QuickStart for Processing Devs

- QuickStart for JavaScript Devs

- Reference

- Find in Reference

- Visit Processingjs.org

Additional Menus

In addition to the Standard mode file menus, Android mode and JavaScript mode include additional menus, titled Android and JavaScript respectively. Figures 1-20 and 1-21 show the menus expanded.

Figure 1-20. Android mode's Android File menu

Figure 1-21. JavaScript mode's JavaScript File menu

Android's expanded menu includes:

- Sketch Permissions: Opens the Android Permissions Selector, shown in Figure 1-22. By default Android applications have no permission to access or adversely affect user data on the device. If your app needs access to certain device resources you can select the specific permission access in the selector. To learn more about Android permissions, see http://developer.android.com/guide/topics/security/security.html#permissions.

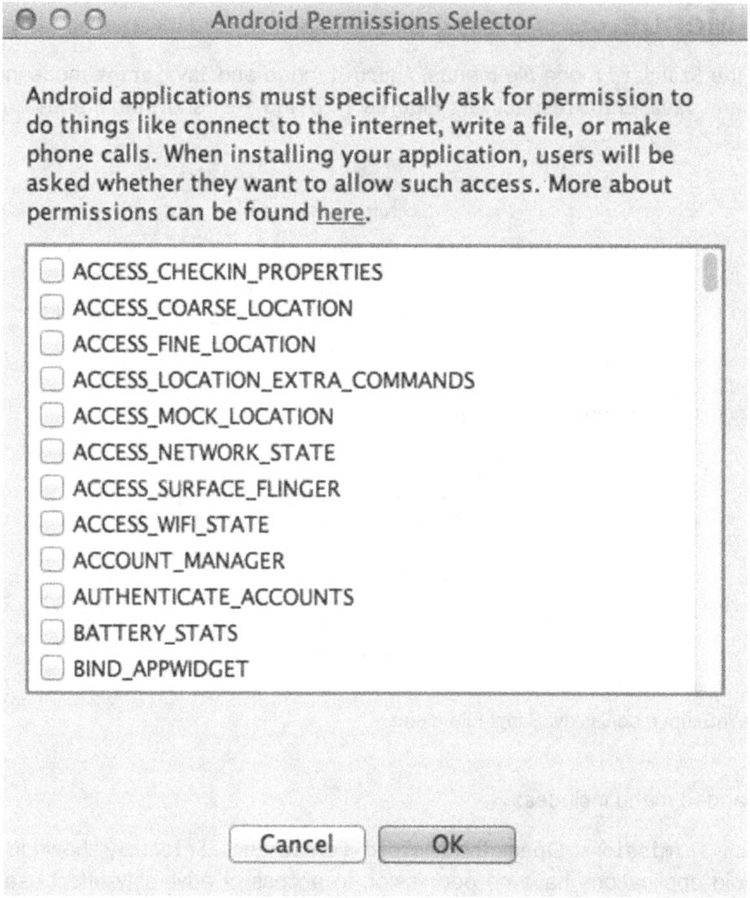

Figure 1-22. Android Permissions Selector

- `Signing Key Setup`: (Not currently implemented as of this writing)

- `Android SDK Manager`: Opens the Android SDK Manager tool, which organizes and simplifies the process of working with the Android SDK. To learn more about the SDK Manager, see `http://developer.android.com/sdk/adding-components.html`.

- `Android AVD Manager`: Opens the AVD (Android Virtual Device) Manager tool, shown in Figure 1-23, which allows you to model different Android devices to be run in the Android software emulator. To learn more about the AVD Manager, see `http://developer.android.com/guide/developing/devices/managing-avds.html`.

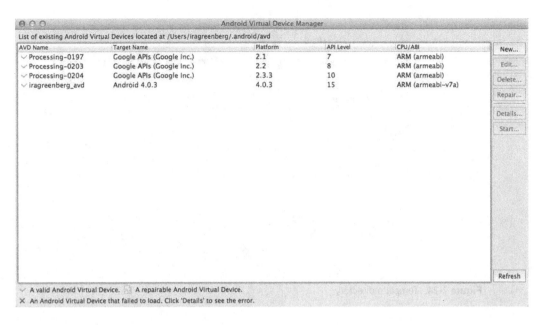

Figure 1-23. AVD Manager

■ **Reset Connections:** If the Android emulator won't load your app, running Reset Connections may clear up the problem.

The JavaScript file menu is simpler than the Android one. The entries are:

■ **Playback Settings (Directives):** Opens the Directives Editor, shown in Figure 1-24, allowing you to set directives. Processing is able to do certain things that JavaScript simply can't do in the browser. For example, Processing is able to wait for images to fully load before attempting to access them. JavaScript mode includes directives to help resolve these sorts of potential problems, such as preloading image data. To learn more about directives, see http://processingjs.org/reference/pjs%20directive/.

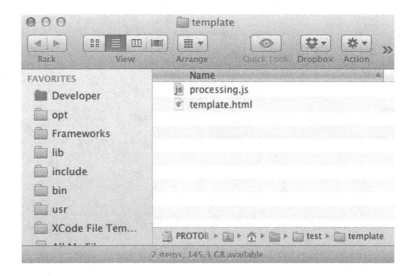

Figure 1-24. Template directory

- `Copy Server Address`: Copies the Web server address of a running Processing.js sketch to the clipboard.

- `Set Server Port`: Opens a dialog box allowing you to manually set the port of the Web server running the Processing.js sketch.

- `Start Custom Template`: By default, Processing sketches in `JavaScript` mode utilize a predefined HTML template, hidden by default, controlling the look and feel of the web page holding the Processing.js sketch. This command creates a copy of the template directory within the current sketch directory, shown in Figure 1-24. You may edit this page in any HTML editor.

- `Show Custom Template`: Opens up the template directory within the current sketch directory. This command requires that the `Start Custom Template` command has been previously selected.

Summary

This chapter presented the requisite 30,000 feet view of creative coding in Processing 2.0. This will be the last (and only) chapter in the book that doesn't include lots of fun, hands-on activities. (We promise!) You learned about the distinction between Computer Science (the discipline) and computer programming (creative coding). Certainly there are overlaps between the two, but you also learned that programming is NOT Computer Science. (Though as we mentioned earlier, it's a really fun part of it!) From bits to bytes, and from low-level languages like Assembly all the way to Processing, you learned a little of what happens underneath the computational hood. Processing 2.0 is a significant new language release, and you had a quick tour of the new development environment and language reference, including Processing's exciting new modes feature. Next chapter, we'll begin making things and putting theory to practice.

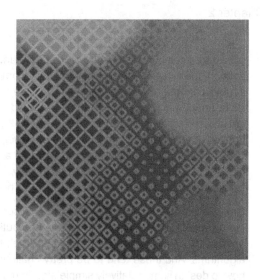

Chapter 2

Art by Numbers

Let the coding fun begin! Roll up your sleeves, insert your pocket protector and grab a large mug of joe. You'll begin this chapter learning about the foundation of coding, *algorithms*, and end with a really cool example that puts everything you learned into practice. Along the way you'll learn about some of the fundamental elements in programming, such as variables and functions. But rest assured, we'll take things slow and ease our way into creative coding. Now's a good time to caffeine up.

Algorithms

Some words just sound complicated, regardless of what they actually mean. Algorithm is one such term. In reality, an algorithm can be quite simple. Here's an example:

1. Buy a yellow, number 2 pencil.

2. Sharpen the pencil.

3. Stick the pencil in your pocket protector.

4. Pat yourself on the back for being a good nerd.

If you completed the steps above, you just implemented an algorithm. According to Dictionary.com, an algorithm is: "...a set of rules for solving a problem in a finite number of steps." Algorithms are fundamental to computing, as computers do things in discreet steps, albeit billions of them per second. For any problem to be solved by a computer, it must be broken down into computable, individual steps. Though this may sound simple enough, the situation can actually get quite complex. For example, think about what you did today before reading this chapter; now write down every single step of everything you did. (Please don't actually do this!) Most likely, nearly everything you did today you did without consciously thinking about each step. We assume you got dressed today (hopefully); but did you think about how you opened the drawer, scanned the contents of the drawer, grabbed the clothes, closed the drawer, etc.? In fact, the process of just getting dressed could take a very, very long time to document, if we try to account for each and every discreet step—especially if we don't make any assumptions. Computers are really, really bad at making assumptions, though they are excellent at following instructions (sort of the opposite of people, right?)

One of the biggest challenges of learning to code, once you get past all the new terminology and rules, is coming up with good algorithms. In fact, in computer science education there are entire semester-long courses, at both the undergraduate and graduate level, that deal exclusively with designing (and ultimately analyzing) algorithms. And these tend to be pretty challenging courses. For our current purposes, we just need to learn how to design some relatively simple algorithms. Though really, and far more importantly, we need to learn how to begin to *think* algorithmically.

> *Try This: Think of the absolute least technical person you know. Write a note to them explaining in detail how to send a group email that includes multiple attachments. Your note will be an algorithm. It's ironic perhaps that our computers need instructions like the least technical among us.*

Pseudocode Example

Next we'll create an initial example algorithm, which we'll develop in a number of stages. First, we'll write the algorithm in narrative form; then we'll simplify and reduce the narrative down to a series of discreet procedural steps; lastly we'll translate the procedural steps into something called pseudocode.

Pseudocode is used to describe the steps of an algorithm as a universal program, not dependent on the specific syntax (the structure and rules) of any particular programming language. Theoretically, programmers who work in different programming languages should be able to implement a program in their respective language, based on pseudocode. Unlike real code, pseudocode is less syntactically strict, but it should still be precise and easily translatable into actual code.

Our initial algorithm will teach someone how to skate. We'll assume that the person is already wearing skates and standing on the ice. Next is the algorithm in narrative form:

Begin with your legs shoulder-width apart, your knees bent, your back straight, your eyes looking straight ahead, and your arms outstretched to the side. Remaining in this position, push back off one of your skates, extending that leg diagonally outward. Bring your outstretched skate back to its initial position. Repeat this process with your other leg and then continue the process, alternating legs.

Next is the narrative broken down into discreet steps:

1. Set your legs shoulder-width apart.

2. Bend your knees.

3. Keep your back straight.

4. Look straight ahead.

5. Outstretch your arms to the side.

6. Push back off one of your skates while extending that leg diagonally outward.

7. Bring the outstretched skate back to its initial position.

8. Repeat steps 6 and 7, alternating legs.

Though we've converted the narrative algorithm into individual discreet steps, it's not quite descriptive enough to be easily converted to code, or understood by a computer. For example, what exactly is the distance of shoulder width, or how far should the person bend the knees, in what direction is "straight ahead"? Computers need much more specific information than people do. Finally, here is the algorithm translated into pseudocode:

```
set skating state equal to true
set shoulder width equal to a fixed distance value
set maximum leg angle equal to a fixed rotation value
set left leg position equal to -(shoulder width)/2
set left leg angle equal to a starting rotation value
set right leg position equal to (shoulder width)/2
set right leg angle equal to a starting rotation value
set knee bend angle equal to a starting rotation value
set back bend angle equal to a fixed rotation value
set eye angle equal to a fixed rotation value
set left arm angle equal to a fixed rotation value
set right arm angle equal to a fixed rotation value
set the active leg equal to left
loop while skating state is equal to true
        loop while the active leg rotation angle is less than the maximum leg angle
                add a value to the active leg rotation angle
        Set the active leg angle to starting rotation value.
        if the active leg is left
        set the active leg to right
        else
        set the active leg to left
```

The pseudocode still uses plain English, but reads less naturally than in the previous stages. Also, notice we quantified the problem by specifying position and rotation values. There is no getting around the fact that programming relies pretty heavily on math. Though, most programming problems don't require very complicated math. (In fact, you'll learn firsthand in this chapter just what you can accomplish with even the simplest math.)

The first thirteen lines of the pseudocode set initial states in the program. Initial states can be thought of as starting conditions. When programming, we almost always want to set some initial states. The states create points of reference for our program. For example, if we know the leg rotation angle starts at 0, as we add to the angle, we can check if the angle reaches a specific target value (maximum leg angle), perhaps telling us that an end or goal state has been reached (the leg is fully extended). Target values might not change in a program, while other values do change. In general, we refer to values that stay fixed in a program as constants, while values that do change we refer to as variables. Later in the chapter you'll learn more about both of these.

After setting initial states, we introduce some loops. Loops are structures we use in programming to do things over and over again. You'll notice we included two loop while statements and also introduced some indenting. The first loop while statement (the outer loop) runs continuously, as long as the skating state is true, which it always is; look at the first line in the pseudocode where we set this state to true and never set it to false anywhere in the program. Therefore, this while loop executes an infinite number of times, so once the skating begins, it never stops. (In real life you'd eventually hit the end boards at an ice rink, or perhaps a tree on a frozen pond.)

The indented statements are what are controlled by the loop. In the case of the outer loop, everything that comes after it is indented, including the other (inner) while loop, and therefore all of it executes an infinite number of times. In a program we could use an infinite loop like this to control continuous animation, or to constantly monitor whether the keyboard or mouse has been pressed, though these types of event loops are a special case, which we'll discuss in Chapter 4. Most of the time, we don't want loops to run infinitely long, as our program can literally hang-up indefinitely while the loop continuously runs. In spite of our best intentions infinite loops are a pretty common programming error. The inner while loop employs some logic to determine when it should run. This is the most common way you'll use a loop. The inner loop will run as long as the active leg rotation angle is less than the maximum leg angle. Notice right after the inner loop, the line "add a value to the active leg rotation angle." As this inner loop runs, the leg rotation angle is increased for each iteration of the loop, until the angle is equal to the maximum leg angle. "Iteration" is the term we use in programming to represent a complete single step in a loop, where all the indented code executes once.

When the logical (or "conditional") test is no longer true–the rotation angle is no longer less than the maximum leg angle–control leaves the inner while loop and proceeds to the next line in the program. The last few lines of pseudocode reset the leg rotation angle and then determine which leg should be the active leg. I used if and else statements to ensure that the active leg keeps changing after each skating stride. if and else are common terms in many programming languages, including Processing, that are used to check for certain conditions or states in a program. if and else will be covered in detail next chapter. For now, just look at the logic to see if you can understand how the active leg changes after each stride. Finally, when the program reaches the bottom of the outer loop, it goes back up to the top of this loop, and it all begins again–*"to infinity and beyond!"* (or until someone quits the program).

The previous skating pseudocode example illustrates that even a relatively simply process, like taking alternating skating glides, requires a fair amount of logic when structuring it algorithmically. If thinking this way feels foreign to you, don't panic. We'll be revisiting all the concepts discussed in greater detail in the next few chapters. Like skating, programming gets much easier with practice, until much of it you'll even be able to do automatically. The important general points to remember for now are:

- Break a problem down into discreet steps

- Set initial program states

- Use constant and variable values to quantify a problem (make it computable)

- Use loops and conditional logic to control the flow of a program

Try This: Using your earlier email note algorithm, create pseudocode.

Generative Algorithm

One of the more interesting things you can do with a computer is have it generate an image. Some computer generated (CG) work attempts to mimic images created using traditional media, such as charcoal or paint. Graphics software applications, such as Adobe's PhotoShop or Corel Painter, can be used to create these types of images, as well as other simulated effects. Figure 2-1 shows a PhotoShop example that transforms a digital photograph into a virtual painting using a built-in filter.

Figure 2-1. PhotoShop virtual painting example

Other CG images are generated more mathematically and tend to either visualize a specific set of equations, such as the famous Mandelbrot plot shown in Figure 2-2, or more simply, generate a random pattern, like the image shown in Figure 2-3.

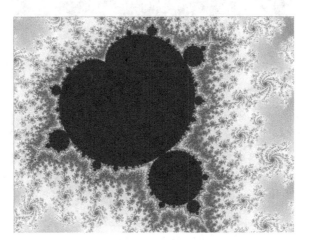

Figure 2-2. Mandelbrot plot

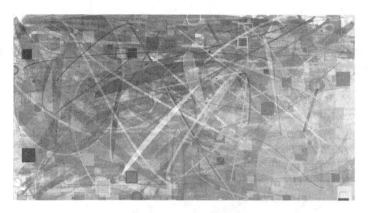

Figure 2-3. Mathematically generated random pattern

Though these approaches may yield interesting results, they can sometimes appear overly predictable, formulaic or random. This type of work is sometimes even referred to as "eye candy"– flashy, but lacking in content or substance.

A more integrative approach to CG involves greater collaboration between the coder and the underlying computation, specifically through the creation of generative algorithms. Generative algorithms ideally synthesize novel, even unexpected creations that feel less deterministic, nor overly random. By selectively balancing equations, conditional logic and randomization, generative algorithms can lead to fascinating and unexpected results, arguably even original works of art. Figure 2-4 shows an image of a virtual organism created using a generative algorithm in Processing.

Figure 2-4. Virtual organism

Later in the chapter you'll develop a generative algorithm to draw a human face. You'll start very simply with predefined values and then slowly open up the generative capacity of the algorithm, which will allow you to create a wide range of interesting and hopefully unexpected results.

Drawing with Code

The human face is an extremely complex form composed of curved surfaces, where the subtlest differences define our unique identities (save for your identical siblings). Before we learn to generate a face, we need to work through some basic algorithmic drawing. Our first example will create a humble abode, literally. Figure 2-5 shows what our initial house drawing will look like.

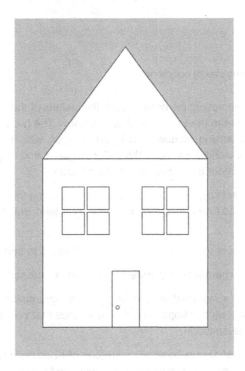

Figure 2-5. Simple house

Drawing with code involves a complex set of coordinated steps, which are mostly handled behind the scenes for us by Processing. For example, to draw a rectangle on the screen in Processing, shown in Figure 2-6, you could simply write:

```
rect(20, 20, 30, 30);
```

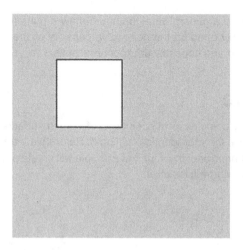

Figure 2-6. Screenshot of Processing's rect() command

The four numbers 20, 20, 30, 30 represent the position and dimensions of the rectangle: 20 pixels to the right of the left edge and 20 pixels down from the top of the sketch window. The two 30's specify the rectangle's width and height respectively. The Processing window is really just a graph with its origin (0,0) at the top left corner of the window; as you move right along the x-axis values of x increase, and as you move down along the y-axis values of y increase. You'll learn more about this later in the chapter.

Look carefully at the syntax of `rect(20, 20, 30, 30);`, as we'll be using this form for many, many other commands in Processing. In fact, if you fully understand the `rect` command, you probably understand nearly 25% of Processing; I kid you not!

Here's a breakdown of the syntax of the `rect` command. I used bullets to better isolate the different parts.

keyword • open parenthesis • arguments separated by commas • closed parenthesis • semicolon

- **Keyword:** A keyword is a reserved word defined in a programming language. If you type the `rect` command in Processing (which I hope you do) you'll notice that `rect` turns orange, showing you it's a reserved keyword in the language.

- **Parentheses:** There must always be an even number of open and closed parentheses, also referred to as balanced pairs; if there's an open one, there needs to be a corresponding closed one. There are many other structures in Processing as well that follow this balanced pair rule (as there are in many programming languages.)

- **Arguments:** Arguments allow you to pass values to a command, enabling it to have more general use. As previously discussed the `rect` command arguments control the rectangle's position and dimensions. Imagine if you weren't able to pass arguments to the `rect` command. All Processing rectangles would then be the same size at the same position, not very useful. However, by including arguments we can easily create 10,000 unique rectangles of varied position and size (actually a trivial thing for the computer to do.) In fact, Figure 2-7 shows exactly that: 10,000 unique rectangles.

Figure 2-7. 10,000 rectangles

- ■ **Semicolon:** We use semicolons in Processing like periods, to end or terminate statements. Every Processing statement must be terminated with a semicolon, or the Processing compiler will yell at you and also refuse to compile your code. You'll learn more about Processing statements later in this chapter.

Now check out at the Processing reference at: http://processing.org/reference/. (You can also view it locally on your hard drive by launching Processing and selecting Help ➤ Reference from the top menu.) Every command listed in the Processing reference that includes parentheses utilizes the same syntax as rect, though of course the argument values you'd include between the parentheses would be different. For example, Processing's point command only takes two arguments:

```
point(50, 50);
```

The triangle command takes six arguments:

```
triangle(50, 20, 80, 80, 20, 80);
```

And the smooth command takes no arguments:

```
smooth();
```

Technically, all these commands are called *function calls*, or even more technically, *function invocations*. The word function is borrowed from math. Programming and math functions work similarly; they can be thought of as little machines, black boxes that take some input, perform processing inside the "box" using the input, and then output *something*. A simple function commonly found on most calculators might just take a number and return the square root of the number. While math functions will almost always do a mathematical operation, functions in programming can do, well, nearly anything you can conceive of–sounds pretty exciting, right?

We refer to the function body as a "black box" because what happens within the function (the function's implementation) should be independent–and hidden–from how we use the function (the function's interface). All you need to know to be able to use a function is its interface, which includes its name (e.g., rect or point) and any input values it requires. Processing's rect command, which we looked at earlier (rect(20, 20, 30, 30);), required four input values. Again, thinking of a calculator's square root example, you don't need to know how your calculator actually calculates a square root to use it; you just need to know how to call it. The same goes for functions when programming.

> *Note: Computer Science, as a relatively young discipline, borrows from numerous other disciplines. The idea of a function in programming borrows from both math and also from engineering. A black box design approach is used in the engineering of physical objects and systems: Most of us have no clue how our microwave oven generates microwaves; we just need to know how to set a cooking time and press start.*

Primitives

Processing's point, rect, and triangle commands are grouped together in the language reference under the heading 2D Primitives. Primitives are basic shape commands included in most graphics programming libraries. Processing includes both 2D and 3D primitive shape commands, which are useful for quickly generating geometry. You can also use the primitives to construct more complex forms, which is what you'll do next when you construct the house example, shown earlier in Figure 2-5.

```
// Simple House
size(400, 600);
// house
rect(50, 250, 300, 300);
// roof
triangle(50, 250, 350, 250, 200, 50);
// door
rect(175, 450, 50, 100);
// door knob
ellipse(185, 515, 6, 6);
// left windows
rect(85, 300, 40, 40);
rect(130, 300, 40, 40);
rect(85, 345, 40, 40);
rect(130, 345, 40, 40);
// right windows
rect(230, 300, 40, 40);
rect(275, 300, 40, 40);
rect(230, 345, 40, 40);
rect(275, 345, 40, 40);
```

If you scan the code you'll notice that all the function calls adhere to the structure we looked at earlier:

keyword • open parenthesis • arguments separated by commas • closed parenthesis • semicolon

Code Comments

Interspersed between the function calls are additional lines that begin with two forward slashes (e.g., `//roof`). Any lines that begin with `//` are treated as comments by the compiler and ignored when the code is compiled. Comments are very useful for organizing your code and also for providing valuable information for other programmers who may work with your code. Commercially, software is usually developed by teams of programmers, often in different locations. In this context, code comments are more a requirement than an option. Even if you're sure you'll be the only person ever looking at your code, you should get in the habit of using comments. It's a sad fact that most of us quickly forget what we were thinking when we coded something in the past. On more than one occasion, we've done a Google search to find help in solving a programming problem, only to find our own solution online, which we had completely forgotten about. Use comments!

In addition to the `//` line comment, Processing includes a block comment: `/* comment */`. The block comment allows you to include multiple lines. For example:

```
/*
This is a multiline comment that
will be ignored by the compiler. You may
include as many lines as you'd like
between the  comment symbols.
*/
```

Though this style can be convenient for commenting out large blocks of code, there is also a potential problem if you nest multiple comment blocks. For example, the following is illegal and will not compile:

```
/*
  multiline comment
  /*
   multiline comment - illegal to nest multiple blocks
   */
*/
```

Processing's Comment/Uncomment command will only add/remove the line style (`//`) comments. Though block comments can cause some issues when you intersperse them throughout your code, they are very useful at the top of your code, for providing initial comments. For example:

```
/*
Processing sketch 0001
By Ira Greenberg
06/20/2012
This sketch explains all the mysteries of the universe
*/
```

Returning to the house example, the code begins with the command `size(400, 600)`, which specifies the size of your sketch window.

By default, all Processing sketches are only 100 pixels wide x 100 pixels high, so you'll almost always want to call size() before any other calls.

> Note: Throughout the rest of the book when we refer to calling functions, we'll often just reference the function name and parentheses, regardless of the number and type of arguments normally included between the parentheses.

The rest of the house example code is all primitive calls that generate the drawing of the house in the sketch window.

> Try This: Change the arguments in some of the function call to see what happens to the house sketch.

If the primitive calls seem a bit mysterious, it helps to understand a little bit of what's going on beneath the surface and to also review the language reference which explains in detail what each of the arguments refer to. One quick way to see useful information is to highlight a command name and then go up to Help ➤ Find in Reference from Processing's top menu.

Coordinate Systems

To better understand the primitive calls, aside from what the specific arguments refer to, you need to better understand how things are drawn in Processing (and by most graphics software systems.) As mentioned earlier the Processing sketch window is really nothing more than a graph. The top left corner of the window is the origin of the graph, (0,0). As you move across the window, from left to right, values increase along the x-axis. As you move down the window, value increase along the y-axis. When you go beyond the Processing window (in any direction) values still exist, though of course you can't see what is drawn. In general, we refer to this built-in graph as Processing's coordinate system.

Processing's coordinate system relates to actual pixel positions filling the window. You can think of pixels as cells in a table. For example, if the default sketch window is 100 pixels wide by 100 pixels high, that's 100 pixels along the x-axis and 100 pixels along the y-axis, and the total number of pixels in the window is: 100 pixels wide x 100 pixels high = 10,000 pixels. Figure 2-8 shows an enlarged 20 x 20 pixels sketch window displaying the 400 pixels.

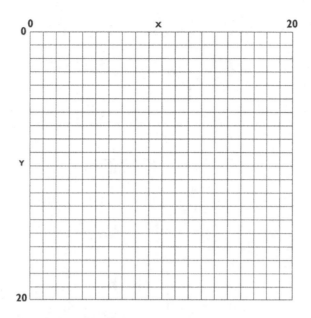

Figure 2-8. 20 x 20 sketch window with blown-up pixels

You can always calculate the total number of pixels making up your sketch window by simply multiplying the values (width and height) you passed into the **size()** command. Referring back to the house example, you can see how the first primitive call–**rect(50, 250, 300, 300);**–draws a 300 x 300 pixel rectangle 50 pixels from the left edge of the window and 250 pixels from the top of the window. If you're still not sure how the 50 and 250 map to the x- and y-axes respectively, refer to the **rect()** command in the Processing reference. You'll see that the first two arguments refer to the x and y position of the rectangle.

The rest of the primitive calls should be self-explanatory, referring to the sketch window's underlying coordinate system. However, the **ellipse()** command introduces one additional complexity that needs clarification. To illustrate the issue, change the first **rect()** call in the Simple House example from **rect(50, 250, 300, 300)** to **ellipse(50, 250, 300, 300)**. Figure 2-9 shows the result. So what happened?

Figure 2-9. Simple house with replacement ellipse() call

The **rect()** and **ellipse()** commands both take four arguments controlling x position and y position, width and height of the respective shape. However, **ellipse()** puts the x and y argument values at the shape's center, or more accurately the ellipse is drawn around the x and y arguments. You can also think of the ellipse's center as its local origin (the rectangle's local origin is its top left corner). While the entire Processing sketch window has a coordinate system, each shape can also be thought of as having its own underlying coordinate system, including an origin from where it's drawn, as illustrated in Figure 2-10.

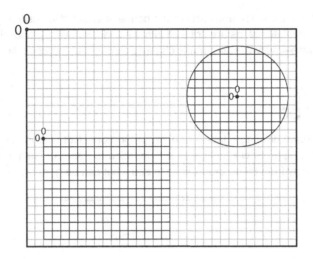

Figure 2-10. Overlapping coordinate systems

By default in Processing, the `rect()` command uses the top left corner of the shape as its origin, while the `ellipse()` command uses its center point. It is possible to override this default behavior using Processing's `rectMode()` and `ellipseMode()` commands, which you'll see an example of later in the chapter.

Try This: Using the primitive commands, create the house shown in Figure 2-11.

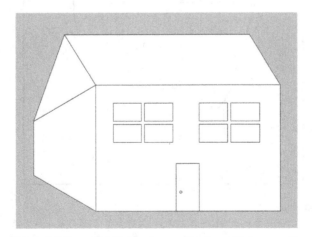

Figure 2-11. Advanced house drawing

You're almost ready to apply your new algorithmic drawing skills to creating a human face. First though take a look at the Simple House code and imagine what you'd have to do to either scale the house or shift it somewhere else in the sketch window. Based on what you know at present, it would very likely involve a fair amount of work, to transform the position or size of the house. The main reason for this is because the house is calculated using a bunch of unrelated values. Though parts of the house are placed in position and sized relative to other details of the house, these relationships are not built into the code, so every global change you make—such as moving or scaling the house—involves many, many changes throughout the code. Next we'll learn a better way to address this problem.

Algorithmic Face

Figure 2-12 shows a diagram dividing a face into basic proportions. Not everyone's face adheres perfectly to these proportions, but the diagram will suffice as a foundation to base an initial face creation algorithm on. Later, we'll purposefully stray from these proportions to see what can be generated.

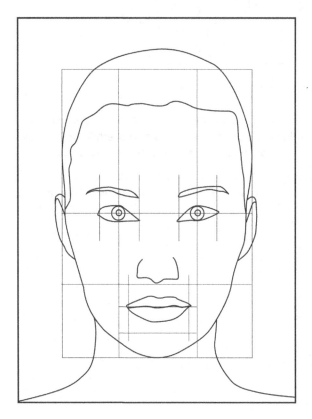

Figure 2-12. Face proportions

Next is pseudocode based on the diagram, including specific positions and size values. Notice that many of the values are based on calculations involving other parts of the face. This is a good example of how to build relationships—in this case facial proportions—into the code:

```
// Algorithmic Face
// set initial states
set the height of the head equal to 600
```

```
set the width of the head equal to the height of the head * 5 / 7
set the position of the eyes along the y-axis equal to the height of the head / 2
set the width of each eye equal to the width of the head / 5
set the height of each eye equal to the width of an eye / 2
set the x-postions of the eyes 1 eye width apart and center them on the face,
set the width of the eyebrows equal to the width of the eyes * 1.25
set the y-position of the eyebrows, above the eyes, equal to the position of the eyes plus the
eye width
set the x-position of each eyebrow equal to the inner point of each respective eye
set the y-position of the nose equal to 1/2 half the distance between the eyes and the bottom of
the head
set the y-position of the mouth equal to 1/3 of the distance between the nose and the bottom of
the head
set the height of mouth equal to 1/3 of the distance between the nose and the bottom of the head
set the height of each lip equal to the mouth height / 2
set the y-position of the top of the ears equal to the eyebrows
set the height of the ears equal to the height of the head / 4
set the width of the ears equal to the height of the ears * .5
draw the face
```

In the pseudocode for the face (as well as in the earlier skating example) we included numerous set statements, specifying initial states in the program. And, as mentioned earlier, we've created relationships in the code between the individual elements. For example, the following lines calculate the head width based on the head height:

```
set the height of the head equal to 600
set the width of the head equal to the height of the head * 5 / 7
```

This approach, if implemented consistently in your code, enables you to easily make global changes to your program. The face pseudocode is based on this approach, where the height of the head will determine the scale of everything else. Another way of thinking about this approach is providing a central command and control structure to your program. It is not uncommon for even simple problems to require hundreds or even thousands of lines of code. Without an organized structure or plan, the code can easily become unmanageable. As much as we love coding, one of our least favorite things to do is to have to work with someone else's code that is poorly structured.

The face pseudocode actually includes a hierarchy of command and control structures, in that individual elements are not only based on the overall height of the head, but on each other. This allows for a lot of flexibility in generating variations, especially when incorporating random number generation, leading to unexpected outcomes—in this case faces. Random variation and generative design is fundamental to the creative coding approach, in which you can discover new possibilities from your code.

Turning the face pseudocode into Processing code requires a new concept. We need a way of structuring the dependencies we described in the pseudocode to provide an efficient command and control structure. Ideally, we should be able to change one value, the head height, and impact the entire scale of the face, including accurate scaling of all the individual elements. The concept we'll use to do this is called variables. Variables are fundamental structures in programming that allow you to write and read to the computer's memory. When setting the head's initial height, you can use a variable to store that value, which is placed in memory for safekeeping.

As long as your program needs access to the variable, Processing will make sure it stays safely in memory and retains the value you assigned to the variable. There are two basic types of variables in Processing: primitive and reference variables. In this chapter we'll focus on primitive variables. When we get to arrays and objects later in the book, you'll also learn about reference variables.

Primitive Variables

As mentioned above, variables give you access to the computer's memory, or really more accurately, access to what's stored in memory. When you create a variable, the computer carves out a little piece of memory and puts it under your control (don't you feel powerful?). The name you give the variable is now associated with the value you store at this location in memory. For example, the following statement declares and initializes a variable representing the height of the head:

```
float headHeight = 600.0;
```

Don't worry about the specific syntax yet; we'll discuss this in detail shortly. When you refer to the variable head-Height later in the program, it will evaluate to 600.0. Since you control this memory now, you're also allowed to change the value associated with headHeight whenever you'd like. For example:

```
headHeight = 575.5;
```

However, once you change the value, the old value (600.0) is gone forever, replaced by the new value (575.5) until you change it again. In this sense, variables do indeed have variable value.

In contrast to variables, constants don't change. Numbers such as 45, 123, -99.9345 are all constants, as are certain special reserved keywords in Processing, such as PI. When programming, you'll use both constants and variables.

Using variables is pretty easy in Processing, but you do need to adhere to some basic rules.

Naming Rules and Conventions

The technical, computer science term for the name of a variable is an *identifier*. In Processing (and Java) all identifiers must begin with a letter, an underscore or a dollar sign. (Though technically legal, you should avoid using the dollar sign, as the Java compiler utilizes this symbol for internal naming.) You may also include numbers in your identifiers, but only after the initial character. Spaces within variable names are never permitted. By convention, variables in Processing should begin with a lower case letter, while constants are written in all caps. Programming conventions are not enforced like rules by the compiler but help ensure consistency, especially when passing code between a team of programmers. Next are examples of some legal variable names:

```
value1
weight
highestScore
isValid
timeLength
bestInShow
```

Here are some illegal identifier names, with a comment as to why they're illegal:

```
Value 3 // can't include spaces in names
5BestFriends // can't begin a variable name with a number
isVery^Strong^ // can't use any characters other than letters, numbers, underscore and the
dollar sign
```

Finally, next is a list of legal names–the compiler will allow them–but conventionally wrong, since other programmers may be confused by them:

```
IAMinconSISTENT // use of inconsistent case
_____a_____ // ambiguous name
I_AM_A_VARIABLE // all capitals is the convention for constants, not variables
perhapsTheLongestVariableNameInTheWorld // variable name is unnecessarily long
```

The best practice when naming variables is finding a balance between clarity and economy. When variable names get too long, even if they're very descriptive, they can become difficult to read and prone to typos. On the other hand, single letter variable names or cryptic abbreviations are equally confusing. In the first list of legal variable names, I tried to create identifiers with enough information to describe the type of value each variable is associated with, without being too verbose. You'll also notice that I used capital letters when combining words into a compound name. This very popular convention is referred to as camel case or humpback notation. Some examples include:

```
fastestTime;
isReadyToRun;
highestValue;
```

Sometimes you need to refer to constant values in your code by name, as with variables. To help differentiate between the two, constant identifiers use all capital letters. Some legal constant names could include:

```
DAYS_IN_WEEK
GRAVITY
POPULATION
MAX_VALUE
```

When multiple words are combined in constant names, as in DAYS_IN_WEEK, the convention is to separate the words using underscores, which helps with legibility.

Strict Typing

In addition to a legal name, variables in Processing must also be declared of a certain data type. A data type tells the compiler what kind of value can legally be associated with a variable. This helps the compiler allocate the right amount of memory for the respective data type and also allows the compiler to help you avoid making a hard to track down truncation error. For example, an integer in Processing requires 32 bits of memory (that's 32 0's or 1's, or 2^{32}). When you declare a variable of type integer, the compiler reserves at least that much space in memory, associating it with your variable name. Later in your program, if you try to assign a floating point number (a real number with a decimal point) to your integer variable, the compiler generates an error. If it didn't generate this error and allowed the assignment, the float value would be truncated into an integer, probably not in the way you would expect. For example, the values 4.02, 4.5 and 4.995 would all be truncated to 4. Later in the book we'll look at other examples where some conversion between related data types is permitted, even necessary.

> Note: As discussed in Chapter 1, the computer reduces information to 0's and 1's (bits), also known as base-2 or the binary numeral system. In comparison, our decimal system uses the 10 symbols 0–9 (base-10). When evaluating values in base-2, we can begin at the rightmost symbol and multiply it by 2^0 (any number raised to the 0 power is 1) the second symbol from the right by 2^1, the third from the right by 2^2, etc. For example, the binary number 1001101 evaluates to 77, based on the following calculation (looking at the binary values from left to right): $1*2^6 + 0*2^5 + 0*2^4 + 1*2^3 + 1*2^2 + 0*2^1 + 1*2^0$.

There are numerous built-in data types in Processing, including: int, for integers; float, for real numbers; String, for words; boolean, for true or false. You'll learn about others throughout the book. Referring back to our earlier list of variable names, here they are again declared with a data type:

```
int value1;
float weight;
int highestScore;
boolean isValid;
int timeLength;
String bestInShow;
```

These statements are now legal variable declarations that will even compile. However, we still haven't assigned an initial value or state to them.

> Note: Depending on where variables are declared in a program, they may be automatically initialized with default values, based on their respective data type. For example, an int is initialized to 0, while a float to 0.0. However, there are other situations where declared but uninitialized variables may be undefined. As a best practice, it's always a good idea for you, the coder, to explicitly assign initial values to your variables when you declare them.

Finally, here are the variable declarations again, initialized with legal values:

```
int value1 = 1786;
float weight = 168.5;
int highestScore = 200000;
boolean isValid = true;
float timeLen = 55.5;
String bestInShow = "Heidi";
```

Congratulations! You now have enough information to begin to create your algorithmic face.

Face Implementation

The following code is an implementation of the face pseudocode we looked at earlier. The code utilizes variables to capture relative position and scale relationships between the facial features, all based on the initial head height. Output of the code is shown in Figure 2-13.

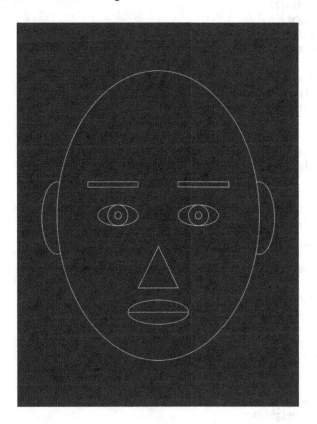

Figure 2-13. Simple algorithmic face

```
// Simple Algorithmic Face

size(600, 800);
background(0);
stroke(255);
noFill();
// draw ellipses from top left corner
ellipseMode(CORNER);

// BEGIN DECLARE/INITIALIZE VARIABLES
// HEAD
float headHeight = 600;
float headWidth = headHeight*5/7;
```

```
float head_x = (width-headWidth)/2;
float head_y = (height-headHeight)/2;

// EYES
float eyeWidth = headWidth/5;
float eyeHeight = eyeWidth/2;
float irisDiam = eyeHeight;
float pupilDiam = irisDiam/3;
float eye_y = head_y+headHeight/2-eyeHeight/2;
// left
float leftEye_x = head_x+eyeWidth;
float leftIris_x = leftEye_x + eyeWidth/2-irisDiam/2;
float leftPupil_x = leftEye_x + eyeWidth/2-pupilDiam/2;
// right
float rightEye_x = head_x+eyeWidth*3;
float rightIris_x = rightEye_x + eyeWidth/2-irisDiam/2;
float rightPupil_x = rightEye_x + eyeWidth/2-pupilDiam/2;

//EYEBROWS
float eyeBrowWidth = eyeWidth*1.25;
float eyeBrowHeight = eyeHeight/4;
float eyeBrow_y = eye_y - eyeHeight - eyeBrowHeight/2;
// left
float leftEyeBrow_x = leftEye_x - (eyeBrowWidth-eyeWidth);
// right
float rightEyeBrow_x = rightEye_x;

// NOSE
float nose_x = head_x+eyeWidth*2;
float nose_y = head_y + headHeight - headHeight/4;

// MOUTH
float mouthWidth = eyeWidth*1.5;
float mouthHeight = headHeight/12;
float mouth_x = leftIris_x+irisDiam/2+eyeWidth/4;
float mouth_y = nose_y + mouthHeight;

// EARS
float earWidth = eyeHeight*1.5;
float earHeight = headHeight/4;
float ear_y = eyeBrow_y;
// left
float leftEar_x = head_x-earWidth/2;
// right
float rightEar_x = head_x+headWidth-earWidth/2;

// BEGIN DRAWING
// Draw head
ellipse(head_x, head_y, headWidth, headHeight);
```

```
// left eye
ellipse(leftEye_x, eye_y, eyeWidth, eyeHeight);
// Draw left iris
ellipse(leftIris_x, eye_y, irisDiam, irisDiam);
// Draw left pupil
ellipse(leftPupil_x, eye_y+eyeHeight/2-pupilDiam/2, pupilDiam, pupilDiam);
// Draw right eye
ellipse(rightEye_x, eye_y, eyeWidth, eyeHeight);
// Draw right iris
ellipse(rightIris_x, eye_y, irisDiam, irisDiam);
// Draw right pupil
ellipse(rightPupil_x, eye_y+eyeHeight/2-pupilDiam/2, pupilDiam, pupilDiam);
// Draw left eyebrow
rect(leftEyeBrow_x, eyeBrow_y, eyeBrowWidth, eyeBrowHeight);
// Draw right eyebrow
rect(rightEyeBrow_x, eyeBrow_y, eyeBrowWidth, eyeBrowHeight);
// Draw nose
triangle(nose_x, nose_y, nose_x+eyeWidth, nose_y, nose_x + eyeWidth/2, nose_y-eyeWidth);
// Draw Mouth - top lip
arc(mouth_x, mouth_y-mouthHeight/2, mouthWidth, mouthHeight, PI, TWO_PI);
// Draw Mouth - bottom lip
arc(mouth_x, mouth_y-mouthHeight/2, mouthWidth, mouthHeight, 0, PI);
// Draw Mouth – crease
line(mouth_x, mouth_y, mouth_x+mouthWidth, mouth_y);
// Draw left ear
arc(leftEar_x, ear_y, earWidth, earHeight, PI/2.3, PI*1.55);
// Draw right ear
arc(rightEar_x, ear_y, earWidth, earHeight, -PI/1.8, PI/1.8);
```

Reviewing the code, notice how the declared variables at the top of the program are named. When naming variables, the goal again should be to strike a balance between clarity and economy. Ideally, the names should be descriptive enough to give a clear sense of their purpose, yet not overly verbose. Also, notice the ample use of comments and whitespace to help organize the code. There is a tendency when coding to just get things working as quickly as possible. This can lead to sloppy and ultimately ugly code. Programmers have a term to describe code like this: "Spaghetti Code." Look at the following two blocks of code: which do you think is easier to comprehend (especially a few months after you've written it, or by another coder trying to work with your code)?

```
// spaghetti code
float ew=hw/5;float eh=ew/2;
float id=eh;float pd=id/3;
float ey=hy+hh/2-eh/2;

// better code
float eyeWidth = headWidth/5;
float eyeHeight = eyeWidth/2;
float irisDiam = eyeHeight;
float pupilDiam = irisDiam/3;
float eye_y = head_y+headHeight/2-eyeHeight/2;
```

In addition to naming and including comments and whitespace, it's also helpful to structure your code in a way that makes it easy to manage. By declaring variables up top, as opposed to interspersed with the drawing code, it's easier to make global changes to the code, as well as debug it, should problems arise—and they will.

Reviewing the Simple Algorithmic Face code more closely, there are a few new commands:

```
background(0);
stroke(255);
noFill();
// draw ellipses from top left corner
ellipseMode(CORNER);
```

The background() command paints the entire sketch window with the color specified by the argument(s) passed between the parentheses. When passing only one argument, values between 0 and 255 will paint the background from black through gray to white respectively. For example, background(0) paints the window black, background(255) paints the window white and any value between 0 and 255 would paint it gray. It is also possible to paint the background a color by passing three arguments (each between 0 and 255) representing red, green, and blue. For example, to paint the background pure red, you'd write background(255, 0, 0), for pure green background(0, 255, 0). Of course, the colors don't have to be pure; background(100, 50, 20) paints a lovely brown. Later in the book you'll learn more about these commands, including the math behind them.

stroke() works similarly to background(), except it controls the color of lines, while fill() controls the inside color of shapes. stroke() and fill() allow you to pass 1, 2, 3, or 4 arguments (each between 0 and 255):

- 1 argument specifies grayscale

- 2 arguments specify grayscale and its degree of opacity (referred to as alpha)

- 3 arguments specify red, green and blue

- 4 arguments specify red, green, blue and alpha (degree of opacity)

noFill() and noStroke() turn off the fill and stroke respectively, until the fill() or stroke() call is made again.

All the commands we've been discussing control Processing's painting system by changing the style states of the system. These states remain constant until another related command is made. For example, after you call fill(255, 255, 0), every shape you draw will be filled with yellow, until you call the fill() command again, specifying a new color. By default, when you start a new Processing sketch the fill state is white and the stroke state is black.

> Note: The default range of values for the arguments you pass to Processing's background(), stroke(), and fill() commands is 0–255, for each of the respective color components (grayscale, red, green, blue and alpha). However, you can change the range of values using Processing's colorMode() command. For example, the following command changes the color range for each component to a range between 0.0–1.0, colorMode(RGB, 1.0). To learn more about this command, see: http://processing.org/reference/colorMode_.html.

Similar to Processing's painting style states, there are default geometry states, controlling how shapes are plotted in the sketch window. As you learned earlier in the chapter, rectangles by default are drawn from their top left corner, while ellipses are drawn around their center. We can override this behavior for each of these shapes with the commands: `rectMode(CENTER)` and `ellipseMode(CORNER)`. In the Simple Algorithmic Face example, using `ellipseMode(CORNER)` simplified the position and scale calculations of the facial features.

After setting the painting and geometry states, we declare and initialize about thirty variables in the code, from `headHeight` down to `rightEar_x`. It may seem like a lot of code, just to draw a relatively simple face, but again computers are lousy at intuiting. Each facial feature needs variables for its position (along both x- and y-axes) and size (specifying width and height). Notice that only the `headHeight` variable is initialized with a constant value (`float headHeight = 600;`). All the other variables are initialized using simple mathematical expressions, based on other facial details. This approach allows us to easily make global changes to the program. For example, Figure 2-14 and 2-15 show dramatic size changes to the head, while maintaining relative scale and positioning between the individual facial features. These images were generated simply by changing `headHeight` to 100 and then 1000.

Figure 2-14. Simple algorithmic face, headHeight = 100

Figure 2-15. Simple algorithmic face, headHeight = 1000

> *Try This: Create a copy of the Simple Algorithmic Face sketch and try entering some different values throughout the code. Try to predict what will happen based on your changes.*

Quick Math Refresher

Some of the variable initialization expressions may initially look a little daunting, as they involve more than one mathematical operation, such as:

```
float mouth_x = leftIris_x+irisDiam/2+eyeWidth/4;
```

Mathematical expressions in programming adhere to similar rules you learned in basic math. For example, the order of operations follows the rules you'd expect: Multiplication and division operations are evaluated first, followed by addition and subtraction. When an expression has multiple operators of the same precedence level (e.g. + and -, or * and /), operation order proceeds from left to right, so the mouth_x assignment operation we looked at earlier is evaluated in the order listed by the superscripts:

```
float mouth_x = ( ( leftIris_x + (irisDiam/2)1st ) 3rd + (eyeWidth/4)2nd )4th;
```

The basic mathematical operators in Processing include:

```
+ (addition)
- (subtraction)
* (multiplication
/ (division)
% (modulus)
```

You're probably familiar with all of these except perhaps the modulus operator. Modulus simply returns the remainder of division. For example, 5 % 2 = 1, 6 % 2 = 0 and 125 % 16 = 13. The operator is actually very handy in programming, and you'll see it in action throughout the book. Modulus has the same precedence level as multiplication and division.

> *Try This: Think of how the modulus operator could be useful in identifying even or odd numbers, as well as numbers occurring only at certain intervals.*

There are other more advanced operators at your disposal in Processing and Java as well, which you can read more about at http://docs.oracle.com/javase/tutorial/java/nutsandbolts/operators.html. One additional symbol (really symbols) you'll use often is parentheses. Parentheses have the highest precedence of all. So when in doubt, you can always place individual operations between parentheses and they'll be evaluated first. For example, to ensure addition occurs before division in the previous expression, you could write:

```
float mouth_x = ( (leftIris_x + irisDiam)/2 + eyeWidth )/4;
```

When parentheses are nested, the inner pair evaluates before the outer.

The last operator to discuss here is =. Unfortunately, = in Processing does not mean *equal to*. Rather, it's called the assignment operator (== means *equal to* in Processing). The expression we've been looking at,

```
float mouth_x = leftIris_x+irisDiam/2+eyeWidth/4;
```

evaluates from right to left relative to the assignment operator(=). This may initially sound contradictory based on what you just learned about order of operations, but it's really not. In regard to how the entire assignment expression is evaluated, first, the operations on the right-hand side of the assignment operator are fully evaluated (following the order of operation rules discussed earlier). Then, the final right hand side value is assigned (across the assignment operator) to the variable mouth_x. Though it may seem like a trivial detail in which direction the assignment operation occurs, it's actually a fundamentally important detail, which we'll return to later in the book.

The rest of the Simple Algorithmic Face code should be self-explanatory. However, there is one new command, arc(), toward the bottom of the code that probably needs some clarification. arc() takes six arguments specifying, position, size, and rotation. We've looked at position and size throughout the chapter, but rotation is a new concept. The last two arguments in the arc() call specify a starting and ending angle for the arc, and these values need to be specified in radians (as opposed to degrees).

Radians are the standard unit of measure on the polar coordinate system, shown in Figure 2-16. The Cartesian coordinate system we've been working with thus far has its origin at the intersection of the perpendicular x- and y-axes, and plotted points are defined in reference to the origin along the respective axes. For example, the point (18, 100) translates to the x-component of the point being 18 units from 0 on the x-axis and the y-component of the point being 100 units from 0 on the y-axis.

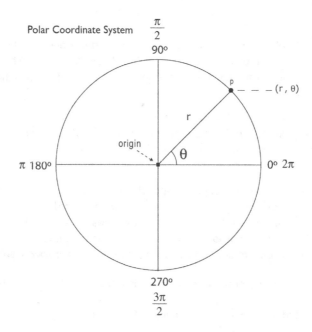

Figure 2-16. Polar coordinate system

The polar coordinate system utilizes a different structure than the Cartesian system. Points are defined relative to an angle of rotation(q) and distance to a central origin. The distance around the entire polar system is Pi * 2, with Pi equal to a half rotation and Pi/2 a quarter rotation. Processing actually includes constants for PI, TWO_PI, HALF_PI and QUARTER_PI. Figure 2-16 shows rotation around the polar system proceeding counterclockwise, which is the standard way it's presented in math texts. However, in Processing, rotation occurs clockwise. Figure 2-17 shows the output of sixteen calls to Processing's arc() command, using random start and end angles, listed below each figure. Please note, the angle values were translated from radians to degrees in the figure for sake of legibility (it's difficult to decipher rotation angles in radians). Throughout the book we'll return to the polar coordinate system, especially when we discuss basic trigonometry (for creating cool effects and imagery).

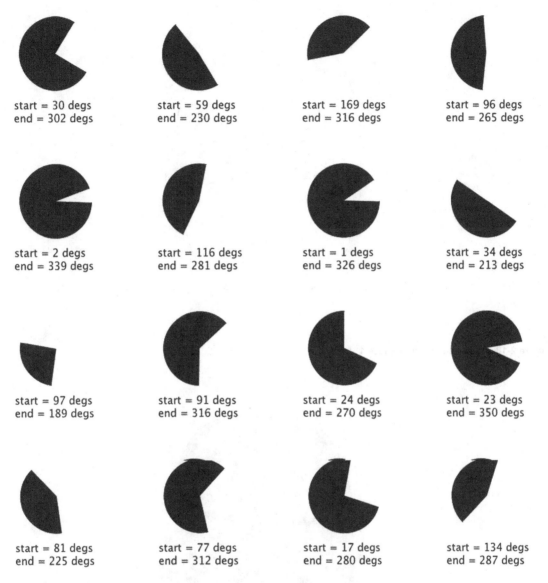

Figure 2-17. Processing's arc() command

Rather than end this chapter on a very technical note, Figures 2-18 and 2-19 show two images created with a more advanced algorithmic face example. This example utilizes curves and additional randomization, leading to many more facial possibilities. Though the code is not included in the text, it can be downloaded from the code repository for the book on the Apress site.

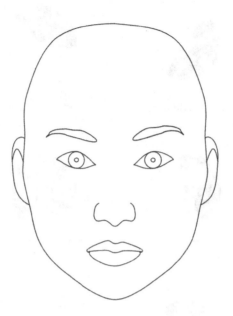

Figure 2-18. Advanced algorithmic face 1

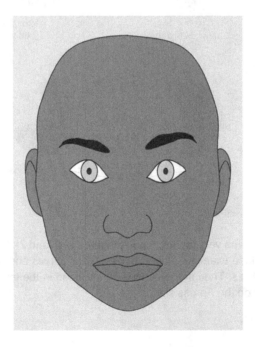

Figure 2-19. Advanced algorithmic face 2

Summary

You've done a lot of hard work this chapter! Hopefully, you're beginning to see the creative and generative possibilities of code. Like with any medium or process, coding includes best practices and conventions that allow you to be most effective. Learning to think algorithmically is a critical skill to master to become a good coder, as is learning how to efficiently (and clearly) translate your algorithm into executable code. Utilizing pseudo-code is a great way to start your coding practice, freeing you to focus on the individual steps, without worrying about specific language syntax. Variables are fundamental structures you'll rely on as a coder, and you learned Processing and Java's simple rules and conventions for their use. Finally, you learned a bit more about Processing, including the 2D primitives and how coordinate systems work, relative to the Cartesian system of the sketch window, as well as the polar coordinate system. In the next chapter you'll dive deeper into drawing in Processing and also learn about functions and loops.

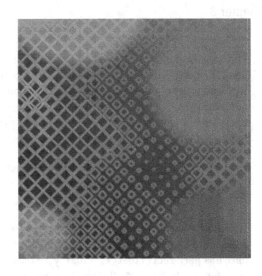

Chapter 3

Processing Boot Camp

In chapters one and two you learned about the Processing environment and how to begin to think algorithmically. You also learned how to draw simple images using Processing's 2D drawing primitives. This chapter you'll dig in much deeper and learn how to begin to structure your code using your own custom functions, loops and conditional statements. You'll also learn how to reimplement (and even override) some of the Processing commands with your own improved advanced drawing commands. We'll also introduce Processing transformations and the drawing context. Finally, you'll put all this knowledge to great use, creating an emergent example showcasing the exciting potential of creative coding with Processing.

Functions

As you learned last chapter, functions are the main programming structures in the core Processing language. All the 2D primitive calls you made last chapter were function calls. You also learned that functions in programming borrow their context from math and engineering and can be thought of as little black boxes, also little machines with an input and output. Functions allow you to create modular structures in your code that can be reused. In fact, you can distribute your functions to other coders who can incorporate them into their programs. This modular aspect of programming is really important in the professional development world, where it's generally more economical to use existing code than to reinvent it.

Revisiting Processing's `rect()` function, here's how you draw a rectangle:

```
rect(20, 20, 60, 60);
```

The way this function works is by calling a function defined in the language with the same name as the function call, in this case "rect." In addition, the arguments passed to the function: 20, 20, 60, 60 need to match the type and order of values defined in the function–the function's parameters. Processing only includes two basic number types, `int` and `float` (though technically you can also use Java's other number types.) Processing's basic rect() function definition includes four parameters of type `float`, which can accept either `int` or `float` number types. The function definition looks something like this:

```
void rect(float x, float y, float w, float h) {
 // rectangle drawing code here
}
```

To simplify things, we won't worry about how the actual rectangle drawing occurs. You'll learn more about that later in the chapter. The really important part of the definition to worry about right now is the function signature, this part: `rect(float x, float y, float w, float h)`. All functions in Processing are evaluated by their signatures, which include the function name and any parameters declared between the function parentheses. Here are some more examples:

```
ellipse(float x, float y, float w, float h)
point(float x, float y)
size(int w, int h)
color(float r, float g, float g, float a)
loadImage(String name)
noFill()
```

Don't worry if you don't know what some of these functions do. The important thing to remember at this point is that Processing evaluates functions by their names and parameter list, including the order and data type of the parameters. In other words, Processing evaluates the following two functions as different, in spite of the fact that they share the same name:

```
foo(int a, float b)
foo(float a, int  b)
```

You'll learn a bit later in the chapter, as well as in other chapters throughout the book, why this language feature is useful. Next, let's try a couple of examples that actually draw something to see functions in action.

Reimplementing rect()

In the next example you'll learn how to recreate (technically **override**) Processing's rect() function. First you'll learn how to break rect() and then you'll try to improve it. As you learned earlier, the basic rect() function looks something like this:

```
void rect(float x, float y, float w, float h) {
 // rectangle drawing code here
}
```

We're hoping you recognize the signature part of the function: rect(float x, float y, float w, float h), but what about the other syntax? All functions in Processing (among other languages) require you to include, at the very beginning of the function, the specific type of data (e.g., int, float, etc.) that the function returns or the word "void" if the function doesn't return anything. A function that returns something literally sends back a value of the declared data type when the function is called. The majority of Processing's built-in functions, as well as our custom rect(), do not return a value and thus must be preceded by void. In the next chapter we'll explore functions that return values.

Though the rect() function doesn't return a value, it does draw to the screen. This can create confusion for new coders. Drawing to the screen is completely different from returning a value; in fact, the two operations are completely independent. A function can draw to the screen and also return a value, or as is the case with rect(), not return a value. Again, the majority of functions in Processing do not return any value and thus are preceded by void in their definitions.

Next we'll add some drawing code to the rect() command, but we'll do so in a subversive way. As I mentioned earlier, first you'll learn how to break rect(). We'll make Processing's rect() call draw ellipses instead of rectangles (probably best not to tell Reas and Fry about this.) Here's the new function:

```
void rect(float x, float y, float w, float h) {
  ellipse(x, y, w, h);
}
```

To test the new rect() function, run the following code:

```
// rect to ellipse example
// overrides Processing's rect function
void setup() {
  size(400, 400);
  background(100);
  rect(width/2, height/2, 300, 300);
} // setup()

void rect(float x, float y, float w, float h) {
  ellipse(x, y, w, h);
} // rect()
```

Notice that we included Processing's setup() function along with our new rect() function. setup() is required in Processing when you include your own custom functions. Going forward, every program you write in Processing should include the setup() function. Also notice that the rect() function exists fully outside of the curly braces of the setup() function. Functions should be defined outside of any other functions. Later in the chapter you'll also learn how to create functions in separate tabs.

When you ran the previous example, shown in Figure 3-1, were you surprised to see that you did indeed break Processing's rect() command? Processing now has two commands to create ellipses, but no command to easily draw rectangles. In fact, if you include your custom rect() command in all future Processing programs, you will indeed not be able to use Processing's original version of rect(). Do you feel the power!

Figure 3-1. Override Processing `rect()` Command

Don't worry: you haven't permanently disfigured Processing, but you have learned how to override a function. Later in the book, when you learn about object-oriented programming, you'll learn more about the concept of overriding. As we discussed earlier, Processing identifies functions by the function's signature: its name and list of parameters, including their respective data types. When you create a custom function that has the exact same signature as a built-in Processing function, your function overrides the built-in one, as you just did in the example. In other words, when someone calls the function you overrode, your custom implementation will run instead of the built-in one.

> *Please note that we refer to the values passed to a function as arguments and the variables declared within the head of the function as parameters.*

Notice in the new `rect()` command that we're using the function's parameters (`float x, float y, float w, float h`) as the arguments we're passing to the `ellipse()` function call (`ellipse(x, y, w, h)`). Function parameters can be thought of as local variables declared within the head of a function that are initialized with the arguments passed to the function when it's called.

> *Remember that declaring a variable means bringing it into existence for the first time, or computationally speaking allocating memory to store data accessible through the variable. When you declare a variable you must include its data type in the declaration statement. However, once it's declared you only refer to the variable thereafter by just its name.*

Local Variables and Scope

Variables are considered local when they are declared within a code block. In Processing, a code block is defined by curly braces. Function parameters, though declared within the head of the function, are still considered local to the function, as if they had been declared between the curly braces. The successful handshake between a function call and the function definition is determined by the data types of the passed arguments and their respective order. If the function signature doesn't match the function call, even by just one argument/parameter, there is no handshake and the function is not called.

> *Try This: Create another function that makes Processing's `ellipse()` command draw rectangles and then another that makes Processing's `arc()` command draw triangles.*

Local variables are only visible within the block where they are declared as well as any nested blocks. This is a very important concept, so you might want to reread the last sentence. The next example illustrates this visibility aspect of local variables.

```
// Local Variable Scope
void setup() {
  int locVar1 = 301;
  println("locVar1 in setup = " + locVar1);

  // nested empty block as an example
  {
    int locVar2 = 290;
    println("locVar1 nested in setup = " + locVar1);
    println("locVar2 nested in setup = " + locVar2);
  }

  // uncommented this will generate an error
  // println("local locVar2 out of scope = " + locVar2);
} // setup()

void myFunction() {
  // uncommented these will both generate errors
  // println("local locVar1 out of scope = " + locVar1);
  // println("local locVar2 out of scope = " + locVar2);
} // myFunction()
```

Processing's println() function outputs information to the text area of the development environment. It's a very useful function for helping you to keep track of values in your program (variable states) and also to eventually debug your code as unexpected problems arise. Notice in the example in each println() call we combined quoted text with a variable. In Processing, we refer to text with quotes around it as a string literal. println() outputs string literals verbatim. A string literal is different from a variable name, which has a symbolic link to a stored value. We wouldn't expect println() to spit back the name of a variable we passed to it, but rather the value assigned to the variable.

As illustrated in the example, you can combine a string literal with a variable as the argument you send to println(). However, you must use the + symbol to do so. The + symbol in this context is referred to as the concatenation operator, not the addition operator; though it is the same exact symbol. Processing figures out the operator's function (concatenating or adding) through the context in which it's used. If the operands on either side of the operator are both numbers, it will add them; if the two types are a string and a number, or two strings, they will be concatenated into a longer string.

Running the program should output:

```
locVar1 in setup = 3

locVar1 nested in setup = 3

locVar2 nested in setup = 290
```

The first `println()` call simply outputs the value of `locVar1` declared right before the statement. The second `println()` call is from within a set of nested curly braces. (Normally, freestanding curly braces would be part of another code structure, but we included them here just to show how the braces control scope.) As mentioned earlier, from within the nested block you can still access `locVar1`. Next we declare `locVar2`, and as expected we can access it with the next `println()` statement.

Leaving the nested block, notice the next `println()` statement is commented out. Try uncommenting it and running the program again; it should generate the following error:

```
Cannot find anything named "locVar2".
```

Do you understand why this error was generated? locVar2 was declared within the nested block in setup(), so it is only visible from within the block or from any other sub-nested blocks. In general, we refer to where and when data is accessible within a program using the term **scope**. The rules of scope of a programming language dictate the visibility of variables, or from the compiler's perspective, when memory can be accessed or even ultimately deallocated and reclaimed as things go permanently out of scope. Though it's probably obvious by now, you can't access locVar1 or locVar2 from within the custom myFunction() function either. If either of the println() calls in myFunction() are uncommented you'll get a compiler error similar to the earlier error.

Returning to our earlier custom rect to ellipse function, perhaps you're feeling a little guilty about seemingly breaking Processing's rect() command and would like to put it back the way it was. However, let's assume you've also grown attached to your new version of rect(). The good news is you can have it both ways. As mentioned earlier, if function signatures don't match exactly, they are evaluated as two different functions, regardless if they share the same name. So the following two functions can exist independently in the same program:

```
void rect(float x, float y, float w, float h)
void rect(float x, float y, float w, float h, boolean isRect)
```

The second rect() function includes the new boolean parameter isRect as a fifth parameter. You looked at the boolean data type very briefly last chapter. boolean values in Processing may only be true or false, which are also both reserved keywords in Processing. boolean variables are useful for setting certain states of a program, such as the function drawing ellipses or rectangles. boolean variables are also commonly referred to as flags in a program.

Processing 2.0 introduced two additional rect() functions enabling you to draw rectangles with rounded corners. The two rect() signatures are:

```
void rect(float x, float y, float w, float h, float r)
void rect(float x, float y, float w, float h, float tl, float tr, float br, float bl)
```

Parameter r specifies the corner radius value for all four corners, while tl, tr, br and bl specify individual values for the top-left, top-right, bottom-right and bottom-left corners respectively. Figure 3-2 shows output using varying argument values.

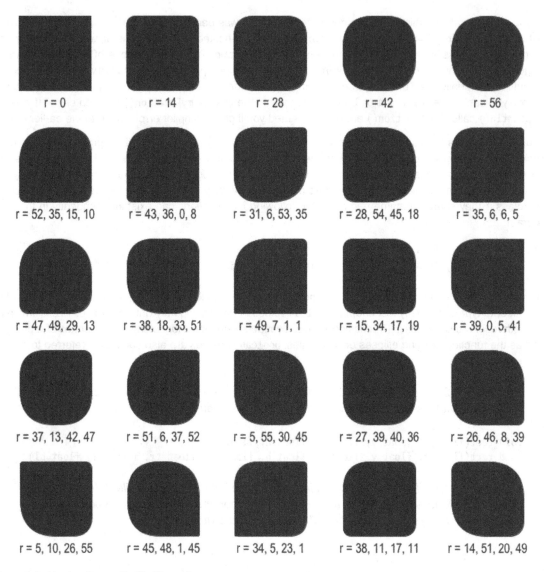

Figure 3-2. Varying Corner Radii with rect()

Adding Some Logic

Our new rect() function will allow users to specify whether they want to draw ellipses or rectangles by passing false for ellipse and true for rectangles as the fifth argument passed to the function. Here's a simple example, with output shown in Figure 3-3:

```
//improved custom rect function
void setup() {
  size(600, 600);
  background(0);
  rect(175, 175, 350, 350, false);
  rect(300, 300, 300, 300, true);
} // setup()

void rect(float x, float y, float w, float h, boolean isRect){
  if (isRect){
    rect(x, y, w, h); // call Processing's rect()
  }

  if (!isRect){
    ellipse(x, y, w, h); // call Processing's ellipse()
  } // rect()
}
```

Figure 3-3. Improved Custom rect()

Now you're able to still use Processing's rect() function as well as your new custom one. In fact, notice in the example that we're actually calling Processing's rect() from within our custom rect(). Pretty cool, eh? Also notice that we snuck in some new syntax as well, including two if statements.

Since we're passing in a boolean argument to specify whether to draw rectangles or ellipses, we need a way of changing our program's flow based on what value the boolean flag evaluates to. There is no way to know ahead of time, from within the function, whether the fifth argument passed to the function will be true or false. Processing includes capabilities for assessing simple logic. You looked at if statements last chapter, at least in theory when you learned about pseudocode. Implementing them is very simple and follows syntax that should look familiar.

Here's the basic structure:

```
if (boolean condition) {
  // this code only runs if condition was true.
}
```

If the condition evaluates to true, any code between the curly brace (the code block) executes. If the condition evaluates to false, the if statement's inner block is skipped and control moves past the closing curly brace. The Boolean condition to test for can be as simple as:

```
if (true) {
}
```

which would always be true of course. The conditional test can also be substantially more complicated, such as:

```
// using pseudocode between the parentheses
if (condition 1 is true and condition is 2 is true and condition 3 is false, etc. ) {
}
```

Obviously we'd need to convert the pseudocode between the parentheses into actual code, but doing so will require a lot more syntax, which we'll look at in the next chapter.

Returning to the previous example program code, hopefully the first if statement now makes more sense:

```
if (isRect){
    rect(x, y, w, h); // call Processing's rect()
}
```

Since the parameter isRect evaluates to true or false, we can simply use the parameter in the conditional evaluation. Also, since we're no longer overriding Processing's rect() function (the signatures of the two rect() functions are now different) we can now use it again.

> Remember: In Processing we always **call** functions from within other functions, but we **define** functions within whitespace, outside of any other function.

The second if statement includes one additional syntactic element, ! (exclamation mark) or very technically the unary logical *compliment* operator. It's unary because it requires only a single operand (versus binary operators such as +, -, *, /, which require two operands). The term compliment simply means the operator inverts the boolean value of the operand (true becomes false, false becomes true).

```
if (!isRect){
    ellipse(x, y, w, h); // call Processing's ellipse()
}
```

The `if(!isRect)` statement will be true if `isRect` evaluates to false, since the complement operator inverts the value. We realize this might seem confusing on the first read. In spite of all the new language syntax and keywords you're learning, ultimately the most challenging part of coding is what you do with the language–your algorithms and program logic.

Conditional logic is fundamental to programming and you'll use it extensively throughout the rest of the book. In addition to the "if " keyword, you'll also utilize "else." For example, to ensure that one of two possible outcomes always occurs you would use if and else in combination:

```
if (condition) {
  // if condition is true this executes
} else {
  // if the condition is not true this executes
}
```

This structure guarantees that only one of the blocks will ever execute. If the condition is true the if block executes and the else block is skipped; if it's false only the else block executes.

You can also use combinations of if, else if, and else blocks, for example:

```
if(condition1) {
  // if condition1 is true this executes
} else if(condition2) {
 // if condition2 is true this executes
} else {
  // if neither is true this executes
}
```

Not only can you use extensive groupings of if else blocks, but you can also nest them, controlling branching logic. For example, if a condition is true, then check a bunch of other conditions, etc. In the upcoming chapters you'll see many examples of conditional logic in action.

Switch and Ternary

Finally, there are two additional language structures used for conditional testing and branching. Both of these are less commonly use than if/else and also less intuitive. Please note that these structures are not commonly used within the book, but we include them here as reference.

Switch Statement

Switch statements are often confusing to newer coders, as they can initially appear redundant (and less useful alternatives) to if/else. Here's an example:

```
switch(val) {
  case 0:
    // do this is if val is equal to 0
    break;
```

```
case 1:
  // do this is if val is equal to 1
  break;
case 2:
  // do this is if val is equal to 2
  break;
default:
  // do this is if val is not equal to any of the cases.
}
```

val must be an exact match to one of the cases (0, 1, 2) for the code under that case to execute. Unlike if/else, which allows for complex conditional logic, switch statements simply evaluate for a matching value, and the values may only be of type byte, short, char and int. Practically speaking we almost always use int. The break; statement within each case prevents what's called fall through, where the following case is evaluated, regardless if the earlier case was true. Without break statements, every case will always be executed, which at times can be useful. For example, a training program may check the last module a user completed. By using a switch statement without break statements, you can ensure all users will progress through to the end of the program, regardless of what module they begin on. Generally speaking though, you want to include break statements in your cases. The default case, like else, will execute if val is not equal to any of the previous cases. Including the default case is optional.

Ternary Operator

The ternary operator works with three operands and is arguably the least intuitive language structure in Processing (among other languages).

The operator is primarily a shorthand syntax for an if else statement that also returns a value. Here's an example:

```
int testVal = -3;
boolean isPositive = (testVal > 0) ? true : false;
```

if the condition (testVal > 0) is true then whatever follows the ? is returned. If the condition is not true then what follows the : is returned.

Moving Beyond the Primitives

Although you can build complex shapes using collections of primitives, you'll want to ultimately be able to draw custom shapes. In the Processing API there is a section titled **vertex**, shown in Figure 3-4.

Vertex
beginShape()
bezierVertex()
curveVertex()
endShape()
texture()
textureMode()
vertex()

Figure 3-4. Processing Vertex Reference

These commands enable you to plots points, technically referred to as vertices (singular is vertex) and then join the vertices to form shapes. You can plot shapes composed of both lines and curves. In this chapter you'll learn about lines, and in the next chapter we'll introduce curves. First, we'll use the new commands to plot some simple shapes and patterns, but we'll slowly build up to some more complex drawing algorithms.

Yet Another Rectangle

I suspect you're getting a bit bored with rectangles, but it will be helpful to recreate one more with the new improved plotting approach, which we'll promise to spice up a bit. The next example is a custom plotted rect-angle function using some of the commands shown in Figure 3-4:

```
// rectangle_plot
void setup(){
  size(600, 600);
  background(255);
  noSmooth(); // enable aliasing ("jaggies")
  plotRect(100, 100, 400, 400);
} // end setup

void plotRect(float x, float y, float w, float h) {
  beginShape();
  vertex(x, y);
  vertex(x, y+h);
  vertex(x+w, y+h);
  vertex(x+w, y);
  endShape();
} // end plotRect
```

Notice in the example we called Processing's noSmooth() command in setup(). noSmooth() turns off anti-aliasing to your sketch. Anti-aliasing is a technique that smooths out the jagged edges ("jaggies") that can occur in computer graphics. You won't notice a big change using noSmooth() with the rectangle, but you'll see bigger changes when you add diagonals and eventually curved lines. Aliasing occurs when you're drawing geometry that doesn't perfectly align to the underlying rectilinear grid of screen pixels, such as with curves and diagonals.

Figure 3-5 shows two triangles: the one on the left is aliased with noSmooth(), and the one on the right is anti-aliased by default. The circled areas are blown up below showing how anti-aliasing attempts to smooth the edges. Processing 2 by default comes with anti-aliasing turned on.

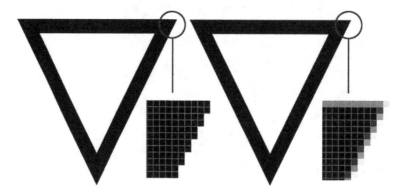

Figure 3-5. Aliasing versus Anti-aliasing

Processing 1 had anti-aliasing turned off by default, and you needed to call smooth() to enable it. You might wonder why in Processing 2 you would ever want to reenable aliasing (jaggies) using noSmooth(). Anti-aliasing does have some impact on performance because of the extra pixel processing. In addition, the smoothing algorithm adds slight blurring to edges, which can sometimes detract from the legibility of fine details, especially with typography. However, in most instances you will want to leave smoothing enabled in Processing 2.

The three commands beginShape(), vertex(), and endShape() work together. You must use all three together. beginShape() can be thought of as an internal record function. Once it's called, any subsequent calls to vertex() will be stored until endShape() is called, which immediately draws the recorded vertex data to the screen. vertex() takes two arguments (in 3D, you'll use additional arguments) specifying the x and y components of the vertex. In the example, we made four calls to vertex(), but you can essentially make as many as you'd like. When you run the example, you'll notice the rectangle seems to be incomplete, missing its top edge, as shown in Figure 3-6.

Figure 3-6. Plotted Rectangle Missing Top Edge

To add the missing edge you could use a fifth vertex call, duplicating the initial vertex. However, Processing includes a better solution utilizing the constant CLOSE as an argument passed to endShape(CLOSE). Including this constant will draw an additional line attaching the last vertex() call to the first one recorded, closing the shape. Here's a revised version of the sketch that draws a closed randomized quadrangle.

```
// randomized Quadrangle plot
void setup() {
  size(600, 600);
  background(255);
  plotRandomizedQuad (200, 200, 200, 200, .2, .2);
} // end setup

void plotRandomizedQuad(float x, float y, float w, float h, float randW, float randH) {
  float jitterW = w*randW;
  float jitterH = h*randH;
  beginShape();
  vertex(x+random(-jitterW, jitterW), y+random(-jitterH, jitterH));
  vertex(x+random(-jitterW, jitterW), y+h+random(-jitterH, jitterH));
  vertex(x+w+random(-jitterW, jitterW), y+h+random(-jitterH, jitterH));
  vertex(x+w+random(-jitterW, jitterW), y+random(-jitterH, jitterH));
  endShape(CLOSE);
} // end plotRandomizedQuad
```

Run the example a couple times. You should see variations in the quadrangle each time the program runs. The new fifth and sixth parameters added to plotRandomizdeQuad() control the range of randomization. Try changing the values of the fifth and sixth arguments passed to plotRandomizdeQuad() in the range 0–1.0. Figure 3-7 shows a page of random quads, progressively changing the argument values (for both width and height) from 0 to .5.

Figure 3-7. Randomized Quadrangles

By using Processing's random() function you can make your program output less predictable. Structured randomization is central to creative coding, where you're encouraged to experiment and discover new aesthetic possibilities. The random() function can take one or two arguments:

- Using one argument produces a random value from 0 up to, but not including, the argument value.

- Using two arguments produces a random value from the first value up to, but not including, the second argument.

We used the range from -jitter to +jitter values for the two axes so the quad would stay approximately centered in the window. Also, notice jitterW and jitterH are local variables declared within the block of the function, meaning again that they are only visible within the function.

Internally, Processing releases the memory used by the local variables after the function completes, since again local variables are not visible outside of the function in which they're declared. Programming languages do this sort of memory management all the time; if they didn't we'd quickly run out of memory. You'll learn more about memory later in the book when we discuss objects.

Expanding the API

Next, we'll expand the Processing API with a new 2D primitive, polygon(). You'll also learn how to create this new function in its own tab, which will enable you to easily reuse the code in another program. However, before we're ready to build a polygon we need to review some trigonometry ("trig"), revisiting the polar coordinate system discussed in the last chapter. Figures 3-8 and 3-9 are a set of cheat sheets that cover essentially everything you need to know about trig for basic computer graphics.

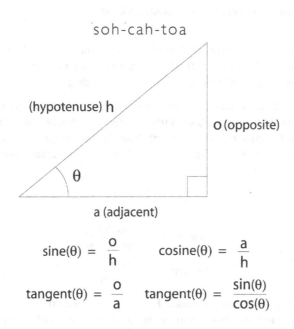

soh-cah-toa

(hypotenuse) h

o (opposite)

θ

a (adjacent)

$$sine(\theta) = \frac{o}{h} \qquad cosine(\theta) = \frac{a}{h}$$

$$tangent(\theta) = \frac{o}{a} \qquad tangent(\theta) = \frac{sin(\theta)}{cos(\theta)}$$

soh-cah-toa is a simple mnemonic device to help you remember how to apply the trig functions in solving for sides or angles of a right triangle.

Figure 3-8. Trigonometry Soh-Cah-Toa Mnemonic

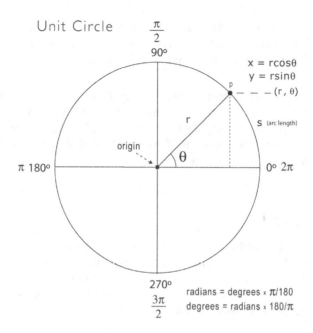

Figure 3-9. Converting between Cartesian and Polar Coordinate Systems

Figure 3-8 illustrates the relationship between the trigonometric functions and right triangles, We're all taught this at some point in school, and then many (probably most) of us summarily forget it. It's hard to appreciate just how useful these relationships are until you begin creative coding.

Take note of how the right triangle is labeled in the figure relative to the angle θ (theta). You'll remember from last chapter that θ is by convention the symbol we use to refer to angles on the polar coordinate system. If you know the value of θ and the length of one side of a right triangle you can easily solve for the lengths of the other sides using the ratios illustrated in Figure 3-8. If it's not obvious, these ratios are condensed in the mnemonic soh-cah-toa as follows:

$$\text{sine}(\theta) = \frac{\text{Opposite}}{\text{Hypotenuse}}$$

$$\text{cosine}(\theta) = \frac{\text{Adjacent}}{\text{Hypotenuse}}$$

$$\text{tangent}(\theta) = \frac{\text{Opposite}}{\text{Adjacent}}$$

Applying these equations is equally straightforward. For example, if you know θ is PI/3 radians and the opposite side of the triangle (the side across from θ, o in the figure) has a length of 6, what is the length of a? Since we know the value for θ and the opposite side of the triangle we can plug our known values into the tangent expression:

$$\tan\left(\frac{\pi}{3}\right) = \frac{6}{a}$$

We need to solve for a, so we'll multiply both side of the expression by a, giving us:

$$a \tan\left(\frac{\pi}{3}\right) = 6$$

Finally, we can divide both sides by the tangent expression to solve for a:

$$a = \frac{6}{\tan\left(\frac{\pi}{3}\right)}$$

It still may not be immediately apparent why this could actually be useful in creative computing, but consider that everything you do on the computer screen involves graphing information. The trig functions, in addition to helping you find the lengths of triangle sides, also enable you to find the angles between lines–lines in computer graphics are more technically referred to as vectors, which you'll learn more about later in the book–among numerous other capabilities. Common applications for the trig functions include aiming, steering behavior and plotting geometry, such as polygons. The trig functions are also extremely useful for simulating smooth periodic motion, such as hanging a weight from a spring.

Figure 3-9 shows the Unit Circle, which is just another representation of the polar coordinate system, where radius r has a length of 1. What's really pertinent in the figure for our polygon function are the expressions:

$$x = r \cos(\theta)$$
$$y = r \sin(\theta)$$

These relatively simple expressions allow you to map any point from the polar coordinate system to the Cartesian coordinate system of your computer screen. To draw a regular polygon with radius r, we just need to plug values of q into the trig functions as we increment q around the center of the Unit Circle (its origin) while multiplying each expression by r. For example, to draw a three-sided polygon (a regular triangle) with a radius of 100, we'd use the following expressions to calculate the first vertex. (To calculate the other vertices we'd increment q in the expressions for each vertex, moving around the Unit Circle:

$$x = 100 * \cos\left(\frac{\pi}{1.5}\right)$$
$$y = 100 * \sin\left(\frac{\pi}{1.5}\right)$$

Polygon Implementation

We'll implement the polygon in its own tab. Select a new tab from the tabs menu, shown in Figure 3-10. Name the new tab "polygon."

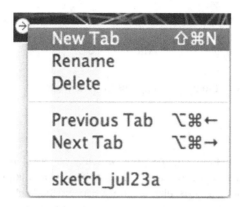

Figure 3-10. Processing's Tabs Menu

Tabs in Processing are primarily for organizational purposes. When Processing compiles your code into Java bytecode, function definitions in their own tabs are copied back into the main left tab behind the scenes. It makes no difference with regard to functionality whether your functions are created in their own tabs. However, it can be very helpful organizationally as well as make it much simpler to reuse your own code. For this reason, it is recommended you create your custom functions in their own tabs.

We'll build the example in a number of steps. Enter the following code in the polygon tab:

```
void polygon(float radius){

  float theta = 0.0;
  float x = 0.0;
  float y = 0.0;

  beginShape();

  // vertex 1
  x = cos(theta)*radius;
  y = sin(theta)*radius;
  vertex(x, y);

  // vertex 2
  theta = theta + PI/1.5;
  x = cos(theta)*radius;
  y = sin(theta)*radius;
  vertex(x, y);

  // vertex 3
  theta = theta + PI/1.5;
  x = cos(theta)*radius;
  y = sin(theta)*radius;
  vertex(x, y);
```

```
  endShape(CLOSE);
} // end polygon
```

To test out the new function, add the following code to the main left tab and run the example:

```
void setup(){
  size(400, 400);
  background(255);
  fill(100);
  polygon(100.0);
}
```

You should have gotten something that looked like Figure 3-11. Can you figure out why most of the polygon seems to be out of the window?

Figure 3-11. Initial Custom Polygon Function Output

The origin (0,0) of the Unit Circle, shown in Figure 3-9, is at its center, and polygons are plotted around this origin. The origin of our sketch window is the top left corner, so the polygon was drawn around this point. We'll shift the polygon to the middle of the sketch window in a moment. Looking at the polygon code, it should be apparent that we really created code for a regular triangle rather than a generalized polygon. Can you see why? What changes would you need to make to the polygon function to draw a pentagon or a dodecagon (12-sided polygon)? Ideally, the polygon function should be able to draw any n-sided polygon by passing a side count argument to the function.

Improved Polygon

The first step we'll take to improving our polygon is shifting it to the center of the window. There are two ways we can achieve this. The first down-and-dirty approach you'll learn simply adds an offset to each of the trig expressions. Edit the trig expressions in the polygon function to include the following offsets (in **bold**):

```
// vertex 1
x = width/2 + cos(theta)*radius;
y = height/2 + sin(theta)*radius;
vertex(x, y);
```

```
// vertex 2
theta = theta + PI/1.5;
x = width/2 + cos(theta)*radius;
y = height/2 + sin(theta)*radius;
vertex(x, y);

// vertex 3
theta = theta + PI/1.5;
x = width/2 + cos(theta)*radius;
y = height/2 + sin(theta)*radius;
vertex(x, y);
```

When you run the revised code you should get the output shown in Figure 3-12.

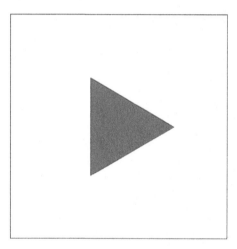

Figure 3-12. Centered Polygon

> *Try This: Edit the polygon() code to be able to draw a triangle pointing in a different direction.*

Transformations

This approach to moving things is fairly intuitive but can lead to some unexpected results. For example, let's add some rotation to the polygon, using Processing's `rotate()` command. In the main tab, add the following line of code right before the `polygon()` call. The output is shown in Figure 3-13.

```
rotate(PI/7);
```

Figure 3-13. Incorrectly Rotated Polygon

The polygon did not rotate around its own center point. What happened instead was that it was rotated around the sketch window origin, the top-left corner. Imagine that if you created a more complex drawing with moving parts like a bicycle, you'd want each tire to rotate around its own axle and not spin off the bicycle and rotate around the window's origin. To resolve this issue, we're going to use Processing's `translate()` function to move our triangle, and we'll remove the offset code we recently added. Your trig expressions in the `polygon()` function should go back to their original form:

```
x = cos(theta)*radius;
y = sin(theta)*radius;
```

In the main tab right, before the `rotate()` call, add the following code and rerun the sketch:

```
translate(width/2, height/2);
```

You should have gotten output that looks like Figure 3-14.

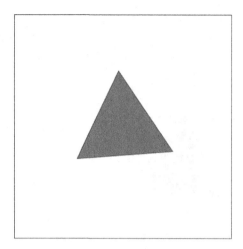

Figure 3-14. Correctly Rotated Polygon

This approach is the recommended way to move geometry in Processing: draw all shapes around the window's origin and then `translate()` them to move them. In general in computer graphics, we refer to operations such as translation, rotation, and scaling as transformations. Under the hood, Processing, as well as other computer graphics' libraries, utilizes matrices and linear algebra to handle transformations, which are beyond the scope of this book.

Perfected Polygon

The last step to perfecting the polygon is to generalize the function, so we can create a polygon of any side count. We can easily add a side count parameter to the `polygon()` function, but utilizing the new parameter will take a bit more work.

Update the signature of the polygon function to:

```
void polygon(int sideCount, float radius)
```

The remaining challenge is to be able to dynamically change the number of vertices plotted, based on the argument value passed to the `sideCount` parameter. Your current code manually creates three vertices, but there is no way to build upon this approach when the number of vertices is unknown until the function receives the argument value. The solution to this problem (and many, many other problems in programming) is to use a loop. We'll take a brief digression to learn about loops and then return to perfect your `polygon()` function.

Loops

You learned a little about loops in theory in the last chapter. Loops are really quite simple. They allow you to run code repetitively as long as a conditional test evaluates to true, similar to what you learned about with `if` statements. The basic logic in pseudocode is:

```
loop(boolean condition){
   // continue to run while the condition is true
}
```

Processing includes three structures for creating loops:

- `for`
- `while`
- `do while`

`for` and `while` loops behave similarly, and which one you choose is sometimes a matter of personal preference. However, there are certain problems that lend themselves more to one than to the other, which we'll illustrate. `do while` loops offer a subtle variation to `while` loops, in that they are guaranteed to run at least one time, which is not the case with `for` and `while` loops. Let's look at a few examples before applying them to the `polygon()` function. Example one outputs the values 0 to 99, first using a while loop and then a `for` loop.

while loop:
```
int i = 0;
while (i < 100) {
  println("i = " + i);
  i = i + 1;
}
```
for loop:
```
for (int i=0; i<100; i=i+1) {
  println("i = " + i);
}
```

The first thing you'll notice about the `while` loop is that the Boolean conditional test (`i < 100`) utilizes a variable external to the `while` loop. Because `int i` is declared outside of the loop, `i` is not local to the loop. In other words, `i` can be seen beyond the `while` loop. Next look at the `for` loop, which at first glance seems much more complicated than the `while` loop. Notice that the variable declaration `int i` occurs within the head of the loop, making it completely local to the loop; it can't be seen outside of the loop's curly braces (its block). Both loops will output exactly the same values: 0–99, and both loops also work by incrementing a counter variable `i`, in this case by 1. Technically, you can use any legal name you want for the loop counter variable, but there is a convention to use `i`, and then `j`, and then `k` if you need additional counters within the same loop structure. You can also increment or decrement the counter in both loops by any legal value or expression you'd like.

`while` loops are straightforward to understand. They continue to run while the test condition is true. If it's always true you'll get an infinite loop, which is generally a bad thing, as discussed in the last chapter. Infinite loops will make Processing lock up as control gets stuck within the loop, causing a standstill. It's a very common error to accidentally generate an infinite loop, even by experienced coders. `while` loops always begin executing with a conditional test; if it evaluates to true, the loops runs, and to false, the loop is skipped. `while` loops are especially useful for repeating processes dependent on a state within the program and not on a preset number of steps. For example, imagine you have a function to randomly search for a value between 1 and 100. Because you need the search to be random, you don't know how many steps it will take. You could create a `boolean` variable called isFound and use that as the conditional test for your while loop. Here's a program to do just this:

```
// randomly find a value between 1-100
void setup() {
  findValue(15);
}
```

```
void findValue(int val) {
  boolean isFound = false;
  int steps = 0;
  while (!isFound) {
    steps = steps + 1;
    if (1+int(random(100)) == val) {
      isFound = true;
    }
  }
  println("It took " + steps + " steps to find " + val+".");
} // findValue
```

We snuck some new code snuck in this example, int(random(100)). The random() function returns a float value, but the example is checking for an integer. Processing's int() function truncates float values to integers by removing any numbers after the decimal point. This means that the following values would all be converted to 3: 3.0001, 3.567, 3.9998. Processing also includes a round() function which rounds a value to the nearest integer value.

Try This: Search for a value between a different range of numbers.

---

for loops use a very condensed syntax that puts the counter declaration, conditional test, and incrementation (or decrementation) all in the head of the loop. Notice these three elements are separated by two semi-colons. The loop begins execution by declaring and initializing the counter, which only happens once. Then the conditional test occurs; if it evaluates to true, the loop executes; if false, the loop is skipped. After each iteration of the loop, the counter is incremented by the rule in the third part of the loop head. In general, for loops are most useful when you know exactly how many iterations the loops should run.

What's significant about both while and for loops is that they are not guaranteed to run even once if the starting conditional test evaluates to false. For example, in the earlier loop examples that printed out all the values from 0 to 99, if we had started i at 100 instead of 0, neither loop would have run. Try running these:

```
//while loop that won't run:
int i = 100;
while (i < 100) {
  println("i = " + i);
  i = i + 1;
}
//for loop that won't run:
for (int i=100; i<100; i=i+1) {
  println("i = " + i);
}
```

The do while loop is a variation of the while loop guaranteed to run at least once. It uses an inverted structure, running the block prior to the conditional test, shown next.

```
// This loop will run once even though
// the starting condition is false
int i = 100;
```

```
do {
  println("i = " + i);
  i =i+1;
} while (i<100);
```

Logically it would seem that this loop shouldn't run, as the counter i is never less than 100. However, do while loops always execute at least once. This can be useful if you need to ensure that some programmatic event always occurs, regardless of the initial state of the program.

Compound Operators

We'll look at one more for loop example, but first we'll make a small modification to how we're incrementing the counter variable. We've been using the long hand form:

```
i = i + 1;
```

This expression is perfectly legitimate. It is evaluated as follows: addition on the right hand side of the expression occurs first, and then assignment happens from right to left, updating the value of i each iteration of the loop. (We use the term iteration to represent each loop cycle.) Experienced coders however wouldn't write code like this, as there's a far more efficient approach–efficient in the sense that it saves keystrokes for the coder. Because incrementation and decrementation are so common in programming, languages include short cuts for them. The previous expression we looked at included both addition and incrementation. Processing includes operators that combine mathematical and assignment compound operations, including:

- +=
- -=
- *=
- /=
- %/

The previous statement, i = i + 1, can be more efficiently written as i += 1. Here are some more examples, in both long and short form:

```
x = x * 13,   x*= 13
y = y - 34,   y -= 34
z = z / 270,   z /= 270
```

Finally, the most common compound operations involve incrementing and decrementing by 1, and there are additional short cut forms for these as well.

```
// assume counter i
++i and i++
--i and i++
```

These forms may only be used for incrementing/decrementing by 1 and are the most common style you'll see used in for loops. The forms with the two operators on the left are referred to as prefix, and the ones with the two operators on the right are postfix. Prefix versus postfix form dictates when the incrementation occurs in an expression. For example, run the following:

```
int a = 0;
println("a = " + a++);

int b = 0;
println("b = " + ++b);
```

The output is:

```
a = 0

b = 1
```

---

a remains 0 because it is incremented only after it's used as an argument to the `println()` function, while b is incremented prior to being passed.

However, the prefix and postfix forms don't impact the behavior of `for` loops; for example run the following:

```
for (int a=0; a<3; a++) {
  println("a = " + a);
}

for (int b=0; b<3; ++b) {
  println("b = " + b);
}
```

Both loops will output the values 0, 1, 2 as expected.

Putting It All Together

Our last step is to apply all this new knowledge about algorithmic drawing, transformations, trigonometry, loops, and compound operators to our `polygon()` function. Here's the final code:

```
void polygon(int sideCount, float radius) {
  float theta = 0.0;
  float x = 0.0;
  float y = 0.0;

  beginShape();
  for (int i=0; i<sideCount; i++) {
    x = cos(theta)*radius;
    y = sin(theta)*radius;
    vertex(x, y);
    theta += TWO_PI/sideCount;
  }
  endShape(CLOSE);
} // end polygon
```

Now you have a function that can create a polygon of any side count, simply by passing in a different argument value for the sideCount parameter. Notice the conditional test in the for loop (i<sideCount) is now controlled by the value of sideCount, as is the incrementation of theta (theta += TWO_PI/sideCount). This model of using an argument value to dynamically redefine functionality through function parameterization is really the bedrock of procedural programming. Taken to the extreme, can you now imagine how a very complex system, such as for a bank, can simply take your login and produce a running program updated with only your data, propagated throughout the entire system.

To test the new polygon() function, update your code in the main tab with:

```
void setup(){
  size(400, 400);
  background(255);
  fill(100);
  translate(width/2, height/2);
  rotate(PI/7);
  polygon(7, 100.0);
}
```

Running the program now should produce a lovely heptagon, shown in Figure 3-15. Make sure you try changing the argument value from 7 to other integer values to produce different polygons. Notice too when the polygon count gets high, you essentially reproduce the Unit Circle.

Figure 3-15. Lovely Heptagon

Having Some Polygonal Fun

You've worked hard this chapter and it's time to use what you've learned to have some fun (not to diminish the fun of learning). Really, the creative coding journey begins here, where you can take a functioning system, albeit modest such as your polygon function, and play with it, exploring algorithmic possibilities. Along the way, you'll also learn a few more concepts and coding tricks of the trade.

Polygonal Wallpaper

Though we're using a loop internally within the polygon() function, we can also use one in the main tab to call the function. One really interesting aspect of programming is how modular things can be. You'll learn later in the book about a concept called recursion, which takes this idea to the extreme. Your first creative code exploration will be a simple polygonal pattern filling the sketch window. You'll also learn how to reuse the polygon() function by adding it to the new sketch.

Create a new sketch and then go to the **Sketch** menu and select **Add File...** You'll need to navigate to the sketch directory of your last sketch. Within it you'll find the file **polygon.pde**. When you select it, the polygon() function will be copied to your current sketch directory and added to your new sketch as a separate tab. Since the function is copied, not moved, the polygon() function will still remain in your old sketch as well.

Swap out the code in your main tab with the following:

```
void setup() {
  size(800, 800);
  background(255);
  int polyCount = 3000;
  noFill();
  int sideCount = 0;
  float radius = 0.0;
  float rotation = 0.0;

  for (int i=0; i<polyCount; i++) {
    sideCount = int(random(3, 15));
    radius = random(2, 20);
    rotation = random(TWO_PI);
    pushMatrix();
    translate(random(width), random(height));
    rotate(rotation);
    polygon(sideCount, radius);
    popMatrix();
  }
}
```

Figure 3-16 shows the polygonal wallpaper. Again, we were able to create this using the existing polygon() function.

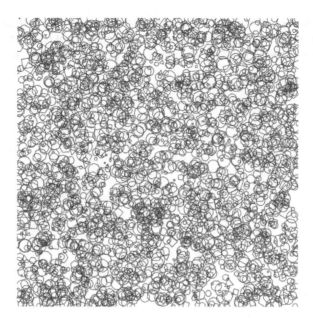

Figure 3-16. Polygonal Wallpaper

Pushing and Popping the Matrix

Look closely inside the `for` loop you just created. You'll notice two new function calls:

```
pushMatrix();
popMatrix();
```

These two mysterious sounding calls were strategically placed around the three lines:

```
translate(random(width), random(height));
rotate(rotation);
polygon(sideCount, radius);
```

This placement was not arbitrary, but actually necessary to get the output we wanted. You'll remember from earlier in the chapter that `translate()` and `rotate()` are considered transformations that seem to operate relative to the sketch window origin, not the shape actually being drawn. We illustrated this point earlier when we rotated a shape that was not drawn centered around the window origin. It seemed to shift around the window instead of rotate around its own center. You then learned to draw shapes centered at the origin and to use `translate()` to move them, allowing you to both move and rotate a shape relative to its own center point.

This process works fine for one shape, but fails with additional shapes. When you call any of Processing's transformations: `translate()`, `rotate()`, or `scale()`, you're effecting something referred to as the graphics context of the sketch window. You can think of this context as a floating canvas within the sketch window where the actual drawing occurs. If you don't call any transformations, the context remains aligned with the sketch window. However, each time you call a transformation, the graphics context is affected. Again, with one shape this is fine, but with additional shapes the context's position is cumulatively transformed by all the individual transformation calls. In other words, by default the graphics context is not reset between transformation calls to realign with the sketch window. Figure 3-17 illustrates a series of transformation calls and the impact to the drawing context.

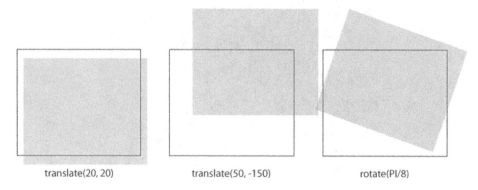

translate(20, 20)   translate(50, -150)   rotate(PI/8)

Figure 3-17. The Drawing Context

Try running the previous sketch now, commenting out pushMatrix() and popMatrix(), as shown in Figure 3-18.

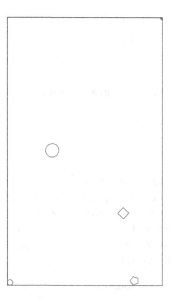

Figure 3-18. Polygonal Wallpaper without pushMatrix() and popMatrix()

Can you figure out why the density of the pattern is lost? Each of the translate() calls in the for loops continues to cumulatively shift the drawing context, putting most of the shapes out of the sketch window. If its not blatantly obvious now, pushMatrix() and popMatrix() are resetting the drawing context between each call. How they do this is actually pretty simple, in spite of their complex sounding names.

As you've learned, variables reference stored information used by your program, which can be changed throughout the lifetime of the running program. Internally, Processing includes a variable that keeps track of the state of the drawing context. Each time you call a transformation, this state is updated. pushMatrix() and popMatrix() simply store the state of the drawing context and then return the current state to the stored state: pushMatrix() copies the current state of the context into memory for safekeeping, and popMatrix() replaces the current state with the stored state. This allows you to issue multiple transformation calls, without cumulatively impacting the graphics context. We'll include one final example this chapter to further illustrate this process.

Star Mandala Table

This last example may push you a bit outside of your comfort zone, but you're ready for it! First, you'll learn how to create a star() function, building upon your knowledge of the polygon(); then you'll use the star() to create an algorithmic mandala; and finally you'll create a table of mandalas. There's really nothing new here, as you'll apply what you've learned thus far in the book creating a more complex example. Here's the star() code:

```
void star(int pointCount, float innerRadius, float outerRadius) {
  float theta = 0.0;
  // point count is 1/2 of total vertex count
  int vertCount = pointCount*2;
  float thetaRot = TWO_PI/vertCount;
  float tempRadius = 0.0;
  float x = 0.0, y = 0.0;

  beginShape();
  for (int i=0; i<pointCount; i++) {
    for (int j=0; j<2; j++) {
      tempRadius = innerRadius;

      // true if j is even
      if (j%2==0) {
        tempRadius = outerRadius;
      }

      x = cos(theta)*tempRadius;
      y = sin(theta)*tempRadius;
      vertex(x, y);
      theta += thetaRot;
    }
  }
  endShape(CLOSE);
} // end star
```

Scan the code. Hopefully it looks similar to the polygon() code. Aside from now drawing a star (as opposed to a polygon) the code has some stylistic improvements. Craft is a part of programming and especially relevant to creative coding, which has a strong emphasis on aesthetics.

Honing Your Coding Craft

`star()`'s function signature replaces the `sideCount` parameter, from `polygon()`, with `pointCount`. As we've discussed before, it is important to try to provide logical semantics in how you name and structure your code. Polygons are commonly thought of as having a specific number of sides, while stars are thought of as having a specific point count. In addition, stars have two distinct radii, an inner and outer, which we also included as parameters.

Because stars have two radii, they require an extra vertex for each inner radius between the outer points (defined by the outer radii). We don't tend to think about these inner vertices when we see stars; we just see their outer point count. This creates a small problem when you build the star compared to the polygon, as the underlying geometry doesn't match the `pointCount` parameter value; it's half the number of needed vertices. We remedied this, shown in the code, with the declaration of an additional local variable:

```
int vertCount = pointCount*2;
```

One subtle improvement we made to the code was to declare another new variable:

```
float thetaRot = TWO_PI/vertCount;
```

If you look back at the `polygon()` example, you'll notice in the for loop we're performing the division (`TWO_PI/sideCount`) when we increment `theta` in each iteration of the loop. This means if a polygon has 500 sides, you're dividing 500 times. However, the value of `TWO_PI/sideCount` never changes in the loop, so it's a waste of processing power, albeit not a big one. In `star()` we fixed this by declaring `thetaRot` outside of the loop and only doing the division once.

Finally, notice the last declaration line:

```
float x = 0.0, y = 0.0;
```

You may declare multiple variables of a single data type (in this case `float`) on the same line. Different coders handle this in different ways. There is no impact to performance whether you put the x and y declarations on one line or their own lines. In the end, it's simply a matter of style. A rule of thumb to consider is if variables are of the same data type and closely related—such as x and y—it might make sense to declare them on the same line. Since `tempRadius` didn't relate enough to x and y, it remained on its own line.

To test the new `Star()` function, enter the following code in the main tab. The output is shown in Figure 3-19.

```
void setup(){
  size(1000, 1000);
  translate(width/2, height/2);
  background(0);
  float radOut = height/2.3;
  float radIn = radOut*.5;
  star(8, radIn, radOut);
}
```

Figure 3-19. star() Function

A Simple Mandala

Nothing new here at all, as the function works very similarly to polygon(). Next, we'll create a single mandala pattern by incorporating a loop to generate numerous overlapping stars. Replace the code in the main tab with the following, the output for which is shown in Figure 3-20.

```
void setup() {
  size(1000, 1000);
  background(0);
  noStroke();
  translate(width/2, height/2);

  int pointCount = 8;
  int steps = 50;
  float outerRadius = width*.5;
  float innerRadiusFactor = .7;
  float innerRadius = outerRadius*innerRadiusFactor;
  float outerRadiusRatio = outerRadius/steps;
  float innerRadiusRatio = innerRadius/steps;
  float shadeRatio = 255.0/steps;
  float rotationRatio = 45.0/steps;

  for (int i=0; i<steps; i++) {
    stroke(255-shadeRatio*i, 100);
    fill(shadeRatio*i);
    pushMatrix();
    rotate(rotationRatio*i*PI/180);
    star(pointCount, outerRadius-outerRadiusRatio*i, innerRadius-innerRadiusRatio*i);
    popMatrix();
  }
}
```

Figure 3-20. Star Mandala

Incorporating variables for steps, shadeRatio, and rotationRatio, you're able to generate beautiful, emergent forms. The steps variable simply controls the number of iterations the for loop runs, while shadeRatio and rotationRatio control the tonal gradient and incremental rotation of the star. These ratios utilize steps to calculate smooth, linear transitions. Make sure you try some different values for the variables—pointCount, steps, innerRadiusFactor, randCol, and rotationRatio—to see the emergent possibilities. Examples are shown in Figures 3-21 through 3-23.

Figure 3-21. Star Mandala Variation 1

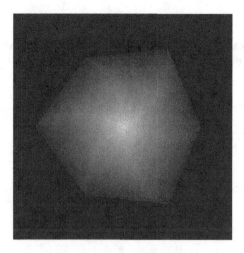

Figure 3-22. Star Mandala Variation 2

Figure 3-23. Star Mandala Variation 3

Create a Mandala Table

Finally, we'll create one more example to programmatically build a table showcasing the emergent possibilities, shown in Figure 3-24. Replace the code in the main tab with the following:

```
void setup() {
  size(1000, 1000);
  background(255);

  //presets
  int rows = 4;
  int cols = 4;
  float outerRadius = width/cols;

  // randomly generated
  int pointCount;
  int steps;
  float innerRadius;
  float outerRadiusRatio;
  float innerRadiusRatio;
  float shadeRatio;
  float rotationRatio;

  translate(outerRadius/2, outerRadius/2);
  for (int i=0; i<rows; i++) {
    for (int j=0; j<cols; j++) {
      pointCount = int(random(5, 15));
      steps = int(random(3, 20));
      innerRadius = outerRadius*random(.3, .9);
      outerRadiusRatio = outerRadius/steps;
      innerRadiusRatio = innerRadius/steps;
      float randCol = random(225, 255);
      shadeRatio = randCol/steps;
      rotationRatio = random(90, 200)/steps;
      pushMatrix();
      translate(outerRadius*j, outerRadius*i);
      for (int k=0; k<steps; k++) {
        fill(shadeRatio*k);
        stroke(randCol-shadeRatio*k, 100);
        pushMatrix();
        scale(.4);
        rotate(rotationRatio*k*PI/180);
        star(pointCount, outerRadius-outerRadiusRatio*k, innerRadius-innerRadiusRatio*k);
        popMatrix();
      }
      popMatrix();
    }
  }
}
```

Figure 3-24. Star Mandala Table Variations

The variables rows and cols control the structure of the table. Try changing their values to see the effect. Figure 3-25 shows a screenshot with both variables assigned 6. Tables are two-dimensional structures, composed of rows and columns. To traverse tables programmatically you use nested loops. Here's how it works: The outer loop begins at the top row with i equal to 0; then the inner loop processes all the columns across the first row as j is incremented while j<cols; next, control returns to the outer loop, incrementing i and stepping down to the next row, and the process continues until all the rows and columns have been processed. Nested for loops, though a little dense looking, make easy work of processing table structures.

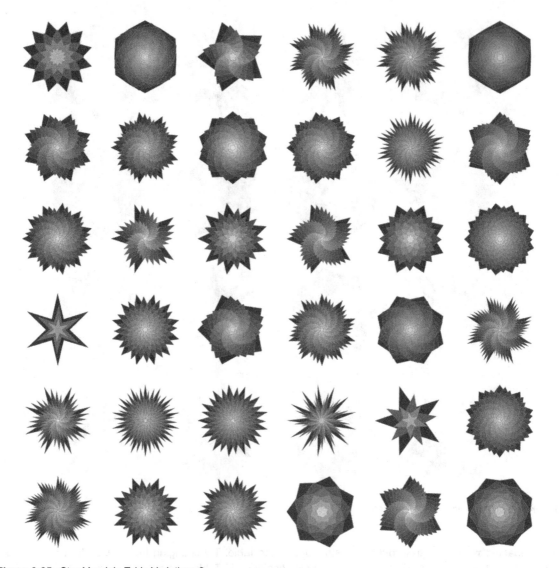

Figure 3-25. Star Mandala Table Variations 2

Because each mandala is composed of component stars, we included a third nested for loop with the counter int k = 0. This inner, inner loop runs for every iteration of the two outer nested loops—rows*cols times. We also introduced numerous random() function calls within the loops, giving us a nice range of mandala output. Finally, the example uses Processing's scale() function to resize the mandalas. scale(), like translate() and rotate(), affects the sketch window's drawing context, so we also needed to include pushMatrix() and popMatrix(), ensuring the drawing context is reset for each mandala. This example is definitely more complex than the others you've looked at thus far in the book, but hopefully it illustrates the exciting emergent possibilities of creative coding.

Summary

This chapter was a deep immersion in Processing and creative coding; consider it the boot camp chapter. You learned about functions, including how they are identified by their signatures (their name and parameter lists). We discussed scope and how the visibility of variables is dictated by where they are declared. You learned more about loops and conditional logic and how to control program flow using Boolean logic. Overriding Processing's `rect()` command, you learned different ways of drawing in Processing, including using the calls `beginShape`, `vertex()`, and `endShape()` to handle custom drawing, which you used to create polygons and stars. Finally, you learned about Processing's transformations and the drawing context, including controlling it using `pushMatrix()` and `popMatrix()`. Whew! Next chapter you'll put all this hard work to great use, as you learn about more advanced drawing techniques and animation in Processing.

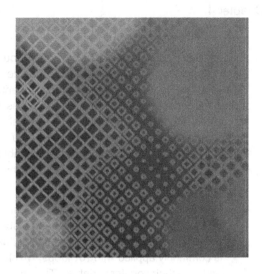

Chapter 4

Creating Across Time and Curved Space

This chapter builds directly upon what you learned in Chapters 2 and 3, expanding your knowledge of variables, scope, conditionals, loops and functions. However, this is really just a warm-up to what comes next: animation and interactivity, where you'll learn to create across time. Processing is a wonderful language and environment in which to explore programmatic animation, greatly reducing many of the under-the-hood complexities. Finally, you'll expand your artist's toolkit and learn about creating interactive curves in Processing, which offers exciting possibilities for generating complex, organic forms.

Keep It Local

You learned in the last chapter that variables declared within function blocks (between curly braces) are local to the function, meaning they can only be seen or accessed inside of the function; we say they have local scope. Exclusively relying on local variables can create some obvious challenges when you're developing a program that needs to maintain global states. For example, if you create a game that includes a player inventory, you'd want to be able to access stuff in your inventory from multiple places within your game. Clearly, if the inventory data only lived within one function, this wouldn't be possible. One solution is to declare the inventory data outside of any function blocks, or in the white space of your program. Variables declared in the white space in Processing have global scope, meaning they are visible from anywhere in your program. This might initially sound like an awesome solution. However as a programming best practice we try to avoid global variables, preferring local ones when possible, which we'll say more about in a moment. Best practices aside, your programs will nearly always include both global and local variables.

One problem with global variables is that you can unintentionally generate logical errors that can be very hard to track down. For example, you may declare a global variable named speed near the top of your ten-thousand-line game program and then accidentally declare a new speed variable locally within some function. When Processing comes across two variables with the same name the more local variable is used. Or more accurately, the local variable hides the global variable of the same name. From within the function with the speed variable, below its local declaration, you won't be able to access the global speed variable. Outside of the function, however, only the global speed variable will be visible, not the previous local one, which is eventually deleted from memory after the closing curly brace of the function. So any changes you made to the value of the local variable speed will have no effect on the value of global speed.

Remember, variables only come into existence when they are declared. The name you give them can be thought of as an alias to a unique place (address) in memory. Technically, you can use the same name when declaring multiple variables, as long as they exist within different scopes. This practice is commonly applied with for loops, which exist throughout your program and often use the letters 'i' and 'j' as their counter variables. That said, it is generally not considered a best practice to reuse variable names willy-nilly, without good reason such as with for loops. It is also illegal to declare multiple variables with the same name within the same global or local scope; trying to do so will generate a compiler error.

First, let's look at an example that illustrates what we've been discussing; then we'll explore another way to work with both local and global variables. (And yes! it won't be long before you're generating programs with ten thousand lines of code.)

```
// global variables
float x, y, radius;

void setup(){
  size(400, 400);
  background(255);
  x = width/2;
  y = height/2;
  radius = width*.5;
  pushMatrix();
  translate(x, y);
  int pts = 600;
  int rots = 10;
  float fall_off = .992;

  drawSpiral(pts, rots, radius, fall_off);
  popMatrix();

  drawFrame();
} // end Setup

void drawSpiral(float pts, int rots, float radius, float fallOff){
  float x = 0;
  float y = 0;
  float theta = 0;
```

```
  beginShape();
  for(int i=0; i<pts; i++){
    x = cos(theta)*radius;
    y = sin(theta)*radius;
    vertex(x, y);
    radius*=fallOff;
    theta += TWO_PI*rots/pts;
  }
  endShape();
} // end drawSpiral

void drawFrame(){
  noFill();
  strokeWeight(20);
  rect(x-radius-1, y-radius-1, radius*2, radius*2);
} // end drawFrame
```

Running the example creates a framed spiral, shown in Figure 4-1.

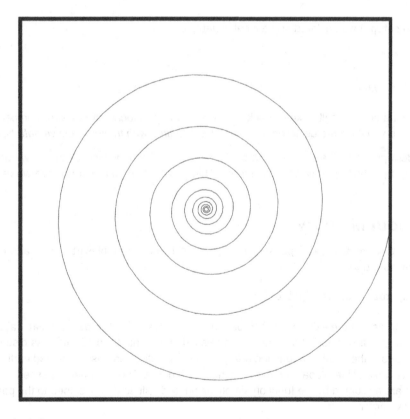

Figure 4-1. Framed spiral

You'll create more interesting visuals later in this chapter. For now, focus on the use of the global versus local variables in the example and how the rules of scope we've been discussing control the accessibility of the variables.

Examining the Variables

At the top of the program, we declare a few global variables:

```
float x, y, radius;
```

Since these are declared in the whitespace, they have global scope and are visible everywhere in the program. Processing's setup() function, though implicitly called when your program executes, still follows the same scope rules discussed: Any variables declared within setup() will only be visible within setup(). Near the top of the setup() function we assigned initial values to the global variables:

```
x = width/2;
y = height/2;
radius = width*.5;
```

Further down in setup() we declared some local variables:

```
int pts = 600;
int rots = 10;
float fall_off = .992;
```

If you're finding it a little difficult to keep track of the global versus local variables, remember that the critical factor is where the variables are declared, or *written the first time with their respective data type.*

> Some coders prefer to use a g_ (or something similar) at the beginning of global variables names (e.g., g_speed), to help quickly recognize them. This is not a bad idea, but not one we've adopted in the book.

Thinking About Memory

Next in setup() we call drawSpiral() passing as arguments the local variables pts, rots, and fall_off, as well as the global variable radius.

```
drawSpiral(pts, rots, radius, fall_off);
```

Notice the function's signature – drawSpiral(float pts, int rots, float radius, float fallOff) – includes the same named parameters for all but one of the passed arguments from setup(). As discussed in the last chapter, parameters in the head of a function are local to the function, and as mentioned earlier in this chapter, declared local variables hide global variables by the same name. The arguments passed to the function as variable names are evaluated by the function simply as passed values and assigned to the parameters based on their respective order.

Within the drawSpiral() function, the only variables visible are the local parameters and any global variables not hidden by a local parameter of the same name. In the example, since radius is the name of both a global variable and also a local parameter, the local parameter radius is what's visible inside drawSpiral(), hiding the global variable radius. What's most important here to remember is that whatever happens to radius within drawSpiral() has absolutely no effect at all on the global variable radius. Also, from a memory perspective, Processing now has two values connected to the name "radius" that are stored at two unique locations in memory. This means that in spite of sharing the same name, the two radius variables have no relationship to one another.

Once program control leaves the drawSprial() function, the compiler has permission to reclaim any memory used by local variables; this is why the local parameter radius no longer is visible anywhere in the program after the closing curly brace of the function. If the drawSprial() function is called again, a completely new local variable radius is created in memory (again at a unique memory address) and then eventually deleted when the function ends. The global variable radius however remains in memory throughout the lifespan of the program, as it never goes out of scope since it was declared in the whitespace.

The drawSpiral() function is similar to the polygon() function from last chapter. It utilizes trig relationships to convert the polar values around the Unit Circle to the Cartesian coordinates of the sketch window. Notice that we reduce the size of the radius parameter each iteration by the expression radius*=falloff. However, as already discussed, this will have no effect on the value of the global variable radius.

After the drawSpiral() function finishes, we call drawFrame(). This function simply draws a frame around the sketch window, using the global variable radius, still equal to the original value it was assigned back in setup(), radius = width*.5.

Returning Value

Not only can functions perform work as independent modules; they can also return values. You've already seen functions do this before, whether you realized it or not. For example, the trig calls using cos() and sin() returned values that we used to calculate vertex positions. In addition, when we used Processing's random() call, it also returned a value.

Functions that don't return values – such as drawSpiral() – are declared with the keyword void in front of the function name. void simply tells Processing that the function does not return a value. Instead of void, you can precede a function name with any legal data type, such as float, int or boolean, just to name a few. However if you do this, the function **must** return a value of that type. Next, is an example function that calculates and returns a factorial (the product of all positive integers less than the input value):

```
int getFactorial(int val) {
  int fact = 1;
  while (val > 0) {
    fact*=val;
    val--;
  }
  return fact;
}
```

To call the getFactorial() function you need to account for the returned value, which you could do by assigning the function call to a variable or using the function call as an argument within another function call; both of these are shown next:

```
// assign function call to a variable
float f = getFactorial(6);
// use function call as an argument within another function call
calcTotal( getFactorial(8) );
```

or

```
println ( getFactorial(8) );
```

The reason you can safely pass a return function call in place of an argument is because Processing evaluates what's inside parentheses first, in effect converting the function call to a single argument.

Notice the last line in the getFactorial(int val) function includes a return statement. This is required for any function that returns a value (any function not preceded by void). You may include multiple return statements in the function, but one must be the last line in the function. Next we show a more interesting example that draws a visual table based on prime numbers and utilizes multiple return statements.

Prime Time

Prime numbers are simply numbers greater than 1 only divisible by 1, as compared to composite numbers that are divisible by additional factors. Numbers 2, 3, and 5 are primes, as each can only be divided by 1, whereas 4, 6, and 8 are composite numbers, as each is divisible by additional factors besides 1 (2, 3, 4). In spite of this very simple rule, prime numbers have intrigued mathematicians since at least the time of the ancient Greeks. The primes form an infinite set of numbers that have some subtle patterns lurking within the set. The most famous of these patterns is probably the Ulam or Prime Spiral, which you can read more about at http://mathworld.wolfram.com/PrimeSpiral.html.

The next example plots a table structure based on the primes, shown in Figure 4-2:

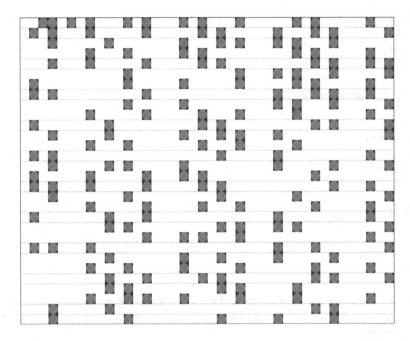

Figure 4-2. Table of primes

```
// Primary Creation
void setup() {
  size(800, 600);
  background(0);
  float cols = 40;
  float rows = 30;
  float cellW = width/cols;
  float cellH = height/rows;
  noStroke();

  for (int i=0, k=0; i<rows; i++) {
    for (int j=0; j<cols; j++) {
      pushMatrix();
      translate(cellW/2+cellW*j, cellH/2+cellH*i);
      if (isPrime(k)) {
        primeCell(cellW, cellH);
      }
      else {
        compositeCell(cellW, cellH);
      }
      popMatrix();
      k++;
    }
  }
} // end setup
```

```
void primeCell(float w, float h) {
  fill(255, 0, 0);
  ellipse(0, 0, w, h);
} // end primeCell

void compositeCell(float w, float h) {
  fill(255);
  rect(-w/2, -h/2, w, h);
} // end compositeCell

// return true or false
boolean isPrime(int val) {
  if (val<2) {
    return false;
  }
  i <= val
  return true;
} // end isPrime
```

You looked at table structures in the last chapter and learned that nesting `for` loops is an efficient way to generate a two-dimensional structure such as a table. Notice within the nested loops in the example code we used the conditional statement

```
if (isPrime(k))
```

to determine whether to draw a prime or composite cell. `isPrime(k)` calls the function signature

```
boolean isPrime(int val)
```

which returns `true` or `false` based on the primality of the argument passed to the `val` parameter. To determine primality we used a very simple brute force approach, iteratively checking if the passed value is divisible by any number other than 1. This is easily accomplished using the modulus operator within the conditional test

```
if (val % i == 0)
```

If `true`, then `val` is not prime, since there is a remainder of 0 by division with a value other than 1.

We began the `for` loop at 2, to avoid a return value of `true` for division by 1.

Finally, notice `isPrime()` included three `return` statements, including the required one in the last line of the function. When the function is evaluated, any of the returns can terminate the function based on the logic flow through the function, which we exploited in this example.

We include one final screenshot with columns and rows set at 400 and 300 respectively. Notice the vertical and diagonal channels running through the image. The vertical channels are simply based on no even numbers besides 2 being prime, so these repeating gaps line up per row. However, the diagonal channels are caused by more interesting numerical properties lurking within the primes.

Figure 4-3. Table of primes with increased density

> *Try This: Try plotting the primes as a Ulam Spiral, and read up on the Sieve of Eratosthenes (http://en.wikipedia.org/wiki/Sieve_of_Eratosthenes) to learn about other more elegant and efficient approaches to finding large quantities of primes.*

Next, you'll learn how to incorporate motion and interactivity into your sketches.

Making Things Move

Simply stated, making things move in Processing is easy! Processing includes a draw() function that when included in your program turns on animation as well as mouse and keyboard interactivity. For example, next is a very simple program that slowly fills the sketch window with random rectangles, as shown in Figure 4-4.

Figure 4-4. Processing's draw() function in action

```
void setup(){
  size(800, 800);
  background(0);
  noFill();
} // end setup

void draw(){
  stroke(255, random(255));
  rect(random(width), random(height), random(5, 20), random(5, 20));
} // end draw
```

Behind the scenes, Java creates animation in Processing using what's called a thread or, more technically, a *thread of execution*. Threads allow programs to manage multiple real time events (seemingly) simultaneously, such as listening for network activity, detecting mouse movements, responding to data input, or running animation, among other processes. In reality, especially on single processor machines, multiple threads don't actually run simultaneously, but they are scheduled to appear that way. Threads are essentially parsed into finer processing strands and interwoven, the way a merge on a highway enables all roads to flow, albeit each more slowly.

In spite of the complexity of threading under the surface, Processing's draw() function manages the entire process for you. By default, draw() executes around 60 f.p.s. (frames per second). Our eyes begin to see continuous motion at around 12 f.p.s., so Processing's default frame rate enables very smooth animation. However, as complexity of an animation increases, the frame rate may also drop.

Moving and Rotating

In the previous example, we let the background get filled up with rectangles, creating an animated painting of sorts. In this next example, we'll repaint the background each draw() cycle, creating a moving and rotating animation:

```
// Rotating Square

// declare global variables
// for moving square
float x, y, w;
float spdX, spdY, theta, rotSpd;

void setup() {
  size(600, 600);
  // initialize global variables
  x = width/2;
  y = height/2;
  w = 150;
  spdX = 2.1;
  spdY = 1.5;
  rotSpd = PI/180;
  fill(0, 175, 175);
  noStroke();
} // end setup

void draw() {
  background(255, 127, 0);
  pushMatrix();
  translate(x, y);
  rotate(theta);
  rect(-w/2, -w/2, w, w);
  popMatrix();
  x += spdX;
  y += spdY;
  theta += rotSpd;
} // end draw
```

The background() command at the top of draw() is what switches the program from a painting system to an animation system. This is essentially what happens behind the scenes for all screen-based computing. For example, your operating system is continuously repainting the screen or your mouse would leave a trail each time you moved it. The rotating square program is relatively simple: spdX and spdY continuously increment x and y, which are used as arguments for the translate() call. We set the square's x and y values both at -w/2, so the square would be drawn centered at (0,0). This enabled the square to rotate around its center point and not around its top left vertex.

Adding Simple Collision

We imagine when you saw the square moving out of the sketch window you wondered how to constrain it within the window. The Processing core language doesn't include pre-made functions to handle collisions, like you might find in a game engine. So we'll code a very simple collide() function, enabling the square to bounce off the walls. Our first version of the function won't be very accurate, but we'll eventually improve it. Here's the initial collide() function:

```
void collide() {
  if (x > width-w/2) {
    spdX *= -1;
    rotSpd *= -1;
  }
  else if (x < w/2) {
    spdX *= -1;
    rotSpd *= -1;
  }
  if (y > height-w/2) {
    spdY *= -1;
    rotSpd *= -1;
  }
  else if (y < w/2) {
    spdY *= -1;
    rotSpd *= -1;
  }
} // end collide
```

The collide() function should either be put below the closing curly brace of draw() or in its own tab; it should be called from within draw().

Progress, Not Perfection

Running the program now, you should see the square bouncing off the walls while rotating around its center point. The collision code detects if the square exceeds any of the edges of the sketch window. We needed to check using '>' (greater than) instead of '==' (equal to) to ensure we didn't miss a collision. The problem with using == to detect collision is that we'll miss most if not all of them. To a computer the values 600 and 600.0001 are different numbers. If you increment the square across the screen at 1.4 pixels per frame, it will never actually be precisely at 600; at frame 428 it will be at 599.2, and at frame 429 it will be at 600.6. By checking using > we ensure the detection occurs. Though at the risk of further complicating this, we also mentioned earlier that `draw()` runs at *approximately* 60 f.p.s., so we actually won't know precisely how far past the boundary the square will go before the detection kicks in. The bottom line is that perfectly accurate collision detection is a complicated problem and beyond the scope of this book. However, our solution using > sufficiently solves the current collision program.

Notice during the collisions that the square's corners go considerably past the edge of the sketch window before the collision detection occurs, as shown in Figure 4-5. This is not because we're using >, but because we based our collision on the `width/2` of the square and not its radius, the distance from its center point to corner. If we had just used the square's radius instead of its `width/2`, collision would then sometimes appear to occur too early, before the flat sides of the square made contact with the window edge. To fix this, we need a dynamic solution that accounts for the square's current rotation in determining collision.

Figure 4-5. Inaccurate collision detection

Calculating a Dynamic Radius

In this final version, we fixed the collision to properly address the square's rotation. New and altered code from the earlier two examples is in **bold**.

```
// Rotating Square with Accurate Wall Collisions
// declare global variables
// for moving square
float x, y, w;
float spdX, spdY, theta, rotSpd;

// enables accurate wall collisions
float cornerRadiusOffset, dynamicRadius, collisionTheta;

void setup() {
  size(600, 600);
  // initialize global variables
  x = width/2;
  y = height/2;
  w = 150;
  spdX = 2.1;
  spdY = 1.5;
  rotSpd = PI/180;
  fill(0, 175, 175);
  noStroke();
} // end setup

void draw() {
  background(255, 127, 0);

  pushMatrix();
  translate(x, y);
  rotate(theta);
  rect(-w/2, -w/2, w, w);
  popMatrix();

  x += spdX;
  y += spdY;
  theta += rotSpd;

  // check for wall collisions
  collide();
} // end draw
```

```
void collide() {
  // calculate dynamicRadius for more
  // accurate wall collisions
  cornerRadiusOffset = w/2/cos(PI/4) - w/2; // calculate difference between corner and side
  dynamicRadius = abs(sin(collisionTheta)*cornerRadiusOffset);

  if (x > width-w/2-dynamicRadius) {
    spdX *= -1;
    rotSpd *= -1;
  }
  else if (x < w/2+dynamicRadius) {
    spdX *= -1;
    rotSpd *= -1;
  }
  if (y > height-w/2-dynamicRadius) {
    spdY *= -1;
    rotSpd *= -1;
  }
  else if (y < w/2+dynamicRadius) {
    spdY *= -1;
    rotSpd *= -1;
  }

  // used to calculate dynamicRadius
  collisionTheta += rotSpd*2;
} // end collide
```

The two lines that handle most of the collision correction are:

```
cornerRadiusOffset = w/2/cos(PI/4) - w/2; // calculate difference between corner and side
dynamicRadius = abs(sin(collisionTheta)*cornerRadiusOffset);
```

The cornerRadiusOffset is simply the distance between the square's width/2 and radius. We solved for this using the basic trigonometric relationship

$$\cos\left(\theta\right)=\frac{adjacent}{hypotenuse}$$

illustrated in Figure 4-6. You'll also use this same approach when you learn how to calculate control point locations for some curves later in the chapter.

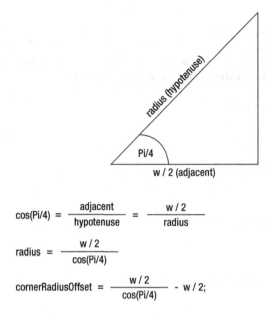

$$\cos(\text{Pi}/4) = \frac{\text{adjacent}}{\text{hypotenuse}} = \frac{w/2}{\text{radius}}$$

$$\text{radius} = \frac{w/2}{\cos(\text{Pi}/4)}$$

$$\text{cornerRadiusOffset} = \frac{w/2}{\cos(\text{Pi}/4)} - w/2;$$

Figure 4-6. Trig used to find cornerRadiusoffset

We use the `cornerRadiusOffset` in the expression: `abs(sin(collisionTheta)*cornerRadiusOffset`

This expression is essentially a sine function that only returns a positive value. Processing's `abs()` function always returns the positive value of whatever argument is passed to it. Both the `sin()` and `cos()` functions return values between -1 and 1, depending upon what angle (theta) value is passed to them. By multiplying the entire `sin()` function by `cornerRadiusOffset`, *while always ensuring it's positive, using abs()*, we're able to generate values from 0 to `cornerRadiusOffset` periodically, as the square rotates. For example, the following table shows some sampled values of the `dynamicRadius` between 0 and Pi (180 degrees) for `collisionTheta`. For reference, the `cornerRadiusOffset` is approximately 31, and all float values in the table have been truncated to integers.

Table 4-1. collisionTheta, dynamicRadius

θ (collisionTheta)	θ (dynamicRadius)
15	8
20	10
30	15
45	22
55	25
70	29
80	30
90	31
100	30
110	29
120	26
130	23
140	19
150	15
160	10
170	5
180	0

Obviously from 180 to 360 degrees (Pi to Pi*2) the values would follow the same pattern (0...31...0). One of the reasons the trig functions are so useful is because of this predictable periodic behavior.

Finally, we incremented collisionTheta with the line:

```
collisionTheta += rotSpd*2;
```

We needed to do this to ensure that the value of collisionTheta in the sin() function was synchronized to the rotation of the square. (Whew!)

If this example feels over your head, rest assured it actually is a bit complex – certainly the most complex thing you've seen in the book thus far. However, if you play with the example a little it should become more obvious what's going on. One of the tenets of creative coding is to *embrace happy coding accidents*! A great way, in general, to better understand a program is to plug in alternate values and see what happens. Sometimes breaking something really is the best way to understand how it works.

> *Try This: Try animating a regular polygon and seeing if you can adjust collisionTheta to create accurate boundary collisions.*

Next, we'll explore some more advanced drawing using Processing's curve functions and also see examples of Processing's interactive capabilities.

Introducing Curves

Simply stated, working with curves is challenging. However, Processing includes a number of functions that make the process much more manageable. The main reason curves are more difficult to work with than lines is because of the underlying math.

To draw a line in Processing we simply code:

```
size(400, 400);
background(255);
float x = 100,y = 100;
beginShape();
vertex(x, y);
vertex(x+200, y+200);
endShape();
```

Hopefully this code is very understandable to you by now. Lines are relatively easy to work with, as the underlying math describing them can almost be intuited, which is generally not the case with curves. There are a number of ways to draw a line. In the example code we simply created two terminal points, (x, y) and (x+200, y+200), and had Processing connect them based on the slope between them. Slope of a line is the ratio of the change of the y-components to the x-components of the terminal points, or more commonly, the *rise over the run*. To calculate the slope of the line in the example, we would use the expression:

$$M = \frac{(Y+200) - y}{(X+200) - x}$$

The slope tells us the direction of the line. Imagine if you were standing on the edge of a desert island with a compass and (of course) a treasure map. The map shows that the treasure is 15 degrees southwest of your position. If you rotate 15 degrees and walk across the island maintaining your bearing you're sure to become rich, *unless of course you fall into the pit of vipers*. What you don't know based on our desert island scenario is how far you need to walk to reach the treasure. So the slope of a line is actually independent of the length of the line. Later in the book you'll work with Processing's PVector class, which is a data type built on this concept – a line divided into its component direction and length, or more commonly magnitude.

Curves are much less predictable than lines. If the treasure map said take a curvy path to the treasure, it wouldn't be very helpful, as there would be infinite possibilities of how the path could curve. Perhaps the map was more specific and included a mathematical expression to describe the curve, something like:

$$f(x) = 3x^2 + 8x - 16$$

This would be more useful if we could determine x- and y-axes on the island. Using the equation, each step we took along the x-axis would give us a corresponding value for f(x) or y. For example, if we assume our second step along the x is 2, then f(x) would be 16 steps on the y-axis. Of course we'd have no idea where along the path the treasure was, but we'd presumably find it before we reached the end of the curve relative to the island (and/or the pit of vipers.)

Figure 4-7 shows the slope of a line at two intervals. Notice the slope for this line will always evaluate to 1, regardless of what interval we look at. By contrast, Figure 4-8 shows the plot of a simple curve. Clearly slope is no longer constant at the two intervals, and to solve for the slope of a curve we now need to employ calculus, which is beyond the scope of this book. We'll reiterate: *curves are challenging!* Fortunately, Processing is here to help.

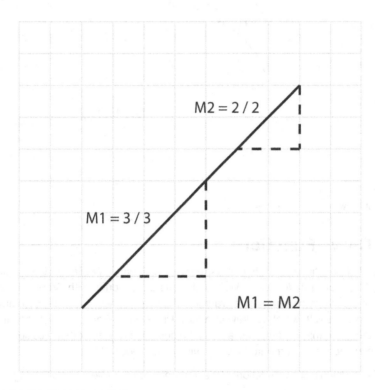

Figure 4-7. Line plot showing slope is constant

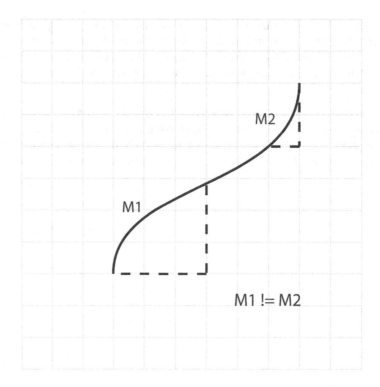

Figure 4-8. Curve plot showing slope changes

Processing's Curve Functions

Processing includes five functions to draw curves: bezier(), curve(), bezierVertex(), curveVertex(), and, new in Processing 2.0, quadraticVertex(). We'll just focus on the ones with "Vertex" in their names, which duplicate behavior of the same named plainer varieties (bezier(), curve()). Initially, you may also wonder why there are so many functions with which to draw curves in Processing. Each of the three functions we'll look at has certain advantages. The main differences among the curves relates to both the underlying math describing them as well as to how they're implemented algorithmically; we'll look at both.

Before we look at Processing's curve functions, let's generate some curves, shown in Figure 4-9, using simple polynomial expressions:

> Polynomials are mathematical expressions made up of a finite number terms using multiplication, addition, and subtraction. They may include constants, such as 2, 34, 187; variables, such as x, y, z; and exponents, such as x^2, y^3, $2x^4$. We often refer to polynomials by degree based on the highest exponent used. For example, the expressions $3x^2 + 24$ and $4x^3 + 2x^2 - 8$ are 2nd degree and 3rd degree polynomials, respectively.

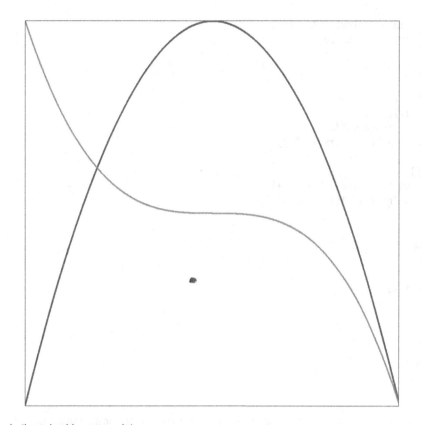

Figure 4-9. Quadratic and cubic curves plot

```
// quadratic and cubic curve examples
void setup() {
  size(600, 600);
  background(255);
  noFill();
  strokeWeight(4);
  translate(width/2, 0);

  // draw quadratic curve
  float fx2Max = fx2(width/2);
  float fx2Scale = height/fx2Max;

  stroke(0, 0, 255);
  beginShape();
```

```
  for (int i=-width/2; i<width/2; i++) {
    vertex(i, fx2(i)*fx2Scale);
  }
  endShape();

  // draw cubic curve
  stroke(255, 127, 0);
  float fx3Max = fx3(width/2);
  float fx3Scale = height/(fx3Max*2);

  beginShape();
  for (int i=-width/2; i<width/2; i++) {
    vertex(i, height/2+fx3(i)*fx3Scale);
  }
  endShape();
} // end setup

// quadratic
float fx2(float x) {
  return x*x;
} // end fx2

// cubic
float fx3(float x) {
  return x*x*x;
} // end fx3
```

Notice the functions fx2() and fx3() in the example. fx2() plots a quadratic curve, based on a 2nd degree polynomial and fx3() plots a cubic curve, based on a 3rd degree polynomial. The polynomial functions themselves are very simple, but it took a bit more work to scale the curves so that they neatly fit within the sketch window. Practically all curves in computer graphics are built out of these types of underlying equations. One of the main differences between quadratic and cubic curves is how they change direction over time, or their points of inflection.

In mathematical terms, an inflection point is where a curve changes concavity. The quadratic curve forms a parabola and never actually changes concavity. Imagine if you were driving a car along the parabola – like driving up and over a mountain – you'd begin steering around the curve and never have to rotate the steering wheel in the other direction. Quadratic curves have no points of inflection. The cubic curve shown, like an s on its side, has one inflection point in the middle of the curve. Using the driving metaphor again, do you see how you'd have to rotate the steering wheel in the middle of the curve to stay on the path? Cubic curves can have up two points of inflection.

Controlling Curves

The challenge of working with curves is not simply plotting them, but plotting them through specific points and controlling their overall curvature. Ultimately in creative coding we're interested in drawing and even sculpting with curves, not simply deconstructing them mathematically. This is where Processing's curve commands come in.

curveVertex() and bezierVertex() both utilize underlying cubic equations, while quadraticVertex() utilizes (obviously) a quadratic equation. The main difference between Processing's cubic and quadratic implementations is that the former enables you to create a more complex single curve (remember the inflection points), while the latter is a bit easier to use.

quadraticVertex()

quadraticVertex() takes four arguments specifying the x and y components of a control point – used to determine how the curve bends – and the plotted curve point, also commonly called an anchor point. This function also requires that an initial vertex() call be made prior to quadraticVertex(). Similar to the vertex() command, quadraticVertex() always needs to be called between Processing's beginShape() and endShape() commands. Next is an interactive example, shown in Figure 4-10 that draws a single quadratic curve, which you can interact with using the mouse. Try dragging both the control and anchor points. We also rendered a handle between the control and vertex points to better illustrate how the control points impact the curvature.

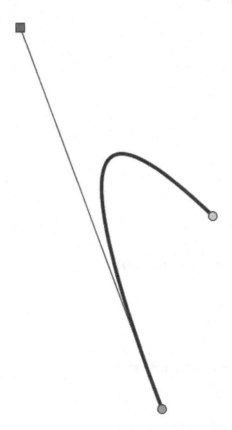

Figure 4-10. Interactive quadraticVertex() example

The quadraticVertex() example includes Processing's mouseDragged() function, which detects mouse drag events – the mouse is pressed in the sketch window while moving it. If you move the mouse without pressing it, Processing's mouseMoved() function detects these events. All of Processing's event detection functions require that the draw() function is included in the sketch.

```
float ax, ay, cx, cy;
boolean isOnControl, isOnAnchor;
float radius = 5;

void setup() {
  size(600, 600);
  cx = random(100, width-100);
  cy = random(100, height-100);
  ax = random(100, width-100);
  ay = random(100, height-100);
} // end setup

void draw() {
  background(255);
  noFill();
  strokeWeight(4);
  stroke(0);

  // draw curve
  beginShape();
  vertex(width/2, height/2);
  quadraticVertex(cx, cy, ax, ay);
  endShape();

  // draw center point
  fill(200);
  strokeWeight(1);
  ellipse(width/2, height/2, radius*2, radius*2);

  // draw connecting handle
  line(cx, cy, ax, ay);

  // draw control point
  fill(0, 0, 255);
  rect(cx-radius, cy-radius, radius*2, radius*2);

  // draw anchor point
  fill(255, 127, 0);
  ellipse(ax, ay, radius*2, radius*2);

  // detect if mouse is on control/anchor point
  if (dist(mouseX, mouseY, ax, ay) < radius) {
    isOnAnchor = true;
  }
```

```
    else if (dist(mouseX, mouseY, cx, cy) < radius) {
      isOnControl = true;
    }
    else {
      isOnAnchor = isOnControl = false;
    }
  } // end draw

  void mouseDragged() {
    // move points
    if (isOnControl) {
      cx = mouseX;
      cy = mouseY;
    }
    else if (isOnAnchor) {
      ax = mouseX;
      ay = mouseY;
    }
  } // end mouseDragged
```

Hopefully you took some time to interact with this sketch. The best way to understand the impact of the control point on the quadratic curve is to play with it, to see its direct impact on the curve. The further the control point is dragged, the more exaggerated the curve becomes. However, no matter how far you move the control point, you still only get a parabolic curve and no inflection point along the curve. Again, this is due to the underlying math, a 2nd degree (quadratic) equation.

Closed Quadratic Curve

In addition to creating a single open curve, you can combine multiple quadraticVertex() commands together to create a more complex form. Again these calls must be preceded by a single vertex() call and all set between beginShape() and endShape(). The next example creates a closed form composed of multiple quadraticVertex() commands.

```
void setup() {
  size(800, 800);
  background(255);
  translate(width/2, height/2);
  quadraticForm(int(random(3, 25)), random(50, 375), random(50, 375));
} // end setup

void quadraticForm(int limbs, float controlRadius, float limbRadius) {
  float theta = 0;
  beginShape();
  float cx = 0;
  float cy = 0;
  float ax = 0;
  float ay = 0;
  float rot = TWO_PI/(limbs*2);
```

```
  for (int i=0; i<limbs; i++) {
    cx = cos(theta)*controlRadius;
    cy = sin(theta)*controlRadius;
    theta += rot;
    ax = cos(theta)*limbRadius;
    ay = sin(theta)*limbRadius;
    if (i==0) {
      // initial vertex required for quadraticVertex()
      vertex(ax, ay);
    }
    else {
      quadraticVertex(cx, cy, ax, ay);
      // draws vertices and controls
      fill(0, 0, 255);
      rect(cx-3, cy-3, 6, 6);
      ellipse(ax, ay, 6, 6);
      line(ax, ay, cx, cy);
    }
    theta += rot;

    // close form
    if (i == limbs-1) {
      cx = cos(0)*controlRadius;
      cy = sin(0)*controlRadius;
      ax = cos(rot)*limbRadius;
      ay = sin(rot)*limbRadius;
      quadraticVertex(cx, cy, ax, ay);

      // draws vertex and control
      rect(cx-3, cy-3, 6, 6);
      ellipse(ax, ay, 6, 6);
      line(ax, ay, cx, cy);
    }
  }
  fill(0);
  endShape();
} // end quadraticForm
```

The sketch utilizes random values for the three quadraticForm(int limbs, float controlRadius, float limbRadius) arguments. Try running the sketch a few times to see the range of possible forms. Figure 4-11 shows a page of examples.

Figure 4-11. Closed quadraticVertex() forms

bezierVertex()

As previously discussed, because of the underlying math, the range of curves you can generate with quadraticVertex() is limited. Processing's bezierVertex() expands your curve possibilities, thanks to the under-the-hood 3rd degree cubic equations. Next is an interactive bezier curve example, with two control points and one anchor point that you can manipulate. Notice in the code that we begin the bezierVertex() curve with an initial vertex() call and place the calls between beginShape() and endshape() which, like quadraticVertex(), is required.

```
float ax, ay, cx1, cy1, cx2, cy2;
boolean isOnControl1, isOnControl2, isOnAnchor;
float radius = 5;

void setup() {
  size(600, 600);
  cx1 = random(100, width-100);
  cy1 = random(100, height-100);
  cx2 = random(100, width-100);
  cy2 = random(100, height-100);
```

```
  ax =random(100, width-100);
  ay =  random(100, height-100);
} // end setup

void draw() {
  background(255);
  noFill();
  strokeWeight(4);
  stroke(0);

  // draw curve
  beginShape();
  vertex(width/2, height/2); // this may be another bezierVertex()
  bezierVertex(cx1, cy1, cx2, cy2, ax, ay);
  endShape();

  // draw center point
  fill(200);
  strokeWeight(1);
  ellipse(width/2, height/2, radius*2, radius*2);

  // draw connecting handles
  line(cx1, cy1, ax, ay);
  line(cx2, cy2, ax, ay);

  // draw control points
  fill(0, 0, 255);
  rect(cx1-radius, cy1-radius, radius*2, radius*2);
  rect(cx2-radius, cy2-radius, radius*2, radius*2);

  // draw anchor point
  fill(255, 127, 0);
  ellipse(ax, ay, radius*2, radius*2);

  // detect if mouse is on control/anchor point
  if (dist(mouseX, mouseY, ax, ay) < radius) {
    isOnAnchor = true;
  }
  else if (dist(mouseX, mouseY, cx1, cy1) < radius) {
    isOnControl1 = true;
  }
  else if (dist(mouseX, mouseY, cx2, cy2) < radius) {
    isOnControl2 = true;
  }
  else {
    isOnAnchor = isOnControl1 = isOnControl2 = false;
  }
} // end draw
```

```
void mouseDragged() {
  // move points
  if (isOnControl1) {
    cx1 = mouseX;
    cy1 = mouseY;
  }
  else if (isOnControl2) {
    cx2 = mouseX;
    cy2 = mouseY;
  }
  else if (isOnAnchor) {
    ax = mouseX;
    ay = mouseY;
  }
} // end mouseDragged
```

Other than the additional code for a second control point, this code is similar to the previous interactive quadraticVertex() example. The second control handle now allows us to generate a more complex curve, including one with an inflection point, as shown in Figure 4-12. Of course, it's not really the extra control point doing the work, but the underlying mathematics.

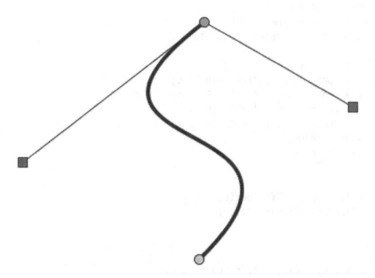

Figure 4-12. bezierVertex() example illustrating a point of inflection

Next we'll generate a closed ellipse using bezierVertex(), shown in Figure 4-13. Notice that due to the extra complexity of the cubic curve, we're able to generate a smooth ellipse with only four points, but needed eight for the quadratic ellipse.

```
// Bezier Ellipse example
void setup() {
  size(800, 800);
  background(255);
  translate(width/2, height/2);

  // draw bezier ellipse
  bezierEllipse(4, 300);
} // end setup

void bezierEllipse(int pts, float radius) {
  //float theta = 0;
  beginShape();
  float cx1 = 0;
  float cy1 = 0;
  float cx2 = 0;
  float cy2 = 0;
  float ax = 0;
  float ay = 0;
  float rot = TWO_PI/pts;
  float theta = 0;
  float controlTheta1 = rot/3.0;
  float controlTheta2 = controlTheta1*2.0;
  float controlRadius = radius/cos(controlTheta1);

  for (int i=0; i<pts; i++) {
    cx1 = cos(theta + controlTheta1)*controlRadius;
    cy1 = sin(theta + controlTheta1)*controlRadius;
    cx2 = cos(theta + controlTheta2)*controlRadius;
    cy2 = sin(theta + controlTheta2)*controlRadius;
    ax = cos(theta+rot)*radius;
    ay = sin(theta+rot)*radius;

    if (i==0) {
      // initial vertex required for bezierVertex()
      vertex(cos(0)*radius, sin(0)*radius);
    }
    // close ellipse
    if (i==pts-1) {
      bezierVertex(cx1, cy1, cx2, cy2, cos(0)*radius,
      sin(0)*radius);
    }
    // ellipse body
    else {
      bezierVertex(cx1, cy1, cx2, cy2, ax, ay);
    }

    // Use cx2, cy2 of current vertex and cx1, cy1 of next vertex
```

```
        // to draw handles between anchor and controls
        float cx1Next = cos(theta + controlTheta1+rot)*controlRadius;
        float cy1Next = sin(theta + controlTheta1+rot)*controlRadius;
        line(ax, ay, cx1Next, cy1Next);
        line(ax, ay, cx2, cy2);

        // draw control and anchor points
        fill(0, 0, 255);
        rect(cx1-3, cy1-3, 6, 6);
        fill(0, 255, 255);
        rect(cx2-3, cy2-3, 6, 6);
        fill(255, 127, 0);
        ellipse(ax, ay, 6, 6);

        theta += rot;
    }
    fill(0, 127);
    noStroke();
    endShape();
} // end bezierEllipse
```

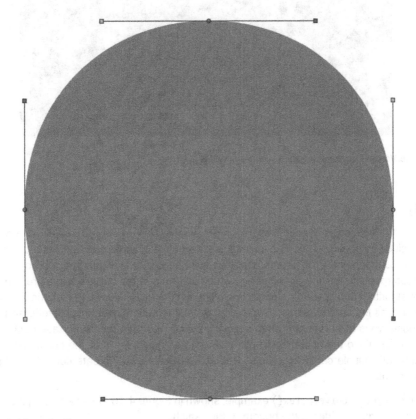

Figure 4-13. bezierVertex() ellipse

By randomizing the placement of the control and anchor points, we can generate a range of interesting, radially symmetric shapes, shown in Figure 4-14.

Figure 4-14. bezierVertex() randomized and radially symmetrical forms

curveVertex()

curveVertex() is the final curve function we'll look at. Like bezierVertex(), it is built on a cubic expression and thus may include inflection points. The main difference between bezierVertex() and curveVertex() is the placement of the control points. You'll remember that both the bezier and quadratic approaches we looked at earlier utilized control points off the actual curve, which determined the curve's curvature. curveVertex() utilizes a different algorithm that places the control points along the actual curve. In fact, the anchor points of the curve also function as the control points. Processing's implementation is technically referred to as a Catmull-Rom spline. These types of curves are often simpler to work with than the earlier approaches we looked at. Having control points along the actual curve provides greater local control of the curve and facilitates piecemeal construction of multiple curve segments. This allows you to easily create complex and smooth curves through specific points.

When you run the following curveVertex() example, shown in Figure 4-15, be sure to drag the points along the curve, as well as the square slider at the bottom of the sketch.

```
// interactive curveVertex() example
float ax0, ay0, ax1, ay1, ax2, ay2, ax3, ay3, ax4, ay4;
boolean isOnAnchor0, isOnAnchor1, isOnAnchor2, isOnAnchor3, isOnAnchor4;
float radius = 5;

// gui to control curvature
float curvature = 0;
float sliderBarX, sliderBarY, sliderBarW;
float sliderHandleX, sliderHandleY, sliderHandleW = 12;
float sliderMin = -3, sliderMax = 3;
boolean isOnSliderHandle;

void setup() {
  size(600, 600);
  background(255);

  ax0 = random(100, width-100);
  ax1 = random(100, width-100);
  ax2 = random(100, width-100);
  ax3 = random(100, width-100);
  ax4 = random(100, width-100);

  ay0 = random(100, height-100);
  ay1 = random(100, height-100);
  ay2 = random(100, height-100);
  ay3 = random(100, height-100);
  ay4 = random(100, height-100);

  // control bar for interactive curvature
  sliderBarW = width/3;
  sliderBarX = width-sliderBarW-40;
  sliderBarY = height-40;
  sliderHandleX = sliderBarX + sliderBarW/2;
  sliderHandleY = sliderBarY;
} // end setup

void draw() {
  background(255);
  noFill();
  strokeWeight(4);
  stroke(0);

  curveTightness(curvature);
  // draw curve
  beginShape();
  curveVertex(ax0, ay0); // double initial point
  curveVertex(ax0, ay0);
  curveVertex(ax1, ay1);
  curveVertex(ax2, ay2);
```

```
    curveVertex(ax3, ay3);
    curveVertex(ax4, ay4);
    curveVertex(ax4, ay4); // double final point
    endShape();

    // draw control/anchor points
    strokeWeight(1);
    fill(255, 127, 0);
    ellipse(ax0, ay0, radius*2, radius*2);
    ellipse(ax1, ay1, radius*2, radius*2);
    ellipse(ax2, ay2, radius*2, radius*2);
    ellipse(ax3, ay3, radius*2, radius*2);
    ellipse(ax4, ay4, radius*2, radius*2);

    // detect if mouse is on control/anchor point
    if (dist(mouseX, mouseY, ax0, ay0) < radius) {
      isOnAnchor0 = true;
    }
    else if (dist(mouseX, mouseY, ax1, ay1) < radius) {
      isOnAnchor1 = true;
    }
    else if (dist(mouseX, mouseY, ax2, ay2) < radius) {
      isOnAnchor2 = true;
    }
    else if (dist(mouseX, mouseY, ax3, ay3) < radius) {
      isOnAnchor3 = true;
    }
    else if (dist(mouseX, mouseY, ax4, ay4) < radius) {
      isOnAnchor4 = true;
    }

    // ensure boolean flags set back to false when mouse released
    if (!mousePressed) {
      isOnAnchor0 = isOnAnchor1 = isOnAnchor2 = isOnAnchor3 = isOnAnchor4 = isOnSliderHandle =
    false;
    }

    // interactively control curvature
    setCurvatureControlGUI();
} // end draw

void setCurvatureControlGUI() {

    line(sliderBarX, sliderBarY, sliderBarX+sliderBarW, sliderBarY);
    fill(0, 0, 255);
    rect(sliderHandleX-sliderHandleW/2, sliderHandleY-sliderHandleW/2, sliderHandleW,
    sliderHandleW);

    if (isOnSliderHandle &&  mouseX>sliderBarX && mouseX < sliderBarX + sliderBarW) {
```

```
    sliderHandleX = mouseX;
  }
  // detect if mouse is on control/anchor point
  if (dist(mouseX, mouseY, sliderHandleX, sliderHandleY) < sliderHandleW/2) {
    isOnSliderHandle = true;
  }

  // ensures slider handle values between sliderMin to sliderMax
  curvature = map(sliderHandleX, sliderBarX, sliderBarX+sliderBarW, sliderMin, sliderMax);
} // end setCurvatureControlGUI

void mouseDragged() {
  // move points
  if (isOnAnchor0) {
    ax0 = mouseX;
    ay0 = mouseY;
  }
  else if (isOnAnchor1) {
    ax1 = mouseX;
    ay1 = mouseY;
  }
  else if (isOnAnchor2) {
    ax2 = mouseX;
    ay2 = mouseY;
  }
  else if (isOnAnchor3) {
    ax3 = mouseX;
    ay3 = mouseY;
  }
  else if (isOnAnchor4) {
    ax4 = mouseX;
    ay4 = mouseY;
  }
} // .end mouseDragged
```

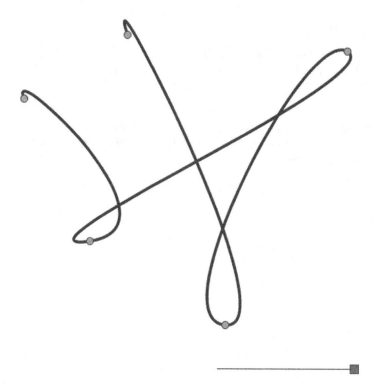

Figure 4-15. Interactive curveVertex() example

In the next chapter you'll learn about arrays, which will allow you to simplify this example considerably, replacing all the individual x and y variables with a single data structure.

Because we added a bit more interactivity and a few more points, the code got a little longer than in the previous examples. However, you'll likely find curveVertex() simpler to use than quadraticVertex() and bezierVertex(). curveVertex() doesn't require an initial vertex() call, and because both control and anchor points lie on the spline curve, we didn't need to do any additional calculations to determine control point offsets. That said, curveVertex() calls also need to be called between beginShape() and endShape(), as with the other curve commands.

Reviewing the code, we began by declaring a bunch of global variables up top. You'll notice some of these variables were initialized when declared, and the rest were initialized in setup(). Any variable initialization dependent on Processing's width or height variables needed to be done after the size() command was called. The coordinate values ax# and ay#, for the five points, were initialized with random values, like in the previous examples. In setup() we initialized variables for a simple slider bar. Processing doesn't include built-in interface elements such as sliders, buttons and menus, though there are some Processing libraries (http://processing.org/reference/libraries/#interface) that include these types of elements.

In draw() we created the curve, rendered the points, and included some conditional statements to enable inter-activity. This is also similar to what we did in the earlier examples. Near the top of draw() you'll notice the line:

```
curveTightness(curvature);
```

curveTightness() is a Processing function allowing you to specify how the curveVertex() spline curve passes through the specified points. The slider bar allows you to see these changes in real time. By default we set the range of the curvature between −3 and 3. You can change this range at the top of the code using the variables sliderMin and sliderMax.

One of the minor challenges of using Catmull-Rom splines is remembering that every point along the curve needs two additional points to act as controls; without them, that point won't be rendered along the curve. For example, the following code will not render a curve, as only the central point has the required two controls:

```
noFill();
beginShape();
curveVertex(20, 20);
curveVertex(60, 40);
curveVertex(80, 80);
endShape();
```

To fix this we need to add some additional points. If we want the curve to go through (20, 20) and (80, 80), we can double up those terminal points:

```
noFill();
beginShape();
curveVertex(20, 20);
curveVertex(20, 20);
curveVertex(60, 40);
curveVertex(80, 80);
curveVertex(80, 80);
endShape();
```

Looking back at the larger example code, you'll notice we doubled up the beginning and ending points as well. The thing to be aware of when you double up points is that you impact overall curvature. In the next example we'll generate an ellipse created with curveVertex() calls that addresses this issue differently.

The rest of the code in the example is stuff you've seen before, except for the line:

```
curvature = map(sliderHandleX, sliderBarX, sliderBarX+sliderBarW, sliderMin, sliderMax);
```

Processing's map() function allows you to convert a value from one range to another. In the example, we wanted the slider to only return values between sliderMin and sliderMax, which we initialized to −3 and 3. When users drag the slider handle, we capture the current mouseX position. However, this value is based on the position of the slider bar in the sketch window – not between −3 and 3. Map() easily scales this value to fall between sliderMin and sliderMax.

curveVertex() Ellipse

In this final example, shown in Figure 4-16, you'll generate an ellipse based on a series of curveVertex() calls using a for loop. Because curveVertex() utilizes an underlying cubic equation, it's possible to generate

Figure 4-16. curveVertex() ellipse

a smooth ellipse with only four points, as you did with bezierVertex(). You'll remember quadraticVertex() required eight points to create a smooth ellipse.

```
// Curve Ellipse
// 4 vertices and tightness

void setup() {
  size(600, 600);
  background(255);
  translate(width/2, height/2);
  curveEllipse(4, 250, 4, -.675);
} // end setup

void curveEllipse(int pts, float radius, float handleRadius, float tightness) {
  float theta = 0;
  float cx = 0, cy = 0;
  float ax = 0, ay = 0;
  float rot = TWO_PI/pts;

  curveTightness(tightness);
```

```
    beginShape();
    for (int i=0; i<pts; i++) {

      // need control before vertex 1 along the ellipse
      if (i==0) {
        cx = cos(theta - rot)*radius;
        cy = sin(theta - rot)*radius;
        ax = cos(theta)*radius;
        ay = sin(theta)*radius;
        curveVertex(cx, cy);
        curveVertex(ax, ay);
      }
      else {
        ax = cos(theta)*radius;
        ay = sin(theta)*radius;
        curveVertex(ax, ay);
      }
      // close ellipse
      if (i==pts-1) {
        cx = cos(theta + rot)*radius;
        cy = sin(theta + rot)*radius;
        ax = cos(theta + rot*2)*radius;
        ay = sin(theta + rot*2)*radius;
        curveVertex(cx, cy);
        curveVertex(ax, ay);
      }

      // draw anchor points/control points
      fill(255, 127, 0);
      ellipse(cos(theta)*radius, sin(theta)*radius, handleRadius*2, handleRadius*2);

      theta += rot;
    }
    fill(0, 127);
    noStroke();
    endShape();
  } // end curveEllipse
```

There's nothing really new in this example. Notice though we didn't double up any points along the curve. For example, when counter variable i in the for loop is 0, we create two different points around the ellipse:

```
    cx = cos(theta - rot)*radius;
    cy = sin(theta - rot)*radius;
    ax = cos(theta)*radius;
    ay = sin(theta)*radius;
```

We do the same thing for the final point as well. Since an ellipse never ends, we can always rotate to the left and right around the ellipse to calculate any required control points for the beginning and ending points.

Figure 4-17. Deformed curveVertex() ellipse

This will ensure that we have smooth and consistent curvature around the curve. If instead we had doubled up the beginning and ending points, our ellipse would have looked like Figure 4-17.

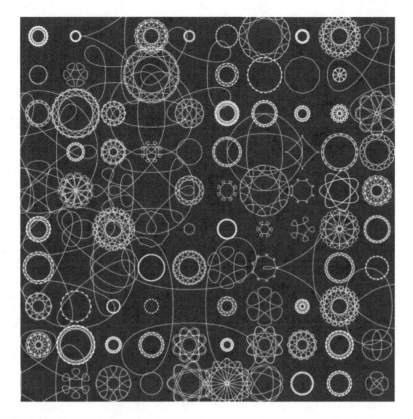

Figure 4-18. curveVertex() ellipse variations

The final figure, Figure 4-18, shows some ellipse variations introducing randomization into the previous example.

Summary

Hopefully this chapter got you more excited about the possibilities of creative coding! Expanding your knowledge of local and global variables, scope, functions, and conditional statements, you now have a deeper understanding about how programs are structured, including some of the benefits and challenges of different strategies. You learned about Processing's draw() and mouse event functions and saw how easy it is to introduce animation and interactivity into your programs. Finally, you expanded your creative coding toolbox by learning about Processing's numerous curve functions. In the next chapter you'll dive even deeper, learning about arrays and the exciting and hot area of data visualization.

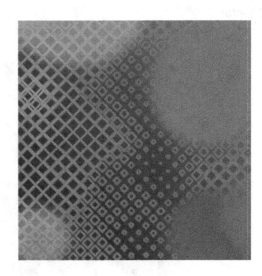

Chapter 5

Expressive Power of Data

The so-called Information Age that we live in is generating exabytes of data on a daily basis (1 exabyte is equivalent to 1 billion gigabytes or 10^{18} bytes). A 2010 article in *The Economist* magazine estimated that in 2005 humans had created a total of 150 exabytes of information, which was estimated to have increased to 1,200 exabytes in 2010. One of the grand challenges of our time has to be the management, storage, and handling such large amounts of data (not to mention the amount of energy this requires). While there are definite advantages to having so much data available, it is also becoming increasingly difficult to process and exploit the data. *The Economist* article calls it "plucking the diamond from the waste." As the self-proclaimed philosopher of information Luciano Floridi puts it, soon we will be drowning in the age of the zettabyte (1,000 exabytes) data deluge.

Such a deluge of data requires computer programs, which can be written in languages like Processing, to acquire, process, and make sense of large amounts of data. Processing of large amounts of data inherently requires sophisticated statistical analyses and thus, in addition to computer programming, a firm foundation in the methods of statistics and machine learning has become essential. Ultimately, we as humans need to be able to see or visualize the patterns in the data to make sense of any information processing outcomes. For example, most of you are perhaps familiar with the phrase "going viral." A phenomenon that is an artifact of our networked and social media-saturated lives wherein a piece of information (some news, a bit of gossip, a video, and so on, almost instantaneously spreads via people's social networks. Figure 5-1 shows how the news of a documentary about exploitation of Ugandan children by the rebel leader Joseph Kony went viral. Within a matter of four days in March 2012 the video, posted on the Internet, was viewed over 50 million times. The graph shows a Twitter analysis of the video going viral.

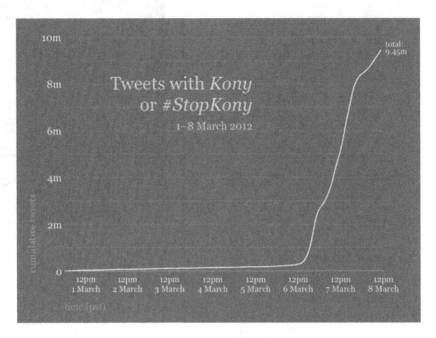

Figure 5-1. An illustration of "going viral" (Created by Isaac Hepworth, *New York Times*, March 9, 2012)

In this chapter you will begin to understand how programs handle large amounts of data and how you can create simple but expressive visualizations.

Arrays

So far, you have seen how to create variables in Processing programs that can be used to store simple values (or primitive types):

```
int x = 0;
float delta = 0.483;
```

In the these definitions, the variables are each associated with a single value (defined by the type int or float). You have also seen instances where multiple values were associated with a single variable name:

```
color darkOliveGreen = color(85, 107, 47);
String colorName = "Dark Olive Green";
PImage castle = loadImage("myCastle.jpg");
```

The types color, String, and PImage each associate a number of values with the variable being defined. The meaning of the values is determined by the type definition itself. Thus, any variable of type color has three RGB values associated with it, a variable of type String can be a string of characters, and a variable of type PImage associates with itself all the pixel values of an image (you will learn more about PImage in a later chapter). In programming language terminology, we distinguish between *simple types* (such as int, float, and so on) that associate a single value with its variables and *compound* or *complex types* (such as `color`, `String`, `PImage`, and so on) that may have several values aggregated together in a single variable. Most modern programming languages provide facilities for creating new aggregate types, which we will see in Chapter 6. Data or values can also be aggregated into *arrays* that are container structures that enable storage of many values of the same type together using a single variable name. For example, consider the set of numbers in Table 5-1:

Table 5-1. A Set of Sample Values

Petroleum	Coal	Natural Gas	Nuclear	Renewable	Hydropower
40.0	23.0	22.0	8.0	4.0	3.0

These numbers represent the percentage of United States national energy consumption, listed by energy source, in 2005. For example, 8% of the overall energy consumed came from nuclear energy sources. It would be easy to create one variable to store each of the values:

```
float petroleum = 40.0;
float coal = 23.0;
float naturalGas = 22.0;
float nuclear = 8.0;
float renewable = 4.0;
float hydropower = 3.0;
```

However, for related values like these that form a dataset it is more convenient to aggregate or group them into a single container, called an *array*. Arrays aggregate as well as structure datasets like these and make them available for use through a single named variable (as opposed to six in the case above). Each individual value is accessed by indexing it in the array. A better way to visualize this representation is shown in Figure 5-2. Note that in Figure 5-2 the first element in the array is indexed as the 0th element. This is true for all arrays. In Processing, the array in Figure 5-2 can be defined as:

```
float[] consumption;
```

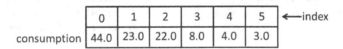

Figure 5-2. Array representation of the table showing name of array and index values

It defines a variable called `consumption` to be an array in which the values will be of type `float`. Notice that it does not define the size or the number of elements it holds. To specify the size of the array, you have to issue the following command:

```
consumption = new float[6];
```

This command is a request to create a new array that is capable of storing six float values. It is possible to combine the preceding two commands:

```
float[] consumption = new float[6];
```

After you have defined and created the array, you can store values in it:

```
consumption[0] = 40.0;
consumption[1] = 23.0;
consumption[2] = 22.0;
consumption[3] = 8.0;
consumption[4] = 4.0;
consumption[5] = 3.0;
```

There is a better way to do this, where you can define, create, and initialize the data in an array in a single command:

```
float[] consumption = {40.0, 23.0, 22.0, 8.0, 4.0, 3.0};
```

That is, you are defining an array of type float; it is called consumption; and it has the six specified float values placed in it. If you look carefully, the format for array initialization is not that different from that of initializing simple variables:

```
float salary = 1000000.00;
```

The only difference is that you have to specify all the aggregate values of the array by placing them inside curly braces. Processing counts the number of values you specify and then implicitly creates an array of exactly that size (six, in this case). The following summarizes all the ways arrays can be defined, created, and/or initialized:

```
TypeName[] arrayName;                           // declaring an array variable to hold
                                                // values of TypeName
arrayName = new TypeName[N];                     // creating an array of size N
TypeName[] arrayName = new TypeName[N];          // declaring and creating an array of size N
TypeName[] arrayName = {v0, v1, ..., vN};        // declaring, creating, and initializing
                                                // an array of size N+1
```

Here are some more examples of array declarations:

```
// An array to hold the names of all the days in a week
String[] weekDays = {"Monday", "Tuesday", "Wednesday", "Thursday", "Friday", "Saturday", "Sunday"};
float[] highTemps, lowTemps;   // two arrays, each containing high and low temperature values
int[] count;                   // an array of integers
PImage[] photos;               // an array of photos

// An array to hold the names of months in a year
String[] months = {"January", "February", "March", "April", "May", "June",
                   "July", "August", "September", "October", "November", "December"};
```

```
// An array of famous mathematical constants. How many can you recognize?
float[] mathConstants = {3.14159, 2.71828, 1.61803, 1.41421, 1.732, 0.57721, 1.32471, 0.66061,
                0.76422};

// The colors in a rainbow
color[] rainbow = {color(255, 0, 0), color(255, 127, 0), color(255, 255, 0),
                color (0, 255, 0), color (0, 0, 255), color (111, 0, 255), color (143, 0, 255)};

// Names of various energy sources
String[] energySource = {"Petroleum", "Coal", "Natural Gas", "Nuclear", "Renewable",
                "Hydropower"};
```

> Try This: For each of the previous array definitions, clearly identify the parts that make up
> an array: its variable name, the type of values it holds, the number of values it can hold
> (its size, if known), and the values it holds (if known).

Indexing, Size, and Loops

Individual elements in the array are accessed by specifying their index using the syntax:

```
arrayName[index]
```

Thus, to access the string value "Natural Gas" from the energySource array shown previously we write:

```
energySource[2]
```

Remember that individual values or items stored in an array are indexed starting from 0 (for the first element) to N-1 (for the last element). Thus, an array of size 6 has its index in the range 0..5. Processing also defines a length attribute for array variables that can be used to find out the size of an array. Thus, the expression

```
energySource.length
```

represents the value 6 because, in the preceding definition, energySource was created with six elements. The length attribute is very useful in designing general purpose functions that operate on arrays, as you will see later.

Most operations on data stored in an array rely on loops to systematically visit each element of the array. For example, if you wanted to store the number 42 in every location of a 1,000-element array

```
int[] n = new int[1000];
for (int i=0; i < n.length; i++) {
    n[i] = 42;
}
```

the for-loop enables an easy mechanism to specify a repetitive set of steps succinctly. The loop control variable, i, also acts as an index into the array. Notice that the initial value assigned to i is 0 (the index of the first element of the array) and it is incremented by 1 after each iteration using i++. Also note that the loop's terminating condition is i < n.length. That is, as soon as the value of i becomes equal to n.length the loop will terminate. You could alternatively specify the for-loop as:

```
for (int i=0; i <= n.length-1; i++) {
...
```

In computing, there is a well-known error that even seasoned programmers tend to make. It is called *off-by-one error* and refers to situations when the number of iterations specified is off by 1. Here are two examples of off-by-one errors:

```
for (int i=0; i <= n.length; i++) {
...
for (int i=0; i < n.length-1; i++) {
...
```

In the first instance, you are specifying the value of i to go from 0 to n.length, including the value of n.length. If, in the loop, i is being used to index into the array n (as in n[i]) the program generates an ArrayOutOfBounds error when the value of i becomes equal to n.length and it tries to access the element n[i]. In the second instance, if i is being used to access all elements of the array n, it will never reach or do anything with the last element in the array (n[n.length-1]) because the loop will terminate before getting there. In this case, the program runs without reporting any errors, resulting in incomplete computation(s) and incorrect results, also known as *bugs*. This is a devious situation that can be hard to *debug*. Always be sure to review and correct all potential off-by-one errors at the time of writing the program!

As another example, if you wanted to store the outcomes of 10,000 rolls of a six-sided die:

```
int[] outcome = new int[10000];
for (int i=0; i < outcome.length; i++) {          // fill it up with random values
    outcome[i] = int(random(1,7));
}
```

As you have seen earlier, when called with two arguments, the function random(n1, n2) returns a floating point value in the interval [n1..n2]. Thus random(1, 7) generates a value in the interval [1.0..7.0], not including 7.0 itself. To generate a number that represents an outcome of throwing a die, we convert the number into an integer using the int() function.

When accessing all elements in an array, you typically need an index variable (like i in the preceding code) that starts from the first index (i = 0) and goes all the way to the end (i < outcome.length), incrementing each time by 1 (i++). If you visualize the array laid out with the first item on the left and stretching out across the page, the index travels from left to right as it allows you to visit each element in succession. For our right-leaning readers, this loop can also be written as:

```
for (int i=outcome.length-1; i >= 0; i--) {       // fill it up with random values
    outcome[i] = int(random(1,7));
}
```

Functionally, the two loops serve exactly the same purpose (that is, filling up the array with random values in the interval [1..7]). In the latter case, you start at the last index (i=outcome.length-1) and go all the way to the first element (i >= 0) decrementing by 1 each time (i--). Also, in both cases, we make use of the length attribute to identify how far (in the first loop) the index variable should go, or where it should start (in the second loop). Where possible, for operations like these, always use the length attribute to control the bounds of your loop.

> *Try This: Write commands to initialize an array to all 0's.*
>
> *Try This: Write commands to initialize an array with the sequence: 1, 1, 2, 3, 5, 8, 13, ...*
>
> *Try This: Create an array called counts to store the number of rolls of each of the six faces of a die using the events generated in the previous outcome array.*

To ensure that you did all the preceding correctly, write complete Processing programs to initialize and print the resulting arrays.

A number of array-based computations require sequential processing all of an array's elements. There is a special form of the for-loop that is provided. It is called the for-each loop and has the following syntax:

```
for (variable : arrayName) {
    // do something with the value of variable
}
```

That is, variable takes on successive values stored in arrayName, from the first to the last, so that it can be used in a computation in the loop.

We should point out here that the for-each loop is useful only in situations where the loop is written purely for the sake of accessing all the values in a given array. You cannot use this loop for modifying values in an array. In general, the for-loop is perhaps the most general and useful form of writing such iterations.

Example: A Simple Bar Graph

As an example, this sketch plots a rudimentary bar graph of the energy consumption data seen earlier (the graph can be seen in Figure 5-3):

```
// Sketch5-1
String[] energySource = {"Petroleum", "Coal", "Natural Gas", "Nuclear", "Renewable", "Hydropower"};
float[] consumption = {40.0, 23.0, 22.0, 8.0, 4.0, 3.0};
void setup() {
 size(400, 400);
 smooth();
} // setup()
```

```
void draw() {
    // set up plot dimensions relative to screen size
    float x = width*0.1;
    float y = height*0.9;
    float delta = width*0.8/consumption.length;
    float w = delta*0.8;
    background(255);
    for (float value : consumption) {
        // draw the bar for value
        // first compute the height of the bar
        // relative to sketch window
        float h = map(value, 0, 100, 0, height);
        fill(0);
        rect(x, y-h, w, h);
        x = x + delta;
    }
} // draw()
```

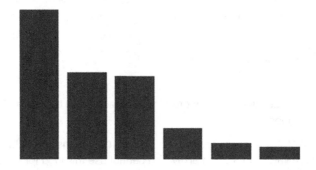

Figure 5-3. Bar graph of energy consumption data

Array Operations

A number of useful array operations are provided in Processing. These include operations for printing, sorting, and computing the minimum and maximum values stored in an array. For these examples, assume the following two array definitions:

```
String[] energySource = {"Petroleum", "Coal", "Natural Gas", "Nuclear", "Renewable",
                         "Hydropower"};
float[] consumption = {40.0, 23.0, 22.0, 8.0, 4.0, 3.0};
```

Printing

Occasionally, it is useful to print the contents of an array (or a variable) in the console window (the one in the bottom part of your IDE where error messages appear). This can be done with the println() command:

```
println(consumption.length);
println(consumption);
```

This prints the number of elements followed by the contents of the array consumption as shown here:

```
6
[0] 40.0
[1] 23.0
[2] 22.0
[3] 8.0
[4] 4.0
[5] 3.0
```

Similarly, for printing energySource:

```
println(energySource);
[0] "Petroleum"
[1] "Coal"
[2] "Natural Gas"
[3] "Nuclear"
[4] "Renewable"
[5] "Hydropower"
```

> Try This: Write commands to print the values from energySource and consumption in the format shown here:
>
> ```
> Petroleum, 40.0
> Coal, 23.0
> Natural Gas, 22.0
> Nuclear, 8.0
> Renewable, 4.0
> Hydropower, 3.0
> ```

Min, Max, and Sorting

Often, as you will see in the following example, it is required to quickly find out the minimum and the maximum values stored in an array, or even sort or rearrange all the elements in an array in ascending/descending order. Processing provides a small handful of useful functions to do these tasks on arrays. We illustrate them here with examples:

```
float smallest = min(consumption);
float largest = max(consumption);
```

The variable `smallest` receives the value 3.0 and `largest` receives 40.0. The functions `min()` and `max()` work only on arrays of `int` and `float` values. Any array of `int`, `float`, or `String` values can be sorted in ascending order using the `sort()` function:

```
println(sort(consumption));
```

```
[0] 3.0
[1] 4.0
[2] 8.0
[3] 22.0
[4] 23.0
[5] 40.0
```

```
println(sort(energySource));
```

```
[0] "Coal"
[1] "Hydropower"
[2] "Natural Gas"
[3] "Nuclear"
[4] "Petroleum"
[5] "Renewable"
```

Processing also provides other array operations as well:

- Reverse the ordering of elements in an array (`reverse()`)

- Expand the size of the array (`append()`, `expand()`)

- Shorten it (`shorten()`)

- Concatenate or split arrays (`concat()`, `subset()`, `splice()`)

- Copy the contents of an array (`arrayCopy()`)

- and so on

Feel free to peek at the Processing Reference for details of these. We introduce them in this text only if, and when, we need to use them.

Example: A Better, Interactive curveVertex

Recall the interactive curveVertex example from Chapter 4 (refer to Figure 4-15). Now, we can rewrite the program to use arrays to store the anchor point coordinates as show here:

```
// Sketch 5-2: Interactive curveVertex() example using arrays

float [] ax;  // x-anchor points
float [] ay;  // y-anchor points
int N = 5;    // number of anchor points

int isOnAnchor;  // anchor point was selected
float radius = 5;

// gui to control curvature
float curvature = 0;
float sliderBarX, sliderBarY, sliderBarW;
float sliderHandleX, sliderHandleY, sliderHandleW = 12;
float sliderMin = -3, sliderMax = 3;
boolean isOnSliderHandle;

void setup() {
  size(600, 600);
  background(255);

  ax = new float[N];  // create anchor point arrays and initialize
  ay = new float[N];
  for (int i=0; i < N; i++) {
    ax[i] = random(100, width-100);
    ay[i] = random(100, height-100);
  }

  // control bar for intractive curvature
  sliderBarW = width/3;
  sliderBarX = width-sliderBarW-40;
  sliderBarY = height-40;
  sliderHandleX = sliderBarX + sliderBarW/2;
  sliderHandleY = sliderBarY;
} // setup()

void draw() {
  background(255);
  noFill();
  strokeWeight(4);
  stroke(0);
  curveTightness(curvature);
```

```
  // draw curve
  beginShape();
  curveVertex(ax[0], ay[0]); // double initial point
  for (int i=0; i<N; i++) {  // specify all anchor points
    curveVertex(ax[i], ay[i]);
  }
  curveVertex(ax[N-1], ay[N-1]); // double final point
  endShape();

  // draw control/anchor points
  strokeWeight(1);
  fill(255, 127, 0);
  for (int i=0; i<N; i++) {
    ellipse(ax[i], ay[i], radius*2, radius*2);
  }

 // detect if mouse is on control/anchor point
 for (int i=0; i<N; i++) {
    if (dist(mouseX, mouseY, ax[i], ay[i]) < radius)
      isOnAnchor = i;
 }
 // ensure boolean flags set back to false when mouse released
 if (!mousePressed) {
   isOnSliderHandle = false;
   isOnAnchor = -1;
 }
 // interactively control curvature
 setCurvatureControlGUI();
} // draw()

void setCurvatureControlGUI() {
  line(sliderBarX, sliderBarY, sliderBarX+sliderBarW, sliderBarY);
  fill(0, 0, 255);
  rect(sliderHandleX-sliderHandleW/2, sliderHandleY-sliderHandleW/2, sliderHandleW,
  sliderHandleW);

  if (isOnSliderHandle &&  mouseX>sliderBarX && mouseX < sliderBarX + sliderBarW) {
    sliderHandleX = mouseX;
  }

  // detect if mouse is on control/anchor point
  if (dist(mouseX, mouseY, sliderHandleX, sliderHandleY) < sliderHandleW/2) {
    isOnSliderHandle = true;
  }
  // ensures slider handle values between to sliderMin to sliderMax
  curvature = map(sliderHandleX, sliderBarX, sliderBarX+sliderBarW, sliderMin, sliderMax);
} // setCurvature()
```

```
void mouseDragged() {()
  // move points
  if (isOnAnchor >=0 && isOnAnchor <N) {
    ax[isOnAnchor] = mouseX;
    ay[isOnAnchor] = mouseY;
  }
} // mouseDragged()
```

One additional change made in the preceding program is to define isOnAnchor as an int variable to hold the index of the anchor point selected (it is set to -1 otherwise). This index is used in mouseDragged to reset the selected anchor point to the mouse location.

Primitive and Reference Types

Now that you are familiar with arrays, it is time to get a little more intimate with some important underlying details. In Processing there are two categories of variables: *primitive* and *reference*. Primitive variables hold values of simple or primitive types (such as int, float, and so on), and reference types are used for values that are aggregates (such as arrays, color, PImage, etc.). The distinction has to do with underlying memory models used in implementing the types, and these manifest in important differences for the programmer. It is therefore crucial to clearly understand this.

In Processing, the only primitive types are int, long, short, byte, float, double, char, and boolean. When you define a variable of a primitive type in Processing

```
int meaningOfLife = 42;
```

you are creating a set of associations, called *bindings*: the variable name (meaningOfLife) takes on values of type (int) and currently associates the value 42 with it. After the preceding definition, any use of the variable meaningOfLife will be associated with the value 42, until the program assigns a different value to it. During the lifetime of most variables in a running program, the values associated with variables change and this is essentially what brings about the fundamental process of computing. Now, think about how inside a computer the value associated with a variable is managed. For primitive types the value is stored in a designated memory location. The previous command results in allocating a designated place in the computer's memory that can hold all values that are possible in the type int. Variables of type int in Processing can take on values in the range -2,147,483,648 to 2,147,483,647 and hence require 4 bytes of computer memory to store an int value. The picture in Figure 5-4 is what you should keep in mind when defining such variables:

Figure 5-4. Bindings for primitive types

The three bindings are clearly shown: the name of the variable on the left, its type on the right, and the memory "cell" containing the current value inside the box in the middle. If commands in your program change the value of meaningOfLife, the value sitting inside the box changes. Any use of the variable picks up the value from this cell. At the machine level the cell itself requires 4 bytes of consecutive memory locations to store the value. But you can imagine that each of the 4 bytes that make up the cell has a unique address in memory. The first address of the first byte of the cell is considered the address of the entire cell. Thus, each time a variable is used in a program, the address of the cell is generated to access the contents of the cell. The address of the cell is also called a *reference*.

The picture for the internal representation of arrays is different. Consider this definition:

```
float[] consumption = {40.0, 23.0, 22.0, 8.0, 4.0, 3.0};
```

To understand the representation of arrays, it is perhaps best to split it into the following:

```
float[] consumption;
```

From what you have just learned, this creates a binding of the name consumption to be an array of type float. Processing interprets this, at the lower level as shown in Figure 5-5:

consumption | null | reference to float

Figure 5-5. Bindings for a reference type

So far this looks almost similar to primitive variable representations: there is a name, a cell, and a type. However, the type is no longer float, but a reference to float (you'll see why later). And the cell contains something called null. A reference, as you saw earlier, is an address of a cell in the memory. In this case, the number of values that will be stored in the array is not yet known. For this and some other reasons, the bindings of array variables is different from those of primitive types: the name, the type of elements in the array, and the cell containing the starting address of the block of cells that store values of an array. If the block has not yet been created, as shown here, a reference has a value null. After you create an array, as in the following, a consecutive block of six cells, each capable of storing a float value (which also require 4 bytes each) is allocated in memory.

```
consumption = new float[6];
```

The starting address of the first cell (that is, the one that becomes consumption[0]) is stored in the cell containing the reference to float. This is shown in Figure 5-6 after the consumption array is filled with the desired values.

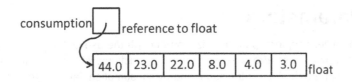

Figure 5-6. Bindings for the consumption array

In Processing, variables that denote arrays and objects (discussed in Chapter 6) are called *reference variables* (or *reference types*). Other reference types you have seen before include String, color, and PImage. Their names are bound to cells containing a reference rather than the actual cells containing the values. This may seem confusing at first but is actually useful in many respects. For instance, a definition of an array, without creating one, is useful in defining an array that can then be associated with values of any size. However, you now have to be a little careful when writing programs with primitive versus reference types. First, consider the following for primitive types:

```
int x = 10;
int y;
y = x;
```

Given that both x and y are primitive types, after the assignment the cells associated with both x and y will contain the value 10. That is, an assignment between primitive types creates a copy of the value to store in the variable on the left-hand side. Next consider what happens in the case of arrays:

```
int[] a = {10, 20, 30};
int[] b;
b = a;
```

What do you think happens? Given that both a and b are reference types, Processing defines the rule that in an assignment, what gets copied is the value of the reference cell. Thus, after the assignment, both b and a will refer to the same set of cells containing the values {10, 20, 30}. You can test this by adding the following lines after the preceding commands:

```
b[0] = 100;
println(a[0]);
```

Before you peek ahead, stop and think. Draw a picture and then write down the value that will be printed. If you wrote down 100, you are correct!

> *Try This: Be sure you run the preceding example to understand what is going on here.*

In the parlance of computer scientists who design programming languages, when two variable names refer to the same data object it is called *aliasing*. Aliasing is a language trap that you have to watch out for, as it is fairly easy to create confusing situations like this one. Aliasing, which is sometimes necessary, can lead to unintended *side effects*.

Arrays As Parameters

As you have seen in earlier chapters, parameterization through the use of functions is a powerful concept in computing. Let's learn how to pass arrays as parameters to functions. We define a function called barGraph() that plots the data in a bar graph. We use the same energy consumption data as previously used. The modified program from earlier in the chapter that uses the barGraph() function is shown here:

```
// Sketch5-3: Bar Graph using a barGraph() function
String[] energySource = {"Petroleum", "Coal", "Natural Gas", "Nuclear", "Renewable", "Hydropower"};

float[] consumption = {40.0, 23.0, 22.0, 8.0, 4.0, 3.0};
void setup() {
   size(400, 400);
   smooth();
} // setup()

void draw() {
   background(255);
   barGraph();
} // draw()

void barGraph() {
   // set up dimensions relative to screen size
   float x = width*0.1;
   float y = height*0.9;
   float delta = width*0.8/consumption.length;
   float w = delta*0.8;
   for (int i=0; i < consumption.length; i++) {
      // draw the bar for ith data value
      // first compute the height of the bar relative to sketch window
      float h = map(consumption[i], 0, 100, 0, height);
      fill(0);
      rect(x, y-h, w, h);
      x = x + delta;
   }
} // barGraph()
```

While this sketch performs just like the previous version, it uses the barGraph() function to draw the bar graph. However, the barGraph() function is still specific to the data in the consumption array. To generalize this, we can parameterize the barGraph() function so that it can draw a bar graph for any given data set (as long as it is an array of float values). This is shown here:

```
// Sketch5-4: Bar Graph using a barGraph() function with array parameter
String[] energySource = {"Petroleum", "Coal", "Natural Gas", "Nuclear", "Renewable", "Hydropower"};

float[] consumption = {40.0, 23.0, 22.0, 8.0, 4.0, 3.0};
void setup() {
   size(400, 400);
```

```
      smooth();
  } // setup()

  void draw() {
    background(255);
    barGraph(consumption);
  } // draw()

  void barGraph(float[] data) {
    // set up plot dimensions relative to screen size
    float x = width*0.1;
    float y = height*0.9;
    float delta = width*0.8/data.length;
    float w = delta*0.8;

    for (float i : data) {
      // draw the bar for ith data value
      // first compute the height of the bar relative to sketch window
      float h = map(i, 0, 100, 0, height);
      fill(0);
      rect(x, y-h, w, h);
      x = x + delta;
    }
  } // barGraph()
```

By creating a formal parameter called data, the barGraph() function is generalized to accept any array of float values to be plotted as a bar graph.

> *Try This: In the preceding sketch, define another data set using an array of float values. Use the barGraph() function to plot it.*

Passing an array as an argument to a function is similar to the way simple variables are passed. Do pay special attention to the function header and notice how an array parameter is defined. One advantage of defining functions that do specialized tasks, as discussed earlier in Chapters 3 and 4, is modularization of your program. Also, notice that the barGraph() function is independent of the size of the actual data array that is provided. We could use it to plot a bar graph of any size data. This is a direct benefit from having the length attribute. It enables us to write the barGraph() function without regards to the size of the array containing the data to be visualized. Additionally, if you wanted, instead, to visualize the data in the form of a pie chart, you can define a similar function called pieChart() to do so.

Time Series Visualization

The data for energy consumption was small enough so we could easily use the array initialization feature in our program. In most cases where data visualization is involved, the amount of data to be visualized is typically too large to use array initialization. In that case it is typically stored in a data file. In many real time applications the data might only be available over a network service, or through a sensing device. Processing provides several means for accessing data from sources whether it is files or another source. In this section, you will learn how to input data from files for doing visualizations.

Long before there was e-mail, correspondents typically used postal services to send mail. Figure 5-7 shows a snapshot of the number of pieces of first-class mail (in billions) shipped by the United States Postal Service each year from 1950 through 2011. This type of data, which varies in discrete time steps (each year, in this case), is called a *discrete time series*. Such a dataset is characterized by values taken from specific points in time, or time blocks (a year in this case), and there is a finite number of possible values. For an example of continuous data, think of the current temperature in a given place. It can be taken at any time and is constantly changing. As you can see, visualizing the data can immediately reveal relevant patterns. You can clearly see how the volume of mail steadily increased from 1950 to 2001 and then reduced by nearly 25% in 2011 from its peak in 2001. The drastic drop in volume since 2001 can be directly attributed to increase in Internet usage and e-mail in the United States over that time.

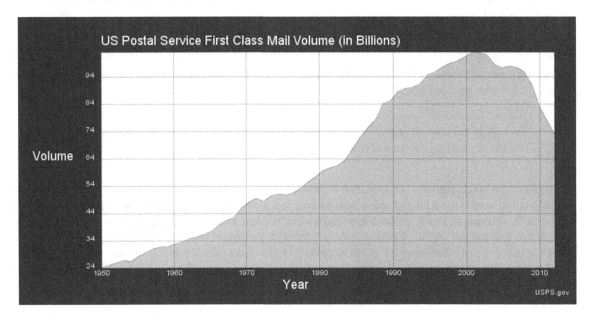

Figure 5-7. A discrete time series visualization

The first step in creating data visualization is to get access to the data. Not only should you ensure that the source is credible (and make sure to cite it); you also need to have it available in a form readable by your program. These days, there are several rich sources of data that you can gain access to through a simple web search. For example, do a search for "USPS first class mail volume" and you will be able to find the data source for the chart shown in Figure 5-7. Also, try to locate the weather data (daily temperature and precipitation log) for your town, city, and so on. After you have identified a credible data source, you have a few options to acquire the data. The data may be freely available or you may have to pay a fee to obtain it. Sometimes, a licensing fee may even be required.

Once you are past the access and usage rights, you have to determine how the data is accessed by your program. Do you have to obtain it and store it on your computer first, or can it be accessed online in real time? In what follows, we will assume that the data is accessible in the form of a file and we have rights of use. As an example, we will download and use historical daily stock price data for Apple Inc. for the year 2010. You can easily locate this data online. For example, we got the data from the Yahoo! Finance site (finance.yahoo.com). You can select any company's stock. For our example we picked AAPL (the ticker symbol for Apple Inc.), the desired range (we chose the entire 2010 year), and then the format in which to receive the data (we chose the Microsoft Excel format). This format option directly loads the data into rows and columns into an Excel spreadsheet that can be saved in different formats. One of these formats is CSV. CSV stands for Comma Separated Values. This is a plain text format in which each row of data is stored on a single line with column entries separated by commas (hence the name CSV). A small snapshot of the data we obtained is shown here:

```
1,4,2010,213.43,214.50,214.01,17633200
1,5,2010,214.60,215.59,214.38,21496600
1,6,2010,214.38,215.23,210.97,19720000
...
...
12,29,2010,326.22,326.45,325.29,5826400
12,30,2010,325.48,325.51,323.66,5624800
12,31,2010,322.95,323.48,322.56,6911000
```

We received 252 lines of data, one for each trading day of 2010, where each line contained the following:

```
MONTH,DAY,YEAR,LO,HI,CLOSE,VOLUME
```

where MONTH, DAY, YEAR represents the date. Thus 1,4,2010 on the first line indicates data for January 4, 2010. The three numbers that follow are the low, high, and the closing stock price. Thus, on December 31, 2010 Apple Inc.'s stock closed at a price of $322.56 trading during the day in the range $322.95 to $323.48 with 6.911 million shares trading hands.

Let's use the preceding data to learn how to create a visualization of a time series. To start simple, we will focus only on the closing stock price (the sixth value in each line). To begin, you should create a new Processing sketch and enter the following code:

```
// Sketch5-5: Visualizing Time Series (AAPL Stock prices)
float[] price;
float X1, Y1, X2, Y2;
void setup() {
  // drawing setup
  size(600, 400);
  X1 = 50; Y1 = 50;
  X2 = width - 50;
  Y2 = height - Y1;
  smooth();
} // setup()
```

```
void draw() {
  background(0);
  // draw plot bounding box
  rectMode(CORNERS);
  noStroke();
  fill(255);
  rect(X1, Y1, X2, Y2);
} // draw()
```

When you run this sketch, you will see a dark background with a white rectangle inset. This is where the plot will be drawn. So far, this sketch defines the plot area and not much else. Next, take the data file and place it in the Data folder of your sketch. All data files required by your sketch should be stored in the Data folder (just like the images). In the sketch above, we also defined an array called price (of float values) that we will use for storing the daily stock prices. At this point, we do not know how large the data set is because we haven't yet read it. Let's do that next.

```
// Sketch5-5b: Visualizing Time Series (AAPL Stock prices)
float[] price;
float minPrice, maxPrice;
float X1, Y1, X2, Y2;

void setup() {
  // drawing setup
  size(600, 400);
  X1 = 50; Y1 = 50;
  X2 = width - 50;
  Y2 = height - Y1;
  smooth();

  // Read the data file...
  String[] lines = loadStrings("AAPLStock.txt");

  // How long is the dataset
  price = new float[lines.length];

  // Parse the needed data
  for (int i=0; i<lines.length; i++) {
    // First split each line using commas as separator
    String[] pieces = split(lines[i], ",");
    // get the closing price of stock
    price[i] = float(pieces[5]);
  }
  println("Data Loaded: "+price.length+" entries.");

  // determine min and max stock price for the year
  minPrice = min(price);
  maxPrice = max(price);
  println("Min: "+minPrice);
  println("Max: "+maxPrice);
} // setup()
```

Most of the additions are in the setup() function. There are no changes in the draw() function so it is not shown here. In setup() we added commands to input and parse the data to store the extracted closing stock prices in the array price. After that, we computed and printed out the minimum and maximum stock prices. When you run the previous sketch, you will see the same output window as before (with an empty plot area) and you will also see the following lines in the console window:

```
Data Loaded: 252 entries.
Min: 192.05
Max: 325.47
```

This indicates that you could successfully input and parse the data and also could compute the stock price range for the year. Quite a year for the stock isn't it? Even simple computations are starting to pay off. Notice how the loadStrings() function is used to input the entire file as an array of strings. Each line in the file gets stored in the array lines as a separate string. Each string is then parsed, inside the for-loop, by first breaking it into pieces using the split() string function resulting in an array of strings for each data item on the line. Next, we convert the needed data item, the closing stock price (at price[5]), into a float value and store it in the price array. Now that you have the data where you need it, in the price array, you are ready to do the next step: visualize.

```
void draw() {
  background(0);
  // draw plot bounding box
  rectMode(CORNERS);
  noStroke();
  fill(255);
  rect(X1, Y1, X2, Y2);
  drawGraph(price, minPrice, maxPrice);
} // draw()

void drawGraph(float[] data, float yMin, float yMax) {
  stroke(0);
  beginShape();
  for (int i=0; i < data.length; i++) {
    float x = map(i, 0, data.length-1, X1, X2);
    float y = map(data[i], yMin, yMax, Y2, Y1);
    vertex(x, y);
  }
  endShape();
} // drawGraph()
```

The sketch now plots the graph shown in Figure 5-8. The drawGraph() function does all the work. Given the data array, the minimum and maximum values in it, and the bounds of the plotting area (X1, Y1) and (X2, Y2) it can plot the daily stock price. It uses the map() function to map each data value to the proper x and y coordinates within the plot area. Carefully study the parameters supplied to the map() function and be sure you understand them. We are using the beginShape() and endShape() functions to specify each data point as a vertex in the plot.

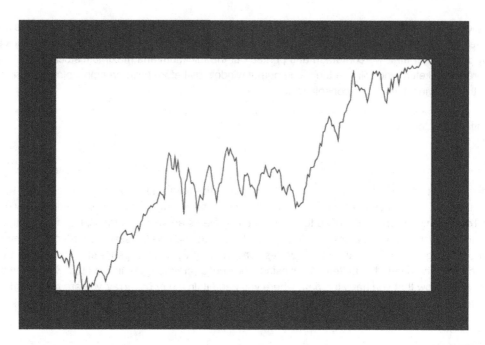

Figure 5-8. Drawing the graph of AAPL stock using drawGraph()

Try This: Now you can start experimenting with different aspects of the sketch. For example, vary the size of the sketch itself (from 600x400 to some other values). Does the plot scale appropriately? Why?

Try This: Change the stroke color of the graph to red or another color of your choosing.

Try This: Change the vertex() command to the curveVertex() command to draw a smooth curve. You will additionally need to define the start and end anchor points.

Try This: Turn this graph into an area plot. An area plot shows the entire area under the graph in a different color. Hint: You will need to experiment with optional parameters of beginShape() or endShape().

It is time to further refine the graph. This time you will add the legend, and label axes. For this, you need to create a font by adding the following at the top of the sketch (above setup()):

```
PFont legendFont = createFont("SansSerif", 20);
```

And then add this command in drawing setup section of setup():

```
textFont(legendFont);
```

The new version of draw() function is shown here:

```
void draw() {
  background(0);
  // draw plot bounding box
  rectMode(CORNERS);
  noStroke();
  fill(255);
  rect(X1, Y1, X2, Y2);
  drawGraph(price, minPrice, maxPrice);

  // draw legend
  // title
  fill(255);
  textSize(18);
  textAlign(LEFT);
  text("(AAPL) Apple Inc. 2010", X1, Y1 - 10);
  textSize(10);
  textAlign(RIGHT, BOTTOM);
  text("Source: Yahoo! Finance (finance.yahoo.com)", width-10, height-10);

  // axis labels
  drawXLabels();
  drawYLabels();
} // draw()
```

The drawYLabels() function is shown next:

```
void drawYLabels () {
  fill(255);
  textSize(10);
  textAlign(RIGHT);
  stroke(255);

  for (float i=minPrice; i <= maxPrice; i += 10) {
    float y = map(i, minPrice, maxPrice, Y2, Y1);
    text(floor(i), X1-10, y);
    line(X1, y, X1-5, y);
  }

  textSize(18);
  text("$", X1-40, height/2);
} // drawYLabels()
```

We will leave the details of the drawXLabels() function as an exercise. For labeling the x-axis you need the month data from the data file. Declare an integer array to store the month values, just as you did for the price. Extract the month into the array and then use it in the drawXLabels() function. The final visualization is shown in Figure 5-9.

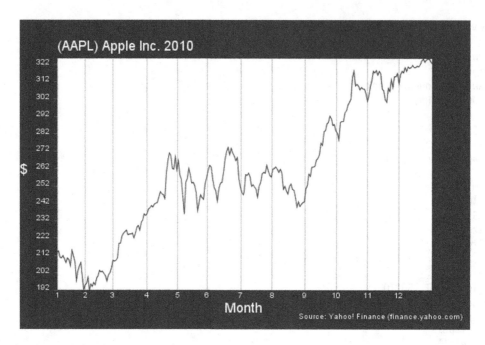

Figure 5-9. A complete, labeled plot of Apple Inc. stock prices in 2010

Simple Data Modeling

We conclude this chapter with a small yet effective computational enhancement to the stock price visualization. First, let's consider the task of computing the average stock price of Apple Inc. stock for the preceding data. We can write a function to compute this as follows:

```
float average(float[] data) {
    float sum = 0;
    for (value : data)
        sum += value;
    return sum / data.length;
} // average()
```

This function accumulates all the stock prices into the variable sum and then returns the average by dividing the sum by the number of elements it accumulated. This function could be used in the sketch by using the command:

```
float avStockPrice = average(price);
```

While an average stock price is a useful indicator, in the financial world, it is more useful to compute the average stock price over a smaller period of time. For example, you may be interested in viewing the price over a 10-day trading range. Computing the 10-day average across the entire year is a useful way to model the movement of a stock. This is called a *simple moving average* and is considered a better indicator of the average price of a stock over a given time period. Over time, this moving average can be plotted along with the daily stock price as shown here:

```
void movingAverage(float[] data, float yMin, float yMax, int MAP) {
  noFill();
  stroke(255, 0, 0);
  strokeWeight(2);
  beginShape();
  for (int i=MAP-1; i < data.length; i++) {
    float sum = 0;
    for (int k=i-(MAP-1); k <= i; k++) {
      sum += data[k];
    }

    float MA = sum/MAP;
    float x = map(i, 0, data.length-1, X1, X2);
    float y = map(MA, yMin, yMax, Y2, Y1);
    vertex(x, y);
  }
  endShape();
} //movingAverage()
```

Adding this to your sketch and calling it from the draw function plots a red curve of the moving average. This is shown in Figure 5-10 for a 25-day moving average (that is, MAP=25).

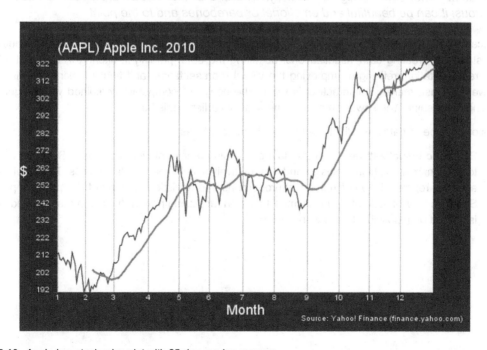

Figure 5-10. Apple Inc. stock price plot with 25-day moving average

As you can see, the moving average plot is a smoother rendering of the price plot as it eliminates the daily ups and downs. In the financial world, a moving average also reflects the stock's momentum. Whenever the stock price curve is above the moving average it implies that the stock price has an upward momentum and generally it is considered a good buy. Whenever the moving average is above the stock curve it reflects a downward momentum of the stock. Thus, in early February, and also in May, July, and August the Apple stock had a downward momentum. The entire years' worth of data, though, depicts a time in history when the stock had an upward momentum for most of the year starting from March 2010. Can you guess why? The iPad was launched on April 1, 2010.

Data Visualization

The previous example illustrates how data, once stored in the array, can be used to create effective plots or other kinds of visualizations. Even simple visualizations can lead to key insights that may not be obvious in a table of numbers. These days data visualization is a growing industry. Beyond business analytics, visualizations enable us to understand and represent complex phenomena. While computers and computational processes have created a richer medium for data visualization, the process of visualization itself pre-dates computers. As you learn more concepts in computing you will be able to store more sophisticated kinds of data, process it in numerous ways, and use the expressive power of Processing to create rich visual representations. We like the following quote from Nathan Yau:

> When you think of visualization as a medium rather than a monolithic tool, it's something much more flexible that can be used for a lot of things. It's also more exciting. You can tell stories with data through analysis, journalism, or art. Visualization can be fun or serious; it can be beautiful and emotional or barebones and to the point.

The process of data visualization itself was formalized by Ben Fry in his PhD thesis in which he outlined the various stages of creating data visualizations: acquiring the data, parsing it, filtering it, mining it, choosing a visual representation, refining or improving the visual representation, and finally making the visualization interactive. The last, making it interactive, is where the power of computers combined with languages like Processing really shine. You saw examples of interactivity earlier in this book.

In terms of the type of data, visualizations can be characterized as:

- **Scientific Visualization**—Scientific data processing/representation algorithms. Scientific data tends to be all numerical, high precision and has relatively simple spatial relationships. The emphasis is on accurate representation of numerical proportions and realistic rendering of the physical properties. Scientific visualization also places importance on facilitating pattern finding in the graphed data that is difficult or impossible to see its raw form.

- **Data Visualization**—Social/economical data and statistical methods. This category of data used to primarily consist of survey data commonly obtained in the social sciences and the census. This type of data tends to be highly categorical and have strong association with physical locations/coordinates on the map. However, with the explosion of social networks, the division between this and information visualization is increasingly blurred.

- **Information Visualization**—Abstract data representation techniques. Information visualization focuses on arbitrary or complex relationships where there are no clearly prescribed spatial representation choices. Communication is an important goal of information visualization, which leads to many visualizations designed solely to illustrate existing results (as compared to data exploration).

Next, we present an overview of a number of simple data visualization techniques for which you could create your own Processing applications using the concepts you have learned thus far. We have already seen a few visualization examples (bar chart, times series plot) in this chapter. The basis of every visualization is the decision over how to represent numbers with visual primitives so that the relative values of numbers (that is, how large or small a number is within a set) can be quickly deduced from visual cues. Most non-trivial data sets are multidimensional, which means they contain multiple sets of numbers related to each other in meaningful ways that complicates a visualization design because those relationships must be clearly and correctly represented.

Mapping Numbers

We begin our exploration of visualization techniques with a simple data set from Jer Thorp, who is a data artist in residence at the *New York Times*. His visualization work is regularly used in the pages of the *New York Times*, *The Guardian*, *Scientific American*, *The New Yorker*, and *Popular Science*. He asked his Twitter followers for a random number between 0 and 99 and collected 225 of them within an hour. Using this data set of 225 whole numbers, each between 0 and 99 he wanted to find out how "random" a particular number is in the human psyche. It has long been reported that primes appear significantly more frequently when a distribution is picked by humans. In particular, 17 is often claimed to be the most (or least) random number between 1 and 20, as demonstrated by a number of psychology experiments. Clearly, humans don't make very good random number generators. Using a mapping visualization can enable one to see if the 225 numbers randomly picked by Thorp's followers bears this out. Using a frequency count of each number in the data set mapping can be employed as a simple visualization technique. Several ways of doing mapping are shown in Figures 5-11 and 5-12 (the visualization is split into two figures due to its wide size) and others are also discussed later.

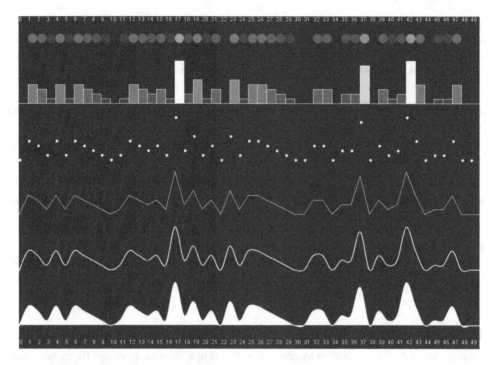

Figure 5-11. Basic plots: mapping Thorp's data set from 0-49

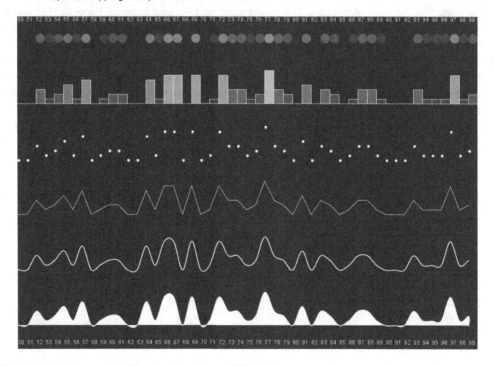

Figure 5-12. Basic plots: mapping Thorp's data set from 50-99

Basic Plots

Given that we have 225 numbers and 100 values, each value should occur 2.25 times if things were truly well distributed. In our data, 17 is indeed well above average. It is the top choice appearing 9 times, along with 42. A disclaimer should be put in for 42 due to its connection to the *Hitchhiker's Guide to the Galaxy*. Also note that most numbers ending in 7 were more frequently occurring than they should.

The dots on the very top are the only visualization generated without the frequency count. Instead, they were created with a clever exploit of the alpha values. A loop was run through all 225 input values and a transparent dot (with alpha value 28) was placed in the appropriate place along the x-axis for each number. Thus, those numbers that were not picked at all (such as 0, 10, 30, etc.) didn't have any dot drawn, and those that appeared multiple times had multiple semi-transparent dots drawn on top of each other, resulting in brighter final dots. Mapping values to color/transparency intensities is a common visualization technique that adds a valuable information dimension.

Also notice the problems introduced by the curved plots, where the curved approximations deviated from the true values, particularly noticeable in consecutive 0 valued numbers such as 48–51 and 90–92. This artifact typically appears when the baseline is chosen too closely to the lowest occurring values in the data set.

An important point to remember about this simple data set is that it is only two dimensional. Each data point has two values - the actual number and its frequency count. However, one of the values - the numerical value is not very meaningful, in that the numbers 17, 42, etc. do not convey any additional information relative to each other. Thus the order in which the numbers are arranged on the X-axis (strictly increasing) is chosen fairly arbitrarily and there is a fair amount of flexibility here that can lead to other visualization choices that we shall see later.

Time Series

A time series visualization generally looks quite similar to the basic visualization forms given here, except that the data set has an added dimension of time, that is, each data point has a value (or values) and an associated time stamp and the X-axis is reserved for visualizing the timeline. You have already seen a detailed example of how to create a time series visualization in this chapter.

Heat Maps

A heat map is a graphical representation where the data values are mapped to color intensities. The name *heat map* refers to the popular color-encoding where high values are encoded to hotter colors such as reds and yellows and smaller values are encoded to greens and blues. However, a heat map can have any color encoding that is convenient. Using the previous Thorp data set from, we can draw a 10x10 heat map grid (see Figure 5-13), In the heat map shown, frequency counts are mapped to reds of different intensities — brighter reds for larger values and darker reds for smaller values. A mouseover interaction was added for each square so that the raw value can be seen interactively. Notice how in this representation, the high frequencies of the 7-ending numbers show much more clearly, because they are aligned in the same column.

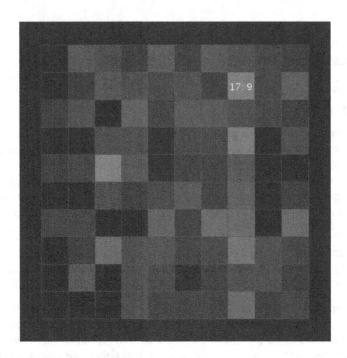

Figure 5-13. A heat map of Thorp's data set

The important advantage of a heat map is its ability to represent data that are fundamentally two dimensional. Traditional charting and plotting schemes like the ones you saw before do not handle that very well, because one of the dimensions (typically the height) is already used up to represent the values of the data. Next we show heat map visualization on true two dimensional data - dates. The data set is taken from a 2006 New York Times article reporting on the numbers of babies born on each day between 1973 and 1999. The original article gave a numerical table only, ranking all 366 days of a year based on the total number of cumulative births. A heat map visualization based on the table is given in Figure 5-14.

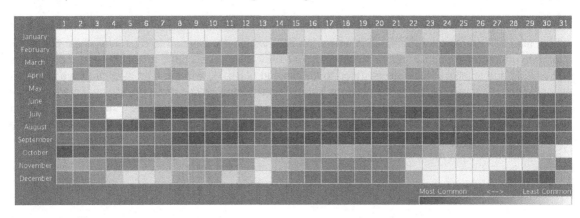

Figure 5-14. Heat map number of babies born in the United States between 1973-1990 *(The New York Times,* "How Common is Your Birthday?", http://www.nytimes.com/2006/12/19/business/20leonhardt-table.html?_r=1, 12/19/2006, referenced 7/26/2012.)

The month of September is clearly the top ranked birthday month, followed by July and August. Also of interest are the lower ranks for major holidays: 4th of July, Thanksgiving, and Christmas. What this visualization does not show us is how much more popular September 16th is (#1) versus September 9th (#2). Was it 1 more baby or 100,000 more babies? This shows the limitation of a heat map visualization, where numerical data must be encoded into colors that are integers and are thus forced into a uniform distribution during the process.

Proportional Symbols

A fundamental challenge of visualization design is how to add more information dimensions to a 2D display space without introducing clutter. Naturally, we can consider 3D visualization techniques, but navigation in a 3D world via a 2D display device introduces other complications and adding dimensions this way is not scalable. Heat maps are great examples of using color to add an information dimension. Besides color, size is another popular encoding choice and is often used in conjunction with colors.

Figure 5-15 shows Jer Thorp's random number data set visualized with proportionally sized circles and text. In addition, placement as well as color were also chosen based on the individual data frequency values. The circles were placed on a spiral starting with the largest from the center, which requires sorting the numbers based on their frequencies.

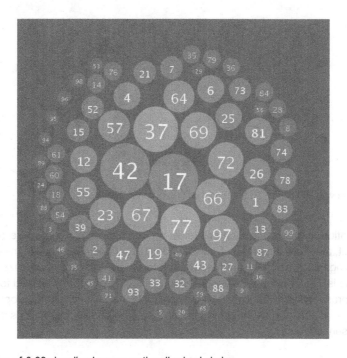

Figure 5-15. Frequencies of 0-99 visualized as proportionally sized circles

Similar techniques are frequently used in word clouds (Wordle, for example) and text-analysis-based visualizations in general. Figure 5-16 is a visualization of a student's tweet word frequency over a three-month period. For more details on the spiral fit as well as word cloud generation, please refer to Chapter 7. In general, such visualizations require parsing, word frequency counting and sorting. After a list of words is sorted by frequency, word tiles with proportionally chosen fonts/colors/transparencies are created based on the frequencies and a packing algorithm is used to fit/arrange the word tiles into the display space.

Figure 5-16. Word cloud visualization of Twitter feed with proportionally sized word tiles

Despite the formalization, data visualization still relies on one's creativity and sense of aesthetics. Also, as Nathan Yau points out, there are a number of do's and don'ts that one must keep in mind. These include obvious, yet important things such as checking the data that forms the basis of a visualization to make sure that it is free of errors and is valid. Moreover, all visualizations should be properly labeled to include the coding(s) used in the visual representations, labeling the axes, including the units, citing the proper sources, and so on. Visual representations, as effective as they may be, can also create false impressions if there are flaws in the geometry of the chosen graphics.

Algorithms and Issues of Space and Time

One of the key aspects of the science of computing is the characterization of algorithms underlying all the programs or sketches we write. Algorithms and pseudocode were introduced earlier in the book. You can think of an algorithm as an abstract description of a way to solve a given problem. Essentially, algorithms are detailed recipes. They have been in existence long before computers were. In fact, for any given problem, there may be several possible ways of solving it. Just think about how many ways there are to get from your campus to your home: you could walk, bike, drive, take a bus, a boat, a train, a plane, or any combination of these. Which way you decide to go may depend on several factors: How long should the trip take? What will it cost? and so on. You will often find yourself making several tradeoffs. For example, you might decide to go home a day later because a friend might be willing to give you a ride. This is also the case with algorithms. If there are many different ways to solve any given problem, how do you decide which one you should use? In this section we give you a brief glimpse into the science of algorithms.

Computers, as you know, come in all shapes and sizes. And hence they also vary in amounts of computational resources: the amount of memory (space), and the capacity and speed of the processor. The speed of a processor can determine how long a given problem will take to solve (time). In the computing industry, computing speeds are classified based on official benchmark computations that calculate speeds in terms of the number of floating-point operations per second, or *flops*. A typical laptop or a desktop these days is capable of delivering speeds between ½ to 1 Gflops (gigaflops or 10^9 flops). The world's fastest computer can deliver computing speeds characterized by Pflops (petaflopsflops or 10^{15} flops). That is over a million times faster and costs many millions of dollars to build one. The amazing thing about characterizing algorithms is that even at these blazing speeds, we know of several problems that would take a gazillion years to solve on even the fastest computers! Theoretical computer scientists tend to characterize a solution to the problem (that is, an algorithm) in terms of an estimate of the number of operations it may take to solve it, without regards to the speed of the computer on which it may be solved. For example, designing a program to play the game of chess so that it guarantees a win, or in the worst case, a draw, requires approximately 10^{65} operations to make a single move. Computer scientists call such problems *uncomputable* because no matter how fast a computer you may have, it will still take several billion lifetimes to make one move. They have created an elaborate vocabulary for discussing problems and classifying them as *solvable* (problems that we know how to solve), *unsolvable* (there is no known solution to the problem), *computable* (a solution can be computed in a reasonable amount of time), or *uncomputable* (a solution cannot be computed in a reasonable amount of time), based on the characterizations, over space and time, of their algorithms.

To make things more concrete, let's look at the stock price visualization sketch from the perspective of a computer scientist. First, let's explore the amount of space or computer memory that will be needed by the sketch. As you already know, every variable that is defined in your program ultimately requires one or more bytes of the computer's memory to store its value(s). For example, the stock visualization sketch has the following variable declarations at the top:

```
float[] price;
float minPrice, maxPrice;
float X1, Y1, X2, Y2;
```

How much space is required for these variables? We will need one cell to store the reference to the array price, and six cells to store the floating point variables. If each cell required four bytes of memory, we would need a total of 28 bytes of memory. Given that even a laptop these days comes with at least a few gigabytes of memory (1 gigabyte = 10^9 bytes), it is not worthwhile to fret over 28 bytes required by a program! However, space requirements do tend to explode very quickly even in the simplest of programs. For example, in the setup() function of the sketch we use the following:

```
String[] lines = loadStrings("AAPLStock.txt");
  // How long is the dataset
  price = new float[lines.length];
```

How much memory is required to store the data in the variables lines and price? If our dataset has 252 entries, as was the case in our sketch, then price would require a total of 252 x 4 = 1008 bytes. Computer scientists would say approximately 1 kbyte (1 kilobyte = 2^{10} or 1,024 bytes), still a miniscule amount considering typical memory sizes in a computer. Now, think about how much memory will be required for reading in the lines array. Each line is input as a string, and each character requires 2 bytes of memory. Each line in the input file is of the form:

```
1,4,2010,213.43,214.50,214.01,17633200
1,5,2010,214.60,215.59,214.38,21496600
1,6,2010,214.38,215.23,210.97,19720000
...
...
12,29,2010,326.22,326.45,325.29,5826400
12,30,2010,325.48,325.51,323.66,5624800
12,31,2010,322.95,323.48,322.56,6911000
```

That is, approximately 40 characters are required to store each line and hence the lines array, for a dataset of 252, would require approximately 20 kbytes of storage. Again, this is not a problem for today's computers. Once you have the sketch completed, you could try it on the entire history of the stock prices of Apple Inc. (or for any other company!). Apple started trading publicly in December 1980 and thus you can estimate that for approximately 250 trading days in each year for the last 32 years (up to 2012) that would be 250 x 20K x 32 bytes of data. That is approximately 160 megabytes of raw data that would need to be read into the lines array!

Let's formalize this a little more. If one line of input data requires 80 bytes of storage, how much storage do N lines of data require? The answer is simple: 40 x N bytes. That is, the storage requirements of the sketch we wrote increase linearly in proportion to N. The number of data items, N, is considered the *size* of the problem. And the space requirements of the program vary linearly in proportion to N.

With several gigabytes making up your computer's memory you seldom worry about the space issue. However, you do need to be aware of your program's space requirements. The more important consideration is the number of operations (or time): the number of operations it will take for the computer to perform all the computations specified in your program. Once again, this is characterized in terms of N, the size of the problem.

Given a dataset of size N, how many operations will be required to do all the computations specified in your sketch? Let's examine the following set of commands from the setup() function first:

```
for (int i=0; i<lines.length; i++) {
    // First split each line using commas as separator
    String[] pieces = split(lines[i], ",");
    // get the closing price of stock
    price[i] = float(pieces[5]);
}
```

For simplicity, we can abstract the preceding into the following algorithm:

```
Do N times {
    from each line, extract the closing stock price
}
```

While it is a simpler version, it captures the essence of the number of computational operations needed. If we assume that extracting the closing stock price takes K operations, then the above loop would require N x K operations. Once again, the relationship between the size of the problem (N) and the amount of time needed to do the computation is linear. These are called *linear time* algorithms. Next, consider the following, also from setup():

```
minPrice = min(price);
maxPrice = max(price);
```

It is not always the case that a single command is equivalent to one operation on the CPU. And this is certainly the case of the two preceding commands. Hidden in each of those commands are operations proportional to N. Here we present an algorithm to compute the smallest number in a given array of N numbers:

```
Assume that MIN is the first element of the array
for each of the remaining N-1 elements do the following {
    if the ith element is less than MIN {
        MIN = ith element of the array
    }
}

MIN now contains the smallest element in the array
```

As you can see, you have to go through all N elements to find and ensure that you have indeed computed the smallest element in the array. And because the loop is executed N–1 times, we can say that this too requires time linearly proportional to N. In the remainder of the sketch there are several loops that each iterate through all N values in the array. For example, look at the function drawGraph(). It is also linearly proportional to N. Thus most computations in the sketch are linearly proportional to N. Let's characterize it as M x N operations (where M << N and represents the total number of loops specified in the program).

For a quick example of a tradeoff, consider finding the smallest (or largest) element in an array of sorted elements (sorted in ascending order). That is easy. Just pick the first element for the smallest and the last one for the largest. You need only one operation. However, what does it take to sort an array of numbers? We introduced the library sort() function earlier. Sorting, it turns out, is worse than linear in its time requirements. Most simple sorting algorithms require time proportional to N^2. We can easily show this in the following sorting algorithm:

```
For each location in the array starting from i = 0 going all the way to N-1
    Let j = location of the smallest element among i..N-1
    Swap the element at i and j
```

With a little more investigation you should be able to confirm that the above algorithm for sorting will take N^2 operations. This particular algorithm for sorting is called *selection* sort. Algorithms like these are called *quadratic time* algorithms. There are several sorting algorithms that we know of. Some are faster, proportional to $Nlog_2(N)$. In many applications where the smallest or largest element is frequently required, it may be better to spend the time required to sort the data once and for all and then use the single operation to find the value.

Also note that the draw() function is repeated 60 times/second. Thus, all the computations specified in draw() are to be executed 60 times each second. Will this have an effect on the performance of the sketch? When the dataset is relatively small (as in N = 252) the sketch will perform smoothly because M x N will be much smaller than 1 Gflop, the typical speed of today's laptops. However, as N increases, say to accommodate the entire 32-year history of Apple's stock, you may find the real time performance of the sketch degrade a little.

In general, developing computer programs to solve any problem requires one to design data representations (like choosing to use an array to store all values in a dataset) and to choose from among a set of alternative algorithms. These decisions lead to the space and time requirements of the program. Solutions vary in the amount of space (or computer memory) and the number of operations or computational time (seconds, minutes, hours, days, years) required on a computer. Here are some examples of problems and their characterizations:

- To compute the product of two numbers requires constant time: to a computer there is no difference between multiplying 5 by 2 or 5,564,198 by 9,256,760. These are called *constant time* algorithms.

- To find a number in an array of N unordered numbers takes time proportional to N, especially if the number you are looking for is not there. These are called *linear time* algorithms.

- To find a number in a list of N ordered numbers (say, in ascending order) requires at most $log_2(N)$ time. How? These are called *logarithmic time* algorithms.

- To transform an N x N pixel image (as you will see later in the book) by manipulating all its pixels takes time proportional to N^2 time. These are called *quadratic* algorithms.

- To find a path from one state to another, in a map of N states, given certain constraints, can take time proportional to b^d where b is the average number of neighbors of each state and d is the number of states that make up the solution. In general, many problems fall into the category N^k where N is the size of the problem. These are called *polynomial time* algorithms.

- There are also several *unsolvable* problems in the world.

You should be sure that you understand the characterization of the size of the problem, and how that leads to the determination of space and time requirements. When an algorithm is characterized as linear, or even quadratic in terms of its time requirements, we can solve fairly large sizes of the problem quite efficiently on today's computers. But you do have to watch out for large problem sizes, polynomial time algorithms, and uncomputable and unsolvable problems.

Summary

In this chapter you learned about how to use arrays to store and process datasets. Data stored in a file can be loaded into arrays, processed in different ways, and finally visualized using the drawing commands you learned earlier. You were introduced to basic data visualization techniques, including a detailed example of how to create time series visualizations. Finally, in this chapter, you got a flavor of thinking about algorithms in the context of issues of space and time complexity of computation.

References

"The Data Deluge." *The Economist*, February 25, 2010.

Floridi, Luciano. *Information: A Very Short Introduction*. New York, NY: Oxford, 2010.

Fry, Ben. *Visualizing Data. Exploring and Explaining Data with the Processing Environment*. Sebastopol, CA: O'Reilly, 2008.

Goodman, J. David, and Jennifer Preston. "How the KONY Tweet Went Viral." *New York Times*, March 9, 2012, http://thelede.blogs.nytimes.com/2012/03/09/how-the-kony-video-went-viral/.

United States Postal Service. http://about.usps.com/who-we-are/postal-history/first-class-mail-since-1926.pdf.

Yau, Nathan. *Visualize This: The Flowing Data Guide to Design, Visualization, and Statistics*. Indianapolis, IN: Wiley, 2011.

Jer Thorp, http://blog.blprnt.com/blog/blprnt/your-random-numbers-getting-started-with-processing-and-data-visualization, 4/11/2010, referenced 7/26/2012.

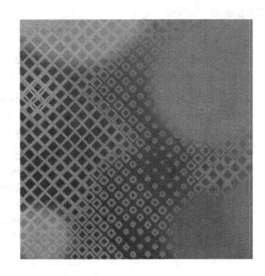

Chapter 6

Organizing Chaos

Prior to the development of modern computers, the word *computing* mostly implied numerical calculation. Today, computing encompasses all forms of electronic manipulation of objects: numbers, text, sound, music, photographs, movies, genes, etc., and even ideas! Computing can be used as an extension of your mind. It is in this form that a computer becomes an enormously powerful device. You might be wondering, how do computers manipulate ideas? Well, not quite in the sense you might have imagined. If you think about objects like numbers, text, sound, music, and even genes and how we are able to process them or do computing with them, then the notion of representing and processing of ideas is not so farfetched. In fact, creative coding is all about the computational representation and manipulation of ideas. The key enabler here is the ability to *represent* the thing that you are interested in inside a computer and then manipulate it. Most modern programming languages provide facilities for specifying and modeling any object. Further, there is also a need to keep programs organized into modules corresponding to their logical components. You have already seen some rudimentary forms of modularization facilitated by functions. Functions help modularize as well as parameterize specific tasks. Subcomponents that make up a program can be further organized into modules that can serve not only to keep the overall program organized but also to provide the ability to design and create *reusable* components that could be used in several programs. In this chapter, we will introduce you to a program design methodology called *object-oriented programming* or OOP. OOP facilitates the design and modeling of objects in an organized and coherent manner.

To get you motivated, consider the popular mobile game app Angry Birds designed by the Finnish video game developer Rovio Entertainment Inc. (www.rovio.com). The game app, originally launched in December 2009, surpassed 1 billion downloads in May 2012. If you have been hiding under a desolate rock the last few years, here is a quick capsule summary of the game: the green pigs have stolen the bird's eggs and are hiding inside buildings and other structures. The birds are angry, have projectile destructive powers and you, the player, can help the birds dish out revenge on the pigs by launching them from a catapult.

Angry Birds is a *physics-based* game. Objects in the game obey simple laws of physics. The genius behind the success of the game lies in a unique combination of artistic design, a simple back story, and requires a combination of logic, skill, and brute force to win the most points.

Imagine if you were part of the team at Rovio that created this app. You would have at least a dozen or more programmers in the team working on designing and coding the app. As mentioned previously, several organizational techniques are employed in keeping a project like this from disintegrating into total chaos. When Niklas Hed, one of the creators of Angry Birds, was young, one of the programs he wrote was to create a bouncing ball (see Figure 6-1 for an idea of what this entails). We are going to use the bouncing ball as an example to help you learn the basics of OOP design and how to implement it in Processing.

Angry Bird	Ball
Properties: type color size position ... **Behaviors:** launch fly screech ...	**Properties:** size position color ... **Behaviors:** move bounce display ...

Figure 6-1. Properties and behaviors of Angry Bird and ball objects

Objects: Attributes and Behavior

The key insight underlying object-oriented design is to think about programming problems the same way you might model problems in the real world. It is a way to identify, extract, and abstract the most important aspects of things in the problem domain. For example, in the Angry Birds game, the birds do not have any feet or feathers to flutter, mostly fly as projectiles, bounce around when hit, and so on. Each problem domain has a set of objects that typically interact with one another. The green pigs are green, sometimes wear helmets, and mostly sit in one place, until hit by another object (a piece of a wall or a bird), and explode or die when the impact of a hit is strong enough. The "castles" or structures themselves are objects. The basic building block in object-oriented design, the most important conceptual basis, is an *object*. Objects possess *properties* or *attributes* and are capable of some functionality or *behavior*. Birds in the game, for example, have properties like their color, size, position, velocity, type of bird, and so on. Functionality of a bird includes a launch operation, the flying motion, the screeching, and so on. The bouncing ball has attributes specifying its size, current position, and color, with behaviors like move, bounce, and display. See Figure 6-1.

> Try This: Think of other kinds of objects you may have come across in solving problems earlier. For example, the dataset of stock prices from Chapter 5 or some other object like a starship, a bank account, or a birthday party. Can you identify the objects, their attributes, and their behavior? Next, think about an entire problem domain, the kinds of objects it might have, and their relevant properties and behaviors.

Classes: Object Factories

In a typical program, or problem domain, there are several objects of the same kind: several Angry Birds, many bouncing balls, several bank accounts, etc. In OOP, objects are defined using *classes*. A class essentially defines the objects and serves as a factory for creating or *instantiating* specific objects. My car, for example, is a specific instantiation of the 2012 VW Passat models made by the Volkswagen Company. It is unique, in that it has a unique VIN or Vehicle Identification Number, but it is similar in most other respects to all the other Passats manufactured in the 2012 edition. They all have several attributes (like color, number of doors, etc.), and functionalities or behaviors whose manifestations might distinguish one from another and yet they all belong to the same class.

The preceding descriptions of Angry Bird and Ball are considered class definitions. Given a class, say Ball, one can create (or *instantiate*) several objects from it. For example, three balls labeled b1, b2, and b3. Each of the balls has the same internal structure as defined by the class and yet they each are distinct objects distinguished by the different values of their properties. Ball b1 might be small in size, green in color as opposed to b2, which might be large and blue. Before we discuss behaviors further, let's make what we have learned more concrete in terms of programming a given object-oriented design in Processing.

Object-Oriented Programming in Processing

Remember, the point of object-oriented design is to organize potentially chaotic large programs into manageable, logical components. After you have outlined the classes or objects required for your program, you can use the object-oriented programming features of Processing to do the coding. Let's begin by defining the Ball class outlined previously. We will start small, so as to grasp the fundamentals of OOP design, as well as their implementation in Processing. As we proceed, we will add more sophistication to our programs by way of extending and enhancing the design. Here is how you can define the Ball class:

```
class ball {      // Define the ball class

    // Attributes
    float x, y;           // the x and y location
    color ballColor;      // its color
    float radius;         // its radius in pixels

} // class ball
```

This code defines a class called ball. Attributes of the class are defined as variables (they are also sometimes called *fields*). Thus, x and y specify the x- and y- coordinates of the ball's position, ballColor, and radius will be used to store the color and size, respectively. The class syntax is very simple:

```
class ClassName {
    // Attributes
    ...
    // Behaviors
    ...
}
```

To define any class, you have to specify the name of the class in the structure as shown previously. Attributes or properties are defined as regular variables inside the body of the class.

Defining a class is essentially equivalent to defining a new *type name* in Processing. That is, just like the type names int, float, etc. you have extended processing's type names by an additional type, ball. Now, you can define variables of type ball:

```
ball b1, b2, b3;
```

As we discussed in Chapter 5, ball is considered as an *aggregate type*. It is an aggregate of all the properties and behavior defined in the class. Also, from what you learned earlier, the variables b1, b2, and b3 are reference variables and after the above definition, their values will be null. Next, we learn how to create an instance of the ball object. For that, the class definition has to include a *constructor*. A constructor is a set of instructions that will be executed each time you create a new object, or instance of a class. The name of the constructor, in Processing, is the same as the name of the class (see below). In addition, there are two things needed here. First, you need to create a new instance of a ball object. This is done, similar to arrays, using the new command:

```
b1 = new ball();
```

The constructor is defined inside the class definition as shown here:

```
class ball {     // Define the ball class

    // Attributes
    float x, y;       // the x and y location
    color ballColor;  // its color
    float radius;     // its radius in pixels

    // Constructor
    ball() {
        // The ball has an initial random location in the sketch window
        x = random(width);
        y = random(height);

        // All balls are red
        ballColor = color(255, 0, 0);
```

```
  // All balls are of radius 25  pixels
  radius = 25;
} // ball()

} // class ball
```

The constructor is invoked whenever a new object is created. It serves the purpose of creating an actual object residing in the computer's memory. The memory allocated contains space for storing all the object's attributes and their values. Additionally, when an object is constructed or instantiated, the constructor is responsible for setting the initial values of the properties of the object being created. In the preceding code, the x- and y- locations (x and y) are set to a random location in the sketch window; the color (ballColor) is set to red, and the radius to 25 pixels. In the following set of commands:

```
b1 = new ball();
b2 = new ball();
b3 = new ball();
```

Three ball objects are created. They will all be red in color, 50 pixels in diameter, and located on three random places in the sketch. To see the three ball objects rendered in the sketch you have to define the display() behavior. Behaviors are defined as functions in the class body following the constructor. For example, the behavior to draw a ball object (display()) is shown here:

```
class ball {     // Define the ball class

  // Attributes
  float x, y;          // the x and y location
  color ballColor;     // its color
  float radius;        // its radius in pixels

  // Constructor
  ball() {
    // The ball has an initial random location in the sketch window
    x = random(width);
    y = random(height);
    // All balls are red
    ballColor = color(255, 0, 0);

    // All balls are of radius 25  pixels
    radius = 25;
  } // ball()

  // Behaviors
  void display() {
    // display the ball
    // set color attributes
    noStroke();
    fill(ballColor);
    // draw the ball
    ellipse(x, y, 2*radius, 2*radius);
  } // display()
} // class Ball
```

We now have a minimal, but usable class definition of a ball object. The structure of the complete program shows how to create and display three balls in the sketch window:

```
// Sketch: 6-1: Creating and displaying three ball objects

ball b1, b2, b3;

void setup() {
  size(400, 400);
  smooth();
  // create the balls
  b1 = new ball();
  b2 = new ball();
  b3 = new ball();
} // setup()

void draw() {
  background(255);

  // display the balls
  b1.display();
  b2.display();
  b3.display();
} // draw()

class ball {     // Define the ball class

  // Attributes
  float x, y;           // the x and y location
  color ballColor;      // its color
  float radius;         // its radius in pixels

  // Constructor
  ball() {
    // The ball has an random location in the sketch window
    x = random(width);
    y = random(height);

    // All balls are red
    ballColor = color(255, 0, 0);

    // All balls are of radius 25  pixels
    radius = 25;
  } // ball()

  // Behaviors
  void display() {
    // display the ball
    // set color attributes
    noStroke();
    fill(ballColor);
```

```
    // draw the ball
    ellipse(x, y, 2*radius, 2*radius);
  } // display()

} // class ball
```

> Try This: Enter the preceding sketch and run it a few times. Try to modify the attributes
> (x, y, radius, ballColor) in the Ball class constructor and observe the outcomes. Try
> creating an array of ten Ball objects and drawing them.

Figure 6-2. Three ball objects

In OOP terminology, functions defined inside classes are also called *messages* or *methods*. Thus, the display()
behavior defined in the ball class is the method for drawing ball objects. The syntax for invoking methods on
an object is shown here:

object.method(...);

The way to read the preceding syntax is to say, "apply **method** to **object**," or "send the message **method** to
object." In your programs, you may have other kinds of objects, like green pigs, for example. How a green pig
is drawn will be specified by a display() method inside the class definition for green pig objects. Thus, in your
program you may have:

```
ball b1, b2, b3;
greenPig p1, p2, p3;
```

After these objects are instantiated, you might want to draw some of these objects:

```
b1.display();
p3.display();
```

Which display() method will be executed for b1? For p3? The ones defined in their respective classes. This is
one of the advantages of OOP-- you can define several methods by the same name (such as display()). The
type of object the method is applied to determines which specific display() method is executed.

Customizing Instances

All the `ball` objects created so far were defined to be of same size and color. What if you wanted to customize each object's size, color, or location? This is done by specifying parameters to the constructor as shown here:

```
ball(float px, float py, float r, color c) {
    // set up ball
    // with position (px, py)
    x = px;
    y = py;

    // radius, r pixels
    radius = r;

    // color, c
    ballColor = c;
} // ball()
```

Now, for example, you can create a completely customized `ball` object:

```
ball b1 = new ball(width/2, height/2, 50, color(0));
```

It assigns to `b1` a `ball` object that is located in the center of the sketch, 100 pixels in diameter, and colored black. Often, it is also the case that you may just want to customize a selection of attributes: Say, the radius and color. Processing allows you to create multiple constructors with different parameters. Thus, in your class definition, you could define all of the following constructors:

```
// Default Constructor
ball() {
    // When created, the ball has a random location
    x = random(width);
    y = random(height);

    // All balls are red
    ballColor = color(255, 0, 0);

    // All balls are of size 50 pixels
    ballSize = 50;
} // ball()

ball(float px, float py, float r, color c) {
    // set up Ball with position (x, y)
    x = px;
    y = py;

    // size, r pixels
    radius = r;

    // color, c
    ballColor = c;
} // ball()
```

```
ball(float r, color c) {
  // set up ball with random position
  x = random(width);
  y = random(height);

  // radius, r pixels
  radius = r;

  // color, c
  ballColor = c;
} // ball()
```

The number and type of arguments used to define a constructor (or a function, or a method) denote its *signature*. For multiple definitions with the same name, as long as the signature is unique, you can define as many constructors (or functions, or methods) as you like. In the preceding code we have defined three constructors with the signatures shown here:

```
ball()
ball(float, float, float, color)
ball(float, color)
```

When you write the following statements:

```
// create the balls
b1 = new ball();
b2 = new ball(width/2, height/2, 50, color(0));
b3 = new ball(25, color(125, 125, 125));
```

The constructor corresponding to the matching signature, as determined by the number, type, and ordering of the arguments in the invocation, is called. A resulting sketch from the preceding statements is shown in Figure 6-3.

Figure 6-3. Customized ball objects

A Useful Keyword: this

Look carefully at the definition of the second ball constructor in the preceding example. Notice that we named its parameters px and py. What would happen if we named them x and y? This is shown here:

```
ball(float x, float y, float r, color c) {
  // set up ball with position (x, y)
  x = x;
  y = y;

  // radius, r pixels
  radius = r;

  // color, c
  ballColor = c;
} // ball()
```

We have only shown one constructor here. Notice that the names of the arguments of ball(), x and y, are the same as the position attributes. Thus, when you see the statements

```
x = x;
y = y;
```

it is not clear whether the attributes are being set to the values of the parameters. Can you tell which is which? If you remember the rules in Processing, if two or more variables with the same name are accessible in the same scope, the names refer to the variables which were defined most recently, and assignment operations occur form right to left. In the preceding, the x and y in both statements, on both sides of the =-operator refer to the parameters x and y and not the attributes. Thus, these statements will not have the desired effect of setting the values of attributes x and y to the values of parameters x and y. You have already seen one solution to this: name them differently. Another way around it, is to make use of the object qualifier, this. this is a variable name that refers to the current object when code inside a class is being executed. Using this you can write the preceding constructor as shown here:

```
class ball {    // Define the ball class

  // Attributes
  float x, y;            // the x and y location
  color ballColor;       // its color
  float radius;          // its size in pixels
  ...
  ball(float x, float y, float r, color c) {
    // set up Ball with position (x, y)
    this.x = x;
    this.y = y;

    // radius, r pixels
    this.radius = r;
```

```
        // color, c
      this.ballColor = c;
   } // ball()


   ...
} // class ball()
```

Now, which variable (attribute or parameter) is being referred is clear. Another convention that avoids using this that is commonly used in these circumstances is to prefix the parameter name with an underscore (_):

```
class ball {      // Define the ball class

   // Attributes
   float x, y;              // the x and y location
   color ballColor;         // its color
   float radius;            // its size in pixels
   ...
   ball(float _x, float _y, float r, color c) {
      // set up Ball with position (x, y)
      x = _x;
      y = _y;

      // radius, r pixels
      radius = r;

      // color, c
      ballColor = c;
   } // ball()


   ...
} // class ball()
```

An underscore (_) is a valid part of a variable name and thus can be used as shown here in these types of situations.

Inside a class, the specification of the this qualifier is optional. In fact, the use of this in setting the radius and color is not necessary because there is no ambiguity. It is a good idea, especially if you intend to use same names to mean different things in different contexts, to explicitly use this as a qualifier.

There are several other uses of the this keyword. For instance, you can use this(...) inside the constructor to invoke a single constructor that initializes objects:

```
// Default Constructor
ball() {
   this(random(width), random(height), color(255, 0, 0), 25);
} // ball()

ball(float r, color c) {
   this(random(width), random(height), r, c);
} // ball()
```

```
ball(float x, float y, float r, color c) {  // The main constructor
  // set up ball with position (x, y)
  this.x = x;
  this.y = y;

  // size, r pixels
  radius = r;

  // color, c
  ballColor = c;
} // ball()
```

Not only do you get more succinct code, you also reduce the chance of errors. Now, all initialization is done inside a single constructor. Other constructors just invoke the 'main' constructor where all initializations occur.

Many object-oriented programming languages use the name this to refer to the object. Others make explicit use of a self-reference name, which can be this, or self, or something else that you can define. It also comes in handy in situations where an object's attributes themselves are other objects. We will show this later in the chapter.

Tabs: Organizing Code

In the preceding example, we presented the code for the ball class in line with the rest of the program: setup(), followed by draw(), followed by the ball class definition. If your program has several classes, as it will later on, the Processing IDE provides an excellent way to organize them into separate files. In fact, from the very beginning in your coding process, you are encouraged to utilize the Tabs feature of the Processing IDE. Take a careful look at your previous program in the Processing IDE. We show a snapshot of our version in Figure 6-4.

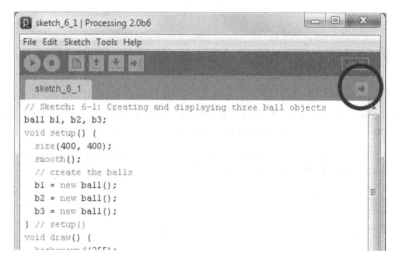

Figure 6-4. The Sketch_6_1 tab and where to look for new tabs (This figure is from a Beta version of Processing 2.0 and may look different.)

Notice how, just above the code, on the top left, the name of the sketch (Sketch_6_1) appears in a tab. In the IDE, your code can be organized into tabs, and each tab corresponds to a separate file in the sketch folder. In programs that use object-oriented design, it is a good idea to place each class separately in its own tab/file. Thus, your "main" program: the setup(), draw(), functions that use the classes and form the main part of your program, will be in the main tab. You can place each new class you define under a separate tab. To create a new tab, click on the small dark arrow, drawn in a shaded box, above the code, on top right (shown circled in Figure 6-4). You get a drop-down menu (see Figure 6-5).

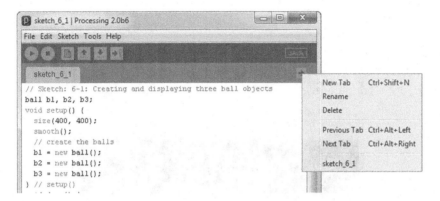

Figure 6-5. Creating a new tab (This figure is from a Beta version of Processing 2.0 and may look different.)

Select New Tab and you see a yellow text box where you have to enter the name of the class you are defining in the new tab. Enter the name of the class (ball) as shown in Figure 6-6, exactly as you intend to define it, and press the OK button. A new tab will be created with a fresh code window. Enter your code for the ball class in this new window. This is shown in Figure 6-7. As you can see, the code that defines the class is now separated from the code that uses it. You can define as many tabs as you like in this manner to keep your programs organized. The contents of each tab is stored in a separate file in the sketch folder. In the situation shown in Figure 6-7, the tab with the ball class is stored as a file ball.pde in the sketch folder.

Figure 6-6. Creating a new tab (This figure is from a Beta version of Processing 2.0 and may look different.)

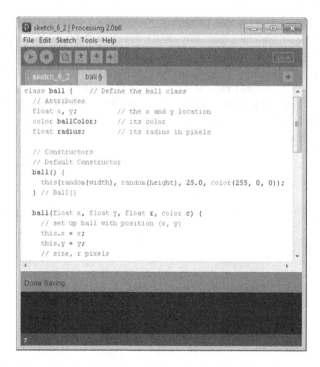

Figure 6-7. The ball tab (This figure is from a Beta version of Processing 2.0 and may look different.)

Defining Additional Behaviors: Motion

A number of creative effects can be generated by defining animations or motions of objects in sketches. Here we use the ball example to illustrate the design and implementation of simple motion. The movement of the object is modeled inside the move() method. To do the animation, the move() method can be used in draw() as follows (in the case of our example with three ball objects):

```
void draw() {
  background(255);

  // display the balls
  b1.move();
  b1.display();
  b2.move();
  b2.display();
  b3.move();
  b3.display();
} // draw()
```

That is, before displaying a ball, its position is updated (that is, moved to its next location). The movement of the ball itself can be modeled using simple approximations of physical behavior utilizing the speed (rate at which a ball travels). Speed can be modeled as an increment of the ball's position. (that is, the change in the balls x- and y- coordinates). Here is a very simple version:

```
void move() {
  x = x + dx;
  y = y + dy;
} // move()
```

You need to define dx and dy as additional attributes for the class ball as follows:

```
float dx = 1;
float dy = 1;
```

We have initialized dx and dy in the definition itself. Alternatively, you can just define the variables and later initialize them inside the constructor.

> Try This: Add the preceding code to your sketch and observe the behavior. Because the position of the ball changes by 1 in both x- and y- directions, the balls move diagonally across the screen, until eventually they leave the sketch window. We address that next. But first, experiment with different values of dx and dy. The way these are defined above, each ball travels at the same speed. You can easily vary each ball's speed by using random values:

```
float dx = random(1, 3);
float dy = random(1, 3);
```

Again, instead of initializing these in the definition, you can choose to initialize these in the constructor(s). To ensure that a ball stays within the bounds of the sketch window, you can additionally define a bounce behavior:

```
void bounce() {

  if (x > (width-radius)) {    // bounce against the right edge
    x = width-radius;
    dx = -dx;
  }

  if (x < radius) {    // bounce against the left edge
    x = radius;
    dx = -dx;
  }

  if (y > (height-radius)) {    // bounce against the bottom edge
    y = height-radius;
    dy = -dy;
  }

  if (y < radius) {    // bounce against the top edge
    y = radius;
    dy = -dy;
  }
} // bounce()
```

Each of the four if-statements tests to see whether the ball has reached an edge of the sketch window. Depending on which edge (left, right, top, or bottom) the displacement (dx or dy) is negated so that the ball reverses direction. Additionally, notice the conditions are checking against the outer edge of the ball and not its center (represented by x, and y). Thus, the condition (x < radius) in the second if-statement is checking to see whether the left edge of the ball is less than the radius of the ball, implying that the ball has displaced beyond the left edge. In that case, we set the ball's center back to align it with the left edge (x = radius), and then reverse the x- direction (dx = -dx). These kinds of adjustments are typical in the world of graphics and animations where the increments, in terms of float values, can lead to the objects crossing the boundaries. By resetting the objects back to the boundary you can avoid situations where the animations go awry. Study this carefully, implement it by adding the bounce() method to the class ball and modifying the move() method as shown here:

```
void move() {
    x = x + dx;
    y = y + dy;

    bounce();   // check for a bounce
  } // move()
```

This implements a ball continuously bouncing from the "walls" of the sketch. Alternatively, you can model a different behavior where the ball behaves like a bouncing ball using a model of *gravity*. Gravity is simply acceleration or the rate at which the speed changes. In this instance, we will be modeling the balls falling from top to bottom. This is implemented in the following definition of move():

```
void move() {
  x = x + dx;
  y = y + speed;
  speed = speed + gravity;

  // check to see if it bounces
  bounce();
} //move()
```

We will need to define four additional attributes for the ball objects:

```
float speed = 5.0;          // The speed at which the ball is moving
float gravity = 0.1;        // the rate of increase of speed
float dx = 1;               // amount of lateral movement
float dampen = -0.9;        // amount of dampening after each bounce
```

Given these definitions, let's try to understand the model of a ball's motion. Each time move() is called, the ball's x- position (x) is updated by dx, its y- position (y) is updated by speed, and speed is updated by gravity. We have used some initial values for speed (5.0), gravity (0.1), and dx (1). You can feel free to experiment with these in your sketch (see below). Further, when a ball reaches the bottom of the sketch window it should bounce. The complete sketch, including the new version of the bounce() method is shown here:

```
// Sketch: 6-2: Creating and displaying three ball objects

ball b1, b2, b3;

void setup() {
  size(400, 400);
  smooth();

  // create the balls
  b1 = new ball();
  b2 = new ball();
  b3 = new ball();
} // setup()

void draw() {
  background(255);
  // display the balls
  b1.move();
  b1.display();
  b2.move();
  b2.display();
  b3.move();
  b3.display();
} // draw()

// Sketch: 6-2: File ball.pde

class ball {     // Define the ball class
```

```
// Attributes
float x, y;            // the x and y location
color ballColor;       // its color
float radius;          // its radius in pixels
float speed = 5.0;     // The speed at which the ball is moving
float gravity = 0.1;   // the rate of increase of speed
float dx = 1;          // amount of lateral movement
float dampen = -0.9;   // amount of dampening after each bounce

// Constructors
// Default Constructor
ball() {
  this(random(width), random(height), 25.0, color(255, 0, 0));
} // Ball()

ball(float x, float y, float r, color c) {
  // set up ball with position (x, y)
  this.x = x;
  this.y = y;
  // size, r pixels
  radius = r;
  // color, c
  ballColor = c;
} // ball()

ball(float r, color c) {
  this(random(width), random(height), r, c);
} // ball()

// Behaviors

void display() {
  // display the ball
  // set color attributes
  noStroke();
  fill(ballColor);

  // draw the ball
  ellipse(x, y, 2*radius, 2*radius);
} // display()

void move() {
  x = x + dx;
  y = y + speed;
  speed = speed + gravity;

  // check to see if it bounces
  bounce();
} //move()
```

```
void bounce() {
  if (x > (width-radius)) {    // bounce against the right edge
    x = width-radius;
    dx = -dx;
  }

  if (x < radius) {    // bounce against the left edge
    x = radius;
    dx = -dx;
  }

  if (y > (height-radius)) {    // bounce against the bottom edge
    y = height-radius;
    speed = speed * dampen ;
  }
} // bounce()
} // class ball
```

Take a close look at the above code. In the bounce() method, if the ball has reached the edge of the sketch, we change the direction of the ball's lateral displacement (dx). Similarly, we check to see whether the ball has reached the bottom of the sketch window, if so, we negate, and decrement the speed. Notice also the use of the dampen variable to reflect a dampening of speed after each bounce. Study this code carefully and make sure you understand it.

> *Try This: Run the preceding sketch (including using a separate tab for the ball class). Next, play with the values of speed, gravity, and dx, as well as the dampening value of speed (dampen). Run the sketch over and over again and carefully observe the motion of each ball. You will need to adjust the values of various attributes to get visually pleasing bouncing behavior. Notice what happens when a ball is no longer bouncing. How can you make it stop? Hint: Think about modeling friction. As defined previously, each ball has the same starting values for speed, gravity, and dx. How can you modify the program so each ball has different starting values of these attributes?*

In the preceding example, we called the bounce() method inside the move() method. Alternatively, you could choose to invoke it from draw():

```
void draw() {
  ...
  b1.move();
  b1.bounce();
  b1.display();
  ...
} // draw()
```

You will notice that object-oriented design and development allows for incremental enhancements and, at the same time, keeps your programs well organized. Also, at each step, there are many decisions that need to be made: What attributes to add? How and when to initialize them? How are object instances customized? What behaviors are needed? How they are invoked? As you make these decisions you will be confronted with choices in the implementation. It is always possible to achieve the same behavior in a sketch out of many possible implementation choices. Which choices you make should be based on keeping a clean design, ensuring future extendibility, and providing as many opportunities for parameterization as might be sensible.

OOP and Encapsulation in Processing

One of the tenets of object-oriented programming is the idea of *encapsulation*. There are two key aspects to encapsulation, one of which you have now seen: it is a way of creating new aggregate types and bundling their data (attributes) and functionality (behavior/methods) together into a separate module (a class). This type of modularization is good for keeping programs organized. Additionally, it allows for reuse of useful classes of objects. The second, perhaps equally important aspect, of encapsulation is *information hiding*. This is a way of restricting access to some parts of an object's definition. For example, in the example in the previous section, the draw() function of the sketch uses the move() and display() methods on specific ball objects. We also saw two different definitions of move(): one to set the ball in linear motion, and one that implements a bouncing behavior. From the perspective of the draw() method (also called a *client* of the class ball), the details of how the motion is implemented are hidden. This type of *procedural abstraction* is already available via functions in any programming language. This type of modularization allows you to change the move() method without requiring any changes to the draw() method. This is considered good program design.

While it is straightforward to restrict the details of implementation of a class's methods, the issue of restricting access to a class's attributes requires further elaboration. Here is the fundamental question: Is it possible to access an object's attributes (and their values) outside the class? For instance, what happens when you do the following?

```
void setup() {
   ...
   b1 = new ball(...);
   b1.x = 42;
   ...
} // setup()
```

Encapsulation in object-oriented programming languages typically allows you, the programmer, to decide whether or not this is something you want to allow. If not, how do you restrict access to an object's attributes?

First of all, in Processing, you are allowed to have complete access to an object's attributes. That is, Processing's manifestation of object-oriented programming does not give you mechanisms for restricting such access. If it did, you would be able to designate each definition (attribute as well as method) in a class to be *public*, or *private*. Once you designate something as private, access to that attribute is no longer permitted outside of the class. In the example, in setup() where b1.x is being modified it will result in a compilation error. The programming language Java, which is an object-oriented language, and which is the underlying implementation substrate for Processing, allows the private or public designation of class definitions. Java allows all definitions to be prefixed with the keyword public or private:

```
public class Ball {
    private float x, y;
    ...
    public void move() {
    ...
    } // move()
    ...
} // class Ball
```

However, this Java feature is not available in Processing. As we mentioned previously, due to the way Processing is implemented on top of Java, all definitions in a sketch are considered public. So, it will be up to you to maintain discipline in your programs so as not to access those things which might be considered private in true object-oriented design. Sometimes, though, it is necessary to be able to do so in many situations (as we see in the next section).

PVector Class in Processing

In most sketches, as you have seen, it is important to keep track of an anchor point or the location, the x- and y- coordinates, of various objects being rendered. Processing provides a useful class, called PVector, to store 2-dimensional or 3-dimensional coordinate data. Now, that you have learned some basics of object-oriented programming, we can introduce this class to you via a preliminary definition:

```
class PVector {
    // Attributes
    float x;
    float y;

    PVector(float px, float py) {    // Constructor
        x = px;
        y = py;
    }  // PVector()

    // Behaviors...
    void add(PVector v) {
        x = x + v.x;
        y = y + v.y;
    } // add()
    ...
} // class PVector
```

That is, a PVector object has two attributes: x, and y. You have to specify values for x, and y when you create a new object. You can add one vector to another by adding their individual x and y components. Processing's PVector class allows for 3-dimensional coordinate data (so it also includes a z attribute). Addition and all other methods available in the PVector class (see Figure 6-9) are based on the concept of a *vector* in Cartesian geometry. Every point in space is described by its coordinates and represents a directional vector from the origin to the point (see Figure 6-8). All behaviors or functions provided in the PVector class implement various vector operations. For example:

```
PVector v = new PVector(7, 11);
PVector w = new PVector(2, 13);

v.add(w);
```

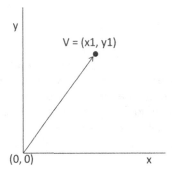

Figure 6-8. A vector

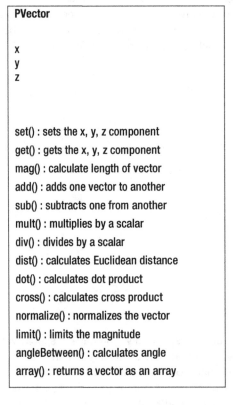

Figure 6-9. The PVector class

Here we define two vectors, v and w with initial values (7, 11) and (2, 13). Next, we add w to v. Vector addition involves adding each individual component (see preceding definition). Thus, after the call to add(), vector v will have values (9, 24) in its x and y components. Using the PVector class, for example, you could now write your ball class as follows (we have left out details of some constructors):

```
class ball {    // Define the Ball class
  // Attributes
  PVector location;          // ball's location (x, y)
  color ballColor;           // its color
  float radius;              // its radius in pixels
  PVector speed;             // dx and dy

  // Default Constructor
  ball() {
   this(random(width), random(height), 25, color(255,0,0));
  } // ball()

  ball(float x, float y, float r, color c) {
    // set up ball with position (x, y), radius r, color c
    location = new PVector(random(width), random(height));
    // radius, r pixels
    radius = r;
    // color, c
    ballColor = c;
    // speed at which the ball travels
    speed = new PVector(random(1, 3), random(1, 3));
  } // ball()

  // Behaviors
  void display() {
    // display the ball
    // set color attributes
    noStroke();
    fill(ballColor);
    // draw the ball
    ellipse(location.x, location.y, 2*radius, 2*radius);
  } // display()

  void move() {
    location.add(speed);
    bounce();
  } // move():

  void bounce() {
    if (location.x > (width-radius)) { // bounce against the right edge
      location.x = width-radius;
      speed.x = -speed.x;
    }
    if (location.x < radius) { // bounce against the left edge
      location.x = radius;
      speed.x = -speed.x;
    }
```

```
    if (location.y > (height-radius)) { // bounce against the bottom edge
      location.y = height-radius;
      speed.y = -speed.y;
    }
    if (location.y < radius) { // bounce against the top edge
      location.y = radius;
      speed.y = -speed.y;
    }
  } // bounce()
} // class ball
```

> Try This: Study the preceding class definition closely and be sure you understand the use of the PVector class. Implement the ball class as defined here. Write a sketch that creates several balls (use an array of Ball objects), and set them to motion.

> Try This: Modify the constructor so that the speed of each ball is set proportional to its size. That is, smaller balls move faster than larger balls.

Ball in a Box

As implemented in the previous section each ball object 'lives' inside the sketch window. Thus, all bounces are checked (inside bounce()) against the limits of the sketch window. In the next example, we will design a box class such that we can have many boxes, and several balls moving about inside each box. First, we give the implementation and design (see Figure 6-10) of the box class:

```
class box {
  float x, y, w, h;  // top left corner (x, y), width (w), height (h)
  int nBalls;        // # of balls in the box
  int ballRadius = 2;
  ball [] balls;     // place to store all the balls in this box

  // Constructor
  box(float x, float y, float w, float h, int n) {
    this.x = x;
    this.y = y;
    this.w = w;
    this.h = h;
    this.nBalls = n;
    // Create balls...
    balls = new ball[nBalls];
    for (int i=0; i < balls.length; i++) {
      balls[i] = new ball(w/2, h/2, ballRadius, color(0), this);
    }
  } // box()
```

```
    void display() {
    // draw box
    pushMatrix();
    translate(x, y);
    stroke(0);
    fill(255);
    rect(0, 0, w, h);

    // draw balls
    for (int i=0; i < balls.length; i++) {
      balls[i].display();
    }
    popMatrix();
    } // display()

    void update() {
    // move each ball...
    for (int i=0; i < balls.length; i++) {
      balls[i].move();
    }
    } // update
} // class box
```

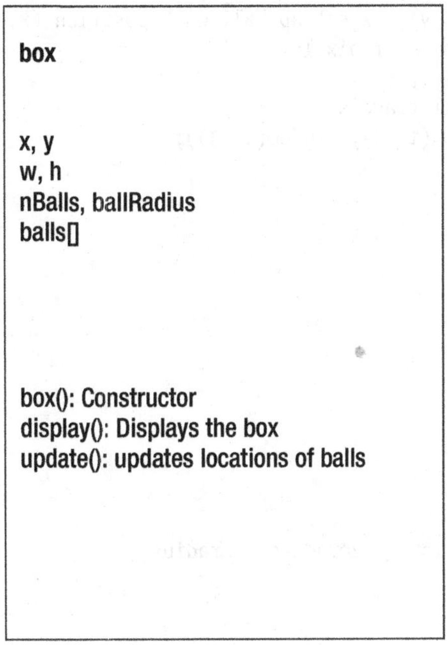

box

x, y
w, h
nBalls, ballRadius
balls[]

box(): Constructor
display(): Displays the box
update(): updates locations of balls

Figure 6-10. The box class

Each box object has attributes for its location (x, y), size (w, h), the number of ball objects in it (nBalls), the size of each ball (ballRadius), and a placeholder to store all the ball objects (balls[]).The first part of the box constructor is pretty straightforward. We are just copying the attribute values supplied as parameters into their respective variables. Next, the constructor creates the balls array, and creates new ball objects. To ensure that each ball object knows which box it is in (and therefore the bounds of the box), we pass a reference to the box object to each ball that is created. This is done using the this keyword variable. It allows a reference to the box object being created to the constructor of the ball class. The ball class has to be modified accordingly to store the enclosing box as an attribute and to use its bounds to decide on bounces. This is shown here:

```
class ball {     // Define the ball class

   // Attributes
   PVector location;        // ball's location
   color ballColor;         // its color
   float radius;            // its radius in pixels
   PVector speed;           // dx and dy

   box b;                   // ball is inside Box, b

   ball(box b) {     // Default Constructor
     this(random(width), random(height), 25, color(255, 0, 0), b);
   } // ball()

   ball(float x, float y, float r, color c, box _b) {
     location = new PVector(x, y); // set up ball with position (x, y), radius r, color c
     radius = r;          // radius, r pixels
     ballColor = c;       // color, c
     // speed at which the ball travels
     speed = new PVector(random(1, 3), random(1, 3));

     // Its enclosing box
     b = _b;
   } // ball()

   // Behaviors...
   void display() {
     // display the ball
     // set color attributes
     noStroke();
     fill(ballColor);

     // draw the ball
     ellipse(location.x, location.y, 2*radius, 2*radius);
   } // display()

void move() {
     location.add(speed);
     bounce();
   } // move()
```

```
void bounce() {
    if (location.x > (b.w-radius)) { // bounce against the right edge of box
      location.x = b.w-radius;
      speed.x = -speed.x;
    }
    if (location.x < radius) { // bounce against the left edge of box
      location.x = radius;
      speed.x = -speed.x;
    }
    if (location.y > (b.h-radius)) { // bounce against the bottom edge of box
      location.y = b.h-radius;
      speed.y = -speed.y;
    }
    if (location.y < radius) { // bounce against the top edge of box
      location.y = radius;
      speed.y = -speed.y;
    }
  } // bounce()
} // class ball
```

Finally, we show here, the main sketch program that creates a 200x200 box with 50 balls moving inside:

```
// Sketch 6-3: balls in a box
box b;

void setup() {
  size(400, 400);
  smooth();
  // Create a 200*200 box with 50 balls
  b = new box(100, 100, 200, 200, 50);
} // setup()

void draw() {
  background(255);
  // display the balls
  b.update();
  b.display();
} // draw()
```

> Try This: Implement the sketch above (an output is shown in Figure 6-11). Play around with various aspects: number of balls, ball colors, box color, ball motion, etc. Can you extend the sketch to incorporate the detection and response to collision between any two particles? Next, create a sketch that shows several boxes with balls moving around inside (see Figure 6-12).

Figure 6-11. Fifty balls in a box

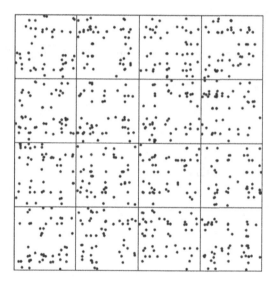

Figure 6-12. Many boxes with balls inside

Composition: Has-a Relationships

In the preceding example, we created the box class to contain several ball objects. That is, a box is an aggregation of several ball objects (in addition to its other attributes). In object-oriented terminology, this is called *composition* or creating *has-a* relationship (as in 'a box has several balls'). This further extends the organizing process such that the overall sketch has no idea that there is a separate ball class. It only knows about the box class and how to create box objects. The box class, in turn, has taken over the management of the existence of ball objects and their behavior. Object composition is considered an important design approach in object-oriented programming. Together with encapsulation it leads to well-organized programs that are considered easier to maintain, and extend over long period of program development and use.

Simulated Physics: Verlet Motion

Two kinds of `ball` motions were introduced so far in the chapter: linear translation at constant speed and an oscillating motion of a bouncing ball that simulates gravity to accelerate as it drops. Most models of motion of objects are due to Isaac Newton and his Laws of Motion. Newtonian motion can be modeled using *dynamics* (which take into account the forces acting upon a moving object) or *kinematics* which is simpler and involves only the temporal and spatial properties of an object. That is, given the current spatial location of an object, where is it going to be in the next time step. We have modeled this by defining the `update()` or `move()` method. Each call to the `move()` me thod is responsible for computing the spatial changes to the object. This can be easily seen here:

```
void move() {
  location.add(speed);
  bounce();
} // move()
```

Here we model velocity in the form of the relative change (as represented in `speed`) in the x and y coordinates of the object. In the bouncing ball model, we additionally added acceleration (in the form of the attribute `gravity`). The `speed` was reduced on each bounce, giving the effect of a dampening oscillation. In general, kinematic models of motion result in recognizable trajectories of particles: translation, rotation, and oscillation. Interesting properties arise when one or more of these are used in combination to define the motion of objects. For example, think about the trajectories of the birds in the Angry Birds game.

Loup Verlet, a physicist at MIT, pioneered the computational modeling of molecular dynamics in the 1960s. He introduced a simple technique for modeling trajectories of motion of particles that is commonly used in computer graphics. *Verlet integration*, as it has come to be called, involves computing the spatial position in the next time step based on the object's previous position. That is, in the simplest case where the object is moving at constant speed (that is, translating); the object continues to move at the same speed, in the same direction from its previous position. This is modeled by keeping track of an object's current as well as previous position:

$$Location_{t+1} = Location_t + (Location_t - Location_{t-1})$$

That is, in order to compute the location of an object in the next time step, add the difference from the previous time step to the current location. This equation also requires the specification of the initial conditions $Location_0$ and $Location_1$. To use Verlet integration to model the motion of the `ball` object, we will define an additional attribute, `oldLocation`:

```
PVector location;        // Current location of ball
PVector oldLocation;    // previous location of the ball
```

Then, the `move()` method can be defined as:

```
void move() {
  PVector temp = location.get();
  location.x += (location.x - oldLocation.x);
  location.y += (location.y - oldLocation.y);
  oldLocation.set(temp);

  bounce();
} // move()
```

215

Notice how you have to save the current position first before computing the next position. The get() method in the PVector class creates a copy of the location object which is then assigned to temp. The saved position is then assigned to the old position (using the PVector method set()). For the initial condition, we create a new variable called nudge that represents the amount of initial nudge (or push) on the object when it is created. Each time a new ball is created, its initial conditions are set up so that its $Location_0$ is the same location where it was created and its $Location_1$ is set to the position where it would end up after it is given the nudge. The attribute definitions of the ball class along with the constructor are shown here:

```
class ball {     // Define the Verlet ball class
  // Attributes
  color ballColor;         // its color
  float radius;            // its radius in pixels

  PVector location;        // current location of ball
  PVector oldLocation;     // previous location of ball
  PVector nudge;           // initial push

  // Default Constructor
  ball() {
     this(new PVector(random(width), random(height)), 10);
  } // ball()

  ball(PVector loc, float r) {
    // set up ball with position (x, y), radius r
    location = loc;
    // radius, r pixels
    radius = r;
    // color
    ballColor = color(0);

    // Set up verlet initial conditions
    oldLocation = location.get();
    nudge = new PVector(random(1, 3), random(1, 3));
    location.add(nudge);
  } // ball()
```

The display() method remains unchanged, however, you do have to make changes in the bounce() method to account for the additional bookkeeping on the old location. Also, each time a bounce is detected, the initial conditions have to be set up again using nudge:

```
void bounce() {
  if (location.x > (width-radius)) { // bounce against the right edge
    location.x = width-radius;
    oldLocation.x = location.x;
    location.x -= nudge.x;
  }
```

```
if (location.x < radius) { // bounce against the left edge
  location.x = radius;
  oldLocation.x = location.x;
  location.x += nudge.x;
}
if (location.y > (height-radius)) { // bounce against the bottom edge
  location.y = height-radius;
  oldLocation.y = location.y;
  location.y -= nudge.y;
}
if (location.y < radius) { // bounce against the top edge
  location.y = radius;
  oldLocation.y = location.y;
  location.y += nudge.y;
}
} // bounce()
```

Make sure to study and understand the preceding code. At each bounce, the current location is saved to the old location (just the x- or the y- location is affected depending on the bounce) and updated by the nudge amount.

> *Try This: Complete and implement the preceding code by writing a sketch program to create one or more balls and then set them to motion. Observe the behavior and compare it to the version with simple translation. Do you see anything different?*

While the behavior appears the same, changing the underlying model to use Verlet integration has several advantages. The payoff occurs, as we will see next, when you have multiple balls that are connected to each other using rigid objects. Consider the simplest situations where two balls are connected using a stick (see Figure 6-13). The stick constrains the individual movement of the balls. If using the Verlet integration model, it is possible to generate a natural spring-like constraint that preserves the motion of the balls yet keeps them springing within the constraints of the length of the stick connecting them. The stiffness (or "springiness") of the stick can be manipulated.

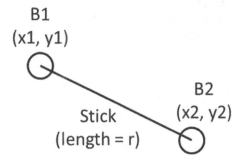

Figure 6-13. Two balls and a stick

Two Balls and a Stick: An Application of Verlet Integration

Figure 6-13 depicts a typical scenario where two balls ($\vec{B1}$ and $\vec{B2}$) are being constrained by a stick of length r. Despite the fact that each ball moves based on its own model of motion, the following Verlet equations restrict the motion of the balls to within the constraints of the length of the stick.

$$\vec{\Delta} = \vec{B1} - \vec{B2}$$

$$Length(\vec{\Delta}) = \parallel \vec{\Delta} \parallel = \sqrt{\Delta_x^2 + \Delta_y^2}$$

$$d = \frac{\parallel \vec{\Delta} \parallel - r}{\parallel \vec{\Delta} \parallel}$$

$$\vec{B1} = \vec{B1} + \vec{\Delta}\, Kd/2$$

$$\vec{B2} = \vec{B2} - \vec{\Delta}\, Kd/2$$

At first, the two ball positions, represented by $\vec{B1}$ and $\vec{B2}$ are unconstrained. The equations that follow determine how to change $\vec{B1}$ and $\vec{B2}$ so that the distance between them is constrained by the length of the stick, r. K is the stiffness constant ($0 \leq K \leq 1$). These simple equations result in interesting simulated behavior of a motion of two balls connected together with a flexible stick. Let us implement this.

First, we will use the same ball class defined previously. The stick is modeled with three attributes: two balls (b1 and b2) and the length of the stick itself (r). The stick constructor copies the two balls provided, and computes the initial distance between the two. This is the length of the stick (r). The display() method for the stick class is also simple: first draw the two balls (using the display() method of the ball class), and then draw the stick connecting the two balls. This is shown here:

```
class stick {
    ball b1, b2;  // the two balls
    float r;       // the length of the stick

    stick(ball b1, ball b2) {
        this.b1 = b1;
        this.b2 = b2;
        // Compute the length of the stick
        // Same as the initial distance between the two balls
        r = b1.location.dist(b2.location);
    } //stick

    void display() {
        // first display the balls
        b1.display();
        b2.display();
        // display the stick
        stroke(255, 0, 0);
        strokeWeight(5);
        line(b1.location.x, b1.location.y, b2.location.x, b2.location.y);
    } // display()
```

```
  void update() {
    b1.move();
    b2.move();
  } // update()
} // class stick
```

We also added the update() method. All it does is asks the balls to move. The following sketch creates a stick with two balls and displays it (see Figure 6-14).

```
// Sketch 6-4: Two balls and a stick
ball b1, b2;
stick s;
int stickLen = 80;

void setup() {
  size(400, 400);
  smooth();

  b1 = new ball(width/2, height/2, 10, color(0));
  b2 = new ball(width/2, height/2-stickLen, 10, color(0));

  s = new stick(b1, b2);
} // setup()

void draw() {
  background(255);
  s.update();
  s.display();
} // draw()
```

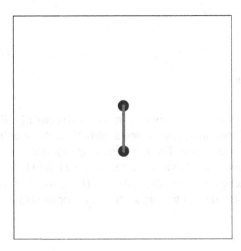

Figure 6-14. Two balls and a stick

Notice that the balls move freely about, based on their own motion parameters. The stick expands to join the two balls (see Figure 6-15). Next, we will add the following constraining method, constrainLength() to the stick class.

```
void constrainLength(){
    float k = 0.1 ;
    PVector delta = PVector.sub(b2.location, b1.location);

    float deltaLength = delta.mag();
    float d = ((deltaLength - r) / deltaLength);

    b1.location.x += delta.x * k * d/2;
    b1.location.y += delta.y * k * d/2;

    b2.location.x -= delta.x * k * d/2;
    b2.location.y -= delta.y * k * d/2;
} // constrainLength()
```

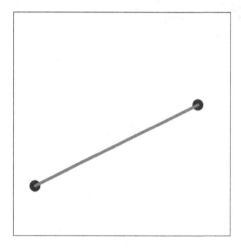

Figure 6-15. The unconstrained stick

The set of equations described here are implemented in constrainLength(). Place a call to constrainLength() as the last command in update() and then observe the sketch. You will notice that the distance between the two balls remains close to the original distance. There is certain springiness in the motion. You can control this by changing the value of the constant k. k = 1 makes the stick appear rigid while k=0 will result in an unconstrained behavior. That is, the stick stretches to where the balls are. This is the main payoff of using Verlet integration for modeling motion. The balls are moved to points where the constraints are satisfied and Verlet integration takes care of the rest.

> Try This: Parameterize the stiffness constant k by adding it as an attribute of the stick
> class. This way it can be customized by its clients.

Now, the fun begins. Let's write a sketch that has a chain of several balls linked together by sticks. Here is the sketch with 10 balls (also see Figure 6-16):

```
// Sketch 6-5: A ball and stick chain
ball [] balls;
stick [] sticks;
int stickLen = 80;
int nBalls = 10;
int nSticks = nBalls - 1;

void setup() {
  size(400, 400);
  smooth();

  // Allocate the ball and stick arrays
  balls = new ball[nBalls];
  sticks = new stick[nSticks];

  // create the balls and sticks and link them up
  for (int i=0; i < nBalls; i++) {
    balls[i] = new ball(width/2+stickLen*i, height/2, 10, color(0));

    if (i > 0) {
      sticks[i-1] = new stick(balls[i-1], balls[i]);
    }
  }
} // setup()

void draw() {
  background(255);

  // Animate

  for (int i=0; i < nSticks; i++) {
    sticks[i].update();
    sticks[i].display();
  }
} // draw()
```

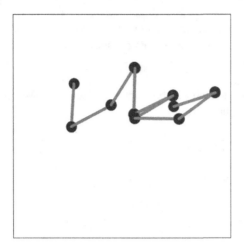

Figure 6-16. A ball and stick chain

The movement of all the balls constrained by the length of the sticks gives a natural way of modeling physical shapes with linkages. This enables you to create what are commonly known as *rag doll* models. If you think of the sticks as limbs and the balls as joints, with a little bit of clever rendering you can create natural shapes that float around in space.

> *Try This: Create a set of circular linkages where the last ball in the chain is connected back to the first ball creating a ring (see Figure 6-17). Once the whole "skeleton" is in motion you will see it fold. To preserve the shape, you can add cross linkages to get an amoeba like organism floating inside the sketch. Render it with some "skin." Further, can you create a stick figure rag doll?*

Figure 6-17. Circular linkage of balls and sticks

Inheritance: Is-a Relationships

Classes enable the capturing of object design in terms of their attributes and behaviors. Different types of objects can be modeled using their own classes to keep a program's components organized and manageable. We saw this earlier in the design of the ball class and then using a box class and a stick class to implement various has-a, or compositional, relationships between a program's objects. Often, in a program, as in the real world, you encounter objects that more or less behave the same way, and yet, have their own differences. Think about vehicles. All vehicles can be used to transport things from one point to another. However, an airplane is a different kind of vehicle than a car, or a ship, or a truck. At the same time, all vehicles have a unique identification tag (like a VIN in a car), have an owner, a home base, and so on. That is, while an airplane is a completely different object from a car or a ship, they still share many common attributes and behaviors. Our understanding of most things in the world tends to be organized in hierarchical manner. OOP provides us the means to further organize our programs in conceptual hierarchies that share common attributes and behaviors and yet differ substantially from one another. As another example, in Processing, we have two kinds of numbers: int and float. While they are different, conceptually, we are still able to do arithmetic on them (+, -, *, /, etc.), compare them, etc. Even though, at the lower level, when you add two int values, you do a different set of computations than when you do addition on two float values. These ideas, as you will soon see, can be captured elegantly using the concepts of *inheritance* in OOP methodology.

Inheritance is a relationship between two classes (a subclass inherits everything from its superclass). That is, it captures the *is-a* relationship between a subclass and its superclass. Additionally, a subclass can differentiate itself from its superclass by defining its own versions of inherited behaviors. For example, even though both airplanes and cars are vehicles, they require very different ways (or *methods*) for washing them. So, while a car (or an airplane) can inherit all the properties common to vehicles, they can differentiate themselves by defining their own wash methods. Let's make these ideas concrete. We will build on (and around) the design of the ball objects. Suppose you want to model all kinds of graphical widgets that can move about in a sketch. Widgets have shapes such as hexagons, squares, circles, stars, and so on. However, they have several common attributes as described here:

Every widget in a sketch has an x- and y- location, it is of a certain size, and color.
Every widget can be displayed in the sketch and it can move about in it.

Here we have outlined some basic (or generic) properties of widgets in a sketch. We can easily capture this description in a Processing class definition. However, at this point, we are only describing the generic properties of widgets. It may not make sense to actually instantiate specific widgets. We will after we specialize widgets (by defining subclasses). Processing enables definitions of these abstract entities by prefixing the class and method definitions by the abstract keyword:

```
abstract class widget {

  // Every shape has a x-, y- location, size, and color
  PVector location;
  float sz;
  color col;

  widget() {
    this(new PVector(random(width), random(height)), 30, color(0));
  } // widget()
```

```
widget(PVector loc, float s, color c) {
  location = loc;"
  sz = s;
  col = c;
} // widget()

// Every shape can be displayed
abstract void display();

// Every shape can move
abstract void move();

// Set the speed at which the widget moves
abstract void setSpeed(PVector s);

} // class widget
```

While most of the preceding code should look familiar, there are two new features here. First, notice that the class definition is preceded by a keyword abstract. This defines an abstract class, which is one that cannot be used to instantiate actual objects. That is, it would be illegal to do the following:

```
widget w = new widget();
```

This is because, from a design perspective, while we are defining some generic properties of objects in the Widget class, it doesn't make sense to create instances of widget objects: these objects, which represent shapes, do not have any geometric features yet. Thus, by putting the keyword abstract in the class definition, all we are saying is that, in the program, there will be things of type widget with the attributes and methods as defined. The second difference you see is the way the display(), move(), and setSpeed() methods have been defined. Only the signatures, or the headers are provided and it too is preceded by the keyword, abstract. There is no code following them. Again, this is deliberate because it is not clear, at this point, how a shape could be displayed or moved. Next, we use inheritance to define two subclasses, disc and hexagon with the properties and behaviors described here:

```
A disc is a circular shape that has a radius and moves in a sketch at a given speed.
It can bounce off the boundaries of the sketch.
A hexagon is a hexagonal shape (with six sides), whose size is specified by a radius.
It is capable of moving around, bouncing off boundaries. While moving, it also spins on its axis.
```

Now, while these two shapes have different attributes and behaviors, they still share the common properties defined for the widget class. We can now create subclasses of the widget such that the generic properties are inherited and additional properties defined. Inheritance in Processing is specified using the extends keyword followed by the name of the superclass. Below, we first show the definition of the disc class:

```
class disc extends widget  {

  // A disc is a circular shape
  float r;
  PVector speed;
```

```
  disc() {
    this(new PVector(random(width), random(height)), 30, color(0));
  } // disc()

  disc(PVector loc, float s, color c) {
    super(loc, s, c);
    r = sz/2;
    speed = new PVector(random(1, 3), random(1, 3));
  } // disc()

  void display() {
    noStroke();
    fill(col);
    ellipse(location.x, location.y, sz, sz);
  } // display()

  void setSpeed(PVector s) {
    speed = s;
  } // setSpeed()

  void move() {
    location.add(speed);
    bounce();
  } // move()

  void bounce() {
    if (location.x > (width-r)) { // bounce against the right edge
      location.x = width-r;
      speed.x = -speed.x;
    }
    if (location.x < r) { // bounce against the left edge
      location.x = r;
      speed.x = -speed.x;
    }
    if (location.y > (height-r)) { // bounce against the bottom edge
      location.y = height-r;
      speed.y = -speed.y;
    }
    if (location.y < r) { // bounce against the top edge
      location.y = r;
      speed.y = -speed.y;
    }
  } // bounce()
} // class disc
```

Notice how the superclass-subclass relationship is defined (class disc extends widget). By doing this, all the attributes and methods from the widget class are inherited. It is as if the attributes location, sz, and color were defined in the disc class. Take a close look at the main disc constructor. It uses the inherited variable sz to set the value of radius. In the constructor, the line

```
super(loc, s, c);
```

is placed to first initialize all the inherited properties by calling the superclass' constructor. Processing enables this by using the super() method. The disc class also inherits the display(), move(), and bounce() methods. However, no definition was provided in widget. They were defined as *abstract methods*. It is required that all subclasses (unless they themselves are abstract!) have to provide concrete definitions of all inherited abstract methods. For disc objects, motion is defined by updating its location with speed. The bounce() method is the same as the one we saw earlier. The hexagon class is shown next:

```
class hexagon extends widget {

    int nSides = 6;        // a hexagon has six sides
    float r;               // the size of the hexagon
    float rot;             // its orientation (rotation)
    PVector speed;         // speed at which it travels

    hexagon() {            // Default Constructor
      this(new PVector(random(width), random(height)), 30, color(0));
    } // hexagon()

    hexagon(PVector loc, float s, color c) {
      super(loc, s, c);
      r = sz/2;
      rot = 0;
      speed = new PVector(random(-2, 2), random(-2, 2));
    } // hexagon()

    void setSpeed(PVector s) {
      s.mult(-2);
      speed = s;
    } // setSpeed()

    void display() {

      float x1, y1;
      float theta = rot;

      noStroke();
      fill(col);

      beginShape();    // Draw the hexagon
      for (int i = 0; i <nSides; i++) {
        x1 = location.x + r*cos(theta);
        y1 = location.y + r*sin(theta);
        vertex(x1, y1);
        theta += PI/3;
      }
      endShape(CLOSE);
    } // display()

    void move() {
      rot += 0.01;
      location.add(speed);
```

```
    bounce();
  } // move()

  void bounce() {
    if (location.x > (width-r)) { // bounce against the right edge
      location.x = width-r;
      speed.x = -speed.x;
    }

    if (location.x < r) { // bounce against the left edge
      location.x = r;
      speed.x = -speed.x;
    }

    if (location.y > (height-r)) { // bounce against the bottom edge
      location.y = height-r;
      speed.y = -speed.y;
    }

    if (location.y < r) { // bounce against the top edge
      location.y = r;
      speed.y = -speed.y;
    }
  } // bounce()
} // class hexagon
```

While most of the structure should be self-explanatory, pay close attention to how the hexagon objects are similar, and yet specialized distinct from the disc objects in the methods: display(), and move(). This sketch uses the three classes defined previously (widget, disc, and hexagon) to populate the sketch with two objects: one disc and one hexagon (see Figure 6-18).

```
// Sketch 6-6: widgets, discs, and hexagons
disc d;
hexagon h;

void setup() {
  size(500, 500);
  smooth();

  d = new disc();
  h = new hexagon();
} // setup()

void draw() {
  background(255);
  d.move();
  d.display();
  h.move();
  h.display();
} // draw()
```

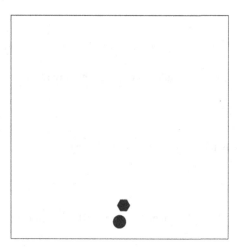

Figure 6-18. Two widget objects: a disc and a hexagon

The preceding sketch demonstrates how objects from different subclasses are organized and used in the same sketch. The real payoff though comes when we need to populate several objects, all of which descend from the same superclass and yet have been specialized in subclasses. For example, consider this sketch:

```
// Sketch 6-7: Several widgets
widget [] pieces;
int N = 10;

void setup() {
  size(500, 500);
  smooth();

  pieces = new widget[N];
  for (int i=0; i < N; i++) {
    color c = color(random(50, 200), random(50, 200), random(50, 200));
    switch (int(random(2))) {
    case 0:
      pieces[i] = new disc(new PVector(random(width), random(height)), 20, c);
      break;
    default:
      pieces[i] = new hexagon(new PVector(width/2, height/2), 40, c);
    }
  }
} // setup()

void draw() {
  background(255);
  for (int i=0; i < N; i++) {
    pieces[i].move();
    pieces[i].display();
  }
} // draw()
```

This sketch uses the same classes as previously used for `widget`, `disc`, and `hexagon`. We define `pieces`, an array of `widgets` (with a maximum of N elements, where N=10 above). Then, in `setup()` we randomly instantiate `disc` or `hexagon` objects (in the `switch` statement). In `draw()`, all `widget` objects stored in the pieces array are moved and updated. That is, since both `disc` and `hexagon` objects are subclasses of `widget`, we can treat them as if they were of the same class while storing them in the same array. Moreover, using the common method interface, we can apply the `move()` and `display()` uniformly to all objects. Study the preceding code carefully. Try running the sketch several times observing outcomes. Vary N, the number of widgets used in the sketch.

> *Try This: Implement another widget: a star or a square or a shape of your choosing. Define its attributes and how it moves and displays and then add it to the preceding sketch. In the sketch above we used the `switch` statement just so you could easily extend the code to use your new widget objects.*

Designing with classes and class hierarchies are the hallmarks of OOP. The superclass, `widget`, as defined previously, is also called a *base class* because it forms the basis for all its subclasses. Using an array of the base class allows you to write more versatile code as shown. Before we move on, there is one more concept that is often found in many programming languages that support OOP, however it is not implemented in Processing (or its base language Java). It is called *multiple inheritance*. That is, a given subclass could inherit from more than one superclass. For example, think about a class hierarchy of animals where animal is the base class. Further down the hierarchy you can expect to see subclasses for mammals, birds, and so on. Perhaps even subclasses for ambulatory animals (animals that walk), or flying animals (birds), can be defined. Now imagine defining a class for bats in this hierarchy: they are mammals and at the same time are also flying animals. Thus, bats could inherit all the modeled attributes of mammals as well as flying animals. This would require using multiple inheritance, something Processing/Java does not have. C++, for example, and other OOP languages support multiple inheritance.

While multiple inheritance is a natural extension of the inheritance idea, it turns out to be a design concept not without controversy. There are strong proponents on each side in the programming language design community. Most practitioners (like you and I), it turns out, seldom find the need for multiple inheritance in their programs. Besides, the implementation of multiple inheritance in a compiler has its own set of technical challenges that we are not going to elaborate here. However, Processing/Java do provide another concept that can be used to simulate the idea of multiple inheritance. It is called *interfaces* and we present that next.

Interfaces Are Doable

In OOP design we have learned to define classes to capture attributes as well as behaviors in a modular fashion. Often, it turns out that there are classes of entities in the world that, while they may belong to different class hierarchies, conform to each other only in their behaviors. Birds and bats, for instance share the flying behavior even though they belong to different animal classes. In the widget sketch shown above, for instance, after you have fleshed out several subclasses of widgets, including perhaps subclasses of `disc` (say a `disc` with a number in it) you might want widgets to be interactive, say being sensitive to and responding to mouse clicks. That is, in the universe of widget instances in your sketch, some widgets respond to mouse clicks. The idea of interfaces has been included in Processing/Java to address exactly such design situations. An interface encapsulates, or packages a set of behaviors that any class could decide to implement. For example, we can create the following interface that widgets could use:

```
Each object of a class can be clicked for interactivity. I.e. it is clickable.
When clicked, the object responds with whatever behavior is specified.
For example, when a mouse is clicked and dragged on an object, it responds by moving in that
direction.
```

Implementing interfaces involves two things: defining the interface; and then specifying that a class implements it. First, let's learn to define interfaces. Below, we show a simple interface, called Clickable that is defined for widgets in our previous sketch.

```
interface Clickable {
  boolean clicked();
} // interface Clickable
```

In a way, the definition of an interface looks just like a class definition. Just the keywork class is replaced by the keyword interface. Inside the body of the interface, one can define additional attributes if needed (we don't in the preceding example). This definition is simply a kind of proclamation that Clickable is an interface that anyone can choose to adopt and implement. However, if one does, they have to ensure that the methods defined in the body of the interface are implemented. Thus, in our example, if we decide that all widget objects are clickable with the behavior as defined previously, we have to specify this in the definition of the widget class as shown here:

```
abstract class widget implements Clickable {

    // all the contents of this class are same as before

} // class widget
```

Next, all subclasses, disc and hexagon, are required to implement the clicked() method. Here we show the definition of the clicked() method that should now be defined in the disc and hexagon classes.

```
boolean clicked() {
  PVector m = new PVector(mouseX, mouseY);
  return (PVector.dist(location, m) < r);
} // clicked()
```

The clicked() method returns true or false depending on whether the current mouse location is inside the bounds of the object. Next, the main sketch program needs to define two mouse event listeners as shown here:

```
PVector pm, cm;
Widget target;
```

```
void mousePressed() {
  // Find out which Widget was clicked
  for (int i=0; i < N; i++) {
    if (pieces[i].clicked()) {
      target = pieces[i];
    }
  }
  pm = new PVector(mouseX, mouseY);
  //noLoop();
} // mousePressed()

void mouseDragged() {
    cm = new PVector(mouseX, mouseY);

    PVector d = PVector.sub(pm, cm);
    d.normalize();
    target.setSpeed(d);
    target.col = color(255, 0, 0);
  //loop();
} // mouseDragged()
```

Whenever the mouse is clicked in the sketch, the mousePressed() method is invoked. It searches through the array of widget objects to see whether the mouse was clicked inside an object's boundaries. If so, that object is set to be the target. Next, when, after clicking the mouse on an object, it is dragged, the new vector corresponding to the dragged direction is computed, normalized, and set as the new speed of the object in the mouseDragged() method.

> *Try This: Run the preceding sketch several times. Try clicking and dragging the objects in the sketch and see how they respond to the mouse. You might find it easier to "slow" down the interaction a little by uncommenting the loop() and noLoop() commands in the mouse methods.*

In this simplified example, you could have easily accomplished the same effect without using interfaces by defining the clicked() method as a part of the widget class itself. Indeed, this turns out to be a design decision. Interfaces are typically used in more complex programs where standardization of an interface is required across several class hierarchies. Our goal here was to show you the concept of interfaces and how they are used in an implementation via a simple example.

Summary

In this chapter you learned the principles of object-oriented programming: thinking about program design in terms of objects. Objects have attributes and behaviors. Classes define factories for objects. They are used to encapsulate the internal details of objects. Further, objects can be composed of other objects and classes can be organized in inheritance hierarchies. Keeping the design of each class separate creates inherent organization in your programs and results in modular, reusable code modules. You learned how to implement object-oriented design in Processing. While Processing supports organization of objects into classes, it does not restrict access to internal details even though Java, its substrate language, has facilities for it. Yet, by self-imposing good discipline, one can write clean programs that capture the essence of encapsulation. You also learned how to model particles or balls and different kinds of physical motion models. Along the way you also learned about Processing's PVector class and some of its methods. Finally, you learned how to model motion of particles using Verlet integration techniques. Verlet integration is a simple, yet powerful model for creating natural looking motions and behaviors in sketches. We began the chapter by motivating you to think about the design of programs like Angry Birds. Successful programs such as these are an outcome of a combination of good design, simple yet intuitive game design, aesthetics, creativity, and interactivity. All these are qualities we hope you have been learning and honing as we progress through these chapters. In the next chapter you will learn more object-oriented programming principles. Finally, we will leave you to think about the Angry Birds game, its design, and programming. It is left as an exercise.

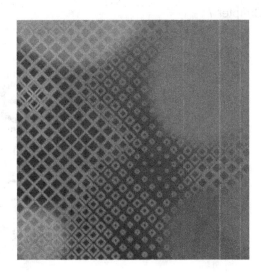

Chapter 7

Creative Abstraction

Abstraction, as you may have come to appreciate by now, is the hallmark of computing. You can compute anything as long as you can create a meaningful abstraction of it in a computer representation. You have seen this repeatedly in this book. Every Processing program you write relies on a number of abstractions. Further, Processing and all other programming languages provide facilities for building your own abstractions. Of course, abstraction is a concept that transcends computing. Abstraction allows us to filter out details and focus on the relevant parts. The graphic shown in Figure 7-1 is an abstraction of President Obama's 2009 Nobel Peace Prize acceptance speech. It uses a popular technique for data visualization called *word clouds*. This particular one was generated using an online program called Wordle (at wordle.net). If you haven't yet seen Wordle in action, go ahead, put this book down and play with Wordle on your computer.

Wordle essentially works by counting frequencies of word occurrence and then drawing each word so that the size of each word is proportional to its frequency—the more often a word appears the larger its size. It is easy to see that in President Obama's speech the three most common words were "war," "world," and "peace." If you have previously not heard or read this speech, you can get a good idea of the theme of the speech just by looking at the word cloud. The dichotomy in the content of the speech clearly shows through, right? Creative abstractions like these can be deconstructed into simple tasks that are easily programmed by someone like you. In this chapter you will learn how to create word clouds. In the process you will learn several new concepts involving strings, text, arrays, as well as some additional concepts in object-oriented programming and continue your own journey into creative abstractions in computing.

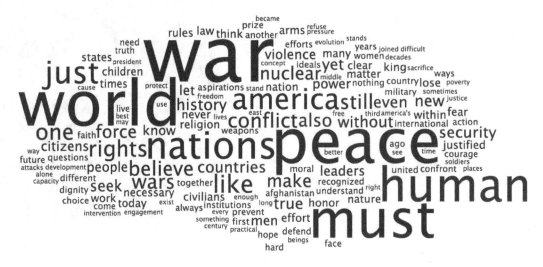

Figure 7-1. A word cloud of President Obama's Nobel Peace Prize acceptance speech as generated by Wordle

Strings

In Processing, the String datatype is used to represent strings of characters. For example,

```
String language = "Processing";
String version = "2.0";
```

The String class is predefined because strings are fundamental to so many computations. Because of this, you also do not have to invoke the constructor to create String objects (as shown in the preceding code). The standard style (that is, using the new command) String() constructor can also be used as shown here:

```
String language = new String("Processing");
String version = new String("2.0");
```

Further, the + operation is defined for String objects to do concatenation:

```
String myProcessing = language + " " + version;
println(myProcessing);
```

The preceding prints

```
Processing 2.0
```

in the console window. There is also a method called concat() to do string concatenation:

```
myProcessing = language.concat(" is a cool language.");  // "Processing is a cool language."
```

The + operator also does implicit conversion to String:

```
String nammoOne = "Processing is Number " + 1;          // "Processing is Number 1"
```

where the int value 1 is first converted to the string "1" and then concatenated. Implicit conversion to string can also be defined for any classes (or new types) that you define. This is done by defining the toString() method in the class definition. For example, you could define the toString() method for the ball objects, from Chapter 6 as shown here:

```
String toString() {
    return "<Ball at location" + location.x + ", " + location.y + ">";
} // toString()
```

The toString() method has to return a String object. What goes in that String object is what you decide to be the *printed representation* of instances of the class. Given a ball object, you can then do the following:

```
ball myBall = new ball(new PVector(100, 200));
println(myBall);
```

will print

```
<Ball at location 100.0, 200.0>
```

String Methods

We will illustrate more examples of the toString() method later in this chapter. The String class provides several other methods that are useful in doing computations with strings. For example, the length() method returns the length of the string:

```
println(language.length());          // will print 10
println(version.length());           // will print 3
```

Two String objects can be compared using the equals() method:

```
String myLanguage = new ("Processing");
String yourLanguage = new ("Processing");
String oldLanguage = new ("FORTRAN");
println(myLanguage.equals(yourLanguage));     // will print true
Println(myLanguage.equals(oldLanguage));      // will print false
```

You might be wondering, why can't you use the == operator to compare if two strings are equal? As in

```
myLanguage == yourLanguage;
```

the == operator is defined only for primitive values (int, float, char, and boolean). For objects, the == operator compares the reference of the two objects (See the section on "Primitive and Reference Types" in Chapter 5). Thus,

```
String herLanguage = myLanguage;       // the two variables refer to the same object
herLanguage == myLanguage;             // will return true
herLanguage == yourLanguage;           // will return false
herLanguage.equals(yourLanguage)       // will return true
```

Study the examples above carefully to ensure that you understand the difference between comparing two primitive values versus comparing objects. The equals() method for strings compares the individual components of the objects whereas the == operator compares the references (or the memory addresses) of the objects.

Given a String object, there are methods to look at its pieces, as well as convert the case of letters in it:

```
myString.charAt(0);          // will return 'P'
myString.charAt(4);          // will return 'o'
myString.indexOf('s');       // will return the index of the first occurrence of 's', which is 5
myString.lastIndexOf('s');   // will return the index of the last occurrence of 's', which is
myString.toLowerCase();      // will return the String "processing"
myString.toUpperCase();      // will return the String "PROCESSING"
```

Working with Strings

These methods from the String class are summarized in Table 7-1. Further, Processing defines several useful string functions to input text from files and to break the text into useful pieces: loadStrings(), split(), join(), and splitTokens(). We used some of these in Chapter 5. This section reviews these.

Table 7-1. List of Some Methods in String Class

Method	Usage	Description
int length()	S.length()	Returns the length of String, S
boolean equals(string)	S1.equals(S2)	Returns true is S1 equals S2, false otherwise
String concat(string)	S1.concat(S2)	Returns S1 + S2
char charAt(int)	S.charAt(n)	Returns the character at index, n in String, S
int indexOf(char)	S.indexOf(C)	Returns index of first occurrence of character, C in String S
int lastIndexOf(char)	S.lastIndexOf(C)	Returns index of last occurrence of character, C in String, S
String toLowerCase()	S.toLowerCase()	Returns the lowercase version of String, S
String toUpperCase()	S.toUpperCase()	Returns the uppercase version of String, S

```
String [] lines;         // an array of strings
lines = loadStrings("myDataFile.txt");
```

The file myDataFile.txt should be present in the Data folder of your sketch. Each line in the data file is input as a String into the entries of the lines array. As many entries in the lines array will be created as the number of lines in the data file. Thus lines[0] will contain the text from the first line of the data file and lines[lines.length-1] will contain the text from the last line.

Next, take a look at the following examples:

```
String line1 = "A man, a plan, a canal, Panama";
String [] pieces;
pieces = split(line1, ", ");
```

The split() function takes a String, followed by a char or a String as parameters. It splits the first string into pieces by splitting it along the character or string provided in the second parameter. Thus, after the preceding statements (where the second parameter is the string containing a comma and a space), pieces will contain the following:

```
pieces[0] = "A man"
pieces[1] = "a plan"
pieces[2] = "a canal"
pieces[3] = "Panama"
```

Here is an example of using a single character to split a string:

```
String line1 = "A man, a plan, a canal, Panama";
String [] pieces;
pieces = split(line1, 'n');
```

That is, the string in line1 is being split across the letter 'n'. After these commands, pieces will contain:

```
pieces[0] = "A ma"
pieces[1] = ", a pla"
pieces[2] = ", a ca"
pieces[3] = "al, Pa"
pieces[4] = "ama"
```

Another way to split a String is to use the splitTokens() function. splitTokens() takes two parameters, the String to be split, and a second String. All characters of the second String specify split points. Thus

```
String line1 = "A man, a plan, a canal, Panama";
String [] pieces;
pieces = splitTokens(line1, ", ");   // split the string across a comma or a space
```

Will result in

```
pieces[0] = "A"
pieces[1] = "man"
pieces[2] = "a"
pieces[3] = "plan"
pieces[4] = "a"
pieces[5] = "canal"
pieces[6] = "Panama"
```

As you can see, the String in line1 is split wherever there is a comma or a space. In text processing it is often required to break an input text into individual pieces. For example, if you want to split a text into individual words. Words in a text file are often delimited by punctuation (characters like a comma ',', a period '.', an exclamation '!', a colon ':', a semicolon ';', and so on). Even the newline character or a tab character is considered a delimiter. Splitting text across all possible delimiters results in *tokens* which, if the text is mostly a written narrative, could be considered as words for language processing. Functions like splitTokens() are also sometimes called *tokenizers*. We will make use of splitTokens() to split texts into words.

Apart from splitting text, you can also join text that may have been split earlier, into a single string using the join() function. To join together the contents of pieces array as shown in the last example above you could do the following:

```
String sentence = join(pieces, ", ");
```

to get the String

```
sentence = "A man, a plan, a canal, Panama"
```

Text Visualization: Creating Word Clouds

We can now begin to design and implement the word cloud application. Because this is essentially a data visualization situation, we will try and follow the methodology outlined in Chapter 5 that includes the following steps:

- Acquiring the data
- Parsing the data
- Filtering the data
- Mining the data
- Choosing a visual representation
- Making the visualization interactive

Our approach here is going to be a *bottom-up*, exploratory program design methodology. However, from time to time during the development process, we will step back, reflect, and redesign our programs to make them more organized, manageable, and extendible.

Acquiring the Data

The word cloud application involves processing a given text. You have to identify a piece of text that you are interested in visualizing. Whether it is an essay you wrote, or a speech, or an entire book, you have to identify a source and acquire it in machine readable form. These days, several rich and freely usable text resources are available on the web. For web search engines, like Google, the entire web is one giant, highly distributed text. One of the single largest online resources for English language books is the site maintained by Project Gutenberg (gutenberg.org). Project Gutenberg's mission is to encourage the creation and distribution of ebooks. Using the loadStrings() function in Processing, you can directly input an entire text into your programs. Alternatively, you can download any text into the Data folder of your sketch and then process it. You should ensure that the text is readable for input and ready for subsequent processing by your programs. This implies that the text should be in *plain text format*. No PDF documents, or documents created in a proprietary word processing application will be usable. If your document is not in plain text, you can easily convert it into one.

We will work on the text used in the word cloud displayed Figure 7-1: President Barack Obama's Nobel Peace Prize acceptance speech from 2009. The transcript is easily located by searching online. Let's assume that it is saved as a file named, Obama.txt in the Data folder of the sketches we will be writing.

Parsing the Data

The next step is to parse the text file. This involves reading or inputting the file, and processing it into separate words. This is done in the sketch shown here:

```
// Sketch 7-1: Parsing an input text file
String inputTextFile = "Obama.txt";
String [] fileContents;
String rawText;
String tokens[];
String delimiters = " ,./?<>;:'\"[{]}\\|=+-_()*&^%$#@!~";

// Input and parse text file
fileContents = loadStrings(inputTextFile);
rawText = join(fileContents, " ");
rawText = rawText.toLowerCase();
tokens = splitTokens(rawText, delimiters);

// print out the list of tokens
println(tokens.length+" tokens found in file: "+inputTextFile);
for (int i=0; i < tokens.length ; i++) {
  println(tokens[i]);
}
```

The sketch inputs the contents of the text file (Obama.txt) into the String array fileContents. Each line in the file gets stored as a String in the array. The lines are then joined into a single string (rawText) and converted to lowercase (using the toLowerCase() function). Then, using the splitTokens() function and the delimiters containing all the possible punctuation characters, the string in rawText is split into individual word like pieces stored in the tokens array. Finally, the contents of token array are printed in the Console window. Here is part of the output:

```
4155 tokens found in file: Obama.txt
your
majesties
your
royal
highnesses
distinguished
members
of
the
norwegian
nobel
committee
citizens
of
america
and
citizens
of
the
```

```
world
i
receive
this
honor
...
```

According to the sketch, there were 4155 tokens found. We classify these as tokens because, due to the way we have chosen to split the text, there will be tokens resulting from splitting of certain common contractions. For example apostrophe words like "I'll" or "don't" or "let's", if present, will result in tokens like "ll", "t", and "s". Expanding such contractions prior to splitting into tokens (for example by converting "I'll" into "I will", etc.) can be done if needed by a text processing application. In our example, we will ignore this, and count the orphaned tokens like "ll", "s", and so on, as words.

Filtering the Data

Assuming that the preceding parsing of input text suffices, the next step is to filter the data (i.e. the words contained in the tokens array). In word clouds a word is displayed proportional to the frequency of its occurrence which can be computed by creating a dataset that pairs each word with its frequency using the following algorithm:

```
Create an empty word-frequency list
for each word do the following
    If the word has already been recorded in the word-frequency list
        Increment its frequency count by 1
    Otherwise
        Add the word to the list with a starting count of 1
```

A word-frequency pair is defined as a class (called Word) as you will see later. Using this algorithm, you can easily create a table of these word-frequency pair objects. However, there are some interesting questions to ponder. Among them, the first one is how many unique words/tokens are there in a text? More generally, given a language, say English, how many words are there in the English language? We will return to the more general question later, but there is an immediate need from a programming perspective: Of the 4155 words found in the Obama speech, how many unique words are there? This number is needed because an array large enough to hold these words will have to be created. While Processing does include operations to expand the size of an array, there is also another option when using objects: ArrayList. ArrayList arrays, as you will see next, allow you to create arrays of objects that can shrink or grow as the need arises.

The ArrayList Class

When you want to use an array of objects in a sketch where the size of the array can change during the sketch's lifetime you can use the ArrayList class. The ArrayList class manages the shrinking or growing of an array as elements are removed or added. For example:

```
ArrayList data;              // Defines data to be an ArrayList variable
data = new ArrayList();      // Creates a new, empty ArrayList
data.add("Anaheim");         // Add a few entries into the array
```

```
data.add("Azusa");
data.add("Cucamonga");
data.add("Timbuktu");
```

You can print the contents of the data array as shown here:

```
println(data);
```

to get the output:

```
[Anaheim, Azusa, Cucamonga, Timbuktu]
```

In addition to add() the following methods are also available for ArrayList objects:

- size(). Returns the number of elements stored in the ArrayList object
- get(int i). Returns the object stored at index, i
- remove(int i). Removes and returns the object stored at index, i

The ArrayList class includes several other methods that you can review in the Processing Reference. Here we show how to use these on the previous data array:

```
println("The data ArrayList contains: "+data.size()+" elements.");
println("data[3] = "+data.get(3));
data.remove(3);
println("The data ArrayList contains: "+data.size()+" elements.");
println(data);
```

Here is the output from the preceding commands:

```
The data ArrayList contains: 4 elements.
data[3] = Timbuktu
The data ArrayList contains: 3 elements.
[Anaheim, Azusa, Cucamonga]
```

Match these outputs to the commands and be sure that you understand the operations and usage of ArrayList objects. If the type of objects to be stored in an ArrayList is known (for example, the data array above contains String objects) it is preferable to define the ArrayList as follows:

```
ArrayList<String> data;       // All entries in data will be String objects
```

Next, returning to the word cloud application, you can begin to implement the filtering of tokens into word frequencies. First create a class, called Word, which pairs each word with its frequency and then create and compute the word frequencies of all the words in the text in a table wordFrequency:

```
ArrayList<Word> wordFrequency = new ArrayList();          // The word frequency list
// Compute the wordFrequency using the tokens array of words
```

First, define the Word class:

```
// Sketch 7-2a: The Word class
class Word {
  // Each Word is a pair: the word, and its frequency
  String word;
  int freq;

  Word(String newWord) {   // Constructor
    word = newWord;
    freq = 1;
  } // Word()

  String getWord() {
    return word;
  } // getWord()

  int getFreq() {
    return freq;
  } // getFreq()

  void incr() {  // increments the word count
    freq++;
  } // incr()

  String toString() {  // print representation of Word objects
    return "<"+word+", "+freq+">";
  }
} // class Word
```

Read the definition of the Word class carefully. Notice how the toString() method is defined to enable nicely formatted printing of the word-frequency pairs. Sketch 7-2b uses the preceding Word class to compute the wordFrequency ArrayList.

```
// Sketch 7-2b: Using ArrayLists for word frequencies
String inputTextFile = "Obama.txt";
String [] fileContents;
String rawText;
String [] tokens;
String delimiters = " ,./?<>;:'\"[{]}\\|=+-_()*&^%$#@!~";
ArrayList<Word> wordFrequency = new ArrayList();

void setup() {
  // Input and parse text file
  fileContents = loadStrings(inputTextFile);
  rawText = join(fileContents, " ");
  rawText = rawText.toLowerCase();
  tokens = splitTokens(rawText, delimiters);
```

```
  // print out the number of tokens found
  println(tokens.length+" tokens found in file: "+inputTextFile);

  // Compute the wordFrequency table using tokens
  for (String t : tokens) {

    // See if token t is already a known word
    int index = search(t, wordFrequency);
    if (index >= 0) {
      wordFrequency.get(index).incr();
    }
    else {
      wordFrequency.add(new Word(t));
    } // if
  } // for

  println("There were "+wordFrequency.size()+" words.");
  for (int i=0; i < wordFrequency.size(); i++) {
    println(wordFrequency.get(i));
  }
} // setup()

int search(String w, ArrayList<Word> L) {
  // search for word w  in L.
  // Returns index of w in L if found, -1 o/w
  for (int i=0; i < L.size(); i++) {
    if (L.get(i).getWord().equals(w))
      return i;
  }

  return -1;
} // search()
```

The partial output from this sketch is shown here:

```
4155 tokens found in file: Obama.txt
There were 1254 words.

<your, 3>
<majesties, 1>
<royal, 1>
<highnesses, 1>
<distinguished, 1>
<members, 1>
<of, 160>
<the, 224>
<norwegian, 1>
<nobel, 2>
<committee, 2>
```

```
<citizens, 6>
<america, 16>
<and, 146>
<world, 31>
<i, 38>
<receive, 1>
<this, 35>
<honor, 5>
...
```

It appears that out of 4155 total tokens, 1254 unique words were found.

> *Try This: Acquire some other texts and process them with this sketch. Note the total number of tokens as well as the resulting number of unique words. Linguists claim that there are close to 500,000 words in common use in the English language. Google, based on its analysis of over 5 million books in English has published a list of over 1 million words!*

Filtering Function Words and Stop Words

Next, pay attention to the computed frequencies of individual words in the output. The application needs to focus on the frequency of individual words to generate the abstract visualization of the content of the text. However, in any given text, words like "and", "the", and "of" that have some of the highest frequencies ("and" occurred 146 times, "the" 224 times, and "of" 160 times) do not necessarily signify any relevant context. Linguists broadly classify words as *content words* and *function words*. Words like "the", "of", "and", and so on are classified as function words as they do not necessarily signify the context or lexical meaning of a sentence. Yet, they serve an important structural purpose in sentences, hence their name. Therefore, it would serve well to filter out or eliminate all function words from the frequency table. This is also standard practice in most language processing applications. Computational Linguists collect and often publish lists of such words. These words, also called *stop words,* are then used in further filtering out unwanted words or tokens, like the orphaned pieces of apostrophe words.

You can easily search the web for a list of stop words, acquire it and place it in your Data folder. We will name our stop words file stopwords.txt. It has ~650 words and includes entries like "ll", 've', and so on along with the most common function words like "and", "to", "the", etc. Once you have access to a set of stop words, the preceding filtering algorithm changes just so slightly (shown here in bold):

```
Create an empty word-frequency list
for each word that is not a stop word do the following
    If the word has already been recorded in the word-frequency list
        Increment its frequency count by 1
    Otherwise
        Add the word to the list with a starting count of 1
```

Sketch 7-2 modified with these changes, by declaring a new String array called stopwords, and using it in the setup() function is shown here:

```
// Sketch 7-3: Using ArrayLists for word frequencies
//                      And eliminating stop words
String inputTextFile = "Obama.txt";
String [] fileContents;
String rawText;
String [] tokens;
String delimiters = " ,./?<>;:'\"[{]}\\|=+-_()*&^%$#@!~";
ArrayList<Word> wordFrequency = new ArrayList();

String [] stopWords;

void setup() {
  // Input and parse text file
  fileContents = loadStrings(inputTextFile);
  rawText = join(fileContents, " ");
  rawText = rawText.toLowerCase();
  tokens = splitTokens(rawText, delimiters);

  // print out the number of tokens found
  println(tokens.length+" tokens found in file: "+inputTextFile);

  // Get stop words
  stopWords = loadStrings("stopwords.txt");

  // Compute the wordFrequency table using tokens
  for (String t : tokens) {
    if (!isStopWord(t)) {
      // See if token t is already a known word
      int index = search(t, wordFrequency);
      if (index >= 0) {
        wordFrequency.get(index).incr();
      }
      else {
        wordFrequency.add(new Word(t));
      }
    }// if
  } // for

  // Compute the wordFrequency table using tokens
  for (String t : tokens) {
    // See if token t is already a known word
    int index = search(t, wordFrequency);
    if (index >= 0) {
      wordFrequency.get(index).incr();
    }
```

```
      else {
        wordFrequency.add(new Word(t));
      } // if
    } // for
    println("There were "+wordFrequency.size()+" words.");
    for (int i=0; i < wordFrequency.size(); i++) {
      println(wordFrequency.get(i));
    }
  } // setup()

  int search(String w, ArrayList<Word> L) {
    // search for word w  in L.
    // Returns index of w in L if found, -1 o/w
    for (int i=0; i < L.size(); i++) {
      if (L.get(i).getWord().equals(w))
        return i;
    }
    return -1;
  } // search()
  boolean isStopWord(String word) {  // Is word a stop word?
    for (String stopWord : stopWords) {
      if (word.equals(stopWord)) {
        return true;
      }
    }
    return false;
  } // isStopWord()
```

To run this version, you will also need the Word class defined in Sketch 7-2. The isStopWord() function searches for every token in the stopWords array and returns true if the token is a stop word, false otherwise Here is the partial output from this version of the sketch:

```
4155 tokens found in file: Obama.txt
There were 1023 words.
<majesties, 1>
<royal, 1>
<highnesses, 1>
<distinguished, 1>
<members, 1>
<norwegian, 1>
<nobel, 2>
<committee, 2>
<citizens, 6>
<america, 16>
<receive, 1>
<honor, 5>
<deep, 2>
<gratitude, 1>
...
```

Notice that after filtering out all the stop words, there are now 1023 words left in the table. Thus with the addition of the stop words filter, over 18% of the words in the text's dictionary were eliminated. Above, we took an existing list of stop words and used it. Often you will find that the list requires some hand editing, depending on the type of text. Thus, there is a science as well as an art to creating text-based abstractions. We will return to this issue after we have completed the visualization. The more immediate problem that needs to be addressed is that of program design.

Often, as you incrementally build programs, it becomes necessary to reconsider the organization of the code to make the programs more manageable in terms of their complexity as well as extendibility. Let's redesign the program before proceeding further. In the process of trying to count word frequencies we have developed some useful functionality that could be abstracted into a usable frequency table module. Frequency tables are often used in data analysis applications. For example, rudimentary cryptographic analysis involves the usage of character frequencies. Computational Linguists make extensive use of simple (or first-order word frequencies) as well as higher-order word frequencies, called N-grams to do statistical text analyses. So, it is worthwhile to reorganize the sketch to make use of a word frequency table. A basic design of a word frequency table class is shown in Table 7-2.

Table 7-2. Design of the Word Frequency Class

class WordFreq	Description
ArrayList<Word> WordFrequency	The word-frequency table
WordFreq(String[ ] tokens)	Constructor
void tabulate()	Prints the table in console
int N()	Returns the number of entries in table
String[ ] samples()	Returns the words in the table
int counts()	Returns the frequencies in the table
int maxFreq()	Returns the maximum frequency
String toString()	Print representation of table
Boolean _isStopWord(String w, String[ ] S)	Is w a stop word in S? True/False
int _search(String w, ArrayList<Word> L)	Is w already recorded in the table? Returns index of word if present, -1 otherwise

The WordFreq class is responsible for creating and maintaining a word frequency list (stored in the ArrayList variable wordFrequency). The table is constructed using the WordFreq() constructor, given an array of word tokens. Other methods are described in Table 7-2. Two worth highlighting are the functions, _isStopWord() and _search(). Their names begin with an underscore character ('_') to indicate that these are *internal functions* to the class and are not necessarily used directly on WordFrequency objects. This is not a requirement, but a naming convention commonly adopted by programmers to easily identify methods that are part of a class's main interface and those that are internal. Given the preceding class design, the sketch can be rewritten as shown here:

```
// Sketch 7-4: Using ArrayLists for word frequencies
//                    And eliminating stop words
//                    And using the WordFreq class
```

```
String inputTextFile = "Obama.txt";
WordFreq table;
void setup() {

  // Input and parse text file
  String [] fileContents = loadStrings(inputTextFile);
  String rawText = join(fileContents, " ").toLowerCase();
  String [] tokens;
  String delimiters = " ,./?<>;:'\"[{]}\\|=+-_()*&^%$#@!~";
  tokens = splitTokens(rawText, delimiters);
  println(tokens.length+" tokens found in file: "+inputTextFile);

  // Create the word frequency table
  table = new WordFreq(tokens);
  table.tabulate();
  println("Max frequency:"+table.maxFreq());
} // setup()
```

Using the WordFreq class results in a much cleaner version. The sketch is essentially responsible for creating an array of tokens, creating the word frequency table using the WordFreq class, and then using methods from WordFreq to do operations on the word frequency table. The WordFreq class itself is shown next:

```
// Sketch 7-4a: The Word frequency table class
class WordFreq {
  // A Frequency table class for Words
  ArrayList<Word> wordFrequency;
  String [] stopWords = loadStrings("stopwords.txt");

  WordFreq(String[] tokens) {  // Constructor

    wordFrequency = new ArrayList();

    // Compute the wordFrequency table using tokens
    for (String t : tokens) {
      if (!_isStopWord(t)) {
        // See if token t is already a known word
        int index = _search(t, wordFrequency);
        if (index >= 0) {
          ( wordFrequency.get(index)).incr();
        }
        else {
          wordFrequency.add(new Word(t));
        }
      }
    } // for
  } // WordFreq()

  void tabulate() {  // console printout
    int n = wordFrequency.size();
    println("There are "+N()+" entries.");
```

```
  for (int i=0; i < n; i++) {
    println(wordFrequency.get(i));
  }
} // tabulate

int N() { // Number of table entries
  return wordFrequency.size();
} // N()

String[] samples() {  // Returns all the words
  String [] k = new String[N()];
  int i=0;
  for (Word w : wordFrequency) {
    k[i++] = w.getWord();
  }
  return k;
} // samples()

int[] counts() {  // Returns all the frequencies
  int [] v = new int[N()];
  int i=0;
  for (Word w : wordFrequency) {
    v[i++] = w.getFreq();
  }
  return v;
} // counts()

int maxFreq() {  // The max frequency
  return max(counts());
} // maxFreq()

int _search(String w, ArrayList<Word> L) {
  // search for word w  in L.
  // Returns index of w in L if found, -1 o/w
  for (int i=0; i < L.size(); i++) {
    if (L.get(i).getWord().equals(w))
      return i;
  }
  return -1;
} // _search()

boolean _isStopWord(String word) {  // Is word a stop word?
  for (String stopWord : stopWords) {
    if (word.equals(stopWord)) {
      return true;
    }
  }
  return false;
} // _isStopWord()
```

```
  String toString() {  // Print representation
    return "Word Frequency Table with"+N()+" entries.";
  } // toString()
} // class WordFreq
```

There is no change in the Word class from Sketch 7-2. Functionally, the sketch is exactly the same as before. That is, its output will be as shown for Sketch 7-3. However, the result is a cleaner design of the code.

> *Try This: Complete Sketch 7-4a and examine the resulting list of words and frequencies. Try the sketch on several texts. Add additional functionality to the WordFreq class. For instance, a clear() method to remove all entries from the table, a lookup() method to return the frequency of a given word, and so on.*

Mining the Data: Sorting

So far, the sketch enables input of a given text file, filters out all stop words, and creates a word frequency table. The next step is to visualize. However, even after filtering out all the stop words, over 1000 words were recorded from the input text file. Think about processing larger texts this way. To illustrate, we used the sketch to process Dante's *Divine Comedy*, which resulted in over 114,000 tokens that created over 11,000 entries in the word frequency table. Visualizing 11,000 words in a sketch would require a huge computer monitor (perhaps one of the large wall displays!). Even 1000 words resulting from our sample text is quite large. Thus, the visualization has to provide means for mining for the most relevant words in the text to be displayed. In this application, the answer is obvious: visualize only the first N most frequent words. Where N can depend on the size of the monitor or display area you want to use. This requires us to *mine* for the N most frequent words in the word table.

One of the most common computational operations on a dataset is *sorting*. That is, given a dataset, an array of numbers, or an array of names of states, sort them in ascending or descending order. For example, given the following:

```
int [] data = {42, 7, 23, 19, -22, 11, 19, 5, -8, 5};
String [] states = {"New York", "Pennsylvania", "Alabama", "Wyoming", ..., "Texas"};
```

after the two arrays are sorted in ascending order, you have:

```
data = [-22, -8, 5, 5, 7, 11, 19, 19, 23, 42]
states = ["Alabama", "Alaska", "Arizona", "Arkansas", "California", ..., "Wyoming"]
```

In Chapter 5, we introduced Processing's predefined sort() function for sorting arrays. For example,

```
println(sort(data));
```

will print

```
[0] -22
[1] -8
[2] 5
[3] 5
[4] 7
[5] 11
[6] 19
[7] 19
[8] 23
[9] 42
```

sort() actually leaves the original array unchanged. It returns a new sorted array. Thus, if you wanted the contents of data (or states) to appear sorted, you would write:

```
data = sort(data);
states = sort(states);
```

To sort the data and states arrays in descending order, you could combine this code with the array reverse() operation, also introduced in Chapter 5:

```
data = reverse(sort(data));
println(data);
[0] 42
[1] 23
[2] 19
[3] 19
[4] 11
[5] 7
[6] 5
[7] 5
[8] -8
[9] -22
```

Next, imagine sorting an array of objects like the word frequency array. Each entry in the array is a word-frequency pair. You could choose to sort the array so that all the words are arranged in lexicographic order (that is, dictionary order), or you could sort it by frequency, in descending order. The latter is what we desire in our application. However, the sort() function described previously only works for arrays of int, float, and String. It does not sort ArrayLists, which are arrays of objects. Java, Processing's substrate language, does provide several other sorting functions that can be used to sort ArrayList arrays. For example, the command:

```
Collections.sort(wordFrequency, Collections.reverseOrder());
```

at the end of the WordFrequency() constructor would sort the word frequency table in reverse order by frequencies provided, the Word class implements the Comparable interface that requires the class to define the compareTo() function:

```
class Word implements Comparable<Word> {
    ...
    public int compareTo(Object w) {
        return freq - w.freq;
    }
    ...
} // class Word
```

Here we only show the Word class with the new function added in. The rest remains unchanged. The compareTo() function returns an integer value as follows:

```
int compareTo(<SomeObject> obj) {
    // returns a negative number, if this < obj
    // returns 0, if this is equal to obj
    // returns a positive number, if this > obj
} // compareTo()
```

The compareTo() function defined in the preceding Word class therefore compares the frequencies. To order the array by words, you can replace the frequency comparison with String comparison. A compareTo() function is already defined in the String class so, to order in lexicographic order, you can write Word.compareTo() as:

```
public int compareTo(Object w) {
        return word.compareTo(w.word);
} // compareTo()
```

> *Try This: Modify the sketch to use the Java-based Collections.sort() function to sort the word frequency table and observe the results.*

Learning to Sort

While it is always a good idea to use a predefined function if one is available, in using the Collections.sort() function, we bypassed a number of advanced preliminaries. For example, we completely skipped over the introduction of Collection class. This is an advanced topic and will not be covered here. However, it is also fairly straightforward to learn how to write a sorting function for your own needs. Computer scientists have designed numerous sorting algorithms, any of which could be used here. In this section, we will introduce two: *selection sort*, and *insertion sort*. The sorting algorithms will be implemented in two functions called selectionSort(), and insertionSort() that work as defined here:

```
void selectionSort(int [] A); // Sorts the integer elements in array A in ascending order
                              // using selection sort
void insertionSort(int [] A); // Sorts the integer elements in array A in ascending order
                              // using insertion sort
```

Later, once the algorithms have been introduced for sorting arrays of integers, you will learn how to use them to sort ArrayList objects.

Selection Sort

The selection sort algorithm rearranges the elements of the array in place. This is done by exchanging the array's elements when needed. The basic algorithm can be described as follows (assuming the array A has N entries):

```
For each location in the array starting from i=0 going all the way to N-1
    Let pos = location of the smallest element among A[i..N-1]
    Swap the contents of A[i] and A[pos]
```

The name of the algorithm, *selection sort*, provides a good clue here. The above algorithm specifies that for each position (i) in the array, select the next smallest element and place it there. The following code implements the algorithm:

```
void selectionSort(int [] A) {  // sort the array A in ascending order using selection sort
  int pos;

  for (int i=0; i < A.length; i++) {
    //find pos the position of the smallest element in A[i] .. A[N-1]
    pos = i;
    for (int j = i+1; j < A.length; j++) {
      if (A[j] < A[pos]) {
        pos = j;
      }
    }
    //Swap or exchange the contents of A[i] and A[pos]
    int temp = A[i];
    A[i] = A[pos];
    A[pos] = temp;
  }
} // selectionSort()
```

Insertion Sort

The Insertion Sort algorithm works a little differently:

```
for i=1 through N-1:
    insert A[i] in A[0] .. A[i] such that A[0] <= A[1] <= ... <= A[i]
```

This algorithm is coded here:

```
void insertionSort(int [] A) { // sort the array A in ascending order
  // for i=1 through N-1:
  for (int i=0; i < A.length; i++) {
    // insert A[i] in A[0] .. A[i] such that A[0] <= A[1] <= ... <= A[i]
```

```
    int a = A[i];      // Save A[i] in p
    int pos = i;
    while ((pos > 0) && (A[pos-1] >= a)) {
      // Move A[pos-1] back by 1
      A[pos] = A[pos-1];
      pos--;
    } // while
    // A[pos] is where a gets inserted
    A[pos] = a;
  }// for
} // insertionSort
```

> *Try This: Write a sketch that creates an array of random integers and sorts it. Print the contents of the array before and after the sort function calls to ensure that the data is indeed sorted in ascending order. Modify the sort function(s) to sort in descending order.*

As we discussed in Chapter 5, Selection Sort will take N^2 operations. Because each search for the smallest element will take $(N-1)+(N-2)+ \cdot \cdot \cdot +1$ comparisons, there will be a total of $N(N-1)/2$ comparisons. Additionally, there will be N swaps. Similarly, Insertion Sort, on average, is also a N^2 or quadratic time algorithm. Given a choice of the two algorithms above, which one would you pick? This turns out to be a perennial question in computing because the correct answer depends on various factors having to do with the nature of the data in the given problem, its characteristics, and so on. A rigorous discussion of these issues is out of the scope of this book. We encourage you to refer to books on algorithms for further information. However, we will point out, that on average Insertion Sort turns out to be a better choice than Selection Sort. The short justification for this has to do with fact that Insertion Sort only does the amount of work it needs to do to sort the data. If, for example, the data were already sorted, Insertion Sort would terminate after N operations whereas Selection Sort will still require N^2 operations. Sorting happens to be a fascinating topic of study in computing. Researchers have written, and continue to write, PhD dissertations on aspects relating to sorting. Professor Robert Sedgewick of Princeton University invented the QuickSort algorithm for his PhD dissertation at Stanford University in the 1970s (see References at the end of this chapter). QuickSort's average case performance uses time proportional to $N\log_2 N$.

This Insertion Sort algorithm can be used to write a sorting function to sort the word frequency table in descending order as determined by the frequency count of the words. You can add the following to the WordFreq class:

```
void _sort(ArrayList<Word> A) {

  // sort the array A in ascending order
  // for i=1 through N-1:
  for (int i=0; i < A.size(); i++) {
    // insert A[i] in A[0] .. A[i] such that A[0] <= A[1] <= ... <= A[i]
    Word a = A.get(i);      // Save A[i] in p
    int pos = i;
```

```
    while ((pos > 0) && (a.compareTo(A.get(pos-1))>=1)) {
      // Move A[pos-1] back by 1
      A.set(pos, A.get(pos-1));
      pos--;
    } // while
    // A[pos] is where a gets inserted
    A.set(pos, a);
  }// for
} // _sort()
```

And make the following call at the end of the WordFreq() constructor:

```
// Sort the table in reverse order of frequencies
_sort(wordFrequency);
```

> *Try This: Add the sorting described here to your word cloud sketch and observe the output.*

A partial output from the sketch that includes this sorting approach is shown here:

```
4155 tokens found in file: Obama.txt
There are 1023 entries.
<war, 35>
<peace, 28>
<human, 21>
<nations, 17>
<america, 16>
<rights, 10>
<wars, 9>
<conflict, 9>
<violence, 8>
<nuclear, 8>
<force, 8>
<history, 7>
<seek, 7>
<countries, 7>
<security, 7>
<true, 7>
<citizens, 6>
<king, 6>
<men, 6>
<nation, 6>
...
Max frequency:35
```

Now the relevant words that will be used in the display have been successfully mined from the word frequency table. These words, along with their frequency counts can be used to create word cloud visualization.

Choosing a Visual Representation

Next, the task is to use the word frequency table computed previously to create a graphic visualization of the most frequent words. Choosing a visual representation is an exploratory as well as a creative exercise. In this application, we already have a good idea of the kind of visual representation we desire: a word cloud. In a word cloud, words are displayed in size proportional to their frequency. Also, given that there are over 1000 words in the table generated from the sample text (and there may be many more in case of other texts), you would want to restrict displaying only the first N most frequent words (say N = 150, for starters). You would also want to have good control on other attributes of the visualization: the color in which words are displayed, the font in which they will be displayed, the spatial placement of words, and so on. So that you can experiment and explore these ideas, you will need to learn a little more about fonts and their properties in Processing, and also redesign the program so that it is extendible across various other parameters. First, let's learn about displaying text and customizing fonts and font colors in Processing.

Displaying Text Using Fonts

You saw in Chapter 5 how to display strings in a sketch using the textSize() and text() functions. Just to review, here is an example (its output is shown in Figure 7-2)

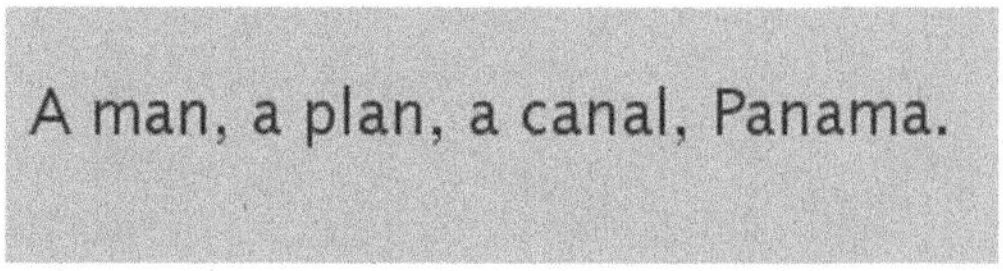

A man, a plan, a canal, Panama.

Figure 7-2. Displaying simple text in a sketch

```
// Sketch 7-5: Displaying Simple Text.
String sentence = "A man, a plan, a canal, Panama.";
void setup() {
  size(400, 100);
  smooth();
} // setup()

void draw() {
  background(200);
  fill(0);
  textSize(24);
  text(sentence, 10, height/2);
} // draw()
```

Text is essentially treated the same as any other graphical object in processing. The fill() command in the preceding sketch is used to specify the color in which the text will be rendered. The textSize() command specifies the font size and the text() command actually draws a given string at the x-, and y- coordinates provided. These coordinates, or anchor points, specify the bottom-left corner of the text.

Processing provides several useful text-related functions that allow you to select a different font and its rendering. In displaying this text, Processing used a default font. If you would like to choose a specific font for the text you want to display, Processing can do this in many different ways. The easiest is to use the createFont() function. createFont() returns an object of type PFont that is a predefined class in Processing. Once a font has been created, it can be used by first selecting the font (using the textFont() function) and various drawing attributes you already know. This is shown here:

```
// Sketch 7-6: Displaying Text in a Specific Font
String sentence = "A man, a plan, a canal, Panama.";
PFont tnr;

void setup() {
  size(400, 100);
  smooth();
  tnr = createFont("Times New  Roman", 48);
  println(PFont.list());
} // setup()

void draw() {
  background(200);
  fill(0);
  textFont(tnr);
  textSize(24);
  text(sentence, 10, height/2);
} // draw()
```

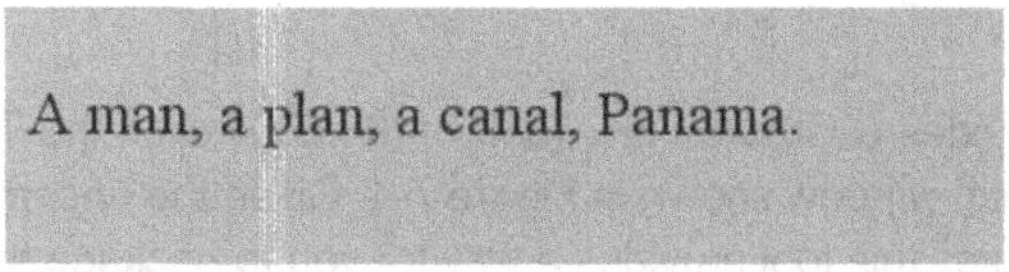

A man, a plan, a canal, Panama.

Figure 7-3. Displaying text in a specific font

To summarize, you first define a PFont variable (tnr), create a PFont object with the specific font using createFont() in setup(), then specify the font using textFont() each time you want to use that font, adjust the size using textSize(), and draw the string using text(). In the example, we used the font named "Times New Roman". Each computer, depending on the kind of operating system it is running, and other factors, has a number of fonts installed on it. Processing is designed to use whatever fonts are available on your computer. To find out what fonts are available, you can issue the simple command:

```
println(PFont.list());
```

The list() method of PFont class returns an array of strings containing a list of all the fonts installed. You can specify any of them in the createFont() function.

> *Try This: Sketch 7-7 prints the number of fonts installed on your system and then prints the font name in the same font whenever you click the mouse in the sketch window.*

```
// Sketch 7-7: List of fonts
String[] fonts;
PFont font;
int N, i;

void setup() {
  size(500, 500);
  background(255);
  fonts =  PFont.list();
  N = fonts.length;
  i = 0;
  println("There are "+N+" fonts installed.");
} // setup()
void draw() {
} // draw()

void mousePressed() {
  font = createFont(fonts[i], 24);
  textFont(font);
  fill(0);
  text(fonts[i], mouseX, mouseY);
  i++;
} // mousePressed()
```

The Processing IDE also provides a Create Font Tool. In the IDE, click the Tools tab and select the Create Font . . . option to get the pop-up window shown in Figure 7-4. Given the uncertainty of the kind and number of fonts available on each computer, this tool provides a way for you to package the font inside your sketch's Data folder so that no matter where anyone uses your sketch it will have the fonts you chose to use. To do this, you use the tool to create a font file (with the extension ".vlw"). Select the font(s) you plan to use, the size, and the filename if you want to change it from the default, and click OK. The font data is sorted as a part of your sketch. Next, to use this data file, you use the loadFont() function instead of createFont(). For example, in the sketch used for Figure 7-3 just replace the line:

```
tnr = createFont("Times New Roman", 48);
```

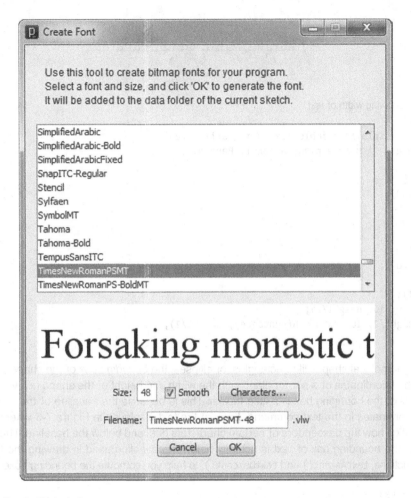

Figure 7-4. The Create Font window

with the line:

```
tnr = loadFont("TimesNewRomanPSMT-48.vlw");
```

The rest of the sketch remains unchanged. You can additionally achieve finer creative control by using some of the font metrics functions that provide access to the width, ascent, and descent, and so on of some text you want to display in a sketch. For example, the textWidth() function returns the width of the text (see Figure 7-5):

A man, a plan, a canal, Panama.

Figure 7-5. Line showing width of text

```
// Sketch 7-8: Displaying Simple Text using attributes
String sentence = "A man, a plan, a canal, Panama.";

void setup() {
  size(400, 100);
  smooth();
} // setup()

void draw() {
  background(200);
  fill(0);
  textSize(24);
  text(sentence, 10, height/2);
  line(10, height/2, 10+textWidth(sentence), height/2);
} // draw()
```

In the case of geometrical shapes like rectangles, or ellipses, the *bounding box* of the shape is clearly marked by specifying the coordinates of a corner along with the width and height of the shape (x, y, w, h). However, in the case of text, the bounding box is a little trickier. This is because the baseline of the text is specified by the x- and y-coordinates in the text command. Look at the text displayed in Figure 7-5 where the baseline is also shown. Notice how the descenders of certain characters descend below the baseline. Thus, the bottom or y-coordinate of the bounding box of text is actually below the baseline used in drawing the text. Processing provides two functions, textAscent() and textDescent(), to help you compute the bounding boxes of any text:

```
float ascend = textAscent();
float descend = textDescent();
```

These two functions return a floating point value denoting the number of pixels the text ascends or descends above/below the baseline. Figure 7-6 illustratzes the ascenders and descenders.

Figure 7-6. Font metrics

Processing offers several additional text-related functions in its API, including additional parameters in some of the functions we have introduced. Consult the Processing Reference for more depth.

> *Try This: Take your favorite poem or song and put it in a plain text file. Write a sketch that inputs the poem and displays each line of the poem one at a time against an image background. Next, modify the sketch so that the next line is drawn only when the mouse is clicked. This is a very simple illustration of how presentation software programs (like Microsoft PowerPoint, Apple Keynote, etc.) work.*

Word Cloud Visualization

Returning now to the sketch that computes the most frequent words, it is now time to design the visualization. Each word in the word cloud is going to be displayed in a chosen font, in size proportional to its frequency, and placed in the sketch in a spatially appealing manner. These requirements force the extension of the design of the code that implements the sketch. Instead of just focusing on the word and its associated frequency, you now have to also keep track of its visual properties: its font, font size, its color, location, and also its boundaries. The main sketch, presented here, uses the WordFreq class to create the word frequency table (table) given an input file (inputTextFile) and then tabulate the resulting frequency table.

```
// Sketch: 7-9: Computing word frequencies using WordFreq & Word
String inputTextFile = "Obama.txt";
WordFreq table;
int N = 150; // The number of words to be displayed

void setup() {
  // Input and parse text file
  String [] fileContents = loadStrings(inputTextFile);
  String rawText = join(fileContents, " ");
  rawText = rawText.toLowerCase();
  String [] tokens;
  String delimiters = " ,./?<>;:'\"[{]}\\|=+-_()*&^%$#@!~";
  tokens = splitTokens(rawText, delimiters);
  println(tokens.length+" tokens found in file: "+inputTextFile);

  // Create the word frequency table
  table = new WordFreq(tokens);
  table.tabulate(N);
    println("Max frequency:"+table.maxFreq());
} // setup()
```

The WordFreq class is presented in Sketch 7-9a. It is essentially identical to the one presented earlier (Sketch 7-4a) with a small change in the parameter of tabulate, which now prints the first n entries.

```
// Sketch 7-9a: The Word frequency table class
class WordFreq {
  // A Frequency table class for Words
  ArrayList<Word> wordFrequency;
  String [] stopWords = loadStrings("stopwords.txt");
```

```
WordFreq(String[] tokens) {  // Constructor

  wordFrequency = new ArrayList();
  // Compute the wordFrequency table using tokens
  for (String t : tokens) {
    if (!_isStopWord(t)) {
      // See if token t is already a known word
      int index = _search(t, wordFrequency);
      if (index >= 0) {
        ( wordFrequency.get(index)).incr();
      }
      else {
        wordFrequency.add(new Word(t));
      }
    }
  } // for
} // WordFreq()

void tabulate(int n) {  // console printout for n entries
  println("There are "+N()+" entries.");
  for (int i=0; i < n; i++) {
    println(wordFrequency.get(i));
  }
} // tabulate

int N() { // Number of table entries
  return wordFrequency.size();
} // N()

String[] samples() {  // Returns all the words
  String [] k = new String[N()];
  int i=0;
  for (Word w : wordFrequency) {
    k[i++] = w.getWord();
  }
  return k;
} // samples()

int[] counts() {  // Returns all the frequencies
  int [] v = new int[N()];
  int i=0;
  for (Word w : wordFrequency) {
    v[i++] = w.getFreq();
  }
  return v;
} // counts()
```

```
  int maxFreq() {  // The max frequency
    return max(counts());
  } // maxFreq()

  int _search(String w, ArrayList<Word> L) {
    // search for word w  in L.
    // Returns index of w in L if found, -1 o/w
    for (int i=0; i < L.size(); i++) {
      if (L.get(i).getWord().equals(w))
        return i;
    }
    return -1;
  } // _search()

  boolean _isStopWord(String word) {  // Is word a stop word?
    for (String stopWord : stopWords) {
      if (word.equals(stopWord)) {
        return true;
      }
    }
    return false;
  } // _isStopWord()

  String toString() {  // Print representation
    return "Word Frequency Table with"+N()+" entries.";
  } // toString()
} // class WordFreq
```

And finally, the Word class, which we shall soon extend, is presented. It is the same as the one presented earlier in Sketch 7-2a.

```
// Sketch 7-9b: The Word class
class Word {
  // Each Word is a pair: the word, and its frequency
  String word;
  int freq;

  Word(String newWord) {  // Constructor
    word = newWord;
    freq = 1;
  } // Word()

  String getWord() {
    return word;
  } // getWord()

  int getFreq() {
    return freq;
  } // getFreq()
```

```
  void incr() {  // increments the word count
    freq++;
  } // incr()

  String toString() {  // print representation of Word objects
    return "<"+word+", "+freq+">";
  } // toString()
} // class Word
```

> *Try This: Assemble the Sketch 7-9 (using all the parts 7-9, 7-9a and 7-9b) and ensure that it runs correctly and gives the output shown here:*

```
4155 tokens found in file: Obama.txt
There are 1023 entries.
<war, 35>
<peace, 28>
<human, 21>
<nations, 17>
<america, 16>
<rights, 10>
<wars, 9>
<conflict, 9>
<violence, 8>
<nuclear, 8>
<force, 8>
<history, 7>
<seek, 7>
<countries, 7>
<security, 7>
<true, 7>
<citizens, 6>
<king, 6>
<men, 6>
<nation, 6>
...
Max frequency:35
```

Next, to add the additional visual properties to the Word class, we will extend it into a subclass called, WordTile, as shown here (we will save these as Sketch 7-10):

```
// Sketch 7-10c: The WordTile class
class WordTile extends Word {
  // A graphical tile containing a word and additional attributes
  PVector location;   // The top left corner of the tile (x, y)
  float tileW, tileH; // width and height of the tile
  color tileColor;    // fill color of word
  float tileFS = 24;  // the font size of tile, default is 24
```

```
WordTile(String newWord) { // Constructor
  super(newWord);
  setSize();
  location = new PVector(0, 0);
  tileColor = color(0);
} // WordTile()

void setXY (float x, float y) {
  location.x = x;
  location.y = y;
} // setXY()

void setFontSize() {
  tileFS = map(freq, 1, 30, 10, 120);
  setSize();
} // setFontSize()

void setSize() {
  textSize(tileFS);
  tileW = textWidth(word);
  tileH = textAscent();
} // setTileSize()

void display() {
  fill(tileColor);
  textSize(tileFS);
  text(word, location.x, location.y);
} // display()
} // class WordTile
```

Because the WordTile class inherits from or extends the Word class, it inherits all the available attributes (word, freq) and methods that are not overridden in WordList. WordTile class adds attributes for location, width, height, color, and font size. The location along with the width and height will be used to compute the bounding box of the word in placing the tiles in the word cloud. For the time being, we are setting the color of all words to black but this can be changed or parameterized. Also, whenever the font size of a WordTile is set or changed, its bounding box is also changed using setSize(). The display() method is responsible for displaying the word tile in the tile's color and font.

You are now ready to use the WordTile class in the sketch. One change you will need to make in the WordFreq (from Sketch 7-9a) class is to now refer to WordTile wherever there was a reference to Word class objects. We show the WordFreq class in the following sketch, reflecting these changes as well as some additions:

```
// Sketch 7-10a: The Word frequency table class
class WordFreq {
  // A Frequency table class for Words
  ArrayList<WordTile> wordFrequency;
  String [] stopWords = loadStrings("stopwords.txt");
```

```
WordFreq(String[] tokens) {  // Constructor
  wordFrequency = new ArrayList();
  // Compute the wordFrequency table using tokens
  for (String t : tokens) {
    if (!_isStopWord(t)) {
      // See if token t is already a known word
      int index = _search(t, wordFrequency);
      if (index >= 0) {
        ( wordFrequency.get(index)).incr();
      }
      else {
        wordFrequency.add(new WordTile(t));
      }
    }
  }  // for
}  // WordFreq()

void tabulate(int n) {  // console printout
  //int n = wordFrequency.size();
  println("There are "+N()+" entries.");
  for (int i=0; i < n; i++) {
    println(wordFrequency.get(i));
  }
}  // tabulate

void arrange(int N) {  // arrange or map the first N tiles in sketch
  for (int i=0; i < N; i++) {
    WordTile tile = wordFrequency.get(i);
    tile.setFontSize();
    tile.setSize();
    tile.setXY(random(width), random(height));
  }
}  // arrange()

void display(int N) {
  for (int i=0; i < N; i++) {
    WordTile tile = wordFrequency.get(i);
    tile.display();
  }
}  // display()

int N() { // Number of table entries
    return wordFrequency.size();
}  // N()

  String[] samples() {  // Returns all the words
    String [] k = new String[N()];
    int i=0;
```

```
    for (WordTile w : wordFrequency) {
      k[i++] = w.getWord();
    }
    return k;
  } // samples()

  int[] counts() {  // Returns all the frequencies
    int [] v = new int[N()];
    int i=0;
    for (WordTile w : wordFrequency) {
      v[i++] = w.getFreq();
    }
    return v;
  } // counts()

  int maxFreq() {  // The max frequency
    return max(counts());
  } // maxFreq()

  int _search(String w, ArrayList<WordTile> L) {
    // search for word w  in L.
    // Returns index of w in L if found, -1 o/w
    for (int i=0; i < L.size(); i++) {
      if (L.get(i).getWord().equals(w))
        return i;
    }
    return -1;
  } // _search()

  boolean _isStopWord(String word) {  // Is word a stop word?
   for (String stopWord : stopWords) {
      if (word.equals(stopWord)) {
        return true;
      }
    }
    return false;
  } // _isStopWord()

  String toString() {  // Print representation
    return "Word Frequency Table with"+N()+" entries.";
  } // toString()
} // class WordFreq
```

The arrange() and display() methods were added to the WordFreq class as shown in the preceding example. arrange() spatially arranges the tiles in the sketch and display() displays them in the sketch after setting the tile's display attributes (font size, size, location, etc.). For the moment, arrange() places each tile randomly in the sketch. This is where we will need to spend some time thinking about how best to arrange the words in a cloud-like fashion. But first, let's write the sketch that uses these functionalities to create a first draft of the word cloud visualization.

```
// Sketch 7-10: Word Cloud Visualization - First Draft
String inputTextFile = "Obama.txt";
WordFreq table;
PFont tnr;       // The font to be used
int N = 150;     // The number of words to be displayed

void setup() {
  // Input and parse text file
  String [] fileContents = loadStrings(inputTextFile);
  String rawText = join(fileContents, " ");
  rawText = rawText.toLowerCase();
  String [] tokens;
  String delimiters = " ,./?<>;:'\"[{]}\\|=+-_()*&^%$#@!~";
  tokens = splitTokens(rawText, delimiters);
  println(tokens.length+" tokens found in file: "+inputTextFile);

  // display stuff
  size(800, 800, OPENGL);
  tnr = createFont("Times New Roman", 120);
  textFont(tnr);
  textSize(24);
  noLoop();
  // Create the word frequency table
  table = new WordFreq(tokens);
  println("Max frequency:"+table.maxFreq());
  table.arrange(N);
} // setup()

void draw() {
  background(255);
  table.display(N);
  table.tabulate(N);
} // draw()
```

You need to reuse the Word class from Sketch 7-9b (rename it to 7-10b) to complete the sketch. Figure 7-7 shows an output from the sketch. While you can clearly see the words displayed proportional to their frequencies, they are scattered all over the sketch because a random positioning strategy is used in arrange(), which is called at the very end of setup(). That will be addressed next and all the work we have done in creating the tiles and their bounds will pay off there.

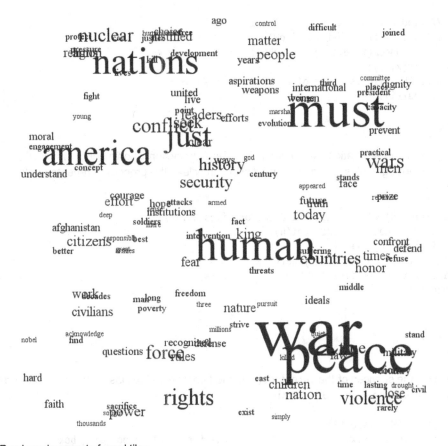

Figure 7-7. Random placement of word tiles

> *Try This: Implement the sketch presented and extend it so that whenever the mouse is clicked, the tile layout is rearranged.*

The next natural extension to the sketch is to try and ensure that each tile is placed so that it doesn't overlap any of the tiles already arranged. The only modification required is in the `arrange()` method, as shown here:

```
For each tile
    pick a random location and ensure that it doesn't intersect any of the previous tiles
```

This is perhaps easier said than done. Here is the code:

```
void arrange(int N) {              // arrange or map the first N tiles in sketch
  WordTile tile;
  for (int i=0; i < N; i++) {
    tile = wordFrequency.get(i);   // the tile to be placed
    tile.setFontSize();
```

```
      do {  // find a random x, y for tile, i
        float x = random(width-tile.tileW);
        float y = random(tile.tileH, height);
        tile.setXY(x, y);
      } // until the tile is clear of all other tiles
      while (!clear(i));
  }
} // arrange()
```

In arrange(), random x, y locations are chosen. The clear() function, shown next, confirms that the tile is clear of all previously arranged tiles. If the chosen location isn't clear, the process is repeated until a clear location is found.

```
boolean clear(int n) { // Is tile, i clear of tiles 0..i-1?
  WordTile tile1 = wordFrequency.get(n);
  for (int i=0; i < n; i++) {
    WordTile tile2 = wordFrequency.gct(i);
    if (tile1.intersect(tile2)) {
      return false;
    }
  } // for
  return true;
} // clear()
```

clear() requires the services of the intersect() method from WordTile class. intersect() returns true if two tiles intersect, false otherwise and is shown here:

```
boolean intersect(WordTile t2) {
    float left1 = location.x;                 // the first tile's bounding box
    float right1 = location.x+tileW;
    float top1 = location.y-tileH;
    float bot1 = location.y;
    float left2 = t2.location.x;              // the second tile's bounding box
    float right2 = left2+t2.tileW;
    float bot2 = t2.location.y;
    float top2 = bot2-t2.tileH;

    return !(right1 < left2 || left1 > right2 || bot1 < top2 || top1 > bot2);
    // testing intersection
} // intersect()
```

intersect() uses a simple rectangle-rectangle overlapping test. Please ensure that you understand the logic used here. The condition in the return statement first tests to see whether the two rectangles do not intersect. The negation (!) of that outcome is returned as a result. Figure 7-8 shows an output from this version. Notice now the words are no longer overlapping. If you run the sketch a few times you will notice some overlaps at the bottom or descenders of words. This is because in computing the height of the tile, we only accounted for the ascenders. We will leave it as an exercise for you to address this.

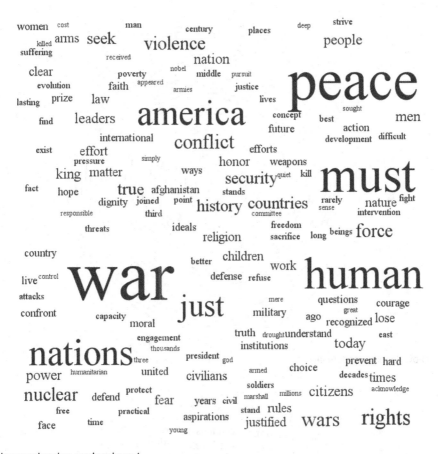

Figure 7-8. Non-overlapping random layout

Spiral Packing a Word Cloud

Above, we created a word cloud by randomly selecting a place in the sketch for the word tile to be placed so that it doesn't overlap any of the previously placed tiles. The resulting visualization contains the end result, the desired set of most frequent words, but lacks a certain aesthetic appeal. We will address this next by presenting an algorithm that was suggested by Jonathan Feinberg, the creator of Wordle (see References at the end of this chapter):

```
For each word w in sorted words:
    while w intersects any previously placed words:
        move w a little bit along a spiral path
```

The only change that needs to be made is in the arrange() function. Instead of assigning a random non-overlapping position to a tile, arrange() has to look for placing each word along a spiral, starting each time, at the center (see Figure 7-9). This version of arrange() is shown in the next example, along with the output produced in Figure 7-10:

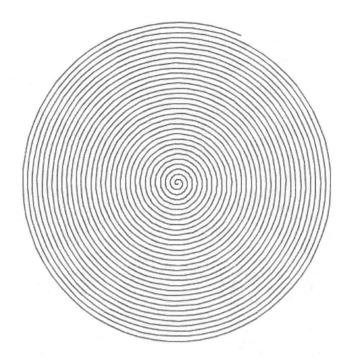

Figure 7-9. Non-overlapping random layout

Figure 7-10. The spiral word cloud

```
void arrange(int N) {   // arrange or map the first N tiles in sketch
  WordTile tile;

  for (int i=0; i < N; i++) {
    tile = wordFrequency.get(i);
    tile.setFontSize();

    // Exploring the spiral layout
    float cx = width/2, cy = height/2, px, py;
    float R = 0.0, dR = 0.2, theta = 0.0, dTheta = 0.5;

    do {  // find the next x, y for tile, i in spiral
      float x = cx + R*cos(theta);
      float y = cy + R*sin(theta);
      tile.setXY(x, y);
      px = x;
      py = y;
      theta+=dTheta;
      R += dR;
    } // until the tile is clear of all other tiles
    while (!clear (i));
  }
} // arrange()
```

The spiral is placed in the center of the sketch (cx, cy). Given a radius (R) and an angle (theta), the next x, y coordinates to explore are computed. To compute the next point in the spiral the previous x,y points area saved (in px, py) and the radius as well as the angle is incremented (by dR and dTheta). Figure 7-9 shows the spiral, or the set of points that are explored.

The resulting design of the program allows you to explore other layout options. In computer science and mathematics, there is a rich body of work relating to tilings and algorithms for laying out tiles. Later in this book you will see examples of alternative visualizations as well.

Making the Visualization Interactive

The last step in a visualization exercise is to make it interactive. We alluded to this in our earlier example in Chapter 5. Given a visualization, you need to first decide what interactivity means in the context of that visualization. Then you also have to think about what interactive modalities are available to the application: keyboard, mouse motions and clicks, finger/gestures, joysticks, gamepads, and so on. The extent and mode of interaction of commonly available devices is continuously increasing and integration of these devices into your visualizations can require creativity as well as technological skills. One of the basic reasons for doing information visualization is to provide a perspective on the underlying data, its context, and interactively allow or engage a user in exploring various aspects of the data. In the word cloud application, for example, mousing over a displayed word could provide more information: its frequency count, rank, perhaps the context of the first occurrence of the word, and so on. There are again many possibilities. From the perspective of program design, all you really have to do is to consider adding a new method, called interact(), to the WordFrequency class. For example, given the position of the mouse in the sketch, you could write the draw function of the sketch as shown here:

```
void draw() {
  background(255);
  table.display(N);
  table.interact(mouseX, mouseY);
} // draw()
```

That is, the interact() method, given the current mouse coordinates, can easily search the table of word tiles to locate the word over which the mouse is hovering. Then, based on what you decide, you could include actions on the tile: to display its frequency, or to change its color, or allow the user to reposition the tile. We will leave you with these ideas to try as exercises.

Before we conclude this chapter, we want to make you aware of the possibility of a redesign of the sketch. Think about when you were playing with the Wordle program. You could consider the word cloud itself as an object. In that case, you can reorganize your sketch so that a word cloud object is created by providing it some raw text (a string long string). Then, you can operate on the word cloud through a number of methods: display(), rearrange(), setFont(), setColor(), setLayout(), and so on. You can imagine how Wordle itself is implemented. This further simplifies your main sketch, and also provides places in your program where you can implement any of the new features.

```
String inputTextFile = "Obama.txt";
WordCloud cloud;

void setup() {
  // Input and parse text file
  String [] fileContents = loadStrings(inputTextFile);
  String rawText = join(fileContents, " ").toLowerCase();
  cloud = new WordCloud(rawText);
} // setup()

void draw() {
  background(255):
  cloud.display();
  cloud.interact(mouseX, mouseY);
} // draw()
```

This is where object-oriented design really pays off. Sketches are better designed so that they are easily maintained and are eminently extensible without too many changes in several portions of the code. You saw a concrete example of this when we were implementing different layout options. All the changes to the layout algorithm were in the arrange() function.

Several immediate extensions are possible to the final sketch. Words could be displayed in different colors or shades: less frequent words appear smaller and lighter. Words could be displayed rotated: a mix of horizontal and vertical, or even rotated a random amount. You could change the number of words displayed.

In the word cloud visualization we used what is considered proportional visual representation of words, where the size of the word (or data item) is proportional to its frequency. Together with proportional representation we also explored the problem of packing the words into a given space without overlapping. In particular, we used rectangles to form bounding boxes of words. You could easily use circles, or other more complex, or tighter shapes. The more complex the bounding shape is, the harder it is to detect overlaps. An alternative to tracking coordinates and computing the intersections is to check with the pixel buffer for non-white pixels instead (see Figure 7-11). We will present pixel buffers in a later chapter. Our goal in this chapter was to deconstruct a popular application that has been used by millions around the world and show you how, using the concepts you have learned, you can design, develop, and implement such applications.

Figure 7-11. Word cloud using pixel buffer

Creative Data Visualization

Doing creative data visualization is fast becoming its own industry within the realm of data analytics or data science. Creative computational artists are applying the visualization process to all kinds of domains and data. Flip through some popular media and look for such visualizations. In Figure 7-12, we show a map-based visualization of wind speed and direction being tracked in real time. The visualization is from Superstorm Sandy that hit the mid-Atlantic region of the eastern United States on October 30, 2012. In this example (taken from `http://hint.fm/wind/gallery/oct-30.js.html`) forecast data from the U.S. National Weather

Service's National Digital Forecast Database is acquired and visualized over the entire geographical area of the 48 contiguous states. Here, to locate the placement of the wind speed (and direction) you need to map the longitude and latitude coordinates of the locations where data was collected. Doing creative visualizations, as we said earlier, is an art as well as a science. A creative combination of both can yield some amazing results.

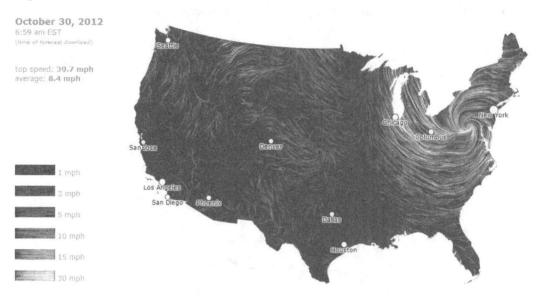

Figure 7-12. Visualizing Superstorm Sandy, October 30, 2012

Summary

This chapter really dove into a specific type of visualization: creating word coulds from input text. We started from scratch, by processing an input text, extracting works, eliminating stop words, and finally doing frequency counts that are later used to display proportionally sized words in the word cloud. Along the way you also learned about strings, ArrayList objects, sorting algorithms, and basic font metrics. You also saw how, in the course of developing a larger application, it is worthwhile redesigning the program. It makes future extensions possible. Principles of abstraction and object-oriented design were exploited to clean up the final program. We hope you enjoyed this hands-on tour of creating word cloud visualizations.

References

Feinberg, Jonathan. "Wordle." In *Beautiful Visualization: Looking at Data Through the Eyes of Experts*, edited by Julie Steele & Noah Ilinsky. Pages 37–58. O'Reilly, 2010.

Obama, Barack. "Just War." Nobel Peace Prize Award Ceremony, Oslo, Norway, 2009. Available at: http://www.nobelprize.org/nobel_prizes/peace/laureates/2009/presentation-speech.html.

Sedgewick, Robert. "Quicksort." PhD. diss., Stanford University, Stanford, CA, 1975.

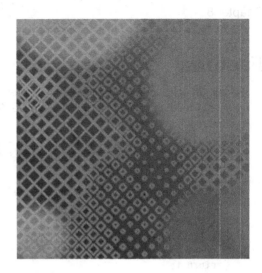

Chapter 8

Drawing with Recursion

Recursion is fundamentally based on the notion of self-similarity and repetition. Fractal art is probably the most well popularized example of mathematical recursion, first made famous by the striking images produced in the 1970s by Benoit Mandelbrot with early computer-aided visualizations. However visual art showing recursive themes appeared much earlier, in particular, M. C. Escher and René Magritte's work comes to mind. Although fundamentally a mathematical construct and immensely applicable in general-purpose programming, recursion exhibits stunning symmetry and aesthetics when used in conjunction with geometric forms and topological patterns. In this chapter we will introduce basic recursion and recursive functions, as well as a data visualization example based on recursive treemaps.

Recursive Functions

Although recursion takes many forms, the essential characteristic that makes something recursive is the creation of a new instance of itself repeatedly. For example, placing two mirrors in front of each other will result in nested images that are a form of infinite recursion. Recursion is a property of many natural languages, which allow clause embedding in sentences. Constructions such as "She knows that he thinks that we don't care that she knows .... " is a demonstration of such in English. Besides the possibility of infinite repetition, recursion also makes it difficult for humans to distinguish the new instances from the old. For this reason recursive definitions are very rare in everyday situations. It is a problem computers can easily overcome however, and the most common application of recursion in computer science is defining recursive functions, in other words, functions that call themselves.

Factorial

Recall the definition of the factorial of a non-negative integer n, denoted by n!, as the product of all positive integers less than or equal to n. For example, 5! = 5x4x3x2x1 = 120. Mathematically, the factorial has a very natural recursive definition

$$n! = \begin{cases} 1, & n = 0 \\ n \times (n-1)!, & n > 0 \end{cases}$$

which has a direct translation into a recursive function in Processing:

```
//factorial.pde, chapter 8
int factorial(int n) {
  if (n == 0) {
    return 1;
  } else {
    return n*factorial(n-1);
  }
}  //end factorial()
```

It is important to trace the series of function calls and realize what actually happens when a call to factorial(5) is made. factorial(5) is expanded to 5*factorial(4) via the else case as 5 is greater than 0, then to 5*4*factorial(3), 5*4*3*factorial(2), 5*3*2*factorial(1), 5*4*3*2*1*factorial(0) and finally 5*4*3*2*1*1 when n is 0. The recursive calls end and the return value of 120 is calculated and returned. During the process the body of the factorial() function is executed 6 times, each time an instance of the function is invoked on a smaller version of the problem, namely to calculate (n-1)!. The condition n==0 tests for the base case, often known as the *stopping condition* for a recursive call. This is important because although a computer can easily keep track of many different instances of the same function, it cannot handle infinite recursion.

> Try This: What do you think will happen if you call factorial() with a negative integer, that is, factorial(-1)?

Recursion is an important abstraction mechanism that allows one to focus on the crux of a solution to many seemingly complicated problems. In computing there are several well-known examples of problems whose recursive solutions are often very intuitive and simple. Notice the Processing function to compute the preceding factorial is essentially a direct translation of the mathematical definition. Moreover, the definition is focused more on specifying *what* is to be computed, and not necessarily *how* it will be computed. This is an important distinction between what is considered *declarative programming* versus *imperative programming*. Declarative programming expresses the logic of a computation without spelling out explicitly how to do the computation. The difference can be easily seen in the coding of another version of the factorial (from Chapter 4), programmed imperatively:

```
int getFactorial(int val) {
  int fact = 1;
  while (val > 0) {
```

```
    fact*=val;
    val--;
  }
  return fact;
}
```

While both functions will compute the correct value of the factorial, the latter is defined imperatively: by explicitly specifying that we begin by setting the variable fact to 1 and then repeatedly multiplying by val, and decrementing val by 1 after each repetition. This is the "how" part of doing a computation. Using recursion it is easy to specify the "what" of computation. The carrying out or execution of the recursive computation is handled by the implementation of the Processing/ Java language.

Recursion is often used to simplify the specification of algorithms. It is a powerful thinking tool. It is used extensively in expressing definitions of mathematical functions (as we saw in the case of the factorial function). In computer science, many programming languages and formalisms have been designed using pure mathematical functions as their basis. This is very different from imperative programming languages like Processing/Java, which are based on a model of computation that is heavily dependent on the underlying computer architecture.

Recursive Circles

We now show a visual example of recursion. We start with the following non-recursive Processing program that draws a single large circle in the middle of the screen (see Figure 8-1). The code should be quite familiar to you, and the only thing worth noting is that we wrapped the call to ellipse() in a function called drawCircle(). At the moment, all drawCircle() does is check the size parameter s to make sure it's greater than 2 and then calls ellipse() with s as both width and height.

```
// recursiveCircle.pde, chapter 8
void setup() {
  size(800, 800);
  background(255);
  smooth();
  noFill();
  translate(width/2, height/2);      // move to the middle of the screen
  drawCircle(0, 0, width/2);         // draws a circle half size of the screen width
} // end setup()

//draw a circle of size s at x, y, s>2
void drawCircle(int x, int y, int s) {
  if (s>2) {
    ellipse(x, y, s, s);
  }
} // end drawCircle()
```

Figure 8-1. Output from recursiveCircle.pde

Now we add one recursive call to the function drawCircle():

```
//draw a circle of size radius s at x, y, s>2
void drawCircle(int x, int y, int s) {
  if (s>2) {
    ellipse(x, y, s, s);
    drawCircle(x-s/2, y, s/2);        // recursive call
  }
}// end drawCircle()
```

Recall that the first two parameters of drawCircle() specify the x and y coordinates of the center of the circle and the third parameter is the size of the circle. The following values are passed into the recursive call: x-s/2, y, and s/2, which means each call will draw a circle half of the current size and move the center to the left by half of the current circle's diameter. The y positions of the circle centers remain unchanged. The drawing stops when the diameter of the circle reaches 2 or less, as guaranteed by the if statement. The drawing results are shown in Figure 8-2. At this point, you might be wondering what the big fuss about recursion is, as you can easily imagine how the code can be rewritten with a loop to do the same thing, but without recursion.

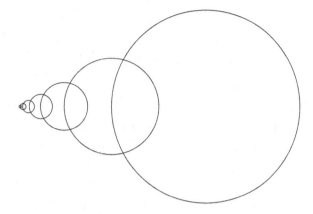

Figure 8-2. Output after a recursive call is added to `drawCircle()`

Next we add one more recursive call to `drawCircle()`, this time to draw a second half-size circle to the right of the current. The results are shown in Figure 8-3.

```
//draw a circle of size radius s at x, y, s>2
void drawCircle(int x, int y, int s) {
  if (s>2) {
    ellipse(x, y, s, s);
    drawCircle(x-s/2, y, s/2);
    drawCircle(x+s/2, y, s/2);
  }
} // end drawCircle()
```

Try This: Before checking out Figure 8-3, can you guess how it would look?

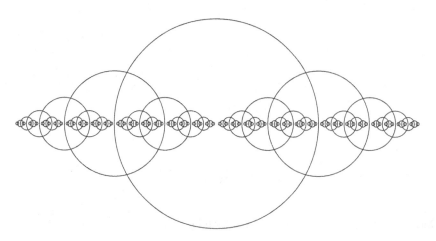

Figure 8-3. Output after a second recursive call is added to drawCircle()

It turns out that Figure 8-2 is usually not a surprise to those who are first introduced to recursion, however Figure 8-3 is. Many expect a mirror image of Figure 8-2, with the left "arrow" of circles reflected and added to the right half. The additional complexity recursion brings is unexpected, because the second recursive call changes the number of additional function calls from linear to exponential. The important thing to note here is that *each* recursive function call generates two additional recursive calls and thus the entire call pattern is tree-like when traced, as illustrated in Figure 8-4, which traces out the first two levels of the recursion. The parameters in the function calls are substituted with actual values to distinguish between different instances of the function calls.

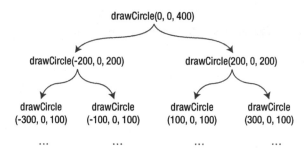

Figure 8-4. Trace of recursive function calls to drawCircle()

Figures 8-5 through 8-8 show which circles are drawn along the way and in what order, if recursion stopped after these first two levels (for example by changing the stopping condition to s>50). For example, Figure 8-5 illustrates the circles drawn after traversing the leftmost branch, that is, drawCircle(0, 0, 400) ⇒ drawCircle(-200, 0, 200) ⇒ drawCircle(-300, 0, 100); and Figure 8-6 shows the circles drawn after traversing the entire left subtree, i.e. drawCircle(0, 0, 400) ⇒ drawCircle(-200, 0, 200) ⇒ drawCircle(-300, 0, 100) ⇒ drawCircle(-100, 0, 100).

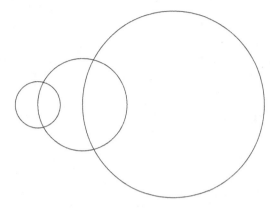

Figure 8-5. Drawing results after call to drawCircle(-300, 0, 100)

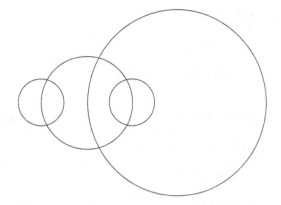

Figure 8-6. Drawing results after call to drawCircle(-100, 0, 100)

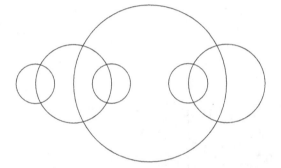

Figure 8-7. Drawing results after call to drawCircle(100, 0, 100)

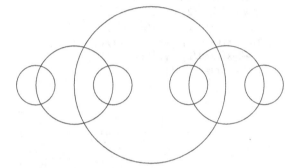

Figure 8-8. Drawing results after call to drawCircle(300, 0, 100)

> *Try This: What would the output look like if you add one more recursive call to drawCircle(), namely drawCircle(x, y-s/2, s/2)? And what about adding a fourth recursive call drawCircle(x, y+s/2, s/2)?*

Recursive Squares

Our next example shows a variation from the recursively drawn circles to squares. The function drawBox() takes three parameters cx, cy, and d and draws a square of side length d centered at cx and cy. Then four additional recursive calls are made to draw squares of half of the current size (all sides), centered on the four corners of the current square. The function terminates when the size of the current square becomes less than 20. The result is shown in Figure 8-9.

```
// recursiveBoxes.pde, chapter 8
void setup() {
  size(500, 500);
  background(255);
```

```
    rectMode(CENTER);
    noFill();
    stroke(0);

    drawBox(width/2, height/2, width/2);
} // end setup()

// Draw boxes recursively, centered at cx, cy, with size d.
void drawBox(float cx, float cy, float d) {
    strokeWeight(0.1*d);
    stroke(d);
    rect(cx, cy, d, d);

    // Base case.
    if (d < 20) return;

    //recursive calls
    drawBox(cx-d/2, cy-d/2, d/2);
    drawBox(cx+d/2, cy-d/2, d/2);
    drawBox(cx-d/2, cy+d/2, d/2);
    drawBox(cx+d/2, cy+d/2, d/2);
} // end drawBoxes()
```

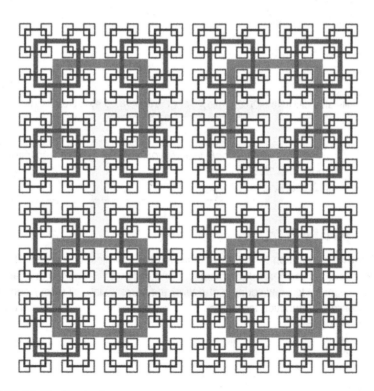

Figure 8-9. Output from recursiveBoxes.pde

Note that the top-level box (first and largest) was indeed drawn but cannot be seen, because the drawing color (in grayscale) is set to be the same as the current size and the first box starts with a size of 250, which is practically full white.

Figure 8-10 shows a variation with one level deeper recursion and colors that vary with the box sizes. The top level box was skipped with an `if` statement for aesthetic reasons.

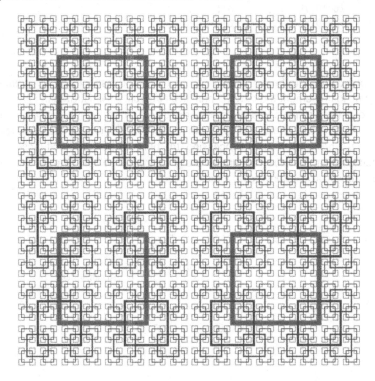

Figure 8-10. Variation of recursiveBoxes.pde

Recursive Tree

In this example, we show a recursive function that draws a tree. More precisely, at every iteration of the recursion, the function draws one branch (one line segment) with the following parameters: x0, y0, len and angle, where x0 and y0 are the x and y coordinates of the starting point, the segment length is given by len and the parameter angle specifies the angle the line segment makes with the horizontal. One end point of the line segment is passed into the function as (x0, y0), and the other (x1, y1) is obtained via simple trigonometric computations involving x0, y0, len and the sine and cosine of angle, which effectively rotates a line segment counterclockwise from horizontal.

```
//recursiveTree.pde, chapter 8
void setup() {
  size(800, 800);
  background(255);
  drawTree(width/2, height, 175, 90);
} //end setup()
```

```
void drawTree(float x0, float y0, float len, float angle) {
  if (len > 2) {
    float x1 = x0 + cos(radians(angle))*len;
    float y1 = y0 - sin(radians(angle))*len;

    line(x0, y0, x1, y1);
    drawTree(x1, y1, len*0.75, angle + 30);
    drawTree(x1, y1, len*0.66, angle - 50);
  }
} // end drawTree()
```

Recall the basic polar-coordinate-based rotation techniques and associated trigonometry we covered in Chapters 2 and 3, e.g., to implement the new 2D primitive Polygon. As illustrated in Figure 8-11, the geometric calculations can be explained by placing a circle centered on (x0, y0) of radius len. Thus, the second end point we want to compute lives on this circle, and trigonometry gives the x coordinate as x0+cos(angle)*len, and the y coordinate as y0-sin(angle)*len. In Processing, the built-in trigonometric functions require input angle parameters specified in radian. Because our angles are given from 0° to 360°, the calls to sin() and cos() have an additional call to the radians() conversion function.

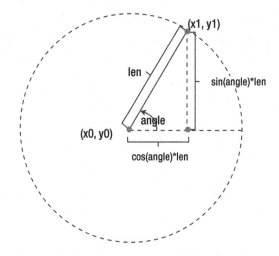

Figure 8-11. Trigonometry and polar coordinates on a circle

After drawing a single line segment of the given length and rotation, the function makes two recursive calls to draw two additional line segments starting at (x1, y1), with reduced lengths (75% and 66% of the original, respectively) and additional rotations (30 degrees to the left and 50 degrees to the right, respectively). Figure 8-12 illustrates a single level of the recursive calls.

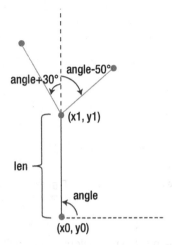

Figure 8-12. Illustration of recursive calls in drawTree()

The top-level call to drawTree() in setup() starts off the drawing with (x0, y0) placed at the coordinates (width/2, height), which is the bottom middle point of the sketch window, as we are growing the tree upward. The initial segment has a length of 175 and a 90-degree angle with the horizontal. Figures 8-13 through 8-16 illustrate the first few levels of recursion and their drawing results. The basic progression can be thought of as drawing a branch, moving to the end of that branch and drawing two child branches rotated 30° to the left and 50° to the right, and repeat for each child branch.

Figure 8-13. Drawing results with no recursion

Figure 8-14. Drawing results after one level of recursion of drawTree()

Figure 8-15. Drawing results after two levels of recursions of drawTree()

Figure 8-16. Drawing results after three levels of recursions of drawTree()

Recall that we also discussed coordinate system transformations in Chapter 3, which is an alternative way to program rotations and movements in general. In this context, our drawing sequence can be thought of as:

1. Rotate counterclockwise (by current angle)

2. Draw horizontal line segment (of current length)

3. Translate to the end of the line segment

4. Recurse on shorter branch 30° to the left

5. Recurse on shorter branch 50° to the right

Thus we can rewrite the program using transformations to move around, as shown next. In this version, the recursive function drawTree() only takes two parameters len and angle, as we are now moving our coordinate system instead and therefore will always draw at (0, 0), eliminating the need to keep track of the starting point.

```
//recursiveTreeTransform.pde. chapter 8
void setup() {
  size(800, 800);
  background(255);
  translate(width/2, height);
  drawTree(175, -90);
} //end setup()

void drawTree(float len, float angle) {
  if (len > 2) {
    rotate(radians(angle));
    line(0, 0, len, 0);
    translate(len, 0);
    pushMatrix();
    drawTree(len*0.75, -30);
    popMatrix();
```

```
    pushMatrix();
    drawTree(len*0.66, 50);
    popMatrix();
  }
} // end drawTree()
```

The two versions of the program are functionally identical. Note that Processing's rotate() rotates clockwise by default, thus all angles are negated in the version implemented with transformations. In addition, the pushMatrix() and popMatrix() function calls are necessary between the recursive calls to return the origin of the coordinate system to the end of the base/parent branch.

Shown in Figure 8-17 is the result of letting the recursion run until current line segment length is less than or equal to 2. Figures 8-18 and 8-19 are variations obtained with different branching angles; segment lengths and recursion stopping conditions (recursion depths).

Figure 8-17. Output from recursiveTree.pde or recursiveTreeTransform.pde

Figure 8-18. Variation 1 of recursiveTree.pde or recursiveTreeTransform.pde

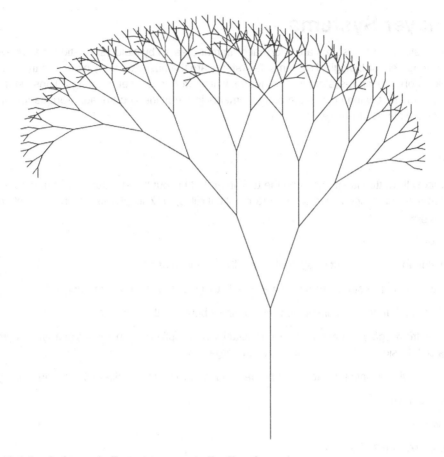

Figure 8-19. Variation 2 of recursiveTree.pde or recursiveTreeTransform.pde

Clearly, more variations can be obtained by varying the number of recursive calls. Moreover, randomness can be introduced to reduce the regularity of the shapes generated by recursion, so that each recursive call is not exactly a scaled-down copy of itself. This is known as *statistical self-similarity* (versus *deterministic self-similarity*).

Much more complex and realistic plants can be generated via recursion with the help of a data structure known as a *stack*. A stack allows backtracking via stored intermediate positions, which makes more complex branching behaviors possible. We introduce the readers to the L-system or Lindenmayer system for more intricate plant growth models in the next section.

Lindenmayer Systems

Lindenmayer systems, or L-systems are a formal grammar created by biologist Aristid Lindenmayer in 1968 to model the development of biological systems. L-systems are the basis for many plant and tree models in computer graphics. Formally, an L-system is a language, which produces a set of strings. These strings are made of specific symbols that when interpreted as movements in the plane and traced, produce remarkable lifelike plants and other systems of nature.

Grammar

We are familiar with written languages and the grammar that lay out the structural rules that govern their compositions. Computer languages have similar grammatical rules, only simpler and more well-defined than most natural languages.

A grammar consists of:

- An alphabet that is a set of symbols (usually variables) used

- An axiom or start string, from which all valid strings of the language are derived

- A rule set that defines substitution relationships between the symbols

L-systems differ from regular grammar in that a substitution rule applies to all instances of a symbol simultaneously. This models cell division in parallel within a growing organism.

Consider the following simple L-system that models Algae, given by Prusinkiewicz and Lindenmayer:

- Alphabet: {**A**, **B**}

- Axiom: **A**

- Rules: (**A** → **AB**), (**B** → **A**)

Tracing the first few rounds of substitutions gives us the following:

1. **A**
2. **AB**
3. **ABA**
4. **ABAAB**
5. **ABAABABA**

Notice that substitutions are simultaneous and happen for all symbols during every iteration. For example going from 2 to 3, **A** was substituted by **AB** with (**A** → **AB**) and **B** by **A** with (**B** → **A**). It is clear that the complexity of the string increases very quickly, particularly with more elaborate rules. Lindenmayer systems were originally conceived as a mathematical theory without geometric interpretation, with the strings as the final output. However, it turns out that only simple extensions are needed to turn them into actual drawings of fractals and plant life.

Rendering

We use a well-known computer graphics paradigm Turtle Graphics, where an imaginary turtle with a pen moves in the plane and traces out its own movement. Consider the following L-system grammar, which generates the Koch Curve:

- Alphabet: **{F}**

- Axiom: **F**

- Rules: (**F → F+F-F-F+F**)

We add the following interpretations:

- **F**: move forward one unit (pen down)

- **+**: turn left (pen up)

- **–**: turn right (pen up)

Note that "pen down" means "move with pen down" and "pen up" means move without drawing. Thus in this example we are only tracing when moving forward. Also, our alphabet only lists variables, that is, those symbols that can be substituted. Symbols that have no substitutions are known as constants, the symbols **+** and **-** are constants in this example. The system starts with the axiom - a straight line of unit length. In the next iteration we apply the single production rule once. The rule says to substitute every **F** (unit-length line) with forward, left turn, forward, right turn, forward, right again, forward, left, and forward. With a 90-degree turn angle, the replacement sequence is shown graphically in Figure 8-20, and this is the result after two iterations (axiom and one substitution).

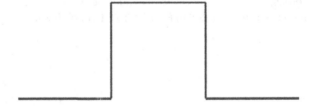

Figure 8-20. Rule (**F → F+F-F-F+F**) graphically

The results after three and four iterations are shown in Figures 8-21 and 8-22.

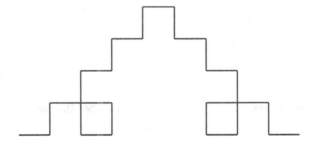

Figure 8-21. After three iterations

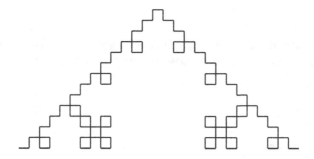

Figure 8-22. After four iterations

Next we introduce a number of variations, which can be easily obtained with small modifications to the turn angle, axiom, and rules.

Koch Snowflake

Grammar:

- Alphabet: {F}
- Axiom: **F++F++F**
- Rules: (**F → F-F++F-F**)

With a turn angle of 60 degrees, this system starts with an equilateral triangle and adds a triangular "bump" to each edge. The first few iterations are illustrated in Figures 8-23 through 8-26.

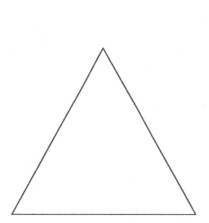

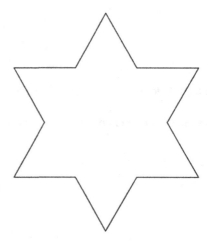

Figure 8-23. After one iteration (Axiom)

Figure 8-24. After two iterations

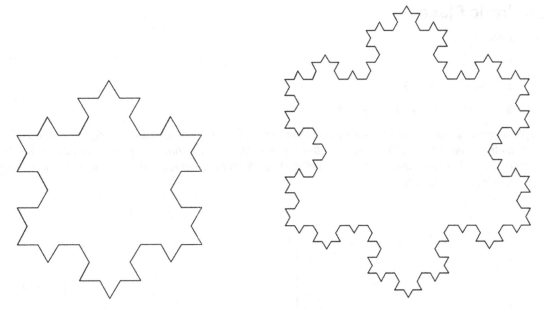

Figure 8-25. After three iterations

Figure 8-26. After Four Iterations

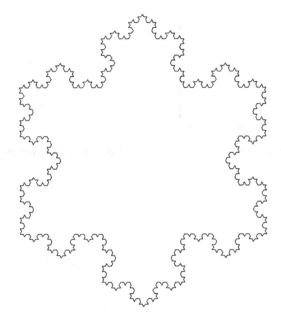

Figure 8-27. After Five Iterations

Quadratic Flake

Grammar:

- Alphabet: {**F**}

- Axiom: **F+F+F+F**

- Rules: (**F → F+F-F-FF+F+F-F**)

With a turn angle of 90 degrees, this system starts with a square and replaces each edge with an edge with two symmetric square "bumps." The results of the first five iterations are shown in Figure 8-28 through Figure 8-31. Figure 8-29 added the outline of the generating shape from the previous iteration to illustrate the replacement relationships more clearly.

Figure 8-28. After one iteration (Axiom)

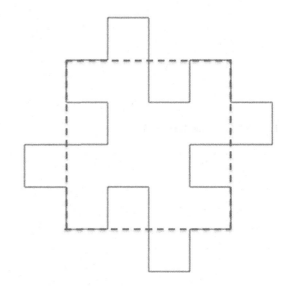

Figure 8-29. After two iterations

Figure 8-30. After three iterations   **Figure 8-31.** After four iterations

Heighway Dragon

Grammar:

- ■ Alphabet: {**FXY**}

- ■ Axiom: **FX**

- ■ Rules: (**X → X+YF+**), (**Y → -FX-Y**)

The dragon curve is a family of self-similar fractal curves, much like all the ones we have seen so far. A distinct shape resembling a dragon emerges after 5-6 iterations, hence its name. Shown in Figures 8-32 through 8-34 are approximations of the dragon curves given by our L-system.

Figure 8-32. After eight iterations

Figure 8-33. After 11 iterations

Figure 8-34. After 15 Iterations

Plants

We now introduce one more addition to our alphabet and rendering rules so that we can use L-systems to approximate plants and trees. We add two additional constants, **[** and **]**, with the geometric interpretations that whenever a **[** is encountered, we will save the turtle's current position and orientation and whenever a **]** is seen, we will restore the turtle to the last saved position and orientation. In other words, this allows us to save the location and heading of the turtle at a branching point, so that we may later return the turtle to that point and branch in a different direction. A similar concept was used in the recursive tree-drawing example in the previous section.

A very rudimentary plant (actually more like a twig), which produces two boughs per branching, is given by the following grammar:

- Alphabet: {**F**}

- Axiom: **F**

- Rules: (**F → F[-F]F[+F]F**)

The rendering results with a turn angle of 27 degrees are shown in Figure 8-35 and Figure 8-36.

Figure 8-35. After two iterations (axiom and one substitution)   **Figure 8-36.** After three iterations

Finally we list a slightly more complex grammar that represents a somewhat weedy looking plant:

- Alphabet: {**FX**}

- Axiom: **X**

- Rules: (**X → XF-[[X]+X]+F[+FX]-X**), (**F → FF**)

Sample outputs of rendering this system with a turn angle of 22.5 degrees are shown in Figures 8-37 and 8-38.

Figure 8-37. After six iterations

Figure 8-38. After seven iterations

Implementation

Now we finally discuss the implementation of an L-system, which involves two parts: the definition and application of a grammar a certain number of times to generate an output string, and the graphical rendering of said string using Turtle Graphics as explained in the previous sections.

We start by designing a class to represent an L-system, which contains three data fields, a String variable axiom that stores the axiom, an ArrayList called rules that stores all substitution rules and a String variable out that stores the output string. The substitution rules are stored as String objects in an ArrayList, and each rule is specified as a plain string without the parentheses or right arrow, that is, rule (**A** → **AB**) is written as "AAB."

```
class Lsys {
  String axiom;
  ArrayList rules;
  String out;                    // final output string
```

```
Lsys() {
  axiom = new String();
  rules = new ArrayList();
  out = new String();
}// end Lsys()

void setAxiom(String s) {
  axiom += s;
  out += axiom;
}// end setAxiom()

void addRule(String rule) {
  String r = new String(rule);
  rules.add(r);
} // end addRule()

// search for a specific rule that starts with character c
// return the arrayList index if found, -1 if not
int searchRule(char c) {
  for (int i=0; i<rules.size(); i++) {
    String r = (String) rules.get(i);
    if (r.charAt(0) == c) {
      return i;
    }
  }
  return -1;
} //end searchRule()

// apply the rules n times and store the result in out
void genString(int n) {
  if (n>0) {
    String temp = "";
    for (int i=0; i<out.length(); i++) {
      int idx = searchRule(out.charAt(i));
      if (idx == -1) {
        temp += out.substring(i, i+1);              //char -> substring of length 1
      }
      else {
        String r = (String) rules.get(idx);
        temp += r.substring(1);                     //substring starting at the 2nd char
      }
    }
    out = new String(temp);
    genString(n-1);
  }
} //end genString()
}// end class Lsys
```

The constructor and the helper functions setAxiom() and addRule() are fairly straightforward. setAxiom() copies the input parameter string s into the axiom variable and then the content of axiom into the out variable, so that the axiom is automatically applied as the first iteration. Note that technically we do not really need the axiom variable, as the only function it serves is so that we remember what the axiom was. The string stored in out will be replaced (and lost) as soon as the next iteration starts. The function addRule() makes a copy of the input parameter string, and adds it to the ArrayList rules.

Function genString(int n) is the recursive function that applies the rules n times and generates and stores the final output string in out. Although symbol substitutions in an L-system are supposed to happen simultaneously, because they are all independent and there is no interference, they can be implemented sequentially with a loop over all symbols. An empty temporary string temp is declared at the beginning of each iteration. As long as n is greater than 0, the function looks at every character in the current string stored in out and calls the function searchRule() to search for a substitution rule that starts with that character. If a rule is found (searchRule() returns an ArrayList index), then the character's substitution is appended onto temp; if not (searchRule() returns -1), then the character is appended onto temp without modification. When done with the current string, temp is copied to out and the function recurses.

This example gives code fragments that can be used in setup() to define an L-system of Koch Snowflake (see grammar listed in previous sections) using the Lsys class implementation and for example generate a string with 5 rounds of the substitutions (axiom + 4 additional).

```
Lsys kochSnowFlake = new Lsys();
kochSnowFlake.setAxiom("F++F++F");
kochSnowFlake.addRule("FF-F++F-F");
kochSnowFlake.genString(4);
```

The last bit of work remaining is to render the generated string with Turtle Graphics. We add the following function to our Lsys class (insert the function into the Lsys class we have been building):

```
void render(float size, float angle) {
  for (int i=0; i<out.length(); i++) {
    switch (out.charAt(i)) {
    case 'F':        // move forward, pen down
      line(0, 0, size, 0);
      translate(size, 0);
      break;
    case '+':        // turn left
      rotate(radians(-angle));
      break;
    case '-':        // turn right
      rotate(radians(angle));
      break;
    case '[':        // save position and orientation
      pushMatrix();
      break;
    case ']':        // restore saved position and orientation
      popMatrix();
      break;
```

```
    default:
      break;
    }
  }
}// end render()
```

render() takes two parameters, a size and an angle, which specifies the step size and turn angle. We implement all movements with Processing's coordinate system transformations, processing the different symbols using a switch/case statement that was first introduced in Chapter 3. The only drawing command is called under the case 'F', where the turtle goes forward with the pen down. This is implemented as drawing a horizontal line of the specified step size.

Using the familiar example of the Koch Snowflake, we can call render() as shown here. Note that this should only happen after you have constructed the appropriate Lsys object (kochSnowFlake), set axiom and rules and generated an output string of the desired recursion levels, as shown in the code fragments previously.

```
translate(0, height/2);            // start at the middle of screen height
kochSnowFlake.render(5, 60);       // step size 5 and turn angle 60
```

It is possible that when rendering certain L-systems you might notice artifacts of misalignment with the default renderer. Renderers, or rendering/graphics engines can be changed with the size() command that specifies the sketch window size in setup(). If given only a width and a height, the default renderer is used. To specify a different renderer, name the desired renderer as the third parameter to size(). For example, size(800, 800, P2D). Besides the default renderer, Processing offers three additional renderers P2D, P3D, and PDF. Both the default renderer (Java2D at the time of writing) and P2D are suited for 2D graphics, but P2D seems to be less prone to artifacts. For more information on renderers as well as 3D rendering, refer to Chapter 11.

It is worth noting that a few simple extensions can make this implementation even more useful/interesting:

1. Use the file input techniques you learned in Chapter 7 to read L-system axioms and rules defined in external text files. This is particularly helpful with large grammars that have numerous or complicated rules that would be a pain to type in.

2. Add additional symbols to represent leaves, flowers, and colors so that more varieties of plant life are represented. For example a symbol **L** can be added to represent a leaf and a corresponding case can be added to the render() function so that whenever an **L** is seen, a function, say drawLeaf(), would be called to draw a leaf.

3. Introduce random and/or stochastic variations so that subparts are not 100% self-similar. For example, randomly skipping the application of a rule to certain occurrences, or instead of one substitution rule per symbol, allowing several, but applying only one of them at a time, making the choices randomly or stochastically.

Advanced Visualization: Treemap

Originally designed for visualizing hierarchies, Treemap is a space filling technique using nested rectangles to represent a tree structure. Since its invention by Shneiderman during the 1990s, treemaps enjoyed great commercial popularity, particularly with newspapers and magazines that used interactive tools to visualize social/economical data, because it turned out to be even more useful for unstructured data than the hierarchies they were originally intended for. Figure 8-39 shows a "Map of the Market," which is a screenshot of an interactive tool on SmartMoney's website that lets you watch more than 500 stocks at once, with updates at 15-minute intervals. The stocks are represented by individual rectangles grouped by sector, proportionally sized to market caps and colored with price performances. The ability of this map to highlight current trends makes it a winner, as well as the ease with which one can pick out the sector over/under-performers. Apps (StockTouch, etc.) that use similar concepts are popular choices for stock watchers who use their mobile phones. Time-lapse videos showing such maps for every close throughout a specified time period are also widely used. Treemaps are known for their efficient use of space and their abilities to display a high density of data items while maintaining a sense of order.

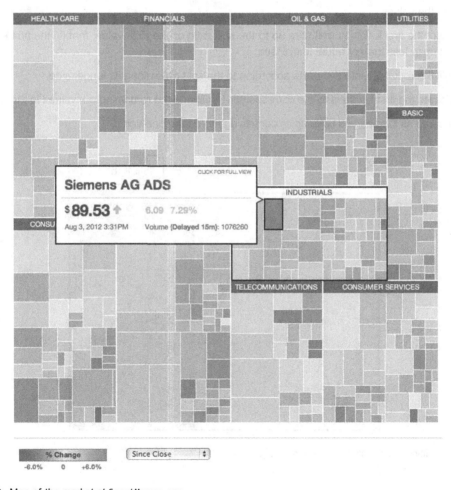

Figure 8-39. Map of the market at `SmartMoney.com`

The key to a treemap implementation is recursive subdivision. The main display area—a rectangle—is repeatedly subdivided into smaller rectangles with sizes proportional to the values. Suppose you start with n values that need to be packed into a given rectangle. This packing is called a *tiling algorithm*. We start with an easy to understand algorithm known as slice-and-dice.

The simplest way of subdividing a rectangle is to split it into two smaller rectangles along the longer side of the original (the longer side is preferred to avoid creating skinny rectangles). The sizes of the two smaller rectangles depend on a split ratio, a floating-point number between 0 and 1 that determines where along the longer side the split should occur. Figure 8-40 shows how a split ratio of 0.6 results in a (light gray) rectangle with 0.6*width of the original and another (dark gray) one with 0.4*width of the original. Also note that because both retain the height, the areas of the resulting rectangles are exactly 0.6 and 0.4 of the original, making the split also area(size)-proportional. How the split-ratio is determined affects the subdivision greatly. Let us start with a simple fixed ratio say 0.6. Consider the following algorithm:

1. Find the sum of all n values, call it sum.

2. Sort the values.

3. Select the first k values that sum up to the split-ratio of the total value, that is, the first k values that add up to less than or equal to 0.6*sum.

4. Split the rectangle into two parts according to the split-ratio along its longer side.

5. Allocate the first k values to the corresponding split and the remaining n-k values to the other.

6. Recurse as long as you have splits containing more than one value.

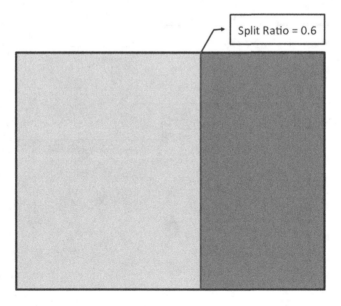

Figure 8-40. Splitting a rectangle with a split ratio of 0.6

Figure 8-41 shows an implementation of this algorithm applied to a word frequency list of President Obama's Nobel Peace Prize acceptance speech in 2009. This is the same data that were used in Chapter 7's word cloud visualization examples. The algorithm generally works on any ordered list of values.

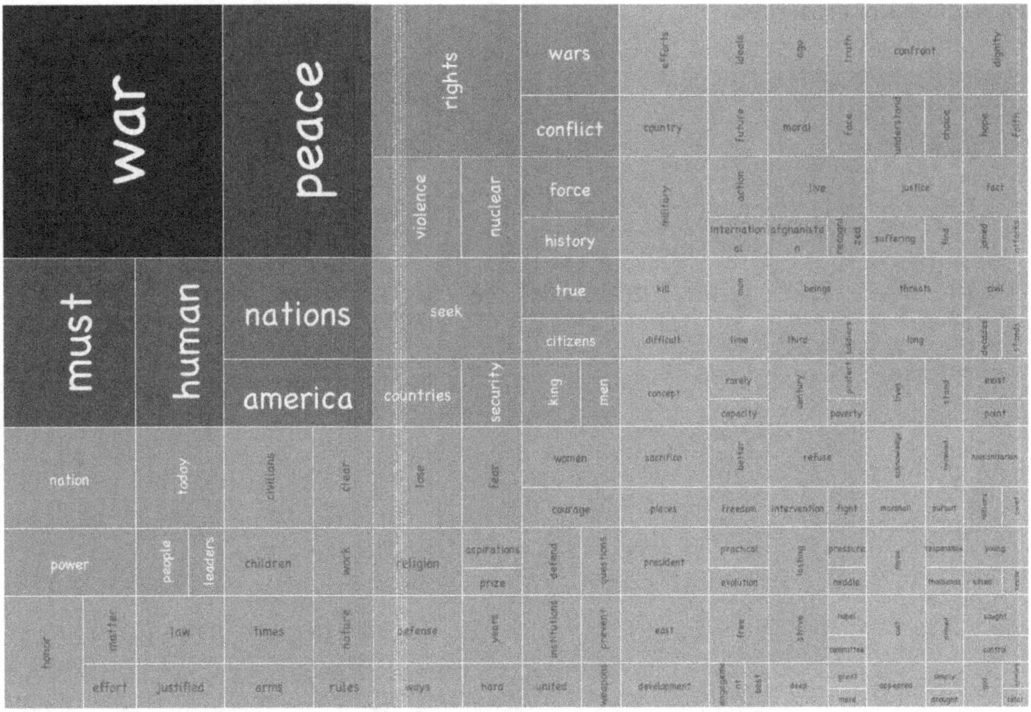

Figure 8-41. Treemap visualization of President Obama's Nobel Peace Prize acceptance speech

On close inspection, an immediate problem arises in that the area proportions do not correspond to the actual word frequencies in the raw data. For example, the words "wars" and "conflict" both occur nine times in the speech and should have been allocated equal-sized rectangles, yet in this implementation "wars" occupies an obviously larger area than "conflict." This is because of step 3, where we assigned the split between the values. Recall that we were going with a fixed geometric split ratio of 0.6 and the first k values that add up to 60% of the total sum were selected. In a list of discrete numbers, one can easily imagine a situation where the first k values add up to much less than 0.6*sum, yet the first k+1 values will exceed 0.6*sum. This means that when we split at k, often the numerical split ratio among the values is not 0.6, but rather something quite a lot less than 0.6. Yet the geometric subdivision always splits with 0.6 regardless. In fact, there is no way to graphically represent a 50/50 split as our data called for. Clearly, a fixed geometric split ratio is not ideal for our application. We now propose a revised algorithm with step 3 updated to:

7. Let k = n/2, that is, select the first n/2 values and find their sum, call it ksum. Set the split ratio to ksum/sum.

The change means we no longer try to find a best-fit split among the values, but rather go with a fixed split ratio there (0.5). However, the geometric split ratio is then calculated based on the split sum versus the total. This results in split ratios changing from split to split but the geometric split is now always proportional to the numerical split. Figure 8-42 shows the result of this change and notice that the words "wars" and "conflict" now occupy rectangles of equal sizes.

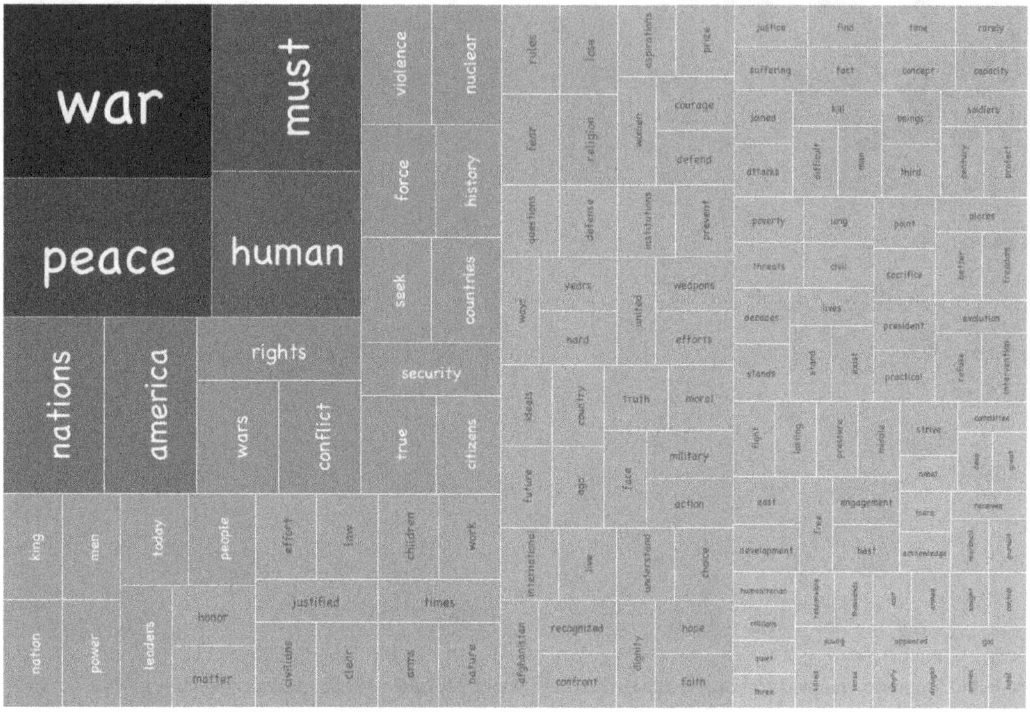

Figure 8-42. Treemap with non-constant split ratios

A major drawback of this tiling algorithm should also become apparent on inspection—it cannot prevent creations of high-aspect ratio rectangles, a problem our previous fixed-ratio algorithm does not suffer from. High-aspect ratio rectangles are those whose lengths are significantly larger than their widths or vice versa, in other words, skinny rectangles. The problem with high-aspect ratio rectangles (besides aesthetic and display challenges) is how we perceive their relative areas. Skinny rectangles appear smaller than fatter rectangles of the same area, which defeats the entire idea of representing data with size. Ideally, a tiling algorithm will preserve proportions/ordering of the input data while generating rectangles with good aspect ratios. Unfortunately, these two goals are inversely related, which results in a variety of proposed algorithms that aim to optimize somewhere in the middle.

Ben Fry implemented a simple treemap library for Processing, which is based on Martin Wattenberg and Ben Bederson's open source Treemap Java algorithms collection with minor adaptation. This library can be downloaded from http://benfry.com/writing/treemap/ and installed as a contributed library.

Summary

In this chapter we introduced the general concept of recursion and experimented with drawing and computing with recursive functions. A number of basic Lindenmayer systems were used to illustrate more systematic ways of recursively modelling iterative functions and biological systems with fractal geometry, such as plants and trees. Much more advanced and complex L-systems exist, and we encourage you to explore creative extensions using the basic framework we provided. Another important application of recursion and fractal geometry that we did not have time to explore is landscape generation, that is, fractal mountains, which create realistic appearances of natural terrain used in many computer graphics applications. Lastly, we gave an advanced visualization example with treemap, using recursively subdivided rectangles. Although we only discussed the algorithm and did not go into details of the implementation, adapting and implementing the treemap algorithm is a fun exercise that will bring a lot of visual gratification and create a natural connection to Chapter 7's word cloud generation example.

References

Deussen et. al., "Realistic modeling and rendering of plant ecosystems," in Proceedings of SIGGRAPH 1998.

Prusinkiewicz, Przemyslaw, and Aristid Lindenmayer. *The Algorithmic Beauty of Plants*. New York: Springer-Verlag, 1990.

Shneiderman, Ben. "Treemaps for space-constrained visualization of hierarchies," http://www.cs.umd.edu/hcil/treemap-history/, 6/25/2009, accessed 8/3/2012.

SmartMoney. "Map of the Market," http://www.smartmoney.com/map-of-the-market/, accessed 8/3/2012.

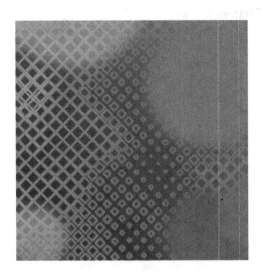

Chapter 9

Painting with Bits

Pictures, or digital images, are an important part of digital artwork. In Chapter 2 we saw how to load an existing image into one's sketch to use as a background or as a component of the sketch. In other words, we are using the images like another drawing primitive. In this chapter we will learn how to create or modify the images themselves. In addition to providing an introduction to Processing's pixel buffers and pixel processing, we will also cover multi-dimensional arrays, bitwise operators, and emergent systems.

Digital Images

In the digital world, a (raster) image is simply a rectangular grid of dots, often rendered as squares (see Figure 9-1). Each dot is of a single solid color and is known as a pixel (short for picture element). The reason why we do not see individual pixels as squares is because they are very small. Resolution of a display device is measured by pixel density, or number of pixels per inch (PPI). Digital displays marketed from 2009 onwards have at least 100 PPI, with the newer and sharper ones reaching 200–300 PPI. For example, the new iPad 3 (2012) boasts a Retina Display with 264 PPI, and LG has just brought a new smart phone (Droid DNA) with a 440 PPI display to market (November 2012). It has been observed that the (unaided) limit of human visual acuity is around 500-600 PPI. Pixels are commonly arranged in a two-dimensional grid, the dimensions of which are specified by the image's size in pixel resolution. For example, when we have a JPEG image of 1920x1080, it means the image has 1920 pixels in its width and 1080 pixels in its height. It has 1920x1080 = 2,073,600 total pixels and thus can also be referred to as a 2-megapixel image. Zooming into an image repeatedly will allow you to reach low enough resolution to see individual pixels, at which point you also lose most recognizable details in the image. This is called pixelation, also known as pixelization when the resolution lowering is done deliberately, a technique often employed in censorship.

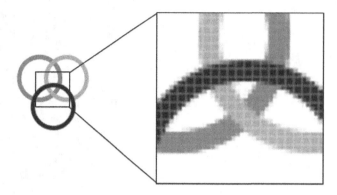

Figure 9-1. An enlarged portion of a picture showing individual pixels rendered as squares

Raster Processing

The word "raster" originally referred to the raster scan of cathode ray tube (CRT) monitors, which paints an image line by line by focusing colored electron beams to the front of a vacuum tube. Today's monitors and display devices employ very different and more advanced display technologies such as LCD, plasma, and LED, but raster and its association with the pixel grid have remained. In Computer Graphics, a raster image is also known as a bitmap, and is a data structure as well as an image representation corresponding to a spatially mapped array of bits, a natural representation of a pixel grid. The color representation of a pixel typically requires more than a single bit, and the number of bits used per pixel is known as color depth. Modern video hardware offers at least 24-bit color, which resolves to 8 bits per red/green/blue (R/G/B) channel, and goes up to 32-bit with the alpha channel. Figure 9-2 shows three pixels with their individual RGB color values and indices at which they are stored in the pixel grid. For example, the leftmost pixel can be found at row 81, column 123 and is colored with a red value of 137, green value of 196, and blue value of 138.

Figure 9-2. Three pixels with RGB color values and pixel grid indices

Processing has two built-in functions, get() and set(), which allow easy access to a pixel. The following code fragment will return the color of the pixel at x = 10, y = 50 (of the display window) and store it in c:

```
PImage img = loadImage("tree.jpg");        //load image tree.jpg into img
image(img, 0, 0);                          //display img at (0, 0)
color c = get(10, 50);
```

The PImage class also provides a similar get() method; thus the following code fragment stores the color of the same pixel into c:

```
PImage img = loadImage("tree.jpg");
color c = img.get(10, 50);
```

Pixelation

The following program samples the color of pixels at the rate of 1/50 of width and 1/50 of height and draws a grid of rectangles with the returned colors. This effectively lowers the resolution of the original image and simulates the pixelation effect (shown in Figure 9-3).

```
// pixelation.pde, chapter 9
void setup() {
  PImage img = loadImage("baby2.jpg");
  int resolution = 50;
  size(img.width, img.height);
  int xInc = width/resolution;          // increment in the x direction in pixels
  int yInc = height/resolution;         // increment in the y direction in pixels
  for (int y=0; y<img.height; y+=yInc) {
    for (int x=0; x<img.width; x+=xInc) {
      fill(img.get(x, y));
      rect(x, y, xInc, yInc);
    }
  }
} // end setup()
```

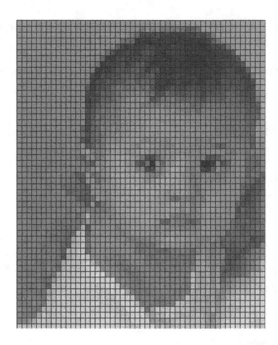

Figure 9-3. With `rect()` command, outlined in black

The nested `for` loops are used to step through the pixel grid. The outer loop indexed with y iterates through the rows, and the inner loop indexed with x iterates through the columns. The entire inner loop accesses one row of the pixel grid and draws one row of rectangles in the output. Changing the rectangles to circles drawn with the `ellipse()` command also recreates the original picture nicely. In fact, the rendering shape hardly matters. It is surprising how well the eye recognizes the original details as long as the relative colors/shading are represented in the drawing primitives. Figure 9-4 shows a variation where each sampled pixel is drawn as a line. We will explore this technique further in the later sections to create more artistic renderings of images.

Figure 9-4. With line() command

Try This: Substitute different drawing primitives for the rect() command; experiment with different sampling resolutions, drawing sizes, strokeWeight(), etc.

Negative Images

The function set(int x, int y, color c) will set the color at x, y to c. Combining get() and set() allows us to alter a pixel's color in many ways. For example, we can create a negative of an image by subtracting each R/G/B component color from the full 255 (see Figures 9-5 and 9-6):

```
// negative.pde, chapter 9
void setup() {
  PImage img = loadImage("prinzipalmarkt.jpg");
  size(img.width, img.height);
  image(img, 0, 0);
  for (int y = 0; y < img.height; y++) {
    for (int x = 0; x < img.width; x++) {
      color c = get(x, y);
      set(x, y, color(255-red(c), 255-green(c), 255-blue(c)));
    }
  }
} // end setup()
```

Figure 9-5. Original

Figure 9-6. Negative

Note that the two parameters x and y to the get() function are the x and y screen coordinates of a pixel. When represented by a grid, a pixel with coordinates (x, y) is located at row y and column x.

> *Try This: Experiment with other possibilities of systematic color modification: set one of the colors to 0, subtract the smallest color value from the other two, multiply each by some fraction, i.e., 0.5, etc.*

Copying Neighbors

Next we show an example where we set a pixel's color by copying randomly from one of its eight neighbors and itself (the local 3x3 grid as illustrated in Figure 9-7).

(x-1,y-1)	(x,y-1)	(x+1,y-1)
(x-1,y)	(x,y)	(x+1,y)
(x-1,y+1)	(x,y+1)	(x+1,y+1)

Figure 9-7. 3x3 neighborhood of (x, y)

```
// randomNeighbor.pde, chapter 9
PImage img;

void setup() {
  img = loadImage("fall.jpg");
  size(img.width, img.height);
  image(img, 0, 0);
} // end setup()

void draw() {
  for (int y = 1; y < img.height-1; y++) {
    for (int x = 1; x < img.width-1; x++) {
      int newX = randInt(x-1, x+1);
      int newY = randInt(y-1, y+1);
      set(x, y, get(newX, newY));
    }
  }
} // end draw()

// returns a randomly generated integer between low and high, including low and high
int randInt(int low, int high) {
  int r =  floor(random(low, high+1));
  //Processing's random(low, high) occasionally returns high,
  //even though the references say it doesn't
  r = constrain(r, low, high);
  return r;
} // end randInt()
```

Figure 9-8. Original photo

The function randInt() is used to randomly select a neighbor with a horizontal index between x−1, x, and x+1, and a vertical index between y−1, y, and y+1. The color of the selected neighbor is copied into the current pixel. We'll use this function throughout the chapter.

Moving the nested for loops that copy the pixels into the draw() function results in repeated copying and overwriting every time draw() is called. Over time, the picture will get increasingly fuzzy as the pixel colors migrate further and further from their original location. Results after 100 and 800 iterations to a photo (shown in Figure 9-8) of a fall landscape are shown in Figures 9-8 and 9-10 respectively. Try also the following variations, copying from the top neighbor (x, y−1), the upper left (x−1, y−1), or the upper right (x+1, y−1). This will cause all the pixel colors to shift straight down or down and to the left or right, creating an interesting dripping effect over time.

Figure 9-9. After 100 iterations

Figure 9-10. After 800 iterations

> *Try This: Notice that the indexing of the nested for loops goes from 1 to img.width-1 or img.height-1. What happens if we wrote the loops to go from 0 to img.width and 0 to img.height instead?*

Note that calling get() with invalid x or y coordinates will result in the color black being returned and trying to set the color of a non-existent pixel will simply be ignored by Processing.

> *Try This: The program copies from a 3x3 neighborhood, including itself. Add a conditional statement to skip the self-copying.*

Like many built-in Processing functions, get() is overloaded, which means the function behaves differently depending on the input parameters given. When called with two integers, get() returns a single pixel color as seen above, however one can retrieve an entire block of pixels (as a PImage), either by giving additional width and height arguments, or by calling get() with no arguments, in which case the entire image will be returned:

```
PImage get(int x, int y, int width, int height)
PImage get()
```

While get() and set() are easy to use, more complex manipulations of images often perform computations based on more than a single pixel color and result in the need of a data structure. We have already seen that an image can be completely specified by the width and height of the image in pixels and the color for each pixel. A natural data structure to represent such a pixel grid is a two-dimensional array of color values (RGB or RGBA), which brings us to the discussion of multi-dimensional arrays.

Multi-dimensional Arrays

In Chapter 5 we learned that an array allows us to store a large number of homogenously typed data in linear order, much like a one-dimensional list. Let's now look at arrays that can store data in more than one dimension.

Two-dimensional Arrays

The concept of an array generalizes into two dimensions readily and a two-dimensional (2D) array is declared and created with two sets of square brackets:

```
int[][] grays = new int[8][10];
```

The statement above creates a 8x10 rectangular array by specifying sizes for each dimension, where the number listed between the first pair of square brackets gives the number of rows and the second number gives the number of columns. Alternatively, like we have seen with the one-dimensional (1D) arrays, we can also create and initialize the array together (example shows 80 randomly generated integer values from 0 to 255):

```
int[][] grays = {
{ 84, 208,  73, 105,  11,  54, 212,  93,   4, 157},
{ 15, 155,  57,  75,   3, 157,  93, 118,  11,  77},
{227,  75, 143,  23, 192, 218,  87,  15,  13,  72},
{ 68, 228,  74,  70,  78, 225, 191, 121, 232, 190},
{162,  22, 119, 255, 179,  45, 166,  96, 135, 200},
{114, 196, 234,  80, 232, 100, 183, 165, 203,  23},
{178,  65, 130,   3,  71, 179,  44,  31,  44, 183},
{ 18,  34, 153,  96, 231,  92, 240, 204, 157,   0}
};
```

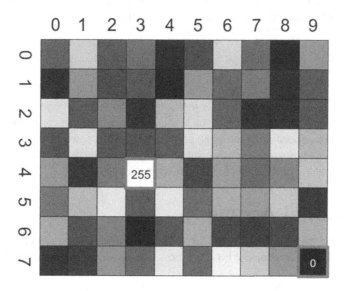

Figure 9-11. Grays array with values visualized as grayscale colors

The initialization values are given as a nested list, where each inner pair of curly braces contains a list of numbers for a row. When done this way, sizes of the array dimensions are inferred from the number of values given. Figure 9-11 shows a visualization of the array grays where the stored integer values are used as fill colors in grayscale for each square in the grid. We will see the code that generates this visualization a bit later.

Indexing a 2D array requires two indices, where the first index specifies which row and the second index specifies which column. In the above example, grays[4][3] was initialized with the value 255 and grays[7][9] was initialized with the value 0 (these two values are shown in bold font in the initialization code). As usual indexing starts from 0 for both dimensions, which means the row with index 4 is in fact the 5th row, for example. To reference a particular location in the array, we follow the same indexing pattern:

```
grays[4][3] = 0;  // assign the color black to row 4 (5th row), column 3 (4th column)
```

Loops and 2D Arrays

Now that we know the basics of a 2D array, we will explore how such arrays can be accessed with loops. Before we look at loops however, we first need to have a discussion of the lengths of a 2D array, which are needed to control the loops. A 2D array is really an array of 1D arrays. That is, each element of the array is again an array. The first dimension specifies the number of 1D arrays (rows) and the second dimension specifies the length of each 1D array. When considered this way, we see that the number of rows is given by the length of the 2D array (with the familiar .length syntax), and the number of columns is also the length of any of the 1D arrays.

The following loops set the values of the entire 6th column (at column index 5) and the entire 7th row (at row index 6) to 255 (white) (see Figure 9-12). Notice that the length of the 2D array is used to terminate the column loop, and the length of the 1D array is used for the row loop.

```
// set the values of column 5 to 255
for (int i = 0; i < grays.length; i++) {
  grays[i][5] = 255;
}
// set the values of row 6 to 255
for(int j = 0; j < grays[6].length; j++) {
  grays[6][j] = 255;
}
```

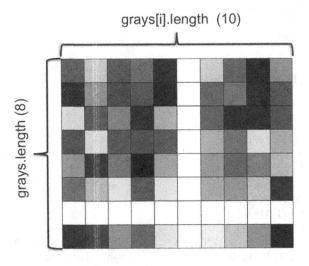

Figure 9-12. Row 6 and column 5 are set to white

A nested for loop is commonly used to index through 2D arrays and the following loop is used to draw the grid of squares shown in Figures 9-11 and 9-12. The outer loop iterates through the rows and the inner loop iterates through the columns, which means i is the row index and j is the column index. The resulting visualization is drawn row by row.

```
int cellSize = 40;
for (int i = 0; i < grays.length; i++) {
  for(int j = 0; j < grays[i].length; j++) {
    fill(grays[i][j]);
    pushMatrix();
    // j is the column index, which correspond to the x screen coordinate
    translate(j*cellSize, i*cellSize);
    rect(0, 0, cellSize, cellSize);
    popMatrix();
  }
}
```

Visualizing 2D Arrays

For rectangular arrays (versus ragged arrays; see next section), it is often more convenient to store the number of rows and columns in two integer variables and use them to declare and create the 2D array as well as serving as loop controls. Below is a complete Processing program that declares and creates a 2D array of 8x10 floats, fills it with values between 0 and 255, and draws a rectangular grid of squares filled with grayscale colors represented by the values stored in the corresponding array element, with output shown in Figure 9-13. The type of the array is changed to float to better accommodate the return values from the map() function, which maps a number from one interval to another. The periodic gradient shading is accomplished by mapping the row and column indices to radians between 0 and 2PI, then passing the resulting angles to the trigonometric functions sine and cosine and calculating their product. The periodicity of the trigonometric functions results in the product repeating values within a certain interval, namely −1 to 1, which is again mapped to 0 to 255, so that −1 is 0 (black) and +1 is 255 (white).

```
// grayScaleTrig.pde, chapter 9
int rows = 100;
int cols = 100;
float[][] grays = new float[rows][cols];
int cellSize = 5;

void setup() {
  size(cellSize*cols, cellSize*rows);
  noStroke();
  //colorMode(HSB);

  //initialize the color values
  for (int i = 0; i < rows; i++) {
    for (int j = 0; j < cols; j++) {
      float x = map(i, 0, rows-1, 0, 2*PI);    // map x index to 0-2PI
      float y = map(j, 0, cols-1, 0, 2*PI);    // map y index to 0-2PI
```

```
      float z = sin(x)*cos(y);
      grays[i][j] = map(z, -1.0, 1.0, 0.0, 255.0); // map product z to 0-255
    }
  }

  // draw all the squares
  for (int i = 0; i < rows; i++) {
    for (int j = 0; j < cols; j++) {
      // fill with color from corresponding location in array
      fill(grays[i][j]);
      //fill(grays[i][j], 255, 255);       // HSB color
      pushMatrix();
      // j is the column index, which correspond to the x  screen coordinate
      translate(j*cellSize, i*cellSize);
      rect(0, 0, cellSize, cellSize);
      popMatrix();
    }
  }
} // end setup()
```

Figure 9-13. Row and column indices and trigonometric functions

Another interesting visualization (shown in Figure 9-14) can be generated by drawing in HSB mode instead and using the stored values as the hue of the fill color, i.e., changing the call fill(grays[i][j]) to fill(grays[i][j], 255, 255).

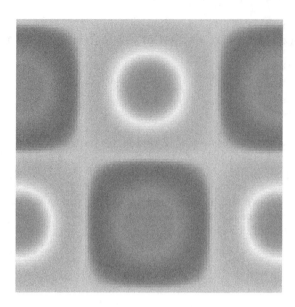

Figure 9-14. Variation with full color drawn in HSB

Try This: Modify the first set of nested for loops above to store values representing grayscale gradient shading of the grid. That is, 0s in the top row, 255s in the bottom row and values that gradually increase from 0 to 255 for all the rows in between, so that when drawn, it will look like the figure below. Can you set the values so that there is also gradient shading from left to right, in addition to top to bottom? Experiment with increasing the array sizes and decreasing the sizes of the squares.

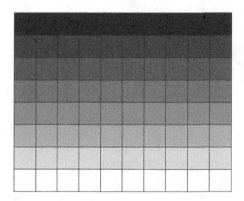

Try This: Declare a 2D array of type color instead and try to replicate all the grayscale examples, but with full color.

Note that if we are just drawing a single image based on the initialization values, the two nested loops can be combined into a single one. That is, as soon as we initialize an array element we immediately draw the square with the corresponding value as fill color. In fact, storing the values into a two-dimensional array isn't even necessary when done this way. A temporary variable can be used to hold the drawing color and the color can be discarded as soon as the square is drawn. However, storing the initial color values are required if we want to animate the base image over time, which necessitates moving the drawing loop into draw() and manipulating the stored color values at every iteration.

Image Animation

We now expand the previous example by repeatedly incrementing the base image colors until 255, and then decrementing until 0. A second two dimensional array incs is added to track the direction of increment/decrement for every array element in grays. At every iteration, the value stored at incs[i][j] is added to grays[i][j], which will be used as the fill color for the corresponding square in the next iteration. All elements in the incs array are initialized to 1 in the first nested loop in setup(), which indicates that we are going to add 1 to all colors. The nested for loop that draws the grid is moved to draw(). We also check to see if the current color in grays[i][j] is 255 or 0, at which point, we negate incs[i][j] so that incrementing will switch direction to decrementing and vice versa.

```
// grayScaleTrigAnimation.pde, chapter 9
int rows = 100;
int cols = 100;
float[][] grays = new float[rows][cols];
float[][] incs = new float[rows][cols];
int cellSize = 5;

void setup() {
  size(cellSize*cols, cellSize*rows);
  noStroke();
  //initialize the color values and values of increment
  for (int i = 0; i < rows; i++) {
    for (int j = 0; j < cols; j++) {
      float x = map(i, 0, rows-1, 0, 2*PI);      // map x index to 0-2PI
      float y = map(j, 0, cols-1, 0, 2*PI);      // map y index to 0-2PI
      float z = sin(x)*cos(y);
      grays[i][j] = map(z, -1.0, 1.0, 0.0, 255.0);    // map product z to 0-255
      incs[i][j] = 1;
    }
  }
} // end setup()

void draw() {
  background(255);
  for (int i = 0; i < rows; i++) {
    for (int j = 0; j < cols; j++) {
      // fill with color from corresponding location in array
      fill(grays[i][j]);
      pushMatrix();
```

```
        translate(j*cellSize, i*cellSize);
        rect(0, 0, cellSize, cellSize);
        popMatrix();
        // reverse direction of color change
        if (grays[i][j] > 255 || grays[i][j] < 0) {
          incs[i][j] = -incs[i][j];
        }
        //increment/decrement color
        grays[i][j] += incs[i][j];
      }
    }
  }  //end draw()
```

> Try This: Note that we set a uniform rate of increment/decrement for all (1), although the program is set up to easily accommodate distinct rates of color change on different squares if so desired. Try setting different rates of color change to select squares, for example, have every other row increment/decrement its colors twice as fast.

2D Perlin Noise

In Processing, there is another way to generate random numbers that relies upon the past history of numbers generated. The Processing library includes a function called noise() that takes the temporal succession of generated numbers into account. As opposed to the random number generator underlying the random() function, it uses a more naturally ordered, harmonic succession of pseudo-random numbers. The result is a much smoother yet unexpected outcome and can be used to model the contours of many natural phenomena.

Here is one way, for example, to generate a set of numbers using noise():

```
float x = 0.0;
for (int i=0; i < 5; i++) {
  println(noise(x));
  x += 0.02;
}
```

Here are the numbers generated from a run of the above commands:

0.74169934, 0.74059266, 0.73735994, 0.7324665, 0.72661906

As you can see, the numbers in the set returned by noise() are random, yet closer to each other than the ones returned by random(). Also, through the argument passed into the noise() function (x), you can control the smoothness of the values returned. You can think of x as representing time in the series of numbers generated. No change in time results in the same values. Larger increments will yield values with greater variation. Processing references recommend incrementing x by values in the range 0.005–0.03, which tends to produce smooth natural-looking noise sequences.

noise() also generates two-dimensional Perlin noise, which are often said to resemble mountain ranges and 2D terrain. The following example generates and stores 2D Perlin noise into a 2D array and visualizes the values as fill colors for drawing tiny 1x1 dots, as shown in Figure 9-15.

```
// noise.pde, chapter 9
import processing.opengl.*;

void setup() {
  float[][] data = new float[500][500];
  size(500, 500, P3D);    // use the P3D renderer instead of the default
  smooth();
  genNoise(data);
  asPoint(data);
} // end setup()

void genNoise(float[][] data) {
  float noiseScale=0.015;
  noiseDetail(2);                                 // use only 2 octaves
  for (int i = 0; i < data.length; i++) {
    for (int j=0; j< data[i].length; j++) {
      data[i][j] = noise(i*noiseScale, j*noiseScale);
    }
  }
} // end getNoise()

void asPoint(float[][] data) {
  for (int i = 0; i < data.length; i++) {
    for (int j = 0; j < data[i].length; j++) {
      //stroke(data[i][j]*255);                   // grayscale colors
      stroke(0, data[i][j]*255, 255-255*data[i][j]);   //blue to green colors
      ellipse(j, i, 1, 1);
    }
  }
} // end asPoint()
```

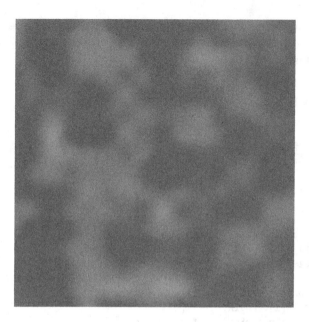

Figure 9-15. 2D Perlin noise visualized as colored points

The function genNoise() generates 2D Perlin noise values based on the current row index i and column index j and stores it in data[i][j]. The function asPoint() takes the 2D array data as an argument, uses each value stored in the array as a stroke color to draw a tiny dot. noise() always returns a floating point number between 0 and 1, thus all values in data are between 0 and 1 and can be easily mapped to a color by multiplying with 255.

Different visualization effects can be achieved by changing the way the shapes are drawn per noise value. Figure 9-16 shows the next example where each value is drawn as a square, using the noise values as a grayscale outline color. In addition, the size of the squares as well as the distances the squares are drawn from the screen (translation along the Z axis) vary depending on the strength of the noise values.

```
void asSquare3D(float[][] data) {
  int s = 10; // size of squares
  for (int i = 0; i < data.length; i+=s) {
    for (int j = 0; j < data[i].length; j+=s) {
      stroke(data[i][j]*255);
      noFill();
      pushMatrix();
      // the larger data[i][j] is, the closer the square is drawn
      translate(j, i, data[i][j]*s*2);
      rect(0, 0, data[i][j]*s, data[i][j]*s);
      popMatrix();
    }
  }
} // end asSquare3D()
```

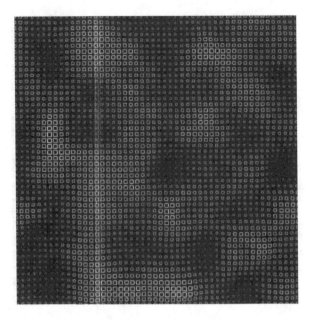

Figure 9-16. 2D Perlin noise visualized as squares with 3D translation

Another variation (shown in Figure 9-17) draws the squares in full color, and the strengths of the noise values are used to vary the green component of the drawing color. The sizes of the squares are doubled to emphasize areas of high noise strength. Notice the difference in this version, which does not visualize with translation along the Z axis.

```
void asSquareColor(float[][] data) {
  int s = 10; // base size of squares
  for (int i = 0; i < data.length; i+=s) {
    for (int j = 0; j < data[i].length; j+=s) {
      stroke(255, data[i][j]*255, 0);
      noFill();
      pushMatrix();
      translate(j, i);
      rect(0, 0, data[i][j]*s*2, data[i][j]*s*2);
      popMatrix();
    }
  }
} // end asSquareColor()
```

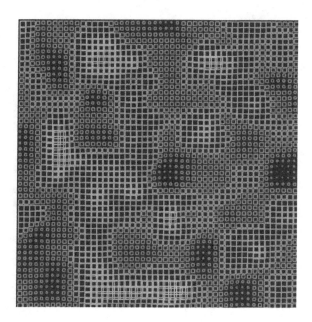

Figure 9-17. 2D Perlin noise visualized as colored squares

```
void asRotation(float[][] data) {
  int s = 5; // base size of lines
  for (int i = 0; i < data.length; i+=s) {
    for (int j = 0; j < data[i].length; j+=s) {
      stroke(255, 50);          // white, semi-transparent
      strokeWeight(2);
      pushMatrix();
      translate(j, i);
      // the larger data[i][j] is, the closer to 2PI we rotate
      rotate(data[i][j]*PI*2);
      line(0, 0, s*4, 0);
      popMatrix();
    }
  }
}  // end asRotation()
```

The last variation draws the noise values as angles of rotation for white, semi-transparent horizontal lines (see Figure 9-18).

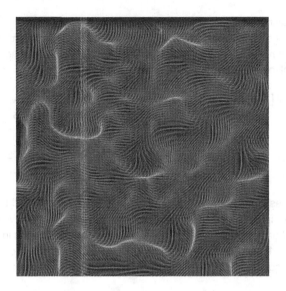

Figure 9-18. 2D Perlin noise visualized as angle of rotation of semi-transparent lines

Ragged Arrays

So far the 2D arrays we have seen are all rectangular. That is, the lengths of all the 1D arrays are the same. This does not have to be the case. When the rows of a 2D have different lengths, it is known as a ragged array. The following is an example of creating a ragged array:

```
int[][] numbers = {
{0, 1, 2, 3, 4, 5, 6, 7, 8, 9, 10},
{1, 3, 5, 7, 9},
{0, 2, 4, 6, 8, 10},
{2, 3, 5, 7},
{0},
};
```

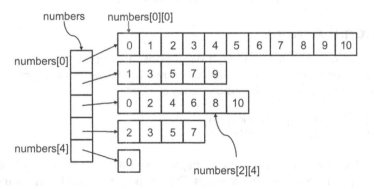

Figure 9-19. Illustration of the ragged array numbers

As it was initialized, the array numbers has five elements, each of which is an array of integers of varying lengths. In other words, numbers.length is 5, numbers[0].length is 11, numbers[1].length is 5, numbers[2].length is 6, numbers[3].length is 4 and numbers[4].length is 1. If initialization values are not immediately available at the time of creation, one can also create ragged arrays based on sizes:

```
int[][] numbers = new int[5][];        //create a 2D array with 5 rows
numbers[0] = new int[11];              //create row 0 with 11 columns - 1D array of 11 integers
numbers[1] = new int[5];               //create row 1 with 5 columns - 1D array of 5 integers
numbers[2] = new int[6];               //create row 2 with 6 columns - 1D array of 6 integers
numbers[3] = new int[4];               //create row 3 with 4 columns - 1D array of 4 integers
numbers[4] = new int[1];               //create row 4 with 1 column - 1D array of 1 integer
```

This declares and creates essentially the same array as before, except that all the elements are uninitialized and will receive the default initialization value of 0 for integers. The 2D array must be created first before creating each individual 1D array and then putting them into the correct location in the 2D array. When creating the 2D array, the number of 1D arrays must be entered as the size of the first dimension. Consider the follow example of generating a ragged array with 20 rows of random lengths between 1 and 100:

```
// ragged.pde, chapter 9
void setup() {
  float[][] ragged = new float[20][];

  for (int i=0; i<ragged.length; i++) {
    int len = randInt(1,100);
    ragged[i] = new float[len];
  }

  for (int i=0; i<ragged.length; i++) {
    println(ragged[i].length);
  }
} // end setup()
```

The function randInt() is used to randomly choose a length. For the sake of space, we will not list the code for randInt() here again, or any other time we use randInt() for the rest of this chapter. Please refer to the Copying Neighbors example for exact implementation of this function.

Multi-dimensional Arrays

As arrays go, there is no limit on the number of dimensions, and everything we did with two-dimensional arrays can be generalized further into n-dimensional arrays. The following statements declare and create a 3-dimensional array of String and a 4-dimensional array of float.

```
String[][][] text = new String[100][200][20];
float[][][][] data = new float[10][20][5][15];
```

While it is difficult to illustrate or visualize arrays beyond three dimensions, working with them is not very different from working with lower-dimensional arrays. The key point to remember is a multi-dimensional array is an array in which each element is another multi-dimensional array, i.e., an array of arrays. For example, the array data is a 4D array of 10 3D arrays, each of which is an array of 20 2D arrays, each of which is an array of 5 1D arrays of 15 floats. We will see an example of using a 3D array of boolean to implement Conway's Game of Life in a later section.

Processing's Pixel Buffer(s)

Now we turn our attention back towards pixel-based image processing. While get() and set() are straightforward to use, they are slow compared to other alternatives. When working with large images, the nested loops can easily result in a high number of iterations because all operations must be done pixel by pixel. For example, a 1920x1080 image has 2,073,600 pixels, which requires a nested loop of 2,073,600 iterations to process. Coupled with more complex computations per pixel, there can be noticeable delays in rendering just a still image. Any attempt to animate the process by putting the loop in the draw() function instead will require even faster access to pixels to prevent plummeting frame rates. For fast access to pixels, Processing provides us a pixel buffer – a built-in global array named pixels[] and two related functions, loadPixels() and updatePixels().

1D and 2D Arrays

It may come as a bit of a surprise that Processing's pixel buffer is a one-dimensional array. The reason for this is partly historical and partly efficiency-based, as Processing's 2D arrays are arrays of arrays, which require more memory references to access than a 1D array. Fortunately, it is not that difficult to convert between 1D and 2D arrays. Processing stores a 2D array in row-major order; that is, it is placed into a 1D array row by row in linear sequence. Figure 9-20 illustrates how a 4x3 2D array converts to a 1D array of 12 elements.

In general, an element in a 2D array with the index (i, j) can be found at index i*rowLength+j in a corresponding 1D array. As illustrated, (2, 1) contains the letter J, which can also be found at index 2*4+1 = 9 in the 1D array. In the particular context of Processing image processing, a pixel with the screen coordinate (x, y) can be found at pixels[y*width+x]. Notice that it's a bit counter-intuitive that the y coordinate indexes the rows while the x coordinate indexes the columns (i.e., while the letter J is located at index (2, 1), it has the screen coordinate (1, 2)).

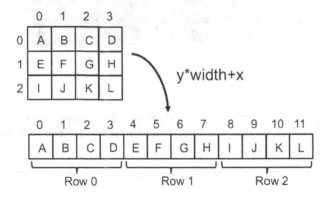

Figure 9-20. Converting 2D indices to a 1D index

For example, the following program loads the pixel buffer of an all-black sketch window and changes the center row of pixels to white (Figure 9-21). Note that the function loadPixels() must be called before accessing the pixels array, and updatePixels() must be called before displaying any modified pixel buffer.

```
// whiteLine.pde, chapter 9
void setup() {
  size(500, 500);
  background(0);
  loadPixels();
  for (int x = 0; x < width; x++) {
    pixels[height/2*width+x] = color(255);
  }
  updatePixels();
} // end setup()
```

Figure 9-21. A Single white line of pixels

> *Try This: Change the program above to additionally affect n rows above the center and n rows below the center, so that a much wider strip of white is drawn in the center of the sketch window.*
>
> *Change the program further so that a cross-shape is drawn centered in the sketch window.*

Gradient Shading

Next we show a sketch that creates a pixel-based grayscale gradient by mapping the pixel index (in the pixel array) to a gray scale color between 0 and 255, which is then used to shade the said pixel. Output is shown in Figure 9-22.

```
// bwGradient.pde, chapter 9
void setup() {
  size(400, 400);
  loadPixels();
  for (int i=0; i<pixels.length; i++) {
    float gray = map(i, 0, pixels.length-1, 0, 255);
    pixels[i] = color(gray);
  }
  updatePixels();
} // end setup()
```

Figure 9-22. Grayscale gradient via pixels

> *Try This: Change the program so that a color gradient is drawn from red to green.*

In general, it is easier to keep to the natural grid structure of an image and access pixels using two indices, but convert from 2D indexing to 1D indexing using the y*width+x formula when necessary. The following shows an example of mapping the pixels from blue (20, 20, 140) to orange (200, 100, 0), depending on the particular pixel's distance from the center of the sketch. The closer it is to the center, the bluer it gets and the further away, the more orange (Figure 9-23).

```
// cone.pde, chapter 9
void setup() {
  float distance, r, g, b;
  size(400, 400);
  loadPixels();
  // Access pixels as a 2D array
  for (int y=0; y<height; y++) {
    for (int x=0; x<width; x++) {
      // Compute distance to center of sketch
      distance = dist(x, y, width/2, height/2);
      r = map(distance, 0, width/2, 20, 200);
      g = map(distance, 0, width/2, 20, 100);
      b = map(distance, 0, width/2, 140, 0);
      pixels[y*width+x] = color(r, g, b);
    }
  }
  updatePixels();
} // end setup()
```

Figure 9-23. Color gradient based on distance from center of sketch

Grayscale

Occasionally when a program does not need to perform any row or column position-based operations and simply needs to access all pixels sequentially, we can get away with just indexing a 1D array. The following program loads an image to screen and converts it to gray scale by setting all pixels to a linear combination of 30% red, 59% green and 11% blue of the original, a standard formula that is based on luminance matching (see Figure 9-24).

```
// blackWhite.pde, chapter 9
void setup() {
  PImage img = loadImage("baby.jpg");
  size(img.width, img.height);
  image(img, 0, 0);
  loadPixels();
  for (int i = 0; i < pixels.length; i++) {
    color c = pixels[i];
    pixels[i] = color(red(c)*0.3+green(c)*0.59+blue(c)*0.11);
  }
  updatePixels();
} // end setup()
```

Figure 9-24. Grayscale filtering

It is important to remember that loadPixels() and updatePixels() as well as the pixels array operate on the pixel buffer of the sketch window. However, the PImage class also implements its own loadPixels(), updatePixels(), and a pixels array. This means that each PImage object has its own separate pixel buffer which is not related to the sketch window, and it is quite possible to work on an image's pixel buffer without displaying it to the sketch window at all. Thus, we can write an equivalent version of the grayscale filtering example as follows:

```
// blackWhite2.pde, chapter 9
void setup() {
  PImage img = loadImage("baby.jpg");
  size(img.width, img.height);
```

```
    img.loadPixels();
    for (int i = 0; i < img.pixels.length; i++) {
      color c = img.pixels[i];
      img.pixels[i] = color(red(c)*0.3+green(c)*0.59+blue(c)*0.11);
    }
    img.updatePixels();
    image(img, 0, 0);
} // end setup()
```

The difference between these two versions is not significant when only a single image is being processed and nothing else is being drawn on screen. However, the ability to obtain a pixel buffer for each PImage becomes handy when we need to deal with multiple images, or when the sketch window is needed for another purpose (animation of some sort, for example).

Sepia and Other Palettes

We now show how we can convert to sepia tones – a warmer coloring that is used in archiving grayscale photos – by setting all pixels' red, green, and blue to a combination of certain percentages of the original. Simply swap out the body of the for loop of the grayscale filtering (first version) to the following:

```
color c = pixels[i];
float r = red(c)*0.393+green(c)*0.769+blue(c)*0.189;
float g = red(c)*0.349+green(c)*0.686+blue(c)*0.168;
float b = red(c)*0.272+green(c)*0.534+blue(c)*0.131;
pixels[i] = color(r, g, b);
```

The above formula creates an approximation of the sepia toning. Although easy to implement, one might find the resulting image rather yellow and not muted enough. To truly give that old-fashioned and aged look, we need to convert the image to gray scale first and then assign each 0–255 value to a distinct color in a sepia palette, which is not unique. Such palettes can be easily created using a for loop to calculate gradient colors, and stored in an array. The following program generates a yellow-toned sepia palette and stores it in the array palette (visualized as a 32x8 grid in Figure 9-25):

```
// sepiaPalette.pde, chapter 9
void setup() {
  color[] palette = new color[256];
  int r = 255;
  int g = 240;   // change green value to 220 for a red-toned sepia palette
  int b = 192;

  for (int i=0; i<palette.length; i++) {
    palette[i] = color(r*i/255, g*i/255, b*i/255);
  }
} // end setup()
```

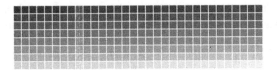

Figure 9-25. Yellow-toned sepia palette

The integers r, g, and b specify the red, green, and blue levels for the lightest color (color in the lower right corner of the grid) in the desired palette. Using a for loop, a gradient of 256 shades between black (0, 0, 0) and the specified final color is calculated by multiplying the loop index i divided by 255 to each color component of the final color.

Once a custom palette is created and stored in an array, we can assign it to a pixel by using its grayscale value to index into the palette array. The following shows how we can change the loop body to accommodate this, assuming that we already created an array palette of type color which stores 256 colors of an appropriate sepia palette. The result is shown in Figure 9-26.

```
color c = pixels[i];
float gray = red(c)*0.3+green(c)*0.59+blue(c)*0.11;
pixels[i] = palette[int(gray)];
```

Figure 9-26. After applying the sepia palette

In general, any custom palette can be created and used to tone a picture, including false and pseudo color palettes. A familiar example is the encoding of altitude using Hypsometric tints in relief maps. The technique of artificially colorizing a grayscale image in order to make details more visible or to encode some physical magnitude is particularly useful in viewing satellite/aerial/geographical images. It is also widely employed in scientific imaging in general. Figure 9-27 shows the same picture assigned to a false color palette.

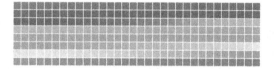
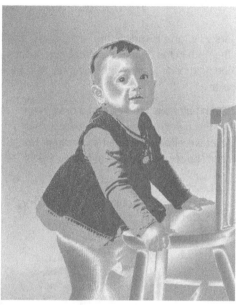

Figure 9-27. A false-color palette

Bitwise Processing and Component Functions

Processing offers a few more tricks for speeding up color-based operations, which are the bread-and-butter of pixel-based manipulations. We have seen that the functions red(), green(), blue(), and alpha() each returns the color value of the appropriate R/G/B/A color channel for a given color. There is a more direct way to extract the individual color values from the color data type, via low-level bitwise operators. This section assumes familiarity with the binary and hexadecimal number systems.

Bitwise Operators

Internally, all data (regardless of type) is represented as a sequence of bits. Each bit only has two states, 0 or 1. Recall that 8 bits form a byte, which is the most basic and smallest addressable unit of memory on most computer architectures. A byte can represent $2^8 = 256$ states, and the color values of Processing (0–255) are designed to fit into a byte. Bitwise operators work on integer types (byte, char, short, int, and long) at the level of the individual bits. They do not work on floating-point types. The speed of the bitwise operators comes from the fact that they are low-level, primitive operations that are directly supported by the processor. Bits are indexed from 0, starting from the right.

The list of bitwise operators is shown below:

Operator	Name	Type	Description
~	bitwise NOT (complement)	Unary	performs logical NOT – sets all 0s to 1s and 1s to 0s
&	bitwise AND	Binary	performs logical AND on each pair of corresponding bits –1 only if both bits are 1
|	bitwise OR	Binary	performs logical OR on each pair of corresponding bits –0 only if both bits are 0
^	bitwise XOR	Binary	performs logical XOR on each pair of corresponding bits –1 only if exactly one bit is 1
<<	left shift	Binary	shifts all bits to the left, 0s are shifted in on the right
>>	arithmetic right shift	Binary	shifts all bits to the right, preserving the sign bit
>>>	logical right shift	Binary	shifts all bits to the right, 0s are shifted in on the left

Bitwise operators are more easily understood if we illustrate all operands (variables values) in binary, which we will do for the remainder of this section.

The bitwise NOT, which performs logical negation on each bit, resulting in one's complement, is the easiest to understand. For example:

~01010101   (decimal 85)
=10101010   (decimal 170)

~	0	1
	1	0

A more concrete example of NOT is given in the following code fragment:

```
color lime = color(0, 255, 0);
println(binary(lime));      // will print 11111111000000001111111100000000
println(binary(~lime));     // will print 00000000111111110000000011111111
```

Notice that the leftmost 8 bits were negated from 1 to 0. In reality the leading 0s are not printed, but it is much easier to read and see the effects of the bitwise operators when they are inserted. For the duration of this section, leading 0s will be inserted when necessary to aid readability. Just remember that if you try some of this code in Processing, the output may look different initially due to the missing leading 0s.

The bitwise AND compares two binary numbers bit by bit and works exactly like the logical operator &&, but on pairs of bits instead.

```
  10001111    (decimal 143)
& 11011010    (decimal 218)
= 10001010    (decimal 138)
```

&	0	1
0	0	0
1	0	1

Because of the way AND works, i.e., resulting in 1 if and only if both bits are 1 and 0 otherwise, it can be used to query if a certain bit is set (equal to 1). For example, if we want to know whether a variable x has bit 7 (8th bit from the right) set, we would bitwise AND it with a binary pattern like this: 10000000 (0x80). If the result is non-zero, then x has the said bit set. Similar patterns can be written for any bit or any bit sequences, and these patterns are known as bit masks. Bit masks are commonly written in hexadecimal, because a hex representation is shorter and yet maintains a direct translation to binary. Combining AND and NOT allows us to use bit masks to clear (set to 0) any bit:

```
x = x & ~0x80          //clear 8th bit from the right (bit 7) of x
x = x & ~0xFF          //clear the rightmost 8 bits (bits 0-7) of x
```

More specifically, the mask is first negated so that the bit locations we are interested in are set to 0 instead and 1 everywhere else, which will result in setting those specific bits to 0 and preserving all others when combined with a bitwise AND on a variable, as shown in the following code fragment:

```
color purple = color(255, 0, 255);
println(binary(purple));            //will print 11111111111111110000000011111111
color fuchsia = purple & ~0x80;
println(binary(fuchsia));           //will print 11111111111111110000000001111111
color red = purple & ~0xFF;
println(binary(red));               //will print 11111111111111110000000000000000
```

The bitwise OR also follows the same pattern of performing the logical operation || on the corresponding pair of bits.

	10001111	(decimal 143)
|	11011010	(decimal 218)
=	11011111	(decimal 223)

|	0	1
0	0	1
1	1	1

The bitwise OR can be used to set a bit or a sequence of bits with the appropriate masks. This operation typically requires that the bits to be set have been cleared first, which means it must be preceded with a bitwise AND on the same bits:

```
color white = ~0;
//clear the rightmost 8 bits (bits 0-7) and set to decimal 224
color lightYellow = white & ~0xFF | 224;
```

Lastly, we have the exclusive OR, or XOR, which has no logical operator equivalent in Java. It results in a 1 only if the two bits are different, i.e., 0 and 1 or 1 and 0. 0 and 0 or 1 and 1 both result in 0.

	10001111	(decimal 143)
^	11011010	(decimal 218)
=	01010101	(decimal 85)

^	0	1
0	0	1
1	1	0

The last three bitwise operators (shaded in the table) are known as the bit shifts. Different from what we have seen so far, these operators do not operate on the numerical values of the corresponding bits; rather, they move the bits to the left or right, i.e., shifting. The following illustrates the result of shifting 10001111 two places to the left, or 10001111<<2. Notice that the leftmost two bits are shifted off the left end and are discarded. The two places emptied on the right end are filled in with 0s.

	10001111	(decimal 143)
<<	2	
=	00111100	(decimal 60)

A left shift by n is equivalent to multiplying by 2^n, provided that the result does not overflow. In the above example, there is overflow because of the leading 1 bit being shifted off. If we did not have that bit set, then the number would be 00001111 which is decimal 15. The result does not change and we still end up with 00111100, which is decimal 60, exactly 15*(2^2).

Right shifts work analogously, except that there is consideration to be made for the sign bit on the left end. If a right shift preserves the sign, it is known as an arithmetic shift, denoted by the operator >>. In contrast, a right shift that always shifts in all 0s on the left end is known as a logical shift, denoted by >>>. There is no difference between the left arithmetic shift and the left logical shift.

	10010111	(signed decimal −105)
>>	1	
=	11001011	(signed decimal −53)

	10010111	(unsigned decimal 151)
>>>	1	
=	01001011	(unsigned decimal 75)

A right shift by n is equivalent to dividing by 2^n.

Retrieving R/G/B/A Values Bitwise

Processing's `color` type is actually just a 32-bit integer whose binary representation associates the bits with a certain structure as follows: AAAAAAAARRRRRRRRGGGGGGGGBBBBBBBB, where each letter is a single bit of 0 or 1. The leftmost 8 bits (byte) pack in the 0-255 value for the alpha channel, the next byte packs in the 0-255 value for the red channel, the 3rd byte from the left packs in the 0–255 value for the green channel, and the rightmost byte packs in the 0–255 value for the blue channel. For example:

```
color lime = color(0, 255, 0);
println(binary(lime));
```

will print lime in binary as 11111111000000001111111100000000. Note that the alpha channel was unspecified and the default alpha is 255, which is 11111111 in binary.

Here is an example when an explicit alpha value is given:

```
color coralTransparent = color(255, 127, 80, 51);
println(binary(coralTransparent));  //will print 00110011111111110111111101010000
```

It is important to remember that while the function color takes the alpha value as the 4th and last argument, it is packed into the leftmost 8 bits in the color data type, rather than the rightmost 8 bits. The following diagram inserted white spaces (and leading 0s) so that the binary representation of coralTransparent shows the color component bits more clearly:

00110011	11111111	011111111	01010000
alpha	red	green	blue

Now it is not difficult to see how Processing's built-in color component functions work. They simply unpack the relevant 8 bits from the correct positions and return the corresponding integer value. We can easily extract the information ourselves using bitwise operators that we learned in the previous subsection. For example, suppose we want to obtain the green value. We first want to shift off the rightmost 8 bits, so that the blue bits are discarded. We start with the same color as in the last example.

```
color coralTransparent = color(255, 127, 80, 51);
println(binary(coralTransparent));          //will print 00110011111111110111111101010000
println(binary(coralTransparent >> 8));     //will print 00000000001100111111111101111111
println(binary(coralTransparent >> 8 & 0xFF)); //will print 00000000000000000000000001111111
```

After shifting, the next goal is to set all the leading alpha and red bits to 0, and then we are done. This can be accomplished by performing the logical AND with a bit mask of all 1s in the rightmost 8 bits, i.e., 11111111, which is 0xFF in hexadecimal. This operation has the effect of preserving the bits in the rightmost 8 bits and zeroing out everything else. Thus the exact formula for obtaining the value of the green bits is to right-shift by 8 bits followed by an AND with 0xFF, i.e. >> 8 & 0xFF. The other color components can be similarly obtained, just with different numbers of bits shifted. In general, the following list shows the Processing color component functions and their equivalent bitwise operations, given a color c:

- alpha(c):   c >> 24 & 0xFF
- red(c):   c >> 16 & 0xFF
- green(c):   c >> 8 & 0xFF
- blue(c):   c & 0xFF

Note that the blue bits do not require shifting, since they are located in the rightmost 8 bits.

A group of consecutive bits is called a bit field. We can clear and set the values of bit fields with masks as well. The following are bitwise operations that clear the corresponding A/R/G/B color bits and then set those to the color value of 171, which is AB in hexadecimal, while leaving the rest of the color untouched. The leading 0s are not necessary in the hex masks, but were put in to aid readability.

```
c = c & ~0x000000FF | 0x000000AB        // set blue to 171
c = c & ~0x0000FF00 | 0x0000AB00        // set green to 171
c = c & ~0x00FF0000 | 0x00AB0000        // set red to 171
c = c & ~0xFF000000 | 0xAB000000        // set alpha to 171
```

We can construct the bit masks with the help of the bit shifts instead of writing the values out directly. The following statements are functionally equivalent. This also allows us to write the numbers in decimal, as we do not need to keep track of the bit positions, which are taken care of by the shifting.

```
c = c & ~0xFF | 171                     // set blue to 171
c = c & ~(0xFF<<8) | (171 <<8)          // set green to 171
c = c & ~(0xFF <<16) | (171 << 16)      // set red to 171
c = c & ~(0xFF<<24) | (171<<24)         // set alpha to 171
```

Lastly, if we have the red, green, blue and alpha values all stored in variables and we want to pack the values into a 32-bit integer color, we have the following equivalent bitwise expression:

■ c = color(r, g, b, a):   c = (a<<24) | (r << 16) | (g <<8) | b

It is clear that bitwise operators are not the easiest way to program. Neither is the resulting code as readable as our earlier examples. We have already explained that sometimes this technique is necessary because of speed requirements. However, there are also other applications where manipulating the bits is essential, and this leads to the subject of our next section.

Steganography

Steganography is a technique of communicating via secret messages when no one suspects the existence of such messages. Different from cryptography, messages in steganography are often hidden in plain sight, and once the means of transmission is known, are easy to decode. A well-known example of steganography is the use of invisible ink. With the arrival of digital images and files, concealing information in the less-significant bits has become another popular method for steganography. We have learned that 8 bits are used to represent each color. Notice that not all eight bits are equal. The left-most bits encode much more information than the rightmost bits. In fact, the entire right half of the bits, i.e., the rightmost 4 bits, only encode 2^4 = 16 colors. This is the reason why the leftmost bits are called the most significant bits and the rightmost the least. Knowing this, we can encode a secrete image in a cover image by sacrificing a certain number of least significant bits per color, and pack in the most significant bits of the corresponding colors in the secret image.

In general, the more bits one overwrites, the noisier the cover image will become. Typically 1-2 bits do not change the cover discernibly, but the extracted hidden image is noisy, as much loss occurs. If the hidden image is grayscale, particularly black/white text dominated, then 2 bits per color channel is more than enough to encode most of the 8-bit grayscale or 2-bit b/w colors. Three to four bits are usually needed for more complicated color images. When more than 2 bits are to be discarded, it's better to choose a cover image that does not contain large patches of similar colors, i.e., lots of sky, water, single color background, etc., because the loss will show first in the gradients. Busy images make better covers. Also important to note is that the encoded image should be saved in a lossless compression format like PNG, otherwise the bit-packing will be altered by compression. The following is a Processing program that encodes an image into the least significant 4 bits of a cover image.

```
// encode.pde, chapter 9
// encodes the most significant 4 bits of each color from the msg image into the least
// significant 4 bits of the cover image

PImage cover;                     // To hold unencoded cover picture
PImage secret;                    // To hold image to be encoded into the cover
// & with color to remove rightmost 4 bits from all R/G/B/A channels
// and all 8 bits from the entire Alpha channel
int clearSecretMask = 0xFF0F0F0F;
// & with color to remove rightmost 4 bitsfrom all R/G/B channels
int clearCoverMask = 0x000F0F0F;

void setup() {
  cover = loadImage("woods.jpg");
  secret = loadImage("fall.jpg");
  size(cover.width, cover.height);      //Size the sketch to be the same size as the cover
  image(cover, 0, 0);
} // end setup()

void draw() {}

// When the mouse is clicked, encode image into cover
void mousePressed() {
  cover.loadPixels();              // Load pixels for the cover picture
  secret.loadPixels();             // Load pixels for the image to be encoded
  for (int i=0; i<cover.pixels.length; i++) {
    // Get pixel colors from both the cover and the secret images
    color cp = cover.pixels[i];
    color sp = secret.pixels[i];
    //strip off the alpha and the least significant 4 bits of R, G and B
    sp = sp & ~ clearSecretMask;
    // right shift so that the most significant 4 bits are now in the least significant
    // 4 bit position
    sp = sp >> 4;
    // Strip off least significant 4 bits of R, G, B from cover image
    cp = cp & ~clearCoverMask;
    // Add the significant bits from the secret image to the cover's least significant bits
    cp = cp | sp;
    // Replace the encoded pixel back
    cover.pixels[i] = cp;
  }
  cover.updatePixels();
  image(cover, 0, 0);
  cover.save("encoded.png");    // save to named file as PNG
} // end mousePressed()
```

Figure 9-28. Encoded cover image

Figure 9-28 shows the encoded cover and Figure 9-29 shows the extracted image from the cover. Notice the loss that shows in the sky, both in the cover and the extracted image, but more obvious in the extracted image because of the greater expanse of sky. If it is imperative that the secret image be recovered in its entirety, i.e., there is important information in every bit, then we will need a cover image in a larger size. If, as in our example, 4 bits per color channel are available for encoding purposes, then a cover image with twice as many pixels will suffice. We can encode the most significant 4 bits in the first half of the pixels and the least significant 4 bits in the second half of the pixels. The fewer bits available for encoding in the cover, the larger a cover image we will need. Next we show the companion code that decodes the encoded cover image.

```
// decode.pde, chapter 9
PImage img;

int clearMask = 0x00F0F0F0;  // & with color to remove leftmost 4 bits from all R/G/B channels

void setup() {
  img = loadImage("encoded.png"); // Load the encoded picture
  size(img.width, img.height);    // Size the sketch to be the same size as the picture

  img.loadPixels();
  for (int i=0; i<img.pixels.length; i++) {
    color ip = img.pixels[i];
    // Strip off the most significant 4 bits of R, G, and B colors
    ip = ip & ~clearMask;
    // left shift and move the least significant 4 bits into the leftmost position
    ip = ip << 4;
    // Replace the decoded pixel back into the picture
    img.pixels[i] = ip;
  }
  img.updatePixels();
  image(img, 0, 0);
} // end setup()
```

Figure 9-29. Extracted image from cover

Complex Systems

So far we have seen many examples of visually complex effects produced by iteration coupled with randomization. It is a well-known phenomenon that small changes and interactions between components aggregated over time often lead to complex systematic behavior. Complex Systems is a research field in mathematical modeling that studies the ways in which organized but unpredictable behaviors are presented in systems of nature and beyond. Most biological systems for example, and many physical and social systems are considered fundamentally complex, and the challenge to model and simulate these systems is great. In this section we will look at examples of how we can simulate some of these systems with programming techniques you have already acquired.

Emergence

Emergence describes the way complex systems and patterns arise out of a multiplicity of simple interactions. In other words, an emergent system generates much more complexity than the sum of its parts. The concept that the total is greater than the sum of its parts is not new, but only recently do we have the computing power to start to model and systematically study these systems in the hope that one day we will more fully understand how complex behaviors manifest from simple base entities and their interactions.

Emergent Properties

An important principle of emergent systems is the lack of central organization or leadership; it is a form of a spontaneous creation of order. Familiar examples from nature include schooling of fish, swarming of insects, and flocking of birds. All are considered emergent behaviors because they arise from simple rules that are followed by individual group members and do not involve any central coordination.

Figure 9-30. A termite "cathedral" produced by a termite colony (Wikipedia)

For instance, flocking behavior can be fairly accurately described using the following three rules, developed in 1986 by Craig Reynolds:

- Separation: Maintain minimum distance to local flockmates to avoid crowding

- Alignment: Steer toward the average heading of local flockmates

- Cohesion: Move toward the average position (center of mass) of the flock

These movement patterns are very predictable over the short term, as the flock's position in the next iteration is spelled out by the simply computable rules. They appear, however, completely unpredictable over time when the effects aggregate. Living systems, therefore, are believed to be poised on the border between order and randomness – a phenomenon discovered by Christopher Langton, a leading researcher in artificial life, known as "the edge of chaos."

Emergence theory has been used to study many decentralized physical, biological, economic, and social systems, particularly with the rise of the World Wide Web, web-based social systems, and the data sphere. For example, among the more interesting questions in economics are whether the world markets display emergent behaviors (they do), and how or why they emerge in terms of the microeconomic behaviors of the individual players. Many efforts to model the human brain also view it as a complex system, with consciousness as the ultimate emergent property, rising from the neurons and the physiology of the brain.

Emergent Voronoi

A simple yet elegant emergence example is outlined in the following algorithm. Scatter particles into a space containing n points – known as sites. All particles move with only one goal, to get further away from the closest site, until they are equidistant to two or more of the closest sites (i.e., it cannot get further away from one without getting closer to another), at which point they stop. What results from this algorithm is an emergent system in which the particles self-organize into what is known as a Voronoi diagram, a subdivision of space into n regions, each containing one site, where all points in a given Voronoi region are no closer to any other site than the one contained in the region. A sample run with 10 randomly chosen sites and 5,000 particles is shown in Figures 9-31 through 9-34.

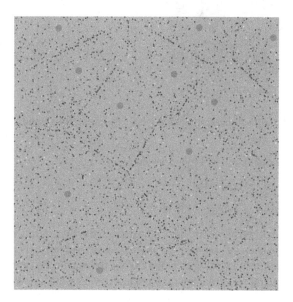

Figure 9-31. After 10 iterations

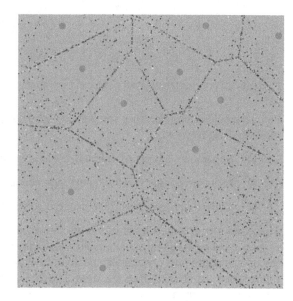

Figure 9-32. After 200 iterations

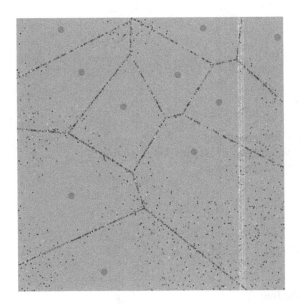

Figure 9-33. After 400 iterations

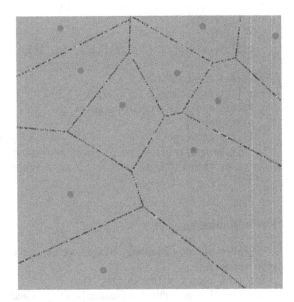

Figure 9-34. After 1,000 iterations

Conventionally, Voronoi diagrams are computed with algorithms from Computational Geometry, implementa-tions of which are non-trivial and typically inaccessible at the introduction level. The elegance of the emergent algorithm lies in its simplicity; i.e., each particle is only responsible for calculating its distance to all the sites, finding the nearest one, then moving away from it. This can be implemented with minimal effort as the code below shows, where the sites are kept as an array of PVector and the particles are kept in an ArrayList. A mouse click calls the function reset() which resets the entire program by generating 10 new randomly chosen sites and 5,000 new particles. The reset() function is also called initially in setup().

```
// emergentVoronoi.pde, chapter 9
PVector[] sites;          // sites
ArrayList ps;             // particles
int numSites = 10;
int numParticles = 5000;

void setup() {
  size(800, 800);
  smooth();
  colorMode(HSB, 360, 100, 100);
  sites = new PVector[numSites];
  reset();
} // end setup()

void draw() {
  background(255);
  // draws the sites as gray circles
  for (int i=0; i<sites.length; i++) {
```

```
      noStroke();
      fill(200);
      ellipse(sites[i].x, sites[i].y, 20, 20);
    }
    // draws the particles
    for (int i=ps.size()-1; i>=0; i--) {
      Particle p = (Particle)ps.get(i);
      p.display();
      if (!p.converge()) {              // if p has not converged
        if (p.update()) {               // move p and if out of screen after moving
          ps.remove(i);                 // remove particle from ps
        }
      }
    }
  } // end draw()

  // creates all new randomly placed sites and particles
  void reset() {
    for (int i=0; i<sites.length; i++) {
      sites[i] = new PVector(random(width), random(height));
    }
    ps = new ArrayList();
    for (int i=0; i<numParticles; i++) {
      ps.add(new Particle(random(width), random(height)));
    }
  } // end reset()

  void mousePressed() {
    reset();
  } // end mousePressed()
```

The draw() function steps through the array sites and draws each site as a gray circle of 20x20. The next loop iterates through the ArrayList ps containing all the particles, which are objects of type Particle. If a particular particle has not yet converged (i.e., it is not yet equidistant to two of the nearest sites), its update() method is called to move it. update() will return true if the particle is outside of the sketch window after moving. It is then removed from the ArrayList.

Most of the work is done in the Particle class shown below. Each Particle object has the following variables: center, radius, v (velocity), c (color) and stable, a boolean variable indicating whether it has converged and should stop moving. The constructor takes the x and y parameters and assigns them as the x and y coordinates of the center of the particle. A radius of 2 and a choice of color are also assigned. Velocity of the particle is set to the normalized vector heading from its center to the nearest site. stable starts off with false.

The two methods nearestSite() and update() are responsible for moving the particle during every iteration, and nearestSite() calculates the distance of the particle to all sites and finds the two nearest. If the particle is considered equidistant to the two nearest sites (distances differ by less than 1 pixel), it sets stable to true. The method then returns the array index of the nearest site. Then update() first moves the particle by adding v to center. It then updates v by setting it to the normalized vector from center to the nearest site. Lastly, it checks the current x and y coordinates of center against the sketch window boundaries and returns true if the particle is out of the screen, and false otherwise.

```
class Particle {
  PVector center;
  float radius;
  PVector v;
  color c;
  boolean stable;

  Particle(float x, float y) {
    center = new PVector(x, y, 0);
    radius = 2;
    // green/blue 50% of the time and yellow/gold 50% of the time
    if (random(1) < 0.5) {
      c = color(random(170, 190), 70, random(100));
    }
    else {
      c = color(random(40, 60), 70, random(100));
    }
    int i = nearestSite();
    v = PVector.sub(center, sites[i]);
    v.normalize();
    stable = false;
  } // end Particle()

  void display() {
    fill(c);
    ellipse(center.x, center.y, radius*2, radius*2);
  } // end display()

  // returns the index of the nearest site
  // also sets stable to true if the two nearest nodes are equidistant
  int nearestSite() {
    // start with first site as nearest and 2nd site as next nearest
    //calculate distance to the current nearest site
    float minDist = PVector.dist(center, sites[0]);
    //calculate distance to the current 2nd nearest site
    float minDist2 = PVector.dist(center, sites[1]);
    int minIdx = 0;                              // index of the current nearest site
    int minIdx2 = 1;                             // index of the current 2nd nearest site
    for (int i=1; i<sites.length; i++) {
      float d = PVector.dist(center, sites[i]);
      if (d < minDist) {        // if site[i] is found closer
        minDist2 = minDist;     // swap nearest site as 2nd nearest site
        minIdx2 = minIdx;
        minDist = d;            // swap site[i] as nearest site
        minIdx = i;
      }
```

```
      else if (d < minDist2) {  // if site[i] is between nearest site and 2nd nearest site
        minDist2 = d;              // swap site[i] as 2nd nearest site
        minIdx2 = i;
      }
    }
    // if equidistant to two nearest sites
    if (minDist2 - minDist < 1) {
      stable = true;
    }
    return minIdx;
  } // end nearestNode()

  // returns true if particle is outside of sketch window, false otherwise
  boolean update() {
    center.add(v);
    int i = nearestNode();
    float d = PVector.dist(center, sites[i]);
    v = PVector.sub(center, sites[i]);
    v.normalize();
    v.mult(2);
    // off the screen, should be removed from ps
    return (center.x > width || center.x < 0 || center.y > height  || center.y < 0);
  } // end update()

  boolean converge() {
    return stable;
  }
} // end class Particle
```

In this implementation a large number of particles are lost through the boundaries because moving out of the screen is also optimal for getting away from the nearest site, depending on the particle's starting point. To avoid this, an additional behavior can be programmed in so that a particle is also generally attracted to the center of the sketch.

> Try This: Modify the mousePressed() function so that each left mouse click adds a new site at mouse point and each right mouse click calls the function reset().

Cellular Automata

Some of the most well known examples of emergent behaviors are exhibited by cellular automata (CA), such as John Conway's Game of Life and its variants (e.g., Seeds, Brian's Brain). A cellular automaton is a discrete mathematical model consisting of these elements:

- A regular grid of cells

- Each cell has a finite number of states (most commonly just 2 – on and off)

- The state of the current cell depends on the neighboring cells from the previous iteration.

Cellular automata were first conceived of in the 1940s by mathematicians Jon von Neumann (often known as the father of the modern computer design, called von Neumann architecture) and Stanislaw Ulam, as a mathematical abstraction to approach the problem of designing self-replicating systems. In 1971 Princeton mathematician John Conway created arguably the most famous CA, "Conway's Game of Life," which brought CA to the popular imagination through an article written about it in *Scientific American*. Although termed as a game, the Game of Life does not require any player input besides the initial values (seeds). Its universe is an infinite 2D grid of cells, which are either alive or dead. At every iteration of the game, a cell's state is changed based on the following rules:

- Any live cell with fewer than two live neighbors dies, as if caused by under-population.

- Any live cell with more than three live neighbors dies, as if by overcrowding.

- Any live cell with exactly two or three live neighbors lives on to the next generation.

- Any dead cell with exactly three live neighbors becomes a live cell, as if by reproduction.

Simply put, a live cell will die in the next generation when it has fewer than 2 or more than 3 live neighbors. A dead cell will become alive in the next generation when it has exactly 3 live neighbors. Everything else remains unchanged. The fame of Game of Life can be largely attributed to its unexpected complexity. More precisely, the surprising ways in which stable, repeating, and self-replicating patterns evolve in the face of such simple rules. The Game of Life exhibits infinite growth and is considered by many to be the key to understanding our world within a discrete framework.

Conway's Game of Life can be easily implemented in Processing using a 3D array of type boolean as shown in the program below. The game grid itself only needs a 2D array of boolean, each of which indicates whether the cell in the corresponding location is alive or dead. A third dimension is needed so that two iterations of the game can be stored at any one time, since the current state of a cell depends on looking up the states of its neighbors in the previous iteration. The program implements a grid of 50x50, from which 20% of the cells are randomly selected to be alive at the start. At each iteration of the draw() loop, the number of live neighbors are counted for each cell with the function countNeighbors(), and the count is then used to determine the cell's state in the next round with the GoL rules.

```
// GOL.pde, chapter 9
// Flags and game parameters
int N = 50;             // Grid Dimension
int cellSize = 10;      // Size of cell
int cur = 0;            // Current grid index
int nxt = 1;            // next grid index
```

```
// CA consists of two grids for current and next step
boolean[][][] CA = new boolean[N][N][2];

void setup() {
  size(500, 500);
  randomizeGrid(cur);
} // end setup()

void draw() {
  background(255);
  drawCells();
  advanceGame();
} // end draw()

void advanceGame() {
  for (int i=0; i<N; i++) {
    for (int j=0; j<N; j++) {
      // Count location neighbors
      int neighbors = countNeighbors(i, j);

      // If the cell is alive
      if (CA[i][j][cur] == true) {
        if (neighbors < 2 || neighbors > 3) {
          CA[i][j][nxt] = false;
        }
        else {
          CA[i][j][nxt] = true;
        }
      }
      else {
        if (neighbors == 3) {
          CA[i][j][nxt] = true;
        }
        else {
          CA[i][j][nxt] = false;
        }
      }
    }
  }

  // Swap grid indices
  int tmp = cur;
  cur = nxt;
  nxt = tmp;
} // end advanceGame

// Count the number of live neighbors of current cell
int countNeighbors(int i, int j) {
  int count = 0;
```

```
   for (int ii=i-1; ii<=i+1; ii++) {
     for (int jj=j-1; jj<=j+1; jj++) {
        // Wrap edges of board
        int iii = (ii + N) % N;
        int jjj = (jj + N) % N;

        // Skip center location
        if (iii!=i || jjj!=j)
          if ( CA[iii][jjj][cur] == true )
            count++;
     }
   }
   return count;
} // end countNeighbors()

void drawCells() {
   for (int i=0; i<N; i++) {
     for (int j=0; j<N; j++) {
        if (CA[i][j][cur] == true) {
          fill(0);
          noStroke();
        }
        else {
          fill(255);
          stroke(240);
        }
        rect(i*cellSize, j*cellSize, cellSize, cellSize);
     }
   }
} // end drawCells()

// Randomly set 20% of cells alive
void randomizeGrid(int c) {
   for (int i=0; i<N; i++) {
     for (int j=0; j<N; j++) {
        // set 20% of cells alive
        if (random(0, 1) < .2) {
          CA[i][j][c] = true;
        }
     }
   }
} // end randomizeGrid()
```

Figure 9-35. Initial grid

Figure 9-36. After 100 iterations

Figure 9-37. After 500 iterations

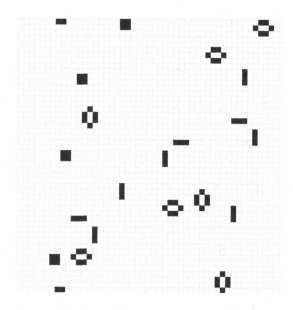

Figure 9-38. After 1,700 iterations

Figures 9-35 through 9-38 show a sample run of the game where the "life" in the grid stabilized after 1,700 iterations.

Von Neumann's CA as well as Conway's Game of Life were two-dimensional and grid-based, but there are even simpler one-dimensional CAs known as elementary cellular automata. These are the simplest non-trivial CAs, in which each cell has two states – on and off – and only has two neighbors, the one to the left and the one to the right. Stephen Wolfram, chief designer of the Mathematica software application and the Wolfram Alpha computational knowledge engine, studied these extensively, and his work culminated in the publication of the volume *A New Kind of Science* in 2002. We refer you to that book if you are interested in finding out more about one-dimensional CAs.

Chapter Project: Truchet Tiling

Truchet tiling is named after Father Sébastien Truchet, who worked on plane coverage with combinations of a single tile in the 1700s. The Truchet tiles are square tiles that may be rotated in the four main orientations (0, PI/2, PI, 3PI/2) in the x-y plane. Shown below in Figures 9-39 through 9-42 are the base tile pattern and its rotational variations that Truchet originally studied.

Figure 9-39. 0   **Figure 9-40.** PI/2   **Figure 9-41.** PI   **Figure 9-42.** 3PI/2

This simple pattern can be schematically tiled with deliberate combinations, for example:

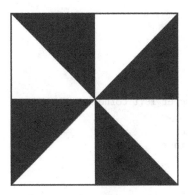  

We first show a Processing program that performs a random Truchet tiling, that is, the rotational orientation of a tile is randomly chosen. Output is shown in Figure 9-43. We implement a Tile class which keeps a tile's x and y coordinates, size, and rotational orientation as data fields and provides a display() method that displays the tile with the chosen orientation via a series of transformations.

```
// truchetRandom.pde, chapter 9
int tileSize = 24;
int rows = 35;
int cols = 35;
Tile[][] tiles = new Tile[rows][cols];

void setup() {
  size(tileSize*rows, tileSize*cols);
  smooth();
  background(255);

  for (int i=0; i < rows; i++) {
    for (int j = 0; j < cols; j++) {
      tiles[i][j] = new Tile(j*tileSize, i*tileSize, tileSize);
      tiles[i][j].display();
    }
  }
} // end setup()

class Tile {
  int sz;         // size of tile
  int x, y;       // x, y coords of top left corner of tile
  int orient;     // orientation of tile

  Tile(int x, int y, int w) {
    this.x = x;
    this.y = y;
    sz = w;
    orient = randInt(0, 3);
  } // end Tile()

  void display() {
    pushMatrix();
    translate(x, y);              // move to tile's x-y location (upper left corner)
    translate(sz/2, sz/2);        // move to the center of the tile
    rotate(orient*PI/2);          // rotate by the appropriate angle
    translate(-sz/2, -sz/2);      // move back to the upper left corner
    fill(0);
    triangle(sz, 0, sz, sz, 0, sz);
    popMatrix();
  } // end display()
} // end class Tile
```

Figure 9-43. 1,225 tiles with random orientation

Now it's time to explore some more interesting tile patterns. When a pair of arcs decorates the tiles as shown in Figure 9-44 and we form a Truchet tiling with these tiles, the arcs join to form a family of simple curves in the plane.

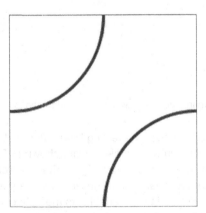

Figure 9-44. Truchet tile decorated with a pair of arcs

This tiling can be easily programmed by swapping out the `fill()` and `triangle()` drawing commands in the `display()` method of the `Tile` class and substituting with the following:

```
stroke(0);
noFill();
arc(0, 0, sz, sz, 0, PI/2);
arc(sz, sz, sz, sz, PI, 3*PI/2);
```

The resulting tiling is shown in Figure 9-45. Note that this is still the result of tiling with randomly chosen orientations. The symmetry of the tile design guarantees that all combinations of the tiles (there are only two unique orientations) result in smoothly joined curves.

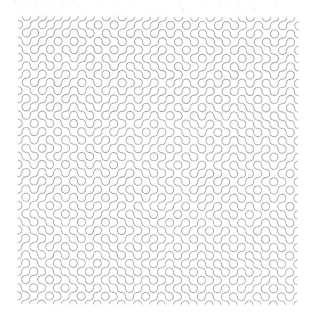

Figure 9-45. Tiling of 1,225 tiles shown in Figure 9-44 with random orientations

We can now introduce colors to produce more interesting tiling patterns. Let us color the areas inside the arcs differently from those outside, resulting in a base tile design, shown in Figure 9-46. Note that we must now manage each tile's orientation and coloring more carefully, so that no breakages in colors will occur between neighboring tiles. This requires that we swap the inside and outside colors depending on the current tile's orientation as well as its neighbor's. We add three variables to the `Tile` class, `ic` and `oc` which store inside and outside colors and a `boolean` variable `swapColors` to indicate whether we should draw the tile with inside and outside colors swapped, as shown in Figure 9-46 on the right column.

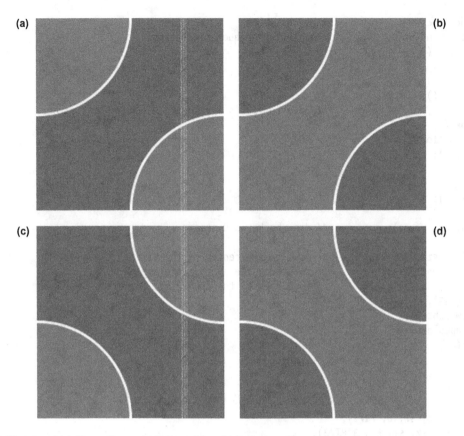

Figure 9-46. (a) and (c): Two unique orientations; (b) and (d): Drawn with swapped colors

The Tile class remains otherwise largely unchanged. ic and oc are initialized in the constructor with parameters passed in. A rect() command is added to display() to add color to the middle section of the tile, and two conditional statements are added to display() to test swapColors and so that a color swap is performed when called for.

```
class Tile {
  int sz;              // size of tile
  int x, y;            // x, y coords of top left corner of tile
  int orient;          // orientation of tile, 0 or 1
  boolean swapColors;  // whether we should swap inside and outside colors
  color ic;            // inside color - fill color of arc if swapColor is false
  color oc;            // outside color - fill color of background square if swapColor is false

  Tile(int x, int y, int w, color ic, color oc) {
    this.x = x;
    this.y = y;
    sz = w;
    this.ic = ic;
```

```
    this.oc = oc;
    orient = randInt(0, 1);        // only two unique orientations
  } // end Tile()

  void display() {
    pushMatrix();
    translate(x, y);               // move to tile's x-y location (upper left corner)
    noStroke();
    if (swapColors) {
      fill(ic);
    }
    else {
      fill(oc);
    }
    rect(0, 0, sz, sz);            // draw background square

    translate(sz/2, sz/2);         // move to the center of the tile
    rotate(orient*PI/2);           // rotate by the appropriate angle
    translate(-sz/2, -sz/2);       // move back to the upper left corner
    stroke(255);
    strokeWeight(3);
    if (swapColors) {
      fill(oc);
    }
    else {
      fill(ic);
    }
    arc(0, 0, sz, sz, 0, PI/2);
    arc(sz, sz, sz, sz, PI, 3*PI/2);
    popMatrix();
  } // end display()
} // end class Tile
```

A swap of the colors is necessary if a row-adjacent neighbor or a column-adjacent neighbor has the same orientation. The swapping is implemented in function colorSwap(), called within the nested for loops in setup(). The condition (i>0 && j==0) checks to see if a tile is the first in a row, starting from the 2nd row. The condition i>0 was added to skip the first row, as tiles[0][0] is the very first tile drawn and no swapping is necessary. If indeed a tile is the first tile in a row, the program checks to see if the tile has the same orientation as the tile directly above. If that is also true, then we set our tile's swapColors to the negation of the swapColors of the tile above, resulting in opposite inside-outside coloring. Note that we cannot simply set swapColors to true or false, because what we really want is for the current tile's color to be a swapped version of the column neighbor's above, which means whether we swap or not depends on whether the tile directly above was swapped or not. If, on the other hand, we have a different orientation as the column neighbor above (the else case), then we copy the column neighbor's swapColors, keeping the coloring the same. The next condition (j>0) looks at all the subsequent tiles in a row (including the first row), performs a similar comparison on the orientations of the current tile and its row-neighbor to the left, and sets swapColors accordingly.

```
// truchetSwap.pde, chapter 9
int tileSize = 100;
int rows = 10;
int cols = 10;
Tile[][] tiles = new Tile[rows][cols];
color ic = color(200, 100, 0);    // orange
color oc = color(20, 100, 255);  // blue

void setup() {
  size(tileSize*rows, tileSize*cols);
  smooth();

  for (int i=0; i < rows; i++) {
    for (int j = 0; j < cols; j++) {
      tiles[i][j] = new Tile(j*tileSize, i*tileSize, tileSize, ic, oc);
      colorSwap(i, j);
      tiles[i][j].display();
    }
  }
} // end setup()

// takes the row and column indices of the current tile and
// decides how to set its swapColor boolean variable
void colorSwap(int i, int j) {
  if (i > 0 && j == 0) {                          // first tile of a row, starting from the 2nd row
    // same orientation as tile directly above
    if (tiles[i-1][0].orient == tiles[i][0].orient) {
      // set to opposite coloring of my neighbor above
      tiles[i][0].swapColors = !tiles[i-1][0].swapColors;
    }
    else {
      // set to same coloring of my neighbor above
      tiles[i][0].swapColors = tiles[i-1][0].swapColors;
    }
  }
  if (j > 0) {                                    // subsequent tiles in a row, including the first
    // same orientation as tile to the left
    if (tiles[i][j-1].orient == tiles[i][j].orient) {
      // set to opposite coloring of my neighbor to the left
      tiles[i][j].swapColors = !tiles[i][j-1].swapColors;
    }
    else {
      // set to same coloring of my neighbor to the left
      tiles[i][j].swapColors = tiles[i][j-1].swapColors;
    }
  }
} // end colorSwap()
```

The result of tiling 100 tiles is shown in Figure 9-47, as well as in Figure 9-48, where each tile is outlined to show the tiling more clearly.

Figure 9-47. Schematic tiling of 100 tiles shown in Figure 9-46

Figure 9-48. Schematic tiling of 100 tiles shown in Figure 9-46

> *Try This: Turn the above tiling into a puzzle by starting with a tiling of random orientations and default colors with no swapping. Add interactive control to enable the user to swap the inside and outside colors of any tile under the mouse point. The goal of the game is for the user to swap the colors of tiles until all neighboring tiles have continuous coloring, that is, to have the user interactively recreate what the swapping algorithm automatically generates.*

Truchet tiling is commonly found on walls and floors and in other architectural contexts. It is also widely used by software programs to generate textures for plane coverage. Much more elaborate and intricate tilings can be created with variations on base tile design and tiling algorithms. Figures 9-49 through 9-52 show some of the simpler variations.

Figure 9-49. Truchet tiling variation 1

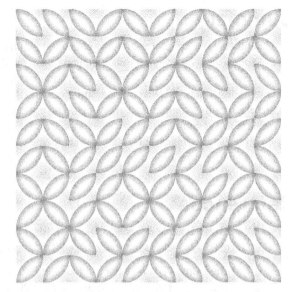

Figure 9-50. Truchet tiling variation 2

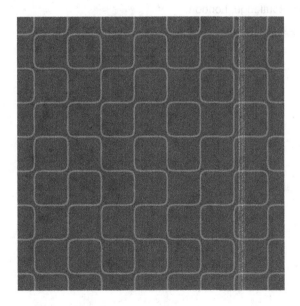

Figure 9-51. Truchet tiling variation 3

Figure 9-52. Truchet tiling variation 4

Summary

This has been a chapter with many challenging and hopefully engaging topics. We began with a look at a few of Processing's basic image manipulation functions, demonstrated with examples of simple image processing. Then we introduced two and multi-dimensional arrays, and from there we discussed Processing's pixel buffers and related functions. Next bitwise operators and their connections to Processing's color component functions are discussed in some detail, and we worked through an example on steganography. Finally, we introduced the readers to a number of advanced areas in Computer Science such as emergence, cellular automata and tiling which all tie into this chapter's topics nicely. We will continue our exploration of image processing in the next chapter, including more advanced techniques such as filtering and video processing.

References

1. ClarkVision.com, R.N. Clark, "Notes on the Resolution and Other Details of the Human Eye", http://clarkvision.com/imagedetail/eye-resolution.html, 11/25/2009, referenced 7/1/2012.

2. The Human Brain Project, "Modeling and Simulating the Brain", http://www.humanbrainproject.eu/modelling_brain.html, referenced 7/1/2012.

3. Craig Reynolds, "Flocks, Herds and Schools: A Distributed Behavioral Model," *Proceedings of ACM SIGGRAPH '87* 21, no. 4 (1987): 25–34.

4. Paul Coates, 2010: *Programming.Architecture*. Routledge, London.

5. Stephen Wolfram, 2002: *A New Kind of Science*. Wolfram Media, Champaign, IL.

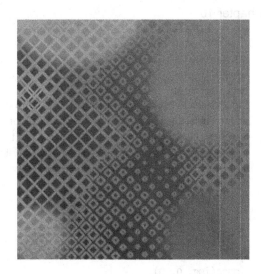

Chapter 10

Expressive Imaging

Image processing refers to the process of digitally analyzing and manipulating an image so that it becomes more aesthetic or useful in some way. Although most of the time the output is also an image, statistical analysis results based on pixel values such as histograms are also common. Photoshop is perhaps the most well-known image editing software and enjoys a tremendous popularity that has seen the name enter the English language as a verb. It is however worth pointing out that image processing is more than just image editing; it encompasses analyzing, enhancing, and compressing as well as reconstructing images. Beyond aesthetic reasons, image processing is widely used in computer vision and robotics for feature recognition and object tracking, as well as in manufacturing and scientific imaging for high-precision inspection and measurement challenges.

In Chapter 9, we have already seen many simpler examples of image processing. In fact, image processing refers to any computation for which the input consists of images, i.e., pixels, and thus any pixel-based operation qualifies. In this chapter, we will focus on more sophisticated techniques and go over Processing's built-in imaging tools.

Image IO

First we do a quick review of image input and output in Processing. Recall that an image can be read into a Processing program with the function call loadImage(), which takes the name of an image and returns a PImage object. Four image formats, GIF, JPG, TGA, and PNG, are supported. Once loaded, PImage objects can be displayed to a sketch window screen via the function call to image(). For example the following code fragment reads the image file tree.jpg into the variable img and then displays it in the sketch window starting at the upper left corner.

```
PImage img = loadImage("tree.jpg");
image(img, 0, 0);
```

Image files to be loaded must be in the same directory as the sketch program itself, or in the data folder of the sketch directory. If the named image file is not found, or cannot be read for any other reason, loadImage() will return null, which will cause the variable img to become null, subsequently generating an error when img gets referenced in the next line of code. In general, it is a good idea to check the return value of loadImage() against null. For example, you could insert the following if statement:

```
PImage img = loadImage("tree.jpg");
if (img==null) {
  println("tree.jpg not found.");
  exit(0);
}
image(img, 0, 0);
```

Error checking is an important programming technique you can use to avoid frequent crashes and minimize debugging time. For the sake of space, we will not be inserting error checking for the return value of loadImage() in any of our subsequent code examples, but we continue to encourage the reader to do so when programming on your own.

Processing also provides an easy way to save a screenshot of the sketch window to an image, via the function call save(). save() takes a String argument, which is used to name the output image. One can specify a TIF, JPG, TGA, or PNG format by naming with the appropriate extensions. If no extension is provided, then the image will be saved in TIF by default. For example the following code fragment loads tree.jpg, displays it in a sketch window and then saves a screenshot of the sketch window to tree.tif, essentially creating a duplicate copy of tree.jpg named tree.tif in TIF format:

```
PImage img = loadImage("tree.jpg");
image(img, 0, 0);
save("tree");
```

Tinting

In Chapter 9 we saw how to modify the colors of individual pixels via the pixel buffer. Another easy way to add a tint or color overlay to an image is to use Processing's tint() function. tint() sets the fill value for displaying an image, which can be thought of as the equivalent of fill() for shapes. The function requires a color value to use for tinting. Additionally, tint() can take an additional alpha value to control the image's transparency. Similar to fill(), the color value can be given in Processing's packed 32-bit integer color data type, or separately as three float values (specifying red, green, and blue), or as a single float value if only grayscale color tinting is desired. The follow program tints a picture with four different colors and displays them in a Warhol-esque collage, as shown in Figure 10-1.

```
// tinting.pde, chapter 10
void setup() {
  PImage img = loadImage("baby2.jpg");
  size(img.width*2, img.height*2);  // 2 times as wide as and 2 times as high as the original image
```

```
  tint(200, 100, 0);                    // orange
  image(img, 0, 0);
  tint(0, 100, 200);                    // blue
  image(img, img.width, 0);             // display at x offset img.width
  tint(100, 100, 200);                  // purple
  image(img, 0, img.height);
  tint(200, 200, 100);                  // yellow
  image(img, img.width, img.height);
} // end setup()
```

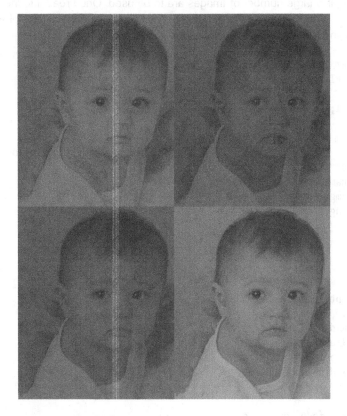

Figure 10-1. Portrait collage created with `tint()`

While easy to use, `tint()` is in general less flexible than the pixel-by-pixel color modifications you saw before, since only a single color can be used as a tint at once, and is applied to the entire image. Knowing about the pixel buffer, you might guess how `tint()` can be easily implemented from scratch. How do we "fill" an image with a single color? An image is usually not all one color; thus the specified fill color is used as a maximum allowable color. That is, a full white pixel (255, 255, 255) will be colored exactly as the fill color. Any pixel with smaller color values (in each red, green, or blue) will be colored with proportionally less fill color. Transparency is managed similarly.

> *Try This: Implement your own `tint()` function using an iteration over the pixel buffer and the algorithm described above. Do not worry about emulating the overloaded arguments in the built-in `tint()`. Take four `float` arguments, each specifying the red, green, blue, and alpha value of the tinting color.*

Our next example demonstrates how `tint()` can be used to alter the alpha values of images. This program slowly fades a group of images in and out. Five images are used in this example. They are named with a specific pattern, i.e., bmc0.jpg, bmc1.jpg, ..., bmc4.jpg so that the images can be loaded into an array with a loop. This is important if a large number of images are to be used. Once read into the array, a current image selected from the array is displayed and slowly faded out by tinting with decreasing alpha values, while the next image is slowly faded in by tinting with increasing alpha values.

```
// fade.pde, chapter 10
PImage[] img = new PImage[5];
int alpha = 255;
int cur = 0, nxt = 1;

void setup() {
  size(600,450);                         // use the largest dimension from all images
  imageMode(CENTER);
  // Load images, named bmc0.jpg, bmc1.jpg, ... etc
  for (int i=0; i<img.length; i++) {
    img[i] = loadImage("bmc"+i+".jpg");
  }
}// end setup()

void draw() {
  background(255);
  // Fade out current image
  tint(255, alpha);
  image(img[cur], width/2, height/2);
  // Fade in next image
  tint(255, 255-alpha);
  image(img[nxt], width/2, height/2);
  alpha--;

  // Swap images when fade completes
  if (alpha < 0) {
    cur = nxt;                     // go to the next image
    nxt = (cur+1)%img.length;      // increment nxt, wrap around if necessary
    alpha = 255;
  }
}// end draw()
```

Tinting can be turned off by calling `noTint()`, or calling `tint()` with full white. Different from most image-related functions, `tint()` is a stand-alone function that only applies to the sketch window. There is no `PImage` version of this function.

Masking

The PImage class provides another useful function called mask(), which is a more flexible way to modify an image's alpha values at display time and can be used to mask out part of an image. It is important to remember that the mask is an alpha mask only. That is, the only thing that it modifies is the transparency of the original image pixels. Processing allows you to use either an image or a pixel buffer as a mask.

Image Mask

When using an image as a mask, the mask needs to be the same size as the original image and should be grayscale. If a full RGB image is given, only the blue channel will be used as the mask. The mask image basically works like an alpha channel but allows alpha values to vary from pixel to pixel (versus tint(), where the same alpha value is applied to all pixels). For each pixel, a value of 0 in the mask will make the corresponding pixel in the displaying image fully transparent and invisible and a value of 255 will make the image pixel fully opaque.

Masking is a popular technique to replace backgrounds in photos or as a first step in many scientific imaging methods to black out unimportant parts of an image. For example, Figures 10-2–10-4 show a mask applied to an image of a Petri dish with a cell culture to mask out all but the center of the dish. Further image processing techniques can be employed to automatically calculate the confluency of the cell culture for example, which we will see later.

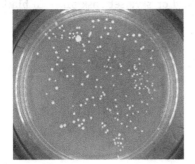
Figure 10-2. Colony.tif

Figure 10-3. Mask.tif

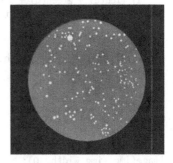
Figure 10-4. Results of masking colony.tif with mask.tif

The Processing program that performed the masking is shown below:

```
// colonyMask.pde, chapter 10
void setup() {
  PImage img = loadImage("colony.tif");
  PImage msk = loadImage("mask.tif");
  background(0);
  size(img.width, img.height);
  img.mask(msk);
  image(img, 0, 0);
} // end setup()
```

It is clear that once a mask is given, the masking process itself is very straightforward. However, how does one create a mask in the first place, particularly if the foreground is not geometrically shaped? One way is to create it in Photoshop, by tracing out the outline manually. It is time-consuming, however. Masks can often be automatically calculated, if the background is clearly distinguishable–that is, if the foreground has a sufficient color difference from the background. In the following example, we automatically create the mask that blocks out the sky and the clouds in the photo of a city street. The program creates the mask by looking at every pixel in the original photo. If the pixel is white or near white (decided by the sum of the red, green and blue values, greater than 600), it is considered part of the clouds. If a pixel is blue or near blue, (decided by the blue value, greater than 190), then it is considered part of the sky. In either case, the corresponding pixel in the mask is set to black. Otherwise, the pixel is set to white. The result of masking the original is shown in Figure 10-5.

```
// imageMask.pde, chapter 10
void setup() {
  PImage img = loadImage("prinzipal.jpg");
  size(img.width*2, img.height);                       //twice the width for side by side display
  PImage msk = createImage(img.width, img.height, RGB); //the mask should be an image of the same size
  background(0);
  img.loadPixels();
  msk.loadPixels();
  for (int y=0; y<img.height; y++){
    for (int x=0; x<img.width; x++){
      color c = img.pixels[y*img.width+x];
      if (red(c) + green(c) + blue(c) > 600 || blue(c) > 190) { // cloud or sky, set mask pixel to black
        msk.pixels[y*img.width+x] = 0;
      }
      else {
        msk.pixels[y*img.width+x] = 255;
      }
    }
  }
  msk.updatePixels();
  image(img, 0, 0);
  img.mask(msk);
  image(img, img.width, 0);
} // end setup()
```

Figure 10-5. Left: original; Right: after masking out the sky and clouds

Pixel Buffer Mask

The mask() function will also take a pixel buffer as a mask. A pixel array used as a mask must have the same number of total pixels as the original image. This feature is often used to generate a dynamic mask at run-time by drawing the mask to the sketch window with Processing's drawing primitives and then masking with Processing's default pixel buffer pixels.

The following program starts by setting the background to green and then draws 3,000 randomly sized rectangles (width and height between 5 and 25) with random placement on the screen. A sample screen shot of what is drawn to screen is shown in Figure 10-6. The resulting pixel buffer is then used to mask off the same city street photo shown in the last example. The result of the masking is shown in Figure 10-7.

```
// pixelBufferMask.pde, chapter 10
void setup() {
  PImage img = loadImage("prinzipal.jpg");
  size(img.width, img.height);
  background(100, 130, 50);                  // green, blue channel used for alpha mask
  for (int i=0; i<3000; i++) {
    rect(random(width), random(height), 5+random(20), 5+random(20));
  }
  loadPixels();
  img.mask(pixels);
  image(img, 0, 0);
} // end setup()
```

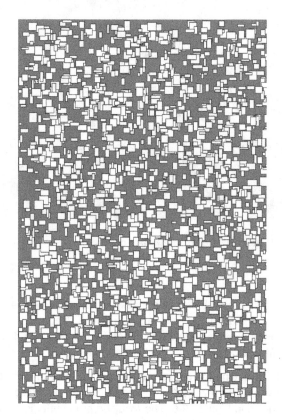

Figure 10-6. Pixel buffer mask drawn in the sketch window

Recall that for the purpose of masking, only the blue component of the pixel color in the mask matters. A 0 in the blue channel will make the corresponding image pixel invisible (fully transparent), 255 will display at full opacity, and everything in between will have varying degrees of translucency. This means that given the mask we drew to the screen, all image pixels within the rectangles will be fully revealed. All those outside acquire the background color (50 in the blue channel) and will be quite translucent, allowing the display window background color to blend through. Lastly those exactly on the outline will be invisible and only the background color will show. Remember that the background is exactly the mask and thus the color on the outline is black.

Figure 10-7. Results of masking with the pixel buffer shown in Figure 10-6

Figure 10-8. Pixel buffer mask drawn with circles

A variation using circles and different background colors is shown in Figure 10-8.

Of course, one could have saved the sketch window pixel buffer to an image with the save() command, and then used the saved image as a mask without bothering with the pixel buffer. In our example, it wouldn't have made much difference either way. The difference of not having to save to an external file and then masking with it matters more when we want to mask continuously with many fast changing masks, for example in creating animation or mouse/keyboard interaction.

> *Try This: The example shown draws all the rectangles in the mask with the same default fill value white (i.e., 255 in the blue channel), which means all pixels within the rectangles have the same level of transparency when masked. Modify the code so that the pixels within the rectangles will have varying degrees of transparency when masked. For example, have the pixels within the rectangles be fully transparent starting on the left side of the image and gradually become fully opaque on the right side.*

Blending

In this section we continue with introducing another one of Processing's built-in functions, blend(). As usual, there are two versions of blend(), the stand-alone version that works on the sketch window and the one associated with PImage. The PImage blend() method is used to blend two PImages together, or more accurately, a parameter-specified PImage into itself. The stand-alone version, on the other hand, blends a parameter-specified PImage with the image that is currently displayed in the sketch window.

In addition to specifying a solid-colored background for the sketch window, the background() function can also be used to specify a background image. However, it requires that the image be of the same size as the sketch window. In the following example, we first load an image into the sketch window background (the familiar city street scene) and then blend a second image (portrait of a baby) into it. The result is shown in Figure 10-9.

```
// blending.pde, chapter 10
void setup() {
  PImage src = loadImage("baby2.jpg");          // blending image
  PImage dest = loadImage("prinzipal.jpg");     // background image for sketch window
  size(dest.width, dest.height);                // size sketch window as background image
  background(dest);                             // load image into background
  blend(src, 0, 0, src.width, src.height, 0, 0, dest.width, dest.height, DARKEST);
} // end setup()
```

Figure 10-9. Blending an image into the sketch window

You may have noticed the long parameter list of blend(), which generally comes in the following signature:

blend(PImage srcImg, int sx, int sy, int sw, int sh, int dx, int dy, int dw, int dh, int mode)

The first argument is a PImage specifying the blending image, also considered the source image for the blending. In the stand-alone blend(), the destination image is always the current sketch window background when blend() is called. It is also possible to leave out the srcImg parameter, in which case the sketch window will be defaulted as the source image. The next four arguments specify the coordinates of the source image used in the blending, given in the usual x and y of the upper left corner plus width and height. In our example, we use the entire image, and thus 0, 0, src.width, and src.height are used. Similarly, the next four arguments specify the coordinates of the destination image used in the blending—again the entire image in our example. Note that the source image we used is not the same size as the destination image; in fact it is much smaller (351x423 versus 639x959). Using the entire source image to blend with the entire destination image effectively stretches the source image.

Now we show an example (results shown in Figure 10-10) where different combinations of coordinates for source and destination images were used; see the exact calls to blend() below. In particular, the same baby portrait was blended four times to the upper left, upper right, lower left, and lower right region of the sketch window. Also, as we are blending each source image into one half of the width of the destination image, but the source image is wider than half of the width of the destination, there are two options. Either we take only a portion of the width of the source image that matches half of the destination width (the left two blending results) or we take the entire width and compress it (the right two blending results).

```
// top left, no resizing
blend(src, 0, 0, dest.width/2, src.height, 0, 0, dest.width/2, src.height, DARKEST);
// top right, width will be resized
blend(src, 0, 0, src.width, src.height, dest.width/2, 0, dest.width/2, src.height, DARKEST);
// bottom left, no resizing
blend(src, 0, 0, dest.width/2, src.height, 0, height-src.height, dest.width/2, src.height,
DARKEST);
// bottom right, width will be resized
blend(src, 0, 0, src.width, src.height, dest.width/2, height-src.height, dest.width/2,
src.height, DARKEST);
```

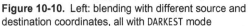

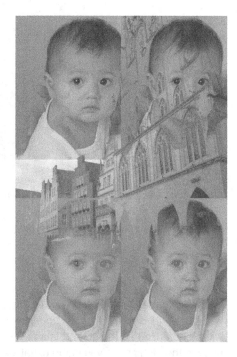

Figure 10-10. Left: blending with different source and destination coordinates, all with DARKEST mode

Figure 10-11. Right: blending with DARKEST mode on top row and LIGHGTEST mode on bottom row

Before we explain the last parameter of blend(), let's take a moment and consider the problem of blending two images together. What should the final blended color be for a pixel? For every pixel, we have two color choices, the color of the pixel in the source image and that of the corresponding pixel in the destination image. Do we take a 50% and 50% blend? Do we take all of one pixel and none of the other? As it turns out, both, and everything in between are perfectly good blending options: the exact ratio of blending depends on the application and the images being blended. Essentially all the different modes of blend() are different built-in blend ratios that the Processing creators deemed to be commonly used.

DARKEST was the mode of blending used in our example, which says that for each pixel, we pick the darker color among the two colors. In fact, the Processing manual lists the exact formula for calculating the blended color C: C = min(A * factor, B), where A is the color of the source pixel, B is the color of the destination pixel and factor is based on the alpha component of the source pixel. In our example, the source image is fully opaque, so the factor is simply 1. Thus the formula simplifies to C = min(A, B), which says take the smaller (darker) color among A and B. This effect shows most obviously in the pavement section as it is full of dark pixels, and only the baby's eyes and hair are visible in the bottom two blending results in Figure 10-10. If we change the mode to LIGHTEST in the last two calls to blend() instead, which means the lighter colors will succeed, then we have the results shown in Figure 10-11. The top two blending calls still use the DARKEST mode because otherwise the lighter colors of the sky and clouds would win out.

Available modes for blend() listed in Processing's manuals are: BLEND, ADD, SUBTRACT, DARKEST, LIGHTEST, DIFFERENCE, EXCLUSION, MULTIPLY, SCREEN, OVERLAY, HARD_LIGHT, SOFT_LIGHT, DODGE, and BURN. Please refer to the manuals for more details.

For example, Figure 10-12 shows the blending of a college campus landscape into the pavement section of the city street using OVERLAY.

Figure 10-12. Blending with OVERLAY

> *Try This: Experiment with all the different modes of* blend( )*.*

We find Processing's decision to base the blend factor on the alpha value of the source pixel somewhat inconvenient. This means that blending options for two non-transparent images are limited, and it's cumbersome to have to covert one of them to a desired level of transparency first. On the other hand, because each pixel can have a different alpha level, Processing's way allows a distinct blending factor per pixel. We recommend implementing your own blending by looping through all the pixels when more flexibility is needed.

> *Try This: Implement blending using* for *loops and Processing's pixel buffers. Experiment with different blending ratios between the source and destination pixel colors. See if you can emulate any of the built-in modes or come up with your own.*

Filtering

Filtering effects on digital images can also be easily generated via the built-in function filter( ). In general, the resulting filters are less flexible than those implemented from scratch, particularly if experimenting and fine tuning are needed as in a typical creative process, but they are convenient and powerful when they do suit your purpose. The aptly named filter( ) function takes a parameter which specifies eight different modes (filters):

- GRAY   converts each pixel to grayscale
- INVERT   sets each pixel to its inverse
- OPAQUE   sets the alpha channel of each pixel to entirely opaque
- THRESHOLD   converts each pixel to black or white depending on a threshold specified by a parameter
- POSTERIZE   limits each channel of each pixel to the number of colors specified by a parameter
- BLUR   executes a Gaussian blur effect on the image, the extent of blurring is specified by a parameter
- DILATE   increases the light areas of the image
- ERODE   reduces the light areas of the image

In Chapter 9 we saw code that implemented exactly the GRAY and INVERT filters (under Grayscale and Negative Images subsections, respectively) with for loops and pixel-by-pixel modifications. OPAQUE works very similarly by setting the alpha value of all pixels to 255. This is in principle exactly how Processing implements the built-in filters as well, except that bitwise operators are used whenever possible for speed.

GRAY and INVERT

The following short program demonstrates how the GRAY and INVERT filter modes can be applied. As usual, the stand-alone filter() function filters the sketch window, yet filter() is also a method of the PImage class. Here we take the opportunity to use an array of PImage objects, because we need to load the original image three times, once just for display, then once each for the GRAY and INVERT filters. Even though three times seem too few to warrant a loop, resist the urge to simply repeat loadImage() three times in your code. This makes your code less extendable and flexible. For example, what if you decided later that you were going to filter the image 20 times or 200 times instead?

```
// filterGrayInvert.pde, chapter 10
void setup() {
  PImage[] imgs = new PImage[3];
  // load the same image into all array elements
  for (int i=0; i<imgs.length; i++) {
    imgs[i] = loadImage("woods2.jpg");
  }
  size(imgs[0].width*imgs.length, imgs[0].height);   // 3 times as wide as the original image
  imgs[1].filter(GRAY);                               //apply  GRAY filter
  imgs[2].filter(INVERT);                             // apply INVERT filter
  // display all images in the array
  for (int i=0; i<imgs.length; i++) {
    image(imgs[i], imgs[0].width*i, 0);
  }
} // end setup()
```

Figure 10-13. Left: original; Middle: GRAY; Right: INVERT

The output of the above code is shown in Figure 10-13. Notice that the implementation tries to minimize the amount of code modification necessary to adapt to a larger array. To filter 20 times for example, the only modification necessary is to change the size from 3 to 20 when declaring the imgs array, and then of course to add code to apply the additional filters (possibly with a loop). The existing two for loops as well as the size() statement require no modification as they incorporate the size of the imgs array and will scale automatically.

OPAQUE

The following program shows the application of the OPAQUE filter to a transparent logo image bmc-logo.png. The original logo is displayed at the top left corner, on top of a background image and the opaque version is displayed at the top right corner. Remember that JPEG images do not support transparencies. We recommend that you use the PNG format for transparent images. The output of the program is shown in Figure 10-14.

```
// filterOpaque.pde, chapter 10
void setup() {
  PImage img = loadImage("bmc-logo.png");          // transparent logo
  PImage bg = loadImage("brynmawr.jpg");           // background image
  size(bg.width, bg.height);
  background(bg);
  image(img, 0, 0);                                // display  original logo on the left
  img.filter(OPAQUE);                              // filter to opaque
  image(img, width-img.width, 0);                  // display opaque logo on the right
} // end setup()
```

Figure 10-14. Transparent logo (left) filtered to opaque (right)

Try This: Referring to the code examples in Chapter 9 that implemented GRAY and INVERT, implement your own function that applies the OPAQUE filter to an image.

THRESHOLD and POSTERIZE

The THRESHOLD filter converts a pixel to white if the original color is above a threshold or to black if it is below. Notice that this is not a grayscale filter and only black and white pixels will result. The threshold level is specified via a second parameter which ranges from 0.0 to 1.0. 0.0 means any pixel with color equal or above 0.0*255 will be set to white, which effectively sets all pixels white. Note that the color we reference here is the maximum component of all three R/G/B channels, that is, a pixel with color (255, 100, 0) is considered to have color value 255 for the purpose of thresholding. Similarly a threshold of 1.0 sets all pixels with colors below 1.0*255 to black, which means all pixels will be set to black except for those with a 255 in either red, green, or blue. If the threshold level parameter is omitted, a default threshold of 0.5 will apply.

The following example demonstrates how to use a for loop to filter an image by a threshold of 0.25, 0.5, and 0.75. The results are shown in Figure 10-15.

```
// threshold.pde, chapter 10
void setup() {
  int n = 4;                            // number of images displayed
  PImage img = loadImage("woods2.jpg");
  size(img.width*n, img.height);
  image(img, 0, 0);                     // original
  for (int i=1; i<n; i++) {
    img.filter(THRESHOLD, i/4.0);       // filter
    image(img, img.width*i, 0);         // display
    img = loadImage("woods2.jpg");      // reload original
  }
} // end setup()
```

Figure 10-15. From left: original, threshold level at 0.25, 0.5, and 0.75

Now we give a variation that dynamically displays filtering results with a threshold level determined by the current mouse y-position. This version uses the stand-alone filter() that affects the sketch window.

```
// thresholdMouse.pde, chapter 10
PImage img;
void setup() {
  img = loadImage("woods2.jpg");
  size(img.width, img.height);
  image(img, 0, 0);
} // end setup()

void draw() {}                          // must include draw() for mouse callbacks

void mouseDragged() {
  float t = map(mouseY, 0, height, 0.0, 1.0);   // map mouse y-position to 0.0-1.0
  image(img, 0, 0);                             // redraw screen with the original
  filter(THRESHOLD, t);                         // filter with new threshold level
} // end mouseDragged()
```

Note that again, while the built-in `filter()` is convenient, it is not very flexible. Particularly, the filtering affects the entire image or the entire sketch window and there is no way to have the filtering effect applied to only a select number of pixels.

> Try This: Implement your own threshold filtering so that only a neighborhood of 50x50 pixels around a mouse click is filtered by a threshold level of 0.5. Be careful to handle the edge/corner cases correctly.

Similarly to masking, threshold filtering is a commonly used computer vision technique for image/video-based feature detection to throw out irrelevant information from images. In safety inspection, cracks and other structural anomalies are more easily identified when wall/building/background colors are filtered out; similarly in computer-aided manufacturing, it is used to automatically count and measure a variety of goods.

POSTERIZE takes the color thresholding concept a step further. The filter limits all three color channels to a specified number of colors supplied by a parameter. The result is a conversion from continuous color gradients to a lower number of tones and abrupt changes from one to the other. Posters were originally created this way from art using photographic techniques. While deliberate posterization is an artistic interpretation popular in contemporary graphic art, unwanted posterization is also known as "banding," which occurs due to insufficient color depth caused by compression (videos with MPEG lossy compression, anyone?) or low bandwidth. Processing's POSTERIZE filter requires a second parameter that specifies the number of colors to down-convert to per color channel. While any integer between 2 and 255 is accepted, the effects are more obvious at the lower end.

We now give an example using the POSTERIZE filter with levels of 2, 3, and 4 on the same image. The results are shown in Figure 10-16.

```
// posterize.pde, chapter 10
void setup() {
  int n = 4;                              // number of images displayed
  PImage img = loadImage("woods2.jpg");
  size(img.width*n, img.height);
  image(img, 0, 0);
  for (int i=1; i<n; i++) {
    img.filter(POSTERIZE, i+1);
    image(img, img.width*i, 0);
    img = loadImage("woods2.jpg");
  }
} // end setup()
```

Figure 10-16. From left: original, POSTERISE with levels 2, 3, and 4

While the number of colors per channel can be customized, more flexible control over the limit colors (i.e., different numbers of colors for each channel, specific combinations of colors, etc.) are not available with the built-in filter. In 2008, the artist Shepard Fairey created a series of posters supporting Barack Obama's presidential compaign, including the iconic "HOPE" poster. The "HOPE" poster basically limited all pixels to exactly four colors, yellow, red, light blue and dark blue, ranging from the lightest to the darkest colors. We now show a Processing program that converts images (particularly portraits) to what is known as an Obamicon. The output is shown in Figure 10-17.

```
//obamicon.pde, chapter 10
void setup() {
  PImage img = loadImage("baby2.jpg");
  color darkBlue = color(0, 51, 76);
  color red = color(217, 26, 33);
  color lightBlue = color(112, 150, 158);
  color yellow = color(252, 227, 166);
  size(img.width, img.height);
  img.loadPixels();
  for (int i = 0; i < img.pixels.length; i++) {
    color c = img.pixels[i];
    float total = red(c)+green(c)+blue(c);
    if (total < 182) {                      // darkest colored pixels
      img.pixels[i] = color(darkBlue);
    }
    else if (total < 364) {                 // 2nd darkest pixels
      img.pixels[i] = color(red);
    }
    else if (total < 546) {                 // lighter pixels
      img.pixels[i] = color(lightBlue);
    }
    else {                                  // lightest pixels
      img.pixels[i] = color(yellow);
    }
  }
  img.updatePixels();
  image(img, 0, 0);
} // end setup()
```

Figure 10-17. Posterized Obamicon

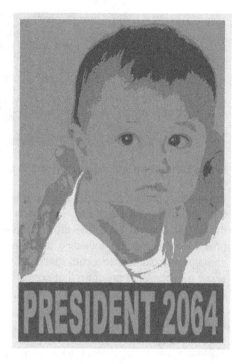

Figure 10-18. Full poster

The algorithm used to posterize is quite straight-forward. For each pixel, we add up the red, green, and blue values of all three channels to a total value. If this total is less than 182 (indicating a dark color), the pixel is set to the dark blue color. Next threshold is set at 364 (182*2), which results in the pixel being set to red. Then below 546 (182*3) gets light blue and finally everything else between 546 and 765 (255*3) gets yellow. Another reasonable algorithm would be to convert to grayscale first and then posterize based on the grayscale values. The result is quite similar.

Additional code can be added to take care of sizing, borders, and the banner, so that we can create a full poster as shown in Figure 10-18. The banner can be added with Processing's text rendering functions covered in Chapter 6.

BLUR, DILATE, and ERODE

The BLUR filter executes a Gaussian blur, where a second parameter specifies the radius for blurring. The larger the radius, the more blurry the result. Figure 10-19 shows the BLUR filter applied to the same image at level 2, 4, and 8.

Figure 10-19. From left: original, BLUR level 2, 4, and 8

The DILATE filter increases the light areas of an image and the ERODE filter decreases those same areas. No parameters are used in these two filters. Figure 10-20 shows the results of applying the DILATE and ERODE filter twice to the same original image on the left. In general, DILATE brightens, causes objects to grow in size and fills small holes. Similarly, ERODE darkens, causes objects to shrink and removes small objects entirely. A common technique to despeckle a noisy image is to erode it first, followed by dilating.

Figure 10-20. Left: original; Middle: DILATE twice; Right: ERODE twice

We have not listed code that generated these figures because the syntax of applying these filters is straight-forward and very similar to all the others we have already covered. What is interesting about these three filters is how they are implemented internally, i.e., how they work on the pixel-level. So far, the filters we have seen change a pixel's color based on a variety of criteria, but all the decisions and computations are based on its own color in the original image. The BLUR, DILATE, and ERODE filters are considered more advanced, because they calculate a pixel's color based on a minimum 3x3 neighborhood of pixels and sometimes larger. These filters are known as spatial (area-based) filters. They are also more computationally expensive. For example, the level parameter of BLUR specifies exactly the size of this neighborhood, i.e., 1 is 3x3, 2 is 4x4, and so on. It is easily noticed that as one increases the level parameter, the BLUR filter takes progressively longer to complete. This is because the number of pixels one must consider increases quadratically as the level parameter climbs. For a small 500x500 image such as the woods2.jpg we used for most of the this section, a 3x3 neighborhood per pixel requires 500x500x9 = 2,250,000 total pixel look-ups; a 5x5 neighborhood per pixel requires 500x500x25 = 6,250,000 total pixel look-ups; and a 10x10 neighborhood per pixel requires 500x500x100 = 25,000,000 total pixel look-ups. In the next section, we will look at how to implement some of the more advanced spatial filters from scratch.

Advanced Filters

In general, a spatial filter calculates the current pixel color based on the colors of the pixels in its immediate neighborhood, including itself. We will base our discussions of these filters on a 3x3 neighborhood, the smallest and simplest; however, please keep in mind that the neighborhood can be larger, as well as differently shaped than a square (box). For a 3x3 box filter, we can think of the calculation performed as defining a function whose input consists of nine pixel colors and outputs a single pixel color. How do we compute a single color from nine? There are a number of choices, and we look at what's known as convolution first.

Convolution

A convolution filter implies that the function we apply is some weighted average of the within-window pixels. Figure 10-21 illustrates the process of how a convolution filter works on a 3x3 neighborhood of the pixel labeled E to produce E'. A kernel of weights is chosen for each neighboring pixel—for example, w1 for A, w2 for B, w3 for C, and so on. E' is obtained by multiplying the weights with the corresponding pixel color and summed together, as given by the equation in Figure 10-12. The larger a weight is, the more the corresponding pixel influences the final output.

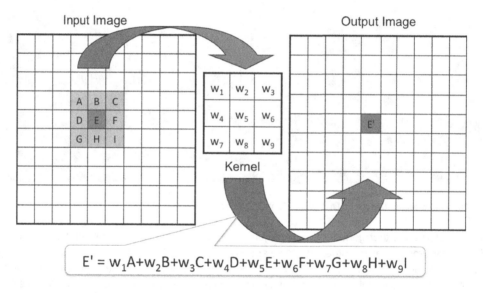

$$E' = w_1A + w_2B + w_3C + w_4D + w_5E + w_6F + w_7G + w_8H + w_9I$$

Figure 10-21. Convolution filter

Identity

The kernel of weights completely determines the final output pixel color values and thus different choices of these weights result in completely different filter behaviors. The easiest (but trivial) convolution filter is the identity filter, which simply gives back the color of the pixel itself. It is given by the kernel shown in Table 10-1. In signal processing, this is known as an all-pass filter, because it lets everything pass without modification.

Table 10-1. Identity Kernel

0	0	0
0	1	0
0	0	0

In the Chapter 9 example titled Copying Neighbors we implemented a spatial filter, although in that particular example only one randomly chosen neighbor is considered at every iteration, which implies a kernel that looks similar to the identity kernel, except that the single 1 is randomly placed into any of the nine locations. Now we list some of the commonly used convolution kernels.

Mean/Average

Represented by kernels shown in Table 10-2 and Table 10-3, this is a smoothing filter that sets a pixel to the average of all colors in the neighborhood—it smoothes out areas of sharp changes. Alternatively, a different kernel can be chosen that ignores the contributions from the corner pixels and only concentrates on the vertical and horizontal direction, as shown in Table 10-3. Notice that the weights are now divided by a normalizing factor to ensure that weights will add up to 1 and the brightness of the output pixel is not compromised. When trying to understand the weights and how they distribute the colors, you can safely ignore the factor. The results of applying this filter are shown in Figure 10-22. We will discuss the implementation details after we have finished listing the kernels. However, if you are impatient, feel free to jump ahead.

Table 10-2. Mean Kernel

1/9	1/9	1/9
1/9	1/9	1/9
1/9	1/9	1/9

Table 10-3. Mean Kernel, Vertical and Horizontal Only

0	1/5	0
1/5	1/5	1/5
0	1/5	0

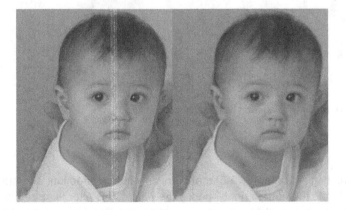

Figure 10-22. Left: original; Right: convolution filter-mean

Gaussian Blur

This is basically Processing's built-in BLUR filter you saw in the last section. The weights (see Table 10-4) are assigned so that a circular effect is created from the center, with the pixels given less weight the further away they are. As a result, the filter will locate significant color transitions in an image and create intermediary colors to soften the edges. This filter is commonly used to blur images and remove detail and noise, similar to the mean filter above, but this one uses a different kernel that represents the shape of a Gaussian (bell-shaped) distribution. The Gaussian Blur filter belongs to a class of filters known as the low-pass filters, because they pass low-frequency signals but attenuate high-frequency signals and are commonly found in audio and signal processing. Figure 10-23 shows the effect of applying a Gaussian Blur to an image.

Table 10-4. Gaussian Blur Kernel

1/16	2/16	1/16
2/16	4/16	2/16
1/16	2/16	1/16

> *Try This: What would a 4x4 or a 5x5 Gaussian Blur Kernel look like?*

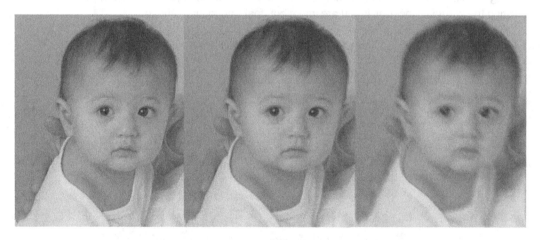

Figure 10-23. Left: original; Middle: Gaussian blur; Right: motion blur

Motion Blur

This is another interesting filter (Table 10-5) that blurs only in one direction. The effect is as if the camera moved from the top left to the bottom right—hence the name. This filter is more obvious with a larger kernel, for example a 9x9 kernel of all 1/9 over the main diagonal. See Figure 10-23 for the result of applying such a 9x9 kernel.

Table 10-5. Motion Blur Kernel

1/3	0	0
0	1/3	0
0	0	1/3

Sharpen

The opposite of low-pass filters are high-pass filters, which enhance the difference between the neighboring pixels. They are also known as sharpen filters (Table 10-6). The greater the difference is between the neighboring pixels, the greater the change in the center pixel. Notice that for the first time, we have negative weights in the kernel. This results in a net effect of subtracting the colors of the neighboring pixels from the center. If all colors concerned are similar (i.e., we are not in a high contrast area) then the filter does little. However, high-contrast pixels (edges) will be enhanced, making the image look sharper. The results of sharpening filters are shown in Figure 10-24.

Table 10-6. Sharpen Kernel

0	−2/3	0
−2/3	11/3	−2/3
0	−2/3	0

Mean Removal

This is also a sharpening filter (Table 10-7), but this one works by incorporating the diagonals as well. Results of applying this filter are shown in Figure 10-24. Compared with the previous sharpen filter, this one has a more "sketchy" effect and the results are harsher and more artificial. This is probably not the filter you want for photo editing but may be the filter of choice if you are preprocessing images to prepare for computer-aided measurements or inspection.

Table 10-7. Mean Removal Kernel

−1	−1	−1
−1	9	−1
−1	−1	−1

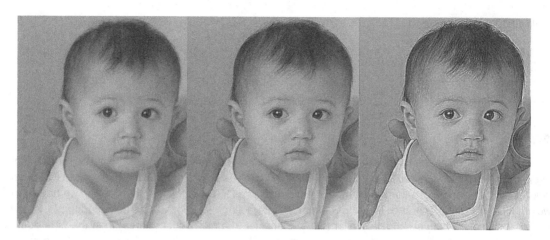

Figure 10-24. Left: original; Middle: sharpen; Right: mean removal

> *Try This: What does the kernel shown in Table 10-8 do? Can you predict its effect by examining the weights, without trying it with code? If you are really stumped, look ahead to the implementation subsection where you can obtain a Processing program applying many different convolution filters, including this one.*

Table 10-8. Mystery Kernel

1	1	1
1	−7	1
1	1	1

Edge Detection

Edge detection works on the same principle as the sharpening filters, in that they are concerned with enhancing the differences between the center pixel and those that surround it. When you perceive an edge in an image, you are simply noticing that there is a (sharper) change in color. Thus, edge detection means to come up with a way to set a pixel to black if it's not very different from its neighbors, and trend towards white the more different it is. Table 10-9 shows an edge-detection kernel that detects both the horizontal and vertical edges, and Table 10-10 shows a kernel that detects the diagonals as well. Notice that for the first time, the weights add up to 0 instead of 1 in these kernels. Consider what happens when these filters are applied to an area of similar colors. The sum will trend towards zero, which will cause a general darkening of the image: anything that is not high-contrast will clamp to black. This is usually undesirable but is not a problem in edge detection, because we do want to black out everything that is not an edge. Also notice how closely Table 10-10 resembles the mean removal kernel in Table 10-7. The results of applying these two kernels are show in Figure 10-25.

Table 10-9. Edge-Detection Kernel (Horizontal and Vertical Only)

0	−1	0
−1	4	−1
0	−1	0

Table 10-10. Edge-Detection Kernel (with Diagonals)

−1	−1	−1
−1	8	−1
−1	−1	−1

Figure 10-25. Left: original; Middle: edge detection (horizontal/vertical only); Right: edge detection with diagonals

> *Try This: How would you modify the kernels so that you can detect ONLY horizontal edges, or ONLY vertical edges?*

There are a great variety of edge detection kernels, because edge detection is basically contrast detection and can be done in a number of different ways. Other well-known ones are, for example, Sorbel, Prewitt, Kirsh (all named after their inventors), etc. Look them up and play with them using the convolution filter implementation given next.

Emboss

This kernel is a simple variation on the edge detection kernels that subtracts pixels from one side of the center from those on the other side and creates a 3D shadow effect to the image. The kernel given in Table 10-11 is a 45° emboss, but clearly the kernel can be modified to create shadows in other directions. One important difference of this kernel is that the resulting pixels can be either positive or negative. To use the negative pixels as shadows and the positive ones as light, an offset of 127 (medium grey) needs to be added to all pixels to brighten the image. Figure 10-26 shows the effects of the emboss filter.

Table 10-11. Emboss Kernel

−1	−1	0
−1	0	1
0	1	1

Figure 10-26. Convolution filter: emboss

Implementation

Now we finally show an implementation that applies these convolution filters to an image. We first create a class Filter to store and apply individual convolution filters. Note the decision to store the normalizing factor separately, which makes the kernel a bit easier to type in and more readable.

```
class Filter{
   float[][] kernel;          // convolution kernel
   float normalizer;          // normalizing factor
   float offset;              // brightening offset
   String name;               // display label

   Filter(float[][] kernel, float normalizer, float offset, String name) {
     this.kernel = kernel;
     this.normalizer = normalizer;
```

```
        this.offset = offset;
        this.name = name;
    }

    // returns the color for pixel(x, y) after applying filter
    color apply(int x, int y, PImage img) {
        int halfSize = kernel.length/2;        // used for moving from the center out to the corners
        float r = 0.0, g = 0.0, b = 0.0;

        for (int i = 0; i < kernel.length; i++) {
            for (int j = 0; j < kernel[i].length; j++) {
                // Which neighbor are we using
                int newX = x+i-halfSize;
                int newY = y+j-halfSize;
                int idx = img.width*newY + newX;
                // make sure we get valid neighbors for the edge pixels
                idx = constrain(idx, 0, img.pixels.length-1);
                // Calculate the convolution
                r += (red(img.pixels[idx]) * kernel[i][j]/normalizer);
                g += (green(img.pixels[idx]) * kernel[i][j]/normalizer);
                b += (blue(img.pixels[idx]) * kernel[i][j]/normalizer);
            }
        }
        return color(r+offset, g+offset, b+offset);
    } // end apply()
} // end class Filter
```

The method apply(int x, int y, PImage img) calculates the new color values for a single pixel (x, y) given the associated original image img. Essentially we want to multiply a 3x3 array of float with appropriate pixels in the img pixel buffer. There is the slight complication that we need to do this by separate color components. In addition, the indices x and y mark the center instead of the upper left corner so they need to be offset by one half of the length of the kernel array.

The rest of the program is fairly straight-forward. Filters are created and stored in an array of type Filter called filters. A temporary array ks is used to stored the filter kernels. Instead of storing the modified pixel values back into the original image, we keep two images around at all times. The variable img stores the original and img2 stores the modified copy. The reason why this is necessary is that with a spatial filter, original/unmodified values of the neighbors are needed for calculations of every output pixel. If we overwrite a pixel with the new values, its neighbors who are processed later will not be able to look up the original colors. img2 is initialized with the command createImage(), which creates a new PImage of a given size and format.

The program is set up to always display the original image on the left and a filtered copy on the right. It starts up with the first filter (Mean) already applied. There are 9 filters in the filters array, but more can be added. The filters can be dynamically swapped by pressing the keys 0 through 8, each corresponding to the filter stored at that particular index in the filters array. An appropriate String label is also displayed so that the exact filter applied is apparent.

The function `applyFilter()` loops through all pixels and calls the selected filter's `apply()` method on each. It also takes care of displaying filtered results and the name of the filter in the top left corner.

```
// convolution.pde, chapter 10
float[][][] ks = {{{1, 1, 1}, {1, 1, 1}, {1, 1, 1}},
                  {{1, 2, 1}, {2, 4, 2}, {1, 2, 1}},
                  {{1, 0, 0, 0, 0, 0, 0, 0, 0},
                   {0, 1, 0, 0, 0, 0, 0, 0, 0},
                   {0, 0, 1, 0, 0, 0, 0, 0, 0},
                   {0, 0, 0, 1, 0, 0, 0, 0, 0},
                   {0, 0, 0, 0, 1, 0, 0, 0, 0},
                   {0, 0, 0, 0, 0, 1, 0, 0, 0},
                   {0, 0, 0, 0, 0, 0, 1, 0, 0},
                   {0, 0, 0, 0, 0, 0, 0, 1, 0},
                   {0, 0, 0, 0, 0, 0, 0, 0, 1}},
                  {{0, -2, 0}, {-2, 11, -2}, {0, -2, 0}},
                  {{-1, -1, -1}, {-1, 9, -1}, {-1, -1, -1}},
                  {{1, 1, 1}, {1, -7, 1}, {1, 1, 1}},
                  {{0, -1, 0}, {-1, 4, -1}, {0, -1, 0}},
                  {{-1, -1, -1}, {-1, 8, -1}, {-1, -1, -1}},
                  {{1, 1, 0}, {1, 0, -1}, {0, -1, -1}}};
Filter[] filters = {new Filter(ks[0], 9, 0, "Mean"),
                    new Filter(ks[1], 16, 0, "Gaussian Blur"),
                    new Filter(ks[2], 9, 0, "Motion Blur"),
                    new Filter(ks[3], 3, 0, "Sharpen"),
                    new Filter(ks[4], 1, 0, "Mean Removal"),
                    new Filter(ks[5], 1, 0, "Mystery"),
                    new Filter(ks[6], 1, 0, "Edge Detection Horizontal/Vertical"),
                    new Filter(ks[7], 1, 0, "Edge Detection with Diagonal"),
                    new Filter(ks[8], 1, 127, "Emboss")};
PImage img, img2;

void setup() {
  img = loadImage("prinzipal.jpg");                     //original image
  img2 = createImage(img.width, img.height, RGB); // new image to store the changed pixels
  size(img.width*2, img.height);

  img.loadPixels();
  img2.loadPixels();
  applyFilter(0);                                       // apply first filter - Mean
} // end setup()

void draw(){}

void keyPressed() {
  if (key >= '0' && key <= '8') {
    applyFilter(key-'0');                               // convert character to int
  }
} // end keyPressed()
```

```
void applyFilter(int n) {
  for (int y=0; y<img.height; y++ ) {
    for (int x=0; x<img.width; x++) {
      img2.pixels[y*img.width+x] = filters[n].apply(x, y, img); // new color for pixel(x, y)
    }
  }
  img2.updatePixels();
  image(img, 0, 0);
  image(img2, width/2, 0);                                     // display filtered image
  textSize(20);
  text(filters[n].name, width/2+width/25, height/25);          // display filter label
} // end applyFilter()
```

Other Spatial Filters

It might seem like convolution filters are the only spatial filters out there, but that's far from the truth. For example, Processing's DILATE and ERODE filters are considered morphological filters which apply mathematical functions of morphology. A dilation filter replaces the center pixel with the maximum color found in the neighborhood, and an erosion filter replaces with the minimum. There is also a median filter that will replace the center pixel with the median value of all colors in the neighborhood. The Median filter is commonly used for noise reduction. All three algorithms require sorting all the colors in the neighborhood, which adds more complexity and computation time to the filter.

Image specialFX

We now show a few more neat things one can do with image processing that are not particularly filter focused.

Pointillism

Pointillism is a technique of painting in which small dots (instead of brush strokes) are applied all over to form an image. We can give an image a "pointillism" effect by first displaying the image in the background and then adding a large number of small dots filled with colors sampled from the pixel buffer at randomly chosen locations. Figure 10-27 shows the result after 10,000 such points were added to a photo of a winter landscape.

```
// pointillism.pde, chapter 10
void setup() {
  PImage img = loadImage("pembroke.jpg");
  size(img.width, img.height);
  imageMode(CENTER);
  image(img, width/2, height/2);
  noStroke();
  loadPixels();
  // Cover with random circles
  for (int i=0; i<10000; i++) {
    addPoint();
  }
} // end setup()
```

```
// Add a random filled circle to screen
void addPoint() {
  int x = (int)random(width);
  int y = (int)random(height);
  int i = x + width*y;
  color c = pixels[i];
  fill(c);
  ellipse(x, y, 7, 7);
} // end addPoint()
```

Figure 10-27. Pointillism

Confluency

In cell culture biology, confluency is a frequently taken measurement, referring to the level of coverage of a Petri dish by cell growth. Confluency is a percentage and 100% confluency means the dish is completely covered. We can automate confluency measurements in the labs by having cameras take periodic images of the Petri dishes, computing the confluency from the images, and alerting the biologist when necessary. We already saw in the Masking section how to mask off the uninteresting parts of the images leaving only the center of the dish, as shown in Figure 10-28, which is repeated from Figure 10-4.

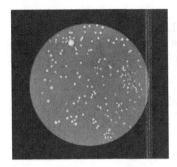 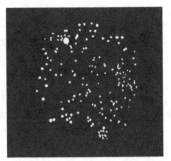

Figure 10-28. Masked Petri dish   **Figure 10-29.** Filtered with threshold 0.6

Given such an image, how do we calculate confluency? First, we want to further separate the dish background (dark grey pixels) from the cells (whiter pixels). This calls for a threshold filter. In this particular image, it turns out that a threshold of 0.6 is a good value for our purposes, which results in Figure 10-29. Now all that is needed is to write a loop and count all the pixels that are white and divide the number by the total number of pixels that weren't black in Figure 10-28. It turns out that the confluency of this particular image is 2272/41898 = 5.42%.

Similar image-based feature recognition and measuring techniques can be employed in many areas of scientific experimentation and manufacturing.

Video Processing

Videos are essentially a series of still images displayed in quick succession, the frequency of which is typically defined by how many images (frames) are displayed per second (FPS), known as a frame rate. Higher frame rates result in higher quality video, particularly with a combination of fast motion and HD displays. On average, 30–60 FPS is sufficient.

Set Up

Processing did most of the hard work allowing us to easily connect to a live camera, and one of the big changes of Processing 2.0 is moving video to the GStreamer framework, an open source video framework now comes bundled with the Processing distribution. This removes the Processing 1.x reliance on the QuickTime libraries to handle video, which are preinstalled on Apple computers but not on Windows. In general, it is a good idea to first test to make sure your camera is working (with Skype for example) before attempting video.

Basic Playback

Video brings a new built-in object called Capture. Like PImage, Capture provides a variety of video related functionalities. Without further ado, we now show a short program that displays a live video stream from your webcam onto your sketch window.

```
// video.pde, chapter 10
import processing.video.*;              //video libraries
Capture vid;                           //Capture object for our video

void setup() {
  size(640, 480);
  vid = new Capture(this, width, height);    // initialize camera
  // Start capturing frames, new method in 2.0, not available in 1.5.1
  vid.start();
} // end setup()

void draw() {
  if (vid.available()) {               // if a new image is available
    vid.read();                        // read the current image
    image(vid, 0, 0);                  // display the current video image to screen
  }
} // end draw()
```

We start by importing Processing's video libraries and declare a global variable vid of type Capture. As usual, we call the constructor to create a Capture object in setup(). The version of the constructor we use requires three parameters, a reference to the current applet and a width and a height. We want the video to be full screen, so we simply give the sketch window width and height. Alternatively, the constructor can also be called with a desired FPS (default is 30) as well as a camera name (if more than one camera is attached). Next we call the start() method to start capturing frames. Note that the start() method is new in Processing 2.0 and if you are running Processing 1.5.1 instead, this call needs to be commented. Video capturing should still work in 1.5.1 without the explicit start.

In the draw() loop, we continuously check to see if a new image is available and once it is, call the method read() to obtain it. It is important that the method available() is always called first to check if a new image is available before anything else is attempted, because of the unpredictable nature of the video stream speed and band-width. Once read, we can display a Capture object as if it is a PImage object, with the familiar function image(), because the Capture class is implemented as a child of the PImage class and inherits most of its functionalities.

Now that we have simple video playback working, it is time to do something to it. Realize that a video stream is delivered to your sketch window one static image at a time. That means that for every iteration you only have your familiar still picture to deal with – also known as a frame. Remember that Capture is a child of PImage, which means that it comes with a pixel buffer as well as all the built-in image processing methods such as tint(), mask(), blend(), and filter(), and every image processing technique we learned will apply.

Pixel-block Replacement

The following example uses the familiar pixelation technique we saw in Chapter 9 and downscales a video frame so that the details are lost. Notice the size of the display window is set at 1600x1000. We could capture the video at this resolution and then downsample, but why waste the bandwidth? Instead we capture the video at a much lower resolution (1/100) and then blow it up by drawing 10x10 squares for every pixel. Results are shown in Figure 10-30.

```
import processing.video.*;
Capture vid;
int s = 10;                // down sampling resolution

void setup() {
  size(1600, 1000);
  vid = new Capture(this, width/s, height/s);
  vid.start();
} // end setup()

void draw() {
  if (vid.available()) {
    vid.read();
    vid.loadPixels();
    for (int y=0; y<height/s; y++) {
      for (int x=0; x<width/s; x++) {
        color c = vid.pixels[y*vid.width+x];
        fill(c);
        //Also interesting... text(x%2, x*s, y*s);   see Figure 10-31
        rect(x*s, y*s, s, s);
      }
    }
  }
} // end draw()
```

Figure 10-30. Video frame with each pixel drawn as a 10x10 rectangle

What the still image does not convey is that the replacement is carried out faithfully from frame to frame, resulting in pixelated video.

Of course, we didn't have to use rectangles. Like we saw with still images, we could replace the pixel blocks with any drawing pimitives and the original image will be largely recovered. Figure 10-31 shows the result of replacing the 10x10 pixel block with text instead. In fact, there are just two numbers, 0 and 1, but they are drawn with the appropriate colors.

Note that Figure 10-31 shows a simple replacement of pixels with the numbers 0 and 1, without any considerations of the typographic features of these numbers. One can of course take this a step further and combine the color matching with a full ASCII art conversion. ASCII art is based on the observation that among the 95 printable characters, some (such as @, m) appear darker than some others (i.e., -, .) and should be used to represent darker (versus lighter) colors in an image.

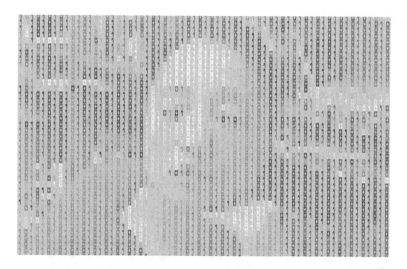

Figure 10-31. Video frame replaced with text

> *Try This: Generate a full ASCII conversion of a video frame by converting to grayscale first, then for each pixel block of your chosen resolution, select an ASCII character that best matches the intensity of the pixels and replace. Try drawing both in grayscale and full color.*

Frame Difference

Next we show an example where instead of displaying the current frame, we keep a copy of the previous frame as well and display the *difference* between these two frames. The difference is obtained simply by subtracting every pixel of the current frame from those in the previous frame using blend() with mode SUBTRACT. As a result, if there are no differences between the two frames, all you get is a black image. If there is a lot of difference, i.e., in video feeds with a lot of motion, a interesting ghostly outline appears where motion is, as shown in Figures 10-32 and 10-33.

```
// diffFrame.pde, chapter 10
import processing.video.*;
Capture vid;
PImage prevFrame;          // image to save the previous frame

void setup() {
  size(640, 480);
  vid = new Capture(this, width, height);
  prevFrame = createImage(width, height, RGB);
  vid.start();
} // end setup()

void draw() {
  if (vid.available()) {
    vid.read();
    // blend the current frame into the previous frame using the SUBTRACT mode
    prevFrame.blend(vid, 0, 0, width, height, 0, 0, width, height, SUBTRACT);
    image(prevFrame, 0, 0);
    // copy the current frame into prevFrame
    prevFrame.copy(vid, 0, 0, width, height, 0, 0, width, height);
  }
} // end draw()
```

Figure 10-32. Output 1 from diffFrame.pde

Figure 10-33. Output 2 from diffFrame.pde

Chapter Project: Image Mosaic

A mosaic is traditionally composed of small pieces of stone or glass. An image mosaic (or photomosaic) is a digital image made up of other digital images, pieced together by software. The collection of small images is arranged in such a way that when they are seen from a distance they suggest a larger image. Let's say your basic image is 100x100 pixels and you have a library of image tiles (small image files such as icons, image fragments, etc.). You want to mosaic the 100x100 image with 400 tiles. This means each tile should be sized 5x5. Here's the basic algorithm:

- For each 5x5 pixel-block in the basic image, determine the average RGB values for those pixels, keeping separate averages for red, green, and blue.

- Determine the average RGB values for each tile in your library.

- Match up the average RGB values of each 5x5 block to the closest match from the tiles, This matching happens between sets of three numbers and can be viewed as a problem of minimizing Euclidean distances to the target color. That is, think of the red, green, blue values as x, y, and z coordinates and calculate the distances of all the tile images to the 5x5 region average color and find the closest one.

- Once the best match is found, resize the tile to 5x5 if necessary and place it in the corresponding location of the final mosaic.

Figure 10-34. Wenlock mosaic

Figure 10-35. Mandeville mosaic

Figure 10-34 and Figure 10-35 show the 2012 London Summer Olympics mascot Wenlock and Paralympics Mascot Mandeville mosaicked with flags of the world.

The algorithm is implemented by first creating a Tile class, which stores a single image tile and its average red, green, and blue colors. The constructor sizes the input image and calls the method calcAvg() to compute the tile's average colors as soon as the object is constructed and stores them in three separate variables avgR, avgG, and avgB.

```
class Tile{
  PImage img;
  float avgR;              // average red of this tile
  float avgG;              // average green of this tile
  float avgB;              // average blue of this tile

  Tile(PImage img, int size){
    this.img = img;
    img.resize(size, size);
    calcAvg();
  }

  void calcAvg(){
    img.loadPixels();
    float r=0, g=0, b=0;

    for(int i=0; i<img.pixels.length; i++) {
      color c = img.pixels[i];
      r += red(c);           // red sum
      g += green(c);         // green sum
      b += blue(c);          // blue sum
    }
    // divide sum by total number of pixels to obtain averages
    avgR = r/img.pixels.length;
    avgG = g/img.pixels.length;
    avgB = b/img.pixels.length;
  } // end calcAvg()
} // end class Tile
```

The rest is fairly easy work, and the hardest part turns out to be getting access to all the stored image tiles. The flag icons we used were all in PNG format and placed in the data directory of the sketch folder; however, to automatically load all images of PNG format in a directory we need a bit of Java magic. The function loadTiles() uses two Java objects, File and FilenameFilter. folder is of type File and is used to specify the directory path, and imgNameFilter is of type FilenameFilter and is created to exclude any files in the specified directory that do not end with .png from being listed. The syntax of setting up the filter is rather unpleasant, but fortunately you can mostly take it as it is and only modify the ".png" part if your icons are in a different format. Once we obtain the list of image names as an array of String, all we need to do is loop through the list, load each image, construct a corresponding Tile object, and place it in the global array called tiles.

```
// imageMosaic.pde, chapter 10
Tile[] tiles;
int size = 5;          // size of pixel block to replace

void setup() {
  PImage img = loadImage("wenlock.jpg");
  size(img.width, img.height);
  background(255);
  loadTiles();
  img.loadPixels();
  for (int x=0; x<img.width; x+=size) {
    for (int y=0; y<img.height; y+=size) {
      color c = avgRGB(img, x, y, size);
      if (red(c) + green(c) + blue(c) < 700) { // only replace those that are not the white background
        int i = findTile(c);
        image(tiles[i].img, x, y);
      }
    }
  }
} // end setup()

// Compute average r, g, b for the pixel block (x, y, s, s) in img, and return as a single color
color avgRGB(PImage img, int x, int y, int s) {
  float r=0, g=0, b=0;
  for (int i=x; i<x+s; i++) {
    for (int j=y; j<y+s; j++) {
      color c = img.pixels[y*img.width+x];
      r+= red(c);
      g+= green(c);
      b+= blue(c);
    }
  }
  r/=s*s;
  g/=s*s;
  b/=s*s;
  return color(r, g, b);
} // end avgRGB()

// load all the files of .png format in data/ into the tiles array
void loadTiles() {
  java.io.File folder = new java.io.File(dataPath(""));    // reads tiles from data folder
  // filter to weed out those that don't end with .png from the file name list
  java.io.FilenameFilter imgNameFilter = new java.io.FilenameFilter() {
    public boolean accept(File dir, String name) {
      return name.toLowerCase().endsWith(".png");
    }
  };
```

```
    // get the list of file names with filter applied
    String[] fileNames = folder.list(imgNameFilter);
    // create the tile array now that we know the length
    tiles = new Tile[fileNames.length];
    for (int i = 0; i < fileNames.length; i++) {
      tiles[i] = new Tile(loadImage(fileNames[i]), size);
    }
  } // end loadTiles()

  // returns the index of the tile that is the closest match to input color c
  int findTile(color c){
    float minDist = 255*3+1;    // initialize to be larger than the largest possible distance
    int minIdx = -1;
    for (int i=0; i<tiles.length; i++) {
      float d = dist(red(c), green(c), blue(c), tiles[i].avgR, tiles[i].avgG, tiles[i].avgB);
      if (d<minDist) {
        minDist = d;
        minIdx = i;
      }
    }
    return minIdx;
  } // end findTile()
```

This simple algorithm works, but the resulting mosaic is crude compared to what a lot of commercial software can produce. The first problem is we do not have a very good tile image library. Ideally, we want a library of tiles that will provide close matches and good coverage for all colors in the target image pixels. Icon files that are freely available are limited in quality and variety and the world flags tend to concentrate on certain primary colors but have poor representation in others.

The second problem is that the algorithm downsamples the original image. That is, it computes a single average color for each pixel block, which is equivalent to downsampling to a single pixel. Similarly, the tiles are also downsampled before matching is attempted. More sophisticated algorithms will compare each target region to the tiles pixel by pixel and attempt to find one that minimizes the differences. This is of course computationally much more expensive. Additionally, it also requires an even more extensive icon library to produce good matches because of the expanded search space.

The bigger problem however is that the uniform-sized tiling does not allow more detailed representations for small or intricate features. Ideally, where we have larger areas of similar colors, we can replace those with larger tiles that match the average colors, and in areas where the color/intensity changes more rapidly, we want to use smaller and more tiles to more accurately reflect the changes. Non-uniform tiling often requires some subdivision of the target image space to zero into the areas containing higher levels of detail, such as a quadtree subdivision algorithm. However, many times a simple greedy algorithm (which tries to always fit the largest tiles first) works surprisingly well.

Image mosaics are frequently used to produce creative photo collages. Sophisticated mosaics require close examinations of space, size, contrast, color selection, and more. There is no one way to create a mosaic, and each mosaic is a creative reinterpretation of the original image. Closely related is the art of typographic design, where the individual tiles are primarily types. The aforementioned ASCII art is but a primitive form of it from the throwback days of limited computing resources. Googling can bring beautiful and inspiring examples of contemporary typography in seconds, and popular apps such as WordFoto are introducing the masses to the possibilities. Figure 10-36 shows our familiar baby photo enhanced by WordFoto with the word set "Got Milk".

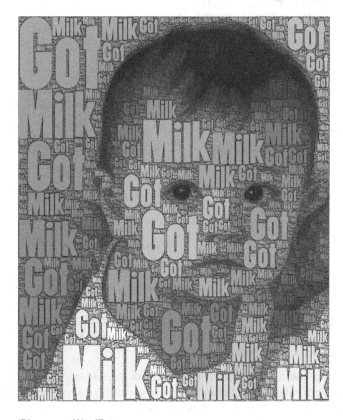

Figure 10-36. Output from iPhone app WordFoto

> *Try This: Design and implement a Processing program that emulates what WordFoto does to an image, given a set of words.*

The replacement decisions are made along the same lines as the image mosaic example. Notice that any single word (regardless of font size) is always written with the same color throughout. Thus, you can think of the individual words as image tiles. In general, the idea is to find the largest pixel block whose within-block pixel color variations are below some threshold – which makes the entire block eligible to be replaced with one color. Then compute the average color for this block and replace with text drawn with this average color and large enough font to fill (most of) the pixel block.

For the non-uniform tiling, try a greedy algorithm similar to the one introduced in the word cloud visualization example in Chapter 7; that is, start by finding pixel blocks to replace with the largest font first, but do not allow overlaps. If the current font no longer fits, but there is still space left in the image, reduce the font and repeat. How well you can track the overlaps will greatly affect how tightly you can pack the text.

Summary

In this Chapter, we looked at Processing's built-in image processing functions `tint()`, `mask()`, `blend()`, and `filter()` in some detail. We then spent some time looking at spatial filters, particularly convolution filters, which determine a pixel's color based on a weighted average of its neighbors' colors. Finally, we looked at other image processing techniques – pointillism, confluency, and video processing as well as image mosaic. Image processing is a powerful tool that has much wider applications beyond the "photo-manipulation" that first comes to mind. We also left out many popular and useful techniques such as histogram equalization or image morphing due to space constraints. We encourage the reader to explore the full potential of image processing. Remember to make use of the built-in functions when they fit the bill, but do not hesitate to implement your own if more flexibility is needed.

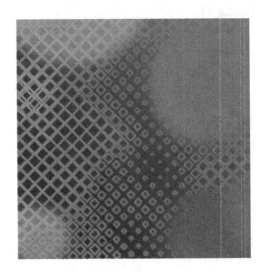

Chapter 11

Spreading Your Creative Coding Wings

If you consider this book a meal, you can think of this final chapter as dessert—a hard earned and guilt free dessert! Beyond Processing's core features, most of which you've learned about throughout the book, Processing also includes numerous advanced features, including 3D, Java integration, custom tool and library development, and an exciting new modes feature, enabling you to run your Processing programs natively in a web browser or on an Android device. Each of these features could easily occupy its own chapter, but we'll have to leave that level of detail for the next book. This chapter offers a taste of what's possible exploring these advanced features, including numerous examples that you can use as a foundation to build on to.

3D

Students are initially very excited to discover Processing's 3D capabilities. With just a few lines of code, you can create slick looking 3D geometry. Figures 11-1 and 11-2 show examples created with 6- and 11-lines of Processing code, respectively. We'll look at the actual code a little later in the chapter.

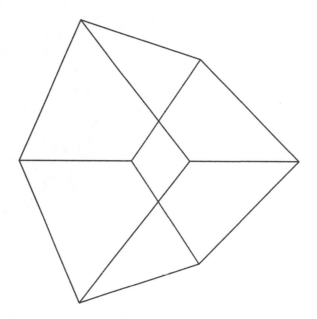

Figure 11-1. 6-line cube example

Figure 11-2. 11-line glossy sphere example

In spite of the initial ease of generating 3D imagery in Processing, it doesn't take long before students' excitement is tempered by the mathematical complexity involved in generating more complex 3D scenes. With the wide-scale popularity of 3D animated feature films, computer enhanced live action blockbusters and of course video games and apps on all our devices, it's easy to forget that all 3D imagery reduces to a bunch of very clever mathematics—lest we forget that we spend much of our time today staring at very flat 2D screens. Interestingly, the underlying calculations simulating 3D on our 2D screens more or less mirror what happens in our own brains—where 2-dimensional data on the surfaces of our retinas is converted into the perceptual 3D world we experience. We won't elucidate how the brain handles this conversion, but we can illustrate how the computer does it, shown in Figure 11-3.

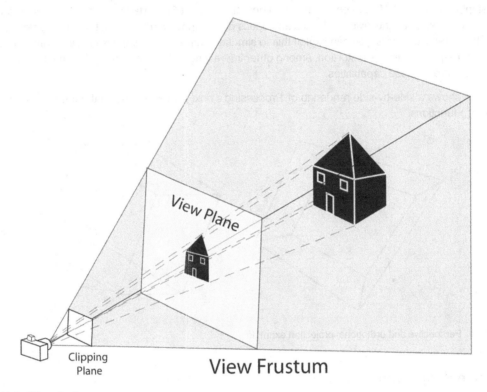

Figure 11-3. 3D projection

View Frustum

Assume the view plane illustrated in Figure 11-3 is your screen. The overall pyramidal shape enclosing the house is called the view frustum, which technically is flat on both ends. The camera in the figure can only see geometry within this view frustum, a fact which is utilized to optimize performance—*don't waste rendering resources on information the camera (really the viewer) can't see.* 3D calculations tax your computer, primarily the video card. Drawing the simple house in Figure 11-3 wouldn't be too difficult, as it can be described with less than 20 vertices, but even a simple character in a video game could include tens of thousands of vertices or many more, not to mention additional image data mapped to the geometry (texture maps) as well as additional per vertex information for calculating lighting. Over the years 3D programmers have come up with very clever algorithms and techniques to enable limited computing resources to render truly remarkable 3D imagery, often calculated in real time. In addition to only rendering data within the view frustum, polygon faces are commonly treated as 1-sided (invisible when not facing the camera) and geometry and textures are dynamically simplified with increasing distance from the camera–just to describe a few optimization techniques.

It's All Virtual

Though Figure 11-3 includes an image of a camera, Processing doesn't really include a camera; it's more of a metaphor for the set of mathematical operations that convert 3D vertex data to 2D screen imagery. And because it's all just math, the laws of physics and optics don't impose the same limitations they do in the physical world. As creative coders, you can exploit this to simulate cameras with impossibly wide- and narrow-angle lens and corresponding image distortion, among other interesting expressive effects. The next set of examples showcases some of these capabilities:

Figure 11-4 shows a side-by-side rendering of Processing's box() command using the perspective() (on left) and ortho() functions.

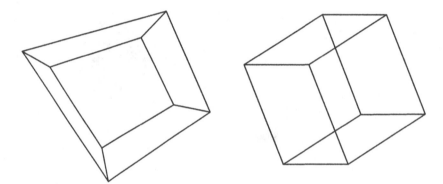

Figure 11-4. Perspective and orthogonal projection example

Perspective Projection

You are probably familiar with perspective drawings, where objects in the distance seem to recede into space by converging toward a vanishing point, as illustrated in Figure 11-5. The cube in Figure 11-5 appears three-dimensional purely by the visual distortion to the form caused by aligning it to the 1-point perspective grid. This drawing convention of course is not purely arbitrary, as we view physical objects in real space receding and converging into the distance, the classic example being railroad tracks converging to a point on the horizon. The math simulating perspective on the computer is surprisingly simple, which we'll look at shortly.

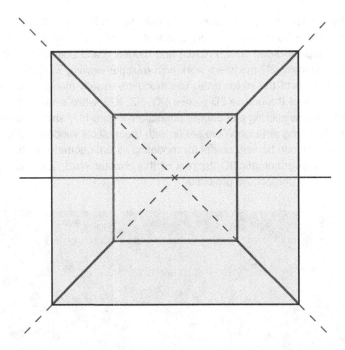

Figure 11-5. Perspective illustration

Orthogonal Projection

In addition to perspective projection, we can also project 3D data orthogonally in Processing, which may be a less familiar concept to you. Orthogonal projection eliminates any perspective cues, including any distortion to the form; so a cube viewed straight-on appears as a rectangle, regardless of the depth of the cube along the z-axis. Figure 11-6 shows two identical boxes with severe depth rendered in perspective (on left) and orthogonal projection.

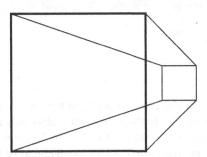 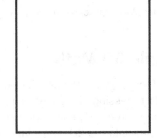

Figure 11-6. Perspective versus orthogonal projection

You might wonder why this rendering approach would ever be useful, as it clearly is not how we view the physical world. It turns out orthogonal projection is actually very useful for modeling 3D geometry and is commonly used in 3D computer-aided design (CAD) and modeling and animation applications (for example, Maya, LightWave, etc.). Typically, 3D modelers work with multiple viewing windows, including both perspective and orthogonal projections of the vertex data. The modelers usually manipulate specific vertex geometry using three orthogonal views of the unique 2D planes (XY, YZ, XZ), while simultaneously interacting with the overall object in a fourth window utilizing prospective projection. Figure 11-7 shows a screenshot of the popular 3D modeling and animation program LightWave set up with the multiple window configuration just discussed. Though orthogonal projection can be very useful for modeling virtual geometry by hand, we'll concentrate on perspective projection and programmatic 3D the rest of this chapter. Next, you'll learn a little bit about how Processing actually calculates perspective projection.

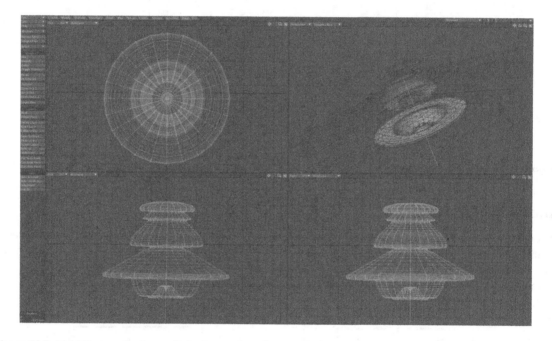

Figure 11-7. LightWave application multiple view configuration screenshot

Some Simple 3D Math

Referring to Figure 11-3, let's assume the view plane is -50 pixels away from our virtual camera, along the z-axis. In Processing, the z-axis is negative as we move into the screen (and obviously positive as we come out of the screen). The following are the expressions we can use to map the 3D point (20, 15, -100) to the point(x, y) onto the 2D view plane. We use the variable d to refer to the distance (-50) of the view plane to the camera, which we simply divide by the value of each vertex's z-component creating a ratio we then multiply by the vertex's x and y-components.

```
float x = p.x*(d/p.z);
float y = p.y*(d/p.z);
```

Plugging in the actual vertex component values, we get:

```
float x = 20*(-50.0/-100.0);
float y = 15*(-50.0/-100.0);
```

Please note, we explicitly used floating point values for the division within the parentheses to avoid integer division, which would evaluate to 0 because of implicit truncation.

Next is an example, shown in Figure 11-8, which uses the simple perspective expressions we just looked at to map 3D cube vertices onto the 2D XY-plane. The figure shows three plots with zFar values of -20, -50, and -200, respectively.

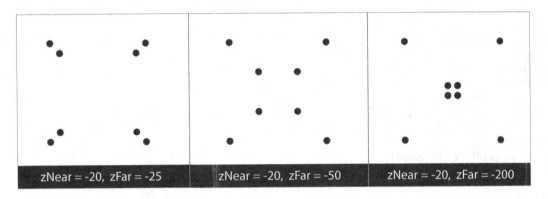

zNear = -20, zFar = -25   zNear = -20, zFar = -50   zNear = -20, zFar = -200

Figure 11-8. Calculating perspective values

```
// Perspective Calculations
PVector[] vecs = new PVector[8];
void setup() {
  size(500, 500);
  background(255);
  strokeWeight(20);
  float d = -10;
  float theta = -PI/4;
  float r = 400;
  float z, zNear = -20, zFar = -50; //z pos of cube front pts
  z = zNear;
  for (int i=0; i<vecs.length; i++) {
    vecs[i] = new PVector(cos(theta)*r, sin(theta)*r, z);
    theta += TWO_PI/4;
    if (i==3) {
      z = zFar; // set z pos of cube back pts
      theta = -PI/4;
    }
  }
}
```

```
    translate(width/2, height/2);
    beginShape(POINTS);
    for (int i=0; i<vecs.length; i++) {
      float x = vecs[i].x*(d/vecs[i].z);
      float y = vecs[i].y*(d/vecs[i].z);
      vertex(x, y);
    }
    endShape();
} // end setup()
```

P3D and OpenGL

Now that you have a little understanding about how 3D vertex data is rendered in Processing, we'll return to the earlier 11-line example that generated the glossy sphere in Figure 11-2. Here's the code:

```
size(600, 600, P3D);
background(30, 30, 50);
noStroke();
sphereDetail(170);
ambient(250, 100, 100);
ambientLight(40, 20, 40);
lightSpecular(255, 215, 215);
directionalLight(185, 195, 255, -1, 1.25, -1);
shininess(255);
translate(width/2, height/2);
sphere(160);
```

Though only 11 lines, there are a number of new commands introduced in this example, including:

- size(600, 600, P3D); - Explicitly enables Processing's P3D renderer, enabling Processing to do 3D calculations.

- sphereDetail(170); - Controls the level of vertex detail to include in the sphere. Higher argument values create smoother looking spheres, but cost more in terms of computing resources.

- ambient(250, 100, 100); - Objects in 3D can both be illuminated by lights in a scene and also have their own material properties (e.g. color), effecting how the objects interact with the respective light sources, in this case ambient light.

- ambientLight(40, 20, 40); - Effects the overall lighting in the scene. Ambient light is usually used in conjunction with more direct light sources. You can think of ambient light as a mixing of all the scattered light sources in a scene with the environment. Ambient light is usually kept pretty low, as it can wash out other lighting effects and visually flatten forms. However, when set too low, the scene can have too dark shadows that appear almost as holes in a scene, with minimal to no detail.

- lightSpecular(255, 215, 215); - Creates hot spots on reflective surfaces. While diffuse light bounces off objects omnidirectionally (in all directions), specular light reflects unidirectionally.

- directionalLight(185, 195, 255, -1, 1.25, -1); - Creates a light source pointing at the scene from a specific position. directionalLight( ) is useful for creating partially illuminated surfaces, like the half lit sphere in Figure 11-2.

- shininess(255); - Works in conjunction with lightSpecular( ) to control the size of specular hot spots. In general, larger shininess values create smaller hot spots and make objects feel more glossy; think about the hot spots on a glossy eyeball.

- sphere(160); - Calculates and renders a sphere.

Recall in Chapters 8 and 9 we saw examples of changing the default renderer. Processing's size( ) function is overloaded and can take an optional third renderer argument. The possible renderer choices are

- P2D: A custom Processing 2D renderer that lacks some of the precision of Processing's default 2D renderer, but is also generally faster.

- P3D: A custom Processing 3D renderer.

- PDF: Writes output to the Acrobat PDF file format.

Processing 1.0 included JAVA2D and OPENGL arguments that have been deprecated in version 2.0. However, the P2D and P3D arguments now utilize OpenGL under the hood. As of this writing Processing's default 2D renderer still relies on Java 2D, although that could change in the future.

As listed, Processing's P3D renderer utilizes OpenGL. OpenGL is an industry standard 3D specification that includes a comprehensive set of 3D commands. Practically all video card manufacturers support the OpenGL specification, enabling you to take advantage of your computer hardware's rendering capabilities. Though it's possible to do all 3D calculations purely at the software level, the underlying video hardware in your computer has been designed and optimized to process vertex data–extremely fast. By providing the bridge between your software programs and the video hardware, OpenGL allows you to do pretty spectacular things with bits.

Simplicity!

Now that you have some sense of how easy it is to do very basic 3D in Processing, it's hard to appreciate just how much Processing manages and simplifies the overall process. Next is a pure Java and OpenGL example that generates a rotating triangle in 3D. (Note: Had we generated an actual 3D object such as sphere instead of triangle, the example would have gotten significantly complex.)

```
import java.awt.Frame;
import java.awt.event.WindowAdapter;
import java.awt.event.WindowEvent;
import javax.media.opengl.*;
import javax.media.opengl.awt.GLCanvas;
import com.jogamp.opengl.util.*;
```

```java
public class SpinningTriangle implements GLEventListener {

    private double theta = 0;
    private float[] xs, ys;

    public static void main(String[] args) {
        GLProfile glp = GLProfile.getDefault();
        GLCapabilities caps = new GLCapabilities(glp);
        GLCanvas canvas = new GLCanvas(caps);

        Frame frame = new Frame("Spinning Triangle");
        frame.setSize(400, 400);
        frame.add(canvas);
        frame.setVisible(true);

        frame.addWindowListener(new WindowAdapter() {
        @Override
        public void windowClosing(WindowEvent e) {
                System.exit(0);
            }
        });

        canvas.addGLEventListener(new SpinningTriangle());
        FPSAnimator animator = new FPSAnimator(canvas, 60);
        animator.add(canvas);
        animator.start();
    }

    @Override
    public void display(GLAutoDrawable drawable) {
        update();
        render(drawable);
    }

    @Override
    public void dispose(GLAutoDrawable drawable) {
    }

    @Override
    public void init(GLAutoDrawable drawable) {
        // calculate vertices
        xs = new float[3];
        ys = new float[3];
            for(int i=0; i<3; i++){
                xs[i] = (float)Math.cos(theta);
                ys[i] = (float)Math.sin(theta);
                theta += (float)(Math.PI*2/3);
            }
    }
}
```

```
@Override
public void reshape(GLAutoDrawable drawable, int x, int y, int w, int h) {
}

private void update() {
}

private void render(GLAutoDrawable drawable) {
    GL2 gl = drawable.getGL().getGL2();
    gl.glClear(GL.GL_COLOR_BUFFER_BIT);
    gl.glRotatef(1.3f, 0, 1, 0);
    gl.glRotatef(-1.3f, 0, 0, 1);

    // rotating triangle
    gl.glBegin(GL.GL_TRIANGLES);
    for(int i=0; i<3; i++){
        gl.glVertex2d(xs[i], ys[i]);
    }
    gl.glEnd();
    }
}
```

While the Processing 3D sphere example was only 11 lines of code, this much simpler Java/OpenGL example was 81 lines. Clearly, Processing is doing lots of stuff for us behind the scenes. Later in the chapter we'll look more closely at Java, but for now just take a moment and quickly read through the code.

What you'll notice are numerous methods for dealing with windows, drawing, and animating, not to mention the long list of import statements up top. Early on in the book we discussed how computers are inherently dumb machines that need to be told very explicit instructions. Clearly by this definition, Processing is not that dumb, as it manages many of these explicit directives to the computer for us. Most importantly though, Processing greatly simplifies 3D creation.

Custom Geometry

As with the 2D primitives, Processing includes very few 3D primitives, just a box and a sphere. However, we can create any other geometry we'd like using the vertex() command, as you've been doing throughout the book. In addition, it's possible to use an external library to import 3D object data. Next, we'll create the simplest of the regular polyhedra, the tetrahedron.

Tetrahedron

A tetrahedron is composed of four equilateral triangles and forms a basic pyramid as shown in Figure 11-9.

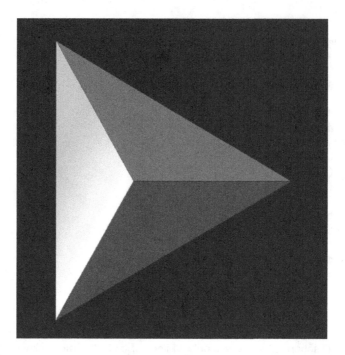

Figure 11-9. A tetrahedron

You can draw a tetrahedron using Processing's vertex() command, similar to how you've built 2D shapes throughout the book. The main challenge in creating the tetrahedron, or any 3D shape, involves calculation of the shape's vertex positions and individual faces.

To simplify this example, we'll utilize precalculated coordinate values for the tetrahedron. To learn more about the underlying vertex calculations used, see: http://www.csee.umbc.edu/~squire/reference/polyhedra.shtml. The coordinates form a tetrahedron whose vertices lay on the surface of a unit sphere—a sphere with a radius of 1. The example includes three classes: Tetrahedron, Face, and Tuple.

The Face class simply groups three vertices. We'll need an array of four faces, making up the surfaces of the tetrahedron. The Tuple class is used to organize the groupings of the tetrahedron's four vertices with its four faces. Figure 11-10 illustrates this grouping.

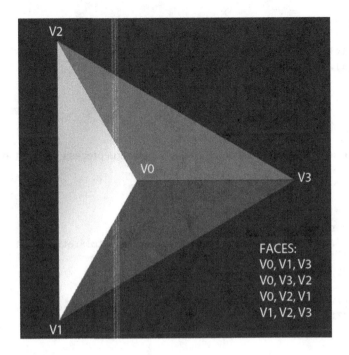

Figure 11-10. Tetrahedron screenshot

A tuple is an ordered list, independent of any specific data type. Our Tuple class includes three integer properties (elem0, elem1, elem2), representing the individual vertices within the vertex array, making up each face of the tetrahedron. We'll need the same number of Tuple objects as Face objects. Next is the code for the Tuple and Face classes:

```
class Tuple {
  int elem0, elem1, elem2;
  Tuple(int elem0, int elem1, int elem2) {
    this.elem0 = elem0;
    this.elem1 = elem1;
    this.elem2 = elem2;
  }
}

class Face {
  PVector[] vecs = new PVector[3];
  Face(PVector v0, PVector v1, PVector v2) {
    vecs[0]=v0;
    vecs[1]=v1;
    vecs[2]=v2;
  }
```

```
  void display() {
    beginShape();
    for (int i=0; i<3; i++) {
      vertex(vecs[i].x, vecs[i].y, vecs[i].z);
    }
    endShape();
  }
}
```

These are simple classes that will help us organize the 3D creation process. Next is the Tetrahedron class:

```
class Tetrahedron {
  float r;

  // Tetrahedron coords from:
  // http://www.csee.umbc.edu/~squire/reference/polyhedra.shtml#tetrahedron
PVector[] verts = {
    new PVector(0, 0, 1), // back
    new PVector(.943, 0, -.333), // right
    new PVector(-.471, -.816, -.333), // left-top
    new PVector(-.471, .816, -.333) // left-bottom
    };

  Tuple[] inds = {
    // wind counter-clockwise (right-hand rule)
    new Tuple(0, 1, 3),
    new Tuple(0, 3, 2),
    new Tuple(0, 2, 1),
    new Tuple(1, 2, 3)
    };

  Face[] faces = new Face[4];

// constructor
Tetrahedron(float r) {
    this.r = r;
    for (int i=0; i<4; i++) {
      faces[i] = new Face(verts[inds[i].elem0], verts[inds[i].elem1], verts[inds[i].elem2]);
    }
  }

  void display() {
    pushMatrix();
    scale(r);
    for (int i=0; i<4; i++) {
      faces[i].display();
    }
    popMatrix();
  }
}
```

This too is a relatively simple class. Notice the integer values passed in the four Tuple instantiation statements:

```
new Tuple(0, 1, 3),
new Tuple(0, 3, 2),
new Tuple(0, 2, 1),
new Tuple(1, 2, 3)
```

The values refer to the individual vertices within the verts arrays. Notice that we reuse the verts shared by the faces of the tetrahedron. By doing this we need only 4 vertices to describe the entire tetrahedron, rather than 3 vertices per face (12 in total). This might not seem like a big savings, but imagine if we had a world of a million tetrahedra, or a more complex form like a dodecahedron (20 unique vertices and 12 pentagon faces).

We use the tuple values when we instantiate the Face objects in the loop:

```
faces[i] = new Face(verts[inds[i].elem0], verts[inds[i].elem1], verts[inds[i].elem2]);
```

It's a little confusing seeing the nested array notation, but remember that the tuples each hold three integer values named elem0, elem1, elem2, which simply evaluate to a position in the verts array.

Final Illumination

Next is code you can put in the main tab to utilize the Tetrahedron, Face, and Tuple classes. You can create a separate tab for each of the classes, put them all in a single tab, or paste them below the following code in the main tab.

```
//Tetrahedron Example
Tetrahedron t;
void setup() {
  size(600, 600, P3D);
  noStroke();
  t = new Tetrahedron(200);
}
void draw() {
  background(50);
  lights();
  translate(width/2, height/2);
  rotateX(frameCount*PI/275);
  rotateZ(frameCount*PI/175);
  t.display();
}
```

Running the example, notice how light defines the faces of the tetrahedron. It's not always obvious how critical lighting is to be able to perceive 3D geometry. We included the lights() call in the example, which enables Processing to automatically calculate simple lighting. Try commenting out lights() and rerunning the example. Without lighting you can't read the 3D form, as the edges between faces disappear.

Processing, and computer graphics in general, calculates lighting in two parts. There are individual light sources and then the geometry itself, which needs to interact with the lights. You can model numerous types of light sources mathematically, such as point or area lights, shaped fluorescent bulbs, and spotlights, among others. Regardless of the light sources, they all interact with the 3D geometry in a similar way–through normal vectors.

Figure 11-11 illustrates a light source illuminating a plane, showing the vector from the light source to the plane and the plane's surface normal. The grayed out plane shows the geometry rotated away from the light source, its normal is now 90 degrees from the light source's vector.

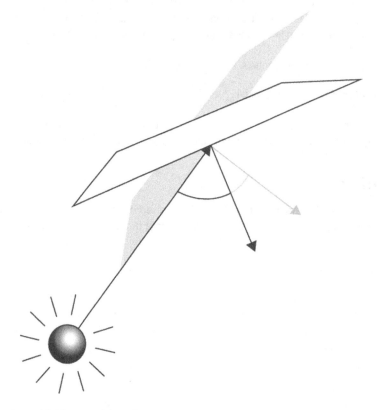

Figure 11-11. Geometry and light source interaction

Surface normals are vectors perpendicular to the surface. Like geometry, lights occupy a location within the 3D world coordinate system, so we can easily find the vectors from each respective light source and the geometry. Once we have this information we can proportionately illuminate surfaces based on the angle between the light and surface normal vectors. For example, 0 degrees would give full surface illumination, which would then fall off proportionately as we moved to -90 or 90 degrees.

Processing's PVector class includes methods to perform multiplication between vectors. cross(v1, v2) calculates a cross-product between v1 and v2. v1 and v2 together describe a surface and cross( ) returns a third vector perpendicular to this surface, which is useful for surface normal calculations. dot(v1, v2) calculates a dot product, also known as the scaler product. This calculation is very useful as it allows us to find the angle between the vectors.

Thinking back on the camera model we discussed at the beginning of the chapter, we also use the vector from the camera's position to the geometry in rendering calculations. For example, when the angle between the camera vector and a surface normal exceeds -90 or 90 degrees, the camera can treat the surface as invisible; this is commonly referred to as *face culling* and saves precious processing resources.

A Very Small Nibble of a Vast and Fascinating Pie

This section barely scratched the surface of 3D, but hopefully it revealed some of the inner workings of Processing's high-level 3D approach. Processing is a great environment to explore 3D and prototype forms, animations, games and even systems. However, as you advance in your 3D understanding we suggest also exploring OpenGL, which you can do to a degree in Processing. However, to fully unleash the power of OpenGL (and there is a lot of power), it's worth taking a lower-level approach than Processing and working directly with a language such as Java.

Advancing to Java

Whether or not you realize it, you already know a great deal of Java. All the Processing syntax, rules, and conventions you've learned throughout this book are straight Java. The single major difference between Processing and Java is that Java is completely object-oriented. There are no standalone functions or global variables in Java; everything must be declared within a class. Other than that, the few additional differences between Processing and Java are trivial.

First Java Dip

To begin to separate from the Processing mothership and explore Java, you'll learn how to work with *pure* Java within Processing. The distinction between a pure Java class and a Processing class is syntactically subtle, though structurally significant. To isolate the differences, we'll code a very simple example both ways. Here's the Processing version:

```
PClass pc;
void setup(){
  size(400, 400);
  background(0);
  translate(width/2, height/2);
  pc = new PClass(200);
}

class PClass {
  PClass(float sz){
    ellipse(0, 0, sz, sz);
  }
}
```

Processing classes, which utilize the .pde suffix, are technically called Java inner classes–classes declared within another class–regardless if they're put in their own tab or included within the same tab as the setup( )/draw( ) functions. The Processing preprocessor is responsible for bundling these inner classes in the main Processing external class. You can actually see the Java code that the preprocessor creates. To do so, export your sketch as an application. When you do this an executable application is generated, including a .java file, named the same as your saved sketch. Here is the Java code generated based on the previous sketch:

```java
import processing.core.*;
import processing.data.*;
import processing.event.*;
import processing.opengl.*;

import java.util.HashMap;
import java.util.ArrayList;
import java.io.BufferedReader;
import java.io.PrintWriter;
import java.io.InputStream;
import java.io.OutputStream;
import java.io.IOException;

public class inner_class_example extends PApplet {

  PClass pc;
  public void setup() {
    size(400, 400);
    background(0);
    translate(width/2, height/2);
    pc = new PClass(200);
  }

  class PClass {
    PClass(float sz) {
      ellipse(0, 0, sz, sz);
    }
  }
  static public void main(String[] passedArgs) {
    String[] appletArgs = new String[] {
      "inner_class_example"
    };
    if (passedArgs != null) {
      PApplet.main(concat(appletArgs, passedArgs));
    }
    else {
      PApplet.main(appletArgs);
    }
  }
}
```

Notice the PClass definition is completely contained within the open and closed curly braces of the outer class inner_class_example. The import statements at the top of the class allow Processing to do things such as create animation, handle mouse and keyboard interaction, render 3D, and input and output data, among other things. Java code is organized as classes within packages, which are simply directories on your computer. Many of these directories are nested, based on logical class relationships. For example, the Java Ellipse2D class lives within a directory named "geom." The geom directory lives within an "awt" directory, which lives within a "java" directory. If you look inside the actual Ellipse2D class, you'll see the following statement declared at the top of the class:

```
package java.awt.geom;
```

To Java, the name of the Ellipse2D class is actually: java.awt.geom.Ellipse2D. In other words, the package directory structure is required to fully identify a class in Java. Because of this approach, we must specify the package structure in the import statements. In our example, the import statements that end in: '*' instead of a class name (the name beginning with a capital letter) simply import all the classes that live within the package. This approach makes sense if there are a bunch of classes in a package you need to import.

You'll notice in our example the use of the "public" keyword. In Processing everything (properties and methods) by default is public, meaning the properties and methods declared within classes can be directly accessed from anywhere you can use objects of the class. In addition, because all Processing classes (classes that include the .pde suffix) are inner classes, the private keyword doesn't actually work.

By contrast, the convention in Java is to declare all properties private, and we may only access and change the properties through public methods, most commonly referred to as *getters and setters*. For example, a float wt property would be declared private like this:

```
private float wt;
```

Using an object of the class (from within another class) that contained the wt property, it would be illegal in Java to do the following, which would also lead to a compiler error.

```
objName.wt = 3.4; // illegal if wt is declared private
```

To access or change the private wt property we'd create the following two public methods to allow users of the class to modify and/or access the property:

```
// setter
public void setWt(float w){
      wt = w;
}
//getter
public float getWt(){
      return wt;
}
```

Also notice in inner_class_example that the class extends PApplet. PApplet is the base class for all sketches that use the Processing core language. PApplet is an enormous class (over 15,000 lines long) that you can freely explore at: http://code.google.com/p/processing/source/browse/trunk/processing/core/src/processing/core/PApplet.java. Remember when you learned about inheritance earlier in the book. When a class extends another class, it inherits the properties and methods of that class. Because all of our Processing sketches ultimately extend PApplet, they all have access to the core language functionality.

Finally, look at the somewhat unfriendly method: static public void main(String[] passedArgs). Every Java program must have a main( ) method. In fact, when you run a Java program, the first thing that happens is control goes to the main( ) method and everything else proceeds from there. If there's no main( ) method, you can't run a Java program. The reason we don't need to add main( ) methods to our Processing sketches is because they're added automatically behind the scenes for us.

Also notice Processing actually calls another main( ) method declared inside the PApplet class. This call may look unusual as the PApplet class itself calls the main( ) method, as opposed to a PApplet object. This is called a static method call. The static keyword is used in Java to ensure that there is only one copy of either a property or method used by a class, regardless of how many objects are created of the class. Static methods are called using the class name, not by objects. You can read more about the static keyword here: http://docs.oracle.com/javase/tutorial/java/javaOO/classvars.html.

Diving Deeper into Java

Perhaps you're wondering if there is a way to utilize Java in Processing so your classes don't get converted into Java inner classes; maybe you want to enforce private access on the class properties or explore Java's static keyword in more depth. The answers are yes.

Processing includes a very clever approach to allow your classes to be standalone Java classes. You simply create a new tab and name it using the .java suffix. When you do so, the .java class remains an independent Java class. Returning to the example we looked at earlier, place the PClass class within its own tab and name it "PClass.java".

```
class PClass {
  PClass(float sz){
    ellipse(0, 0, sz, sz);
  }
}
```

Java requires that standalone classes be named with the same exact identifier (that is, "PClass") as the file. Next, again place the following code in the main tab:

```
PClass pc;
  public void setup() {
    size(400, 400);
    background(0);
    translate(width/2, height/2);
    pc = new PClass(200);
  }
```

Try running the example.

Were you surprised the sketch now generated the following compiler error?

```
The function ellipse(int, int, float, float) does not exist
```

So what happened, why did converting your class to "pure" Java break the sketch? By including the .java suffix in the tab name, the Processing preprocessor left the code in the tab external to the class in the main tab. You'll remember that the preprocessor names the main class with the same name as your sketch, and also extends PApplet; it also encapsulates any variables or functions (including setup() and draw()) within the main tab into the class block. As an example, if your sketch is named "outer_class_example", the main class declaration is

```
public class outer_class_example extends PApplet {
```

The outer_class_example.java and the PClass.java class are now completely independent, so much so that PClass doesn't even have access to code within the Processing library. The ellipse() command lives within the Processing library, not within the Java language. Remember the list of import statements that you looked at earlier, which the preprocessor added to the main class to give it access to required code; we now need to do the same thing within PClass. Add the following import statement at the top of the PClass.java tab.

```
import processing.core.*;
```

There *Really* Are No Functions in Processing

Now we have access to the core Processing code, but there is still one more thing we need to do. Earlier in the chapter we explained that one of the main differences between Processing and Java is that Java has no standalone functions; everything must be structured within a class. The ellipse() function in Processing is actually a Java method (as are all function calls within Processing), and ellipse() is actually being called by the special object "this". Create a new sketch and type and run the following:

```
this.ellipse(50,50,80,80);
```

this is a special keyword in java that means the current object. From within any class object, you can refer to the current object (itself) using this. (Please note: It's often much more complicated to explain the concept of this than to simply implement it.) However, you don't need to explicitly preface all methods within the class with this, as it's implicitly there. Though it looks like all the commands (for example, ellipse(), rect(), fill(), etc.) are simply functions within Processing, they are really not; they're all technically methods of the PApplet class, which your main class extends, pretty clever, huh?

Returning to the outer class example, the easiest way to fix our sketch is to pass the this object from the main tab into our PClass class. In the main tab, add the this argument to the PClass instantiation statement:

```
pc = new PClass(this, 200);
```

In the `PClass.java`, change the constructor to:

```
PClass(PApplet p, float sz) {
    p.ellipse(0, 0, sz, sz);
}
```

You now have a standalone Java class working with your Processing sketch. We realize this news may be somewhat underwhelming, as the sketch doesn't do anything different from the inner class approach. However, building on this knowledge it's now possible to explore Processing as a standalone graphics library for pure Java development, as well as creating your own Processing Tools and Libraries. These exciting next steps are beyond the scope of this book, but the following links will guide you through the respective processes:

To develop a standalone Java application with embedded Processing:

```
http://wiki.processing.org/w/Swing_JSliders
```

To develop a Processing Library:

```
http://code.google.com/p/processing/wiki/LibraryOverview
```

To develop a Processing Tool:

```
http://wiki.processing.org/w/Create_Tools
```

Modes

Last but certainly not least, Processing 2 introduces a new modes feature. This feature arose out of developments external to the Processing software itself. One of these developments was the porting of the Processing API to other languages, most notably JavaScript by well-known developer John Resig. In addition, the explosive proliferation of mobile computing created an almost overnight interest in phone and tablet app development. Processing's Modes feature addresses both these demands, allowing you to easily create both JavaScript web and Android mobile apps (or more accurately convert your Processing sketch directly to these). In addition, the Modes feature is built on an open architecture, allowing Processing to support additional languages in the future.

JavaScript Mode

One of the earliest ports of the Processing API was to JavaScript, by John Resig. HTML5 includes a Canvas element that allows you to draw directly within a web page. For example, here is some code to draw a polygon using native JavaScript. To test it, just enter the code into a text editor (plain text format), save the file with a .html suffix, and open the page in a browser:

```
<!DOCTYPE HTML>
<html>
  <head>
    <style>
```

```
    #canv {
    border:
      2px solid #666666;
    }
    </style>
  </head>
  <body>
    <canvas id="canv" width="400" height="400"></canvas>
    <script>
      var canvas = document.getElementById('canv');
      var ctx = canvas.getContext('2d');
      var x = canvas.width/2;
      var y = canvas.height/2;
      var radius = 75;
      var pts = 5;
      var theta = 0;
      ctx.beginPath();
      ctx.moveTo();
      for (var i=0; i<pts; i++) {
        ctx.lineTo(x+Math.cos(theta)*radius, y+Math.sin(theta)*radius);
        theta += Math.PI*2/pts;
      }
      ctx.closePath();
      ctx.lineWidth = 15;
      ctx.strokeStyle = 'black';
      ctx.stroke();
    </script>
  </body>
</html>
```

However, there's really no need to work in native JavaScript (unless you want to of course) if you just want to post your processing sketches to the web. For example, the following 11-line Processing code gives the same output as the 32-line JavaScript version.

```
size(400, 400);
background(255);
int pts = 5;
float radius = 75, theta = 0;
strokeWeight(15);
beginShape();
for (int i=0; i<pts; i++) {
  vertex(width/2+cos(theta)*radius, height/2+sin(theta)*radius);
  theta += TWO_PI/pts;
}
endShape(CLOSE);
```

To run your Processing code in a browser, simply click the Java mode button in the top-right corner of the Processing IDE and switch to JavaScript mode. Now run your Processing sketch again. Voila! You now have a native JavaScript version of your processing code running in a browser, ready to be uploaded to the web. To learn more about JavaScript mode, check out: `http://processing.org/learning/javascript/`.

Android, et al

In addition to JavaScript, Processing 2 includes numerous other modes. As of this writing these include: Android, CoffeeScript, Experimental, and more are coming (or have already arrived depending on when you're reading this.) A description of each of these is beyond our scope, but you can learn more about each of these using the following links:

- Android mode: `http://processing.org/learning/android/`

- CoffeeScript mode: `https://github.com/fjenett/coffeescript-mode-processing`

- Experimental mode, which introduces debugging into the processing environment. You can view the developers site here: `http://code.google.com/p/processing/source/browse/trunk/processing/experimental/src/processing/mode/experimental/ExperimentalMode.java?r=10571`

In addition to modes, here's a link to a tutorial that shows you how to develop Processing outside of the Processing environment, using the popular Eclipse development environment: `http://processing.org/learning/eclipse/`

Summary

This chapter may have introduced more questions about advanced creative coding than it answered, which was essentially its main purpose. 3D is a vast area of research, development, and learning, and Processing is a wonderful environment to introduce the topic. However, if the 3D bug really bites you (and we hope it does), you'll definitely want to explore additional languages and environments, such as OpenGL and Java, or even C++. In addition, as you gain more expertise in Processing and creative coding in general, think about contributing some new Libraries and/or Tools to the Processing community. One of the best parts of Processing is its large community of passionate users. Finally, in today's ubiquitous world of computation, the boundaries between languages, environments, and devices are blurring, and Processing's modes feature allows you to explore this exciting new hybrid frontier. Happy creative coding!

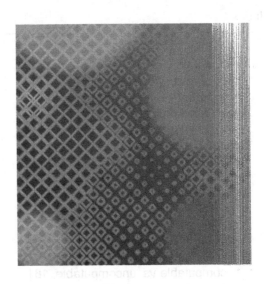

Index

C

D

P